Statius and Epic Games

Epic games are more than just an interlude; they reflect the realities of epic: heroism, power and war. This first major study of the athletic games in Statius' *Thebaid* Book 6 uses them to produce a new reading of the poem as a whole. It explores each event in Statius' games, discussing intertextual manoeuvres, historical context and poetic positioning, developing a theme from each: audience power, cosmic disruption, national identity, masculinity and the body, games and war, kingship and narrative control. This book uses a close reading of one part of one text to range over ancient literature. It casts light on the tradition of games in ancient epic as a whole, examining the works of Homer, Virgil, Apollonius, Ovid and Lucan. It is essential reading for the student of Statius and of ancient epic, and should also appeal to historians of Roman society with an interest in sport and spectacle.

HELEN LOVATT is Lecturer in Classics at the University of Nottingham. She has written numerous articles on Latin epic and its reception.

CAMBRIDGE CLASSICAL STUDIES

STATIUS AND EPIC GAMES

Sport, Politics and Poetics in the *Thebaid*

HELEN LOVATT
University of Nottingham

CAMBRIDGE
UNIVERSITY PRESS

PUBLISHED BY THE PRESS SYNDICATE OF THE UNIVERSITY OF CAMBRIDGE
The Pitt Building, Trumpington Street, Cambridge, United Kingdom

CAMBRIDGE UNIVERSITY PRESS
The Edinburgh Building, Cambridge CB2 2RU, UK
40 West 20th Street, New York, NY 10011–4211, USA
477 Williamstown Road, Port Melbourne, VIC 3207, Australia
Ruiz de Alarcón 13, 28014 Madrid, Spain
Dock House, The Waterfront, Cape Town 8001, South Africa

http://www.cambridge.org

First published 2005

Printed in the United Kingdom at the University Press, Cambridge

Typeface Times 11/13 pt   *System* LaTeX 2$_\varepsilon$ [TB]

A catalogue record for this book is available from the British Library

ISBN 0 521 84742 7 hardback

To those who help make the possible into reality.

The board became both Culture and Empire again. The setting was made by them both; a glorious, beautiful, deadly killing field, unsurpassably fine and sweet and predatory and carved from Nicosar's beliefs and his together. Image of their minds; a hologram of pure coherence, burning like a standing wave of fire across the board, a perfect map of the landscapes of thought and faith within their heads.

He began the slow move that was defeat and victory together before he even knew it himself. Nothing so subtle, so complex, so beautiful had ever been seen on an Azad board. He believed that; he knew that. He would make it the truth.

The game went on.

Breaks, days, evenings, conversations, meals; they came and went in another dimension; a monochrome thing, a flat, grainy image. *He* was somewhere else entirely. Another dimension, another image. His skull was a blister with a board inside it, his outside self just another piece to be shuffled here and there.

He didn't talk to Nicosar, but they conversed, they carried out the most exquisitely textured exchange of mood and feeling through those pieces which they moved and were moved by; a song, a dance, a perfect poem. People filled the game-room every day now, engrossed in the fabulously perplexing work taking shape before them; trying to read that poem, see deeper into this moving picture, listen to the symphony, touch this living sculpture, and so understand it.

Iain M. Banks, *The Player of Games*

CONTENTS

ACKNOWLEDGEMENTS

This has been a very long project; since I first started working on Statius in 1995, until the final revision of the Ph. D. thesis in 2003, so many people have helped me and continue to help me. Michael Sharp, Annie Lovett and Sinéad Moloney provided podiums and victory palms; the sharp eyes of Nina Palmer saved me from many a stumble; Carrie Vout, Helen Asquith, Sara Owen and Jason König helped me down the home straight; friends and colleagues at New Hall, Keele and Nottingham supported and commiserated. My sponsors, without whom I would never have made it to the games, were New Hall for the research fellowship which gave me the time to carry out revisions and the confidence to try, and the AHRB for financial support during M. Phil. and Ph. D. Many generations of friends in the Cambridge Classics Faculty Graduate Common Room cheered on the sidelines; Emily Greenwood, Lucy Grig and Jason König struggled heroically with my thesis. Thanks also to Joanne Brown, Ruth Parkes, Philip Smith, Jason König, Andrew Feldherr and Alison Sharrock for giving me things to read. Now to those who coached and trained: Damien Nelis, my Ph. D. examiner, gave enthusiasm and details with great generosity; Elaine Fantham gave timely encouragement and a clear-minded overview. Michael Reeve, read (and reread), helped and supported; Richard Hunter, without whose encouragement I would never have even attempted this; Philip Hardie, for raising eyebrows and putting up with me over the years; John Henderson, my supervisor, who knew when to leave well alone and when to intervene, and who never encouraged me to take any sort of illegal substances in pursuit of better performance. Back to grass roots in the palaestra, thanks to all those teachers who started me off in the right direction: Neil Wright, who first read Statius with me, and especially Roger Adams, who spent the most enthusiastic hour and a half reading four lines of the *Aeneid* that I have ever encountered. Support on the home front came from: Andrew's parents, who looked after Jonathan (and me) when we needed help; my parents and sister, who coped with my endless obsessions; last, and most importantly, Andrew, for tending to me, fixing computer problems, providing moral support and a sense of proportion, and Jonathan, for making it all worthwhile. A large but inevitably inadequate thank-you to you all. Any errors, omissions or other horrors that remain are my own responsibility.

The text of the *Thebaid* used is that of Hill (1983); all translations are my own and attempt only to explain how I read the Latin, with no pretensions to the status of literature. The extract from *The Player of Games* by Iain M. Banks is reproduced by permission of Time Warner Books (London, 1996).

ABBREVIATIONS

CHCL	E. J. Kenney and W. V. Clausen, eds. (1982) *Cambridge History of Classical Literature II. Latin Literature*, Cambridge
Lewis and Short	C. T. Lewis and C. Short (1879) *A Latin Dictionary*, Oxford
LSJ	H. G. Liddell and R. Scott, rev. S. Jones (1925–40) *Greek English Lexicon* (9th ed.), Oxford
OLD	(1968) *Oxford Latin Dictionary*, Oxford
RE	A. Pauly, G. Wissowa and W. Kroll (1893–) *Real-Encyclopädie der klassischen Altertumswissenschaft*, Stuttgart
SH	H. Lloyd-Jones and P. Parsons, eds. (1983), *Supplementum Hellenisticum*, Berlin; New York
TGF	A. Nauck, ed. (1926) *Tragicorum Graecorum Fragmenta* (2nd ed.), Leipzig
TLL	(1894–) *Thesaurus Linguae Latinae*, Leipzig

INTRODUCTION

nil fixum cordi: pugnant exire pauentque,
concurrit summos animosum frigus in artus.
qui dominis idem ardor equis; face lumina surgunt,
ora sonant morsu, spumisque et sanguine ferrum
uritur, impulsi nequeunt obsistere postes,
claustraque compressae transfumat anhelitus irae.
stare adeo miserum est, pereunt uestigia mille
ante fugam, absentemque ferit grauis ungula campum.
circumstant fidi, nexusque et torta iubarum
expediunt firmantque animos et plurima monstrant.
insonuit contra Tyrrhenum murmur, et omnes
exsiluere loco. quae tantum carbasa ponto,
quae bello sic tela uolant, quae nubila caelo?
amnibus hibernis minor est, minor impetus igni,
tardius astra cadunt, glomerantur tardius imbres,
tardius e summo decurrunt flumina monte.

(*Thebaid* 6.394–409)

Nothing is fixed in their hearts: they fight to get out and they fear,
a spirited shiver runs through to the tips of their limbs.
In the masters, in the horses, the same burning; their eyes shoot flame,
their mouths sound with biting, the iron is burnt with foam
and blood, the posts cannot stand in their way as they push
against them, breath of compressed anger smokes across the bolts.
To stand is so wretched that a thousand footsteps perish
before their flight, the heavy hoof is striking the absent plain.
The faithful stand around, sorting out reins and the twisted
crests, strengthening spirits and offering much advice.
The trumpet blast sounded opposite, and all
leapt out from their places; what sail on the sea,
what weapon in war flies so fast, what cloud in the sky?
The force of the winter floods is less, the force of fire is less,
more slowly fall the stars, the rain storms gather more slowly,
more slowly from the mountain-top torrents run down.

Start at the beginning, *in medias res*, in the middle of the beginning, in this case with the beginning of Statius' first event, the chariot race: the reader is drawn into the fever-pitch excitement of the racehorses straining to explode from the gates, just as the viewer shares the tension waiting for the starting gun to fire. All polarities become paradoxes: master and horse are in one state of mixed excitement and terror; cold mixes with fire; metal burns; breath becomes smoke. The horses and their riders already race the course in their minds, as if caught up in an endless repetition of the act before it even happens. The gun fires; the handkerchief falls; the trumpet blasts: the speed and force of the chariots bursting out, the thunder of horses' hooves, becomes a flood of thundering images, thumping the message home.

We too will play out our own set of games, each chapter an event, each event a chapter. The line between audience and competitors will not necessarily be clear: you are watching me; we are watching Statius; we are watching Statius watch his competitors and their audience; those competitors are watching each other. Will you compete by reading – making a judgement and running your interpretations against mine? It should prove a game worth playing, a spectacle worth watching; perhaps we will be in luck – and catch a spectacular shipwreck, or a controversial verdict or two: no disqualifications, I trust.

This is a book about Statius and about epic games.[1] It rereads Statius and the *Thebaid* through a reading of the games in book 6 and their interaction with the rest of the poem.[2] It rereads epic games from the vantage point of Statius, looking back over all his epic predecessors (and interacting with his contemporaries).[3]

---

[1] Work on Statius' epic games has generally followed two lines: the relationship between Statius' games and those of Homer and Virgil, and the relationship between Statius' games and Roman games. Legras (1905) deals with both, as does Von Stosch (1968) (the only monograph on the subject); Kytzler (1968) concentrates on Virgil and Homer, as does Juhnke (1972); Thuillier (1996b) studies Statius as evidence for historical games. Venini (1961a) introduces a new element with her investigation of foreshadowing, elaborated by Vessey (1970): the relationship between the games and the rest of the poem.

[2] The title of the book refers to the title of Michael Putnam's chapter on the games in *Aeneid* 5 'Game and Reality': he reads Virgil's games as a light-hearted version of the serious events to come, primarily the sacrifice of Palinurus (Putnam (1965) 64–104).

[3] Silius Italicus also wrote a set of games, in *Punica* 16; Juhnke (1972) 229–67 analyses both sets of games. Throughout the book I have attempted to give a sense of the similarities and differences, but I explore the relationship fully elsewhere. Scholarship

It is a book about both intratextuality and intertextuality. Each chapter comes in two halves: the first half is mainly intertextual; each reads one event in the games in detail, looking at the relationships with previous versions; the second half is intratextual, taking a theme from the event and tracing it through the rest of the *Thebaid*. Starting from close reading of a small part of one poem, we move out towards wider interpretation of the whole poem, a sense of the poem's interaction with its genre and predecessors,[4] a new perspective on that genre and on wider issues in Greek and Roman culture.[5] The poetics of athletics meets the poetics of gigantomachy; games are played on and through bodies and audiences; the tripartite power structure of *editor* (producer of the games), audience and spectacle forms one frame for the discussion; the construction of masculinity, ethnicity and poetic identity another. Anyone interested in Statius, epic games, the epic genre in any of its incarnations, ancient or otherwise, anyone interested in representations of sport and the history of games, will find something to watch.[6]

In this introduction, I present Roman ideas about games, examining the ludic through the multifaceted concept of *ludus*. It is also a prelude, a *pompa*, bringing in the characters who will watch

---

has generally placed the publication of the *Punica* after the publication of the *Thebaid*, though acknowledging that the process of composition would have overlapped and that reciprocal influence is probable. See Wistrand (1956); Venini (1970a) xv–xvi; Juhnke (1972) 12–13; Dewar (1991) xxxi–xxxv; Smolenaars (1994) xvii–xviii.

[4] Hardie (1993) shows that Statius is a reader and critic of Virgil, as well as a successor. Cf. Hinds (1998) on Statius and 'secondariness'.

[5] The foundation of my work is an attempt to read and understand the text under consideration: I chose the themes from what I found interesting, disconcerting and difficult in the text. There will be a running dialogue between close reading and broad theory, in which each changes the other. I mean to combine discovery of what is there already in the text with new ideas and new readings of it.

[6] Apology has characterised scholarship on Statius: each generation of apologists creates a defence for studying Statius which becomes the object of attack for the next generation. So the label of 'episodic epic' which started as an apology became a means of criticising and marginalising Statius' *Thebaid*, effectively repudiated by Vessey (Vessey (1970); Vessey (1973); Brown (1994) 6). Vessey's apology centred around the concepts of 'mannerism' and 'baroque epic': Ahl has laid bare the persistent rhetoric of marginalisation in these concepts too (Ahl (1986) 2809–10). It is no empty rhetorical stance, then, when I refuse to apologise for working on Statius. Statius can and should be central to our understanding of ancient epic, and critical work on the *Thebaid* can start from the position that the aim is elaboration and enrichment of understanding, not justification of the poem itself. The extent to which I am indebted to previous work on Statius is clear from the whole text, though it will not be possible to acknowledge these debts in full.

throughout, under the auspices of the Olympian gods watching from their box. Exploration of the poetics of epic games will begin by examining games as 'prelude', and the imagery of games in Statian *recusatio*. Finally, I want to provide background for the events to come (think of it as the thirty days' training, presided over by the *hellanodikai*). What was the system of spectacle in Rome? What are the fundamental dynamics of intertextuality in Statius' games? How does the programme of a set of epic games conjure up a different world?

Concepts of games

In this section, I briefly examine the concepts associated with the Latin noun *ludus* (game) and verb *ludo* (I play); how similar are Roman concepts of games to our own? How do epic poets in particular refer to their games? The *TLL* gives us a baseline for the concept: a *ludus* is fundamentally in opposition to whatever is *serius* ('serious'), and to *labor* ('work'). This fits in very well with our ideas about games, encapsulated in the phrase 'just a game'. Essentially, a game is always something which is set against some sort of reality (though it might be asked whose reality). This study is concerned with the different realities against which Statius sets his games.

Playing is also used of spending one's time idly or frivolously, even wasting one's efforts; there is a hint of disapproval in the way the concept is transferred to other ideas, which suggests that a game in the Roman mind is not only 'just a game', something to be dismissed as unimportant, but even something slightly immoral. To play with someone is not only to tease, but also to ridicule, make mock of, and even to trick or deceive. To act towards someone with less than perfect seriousness is to wound their dignity and even, perhaps, to damage the truth. If anything, the Roman attitude towards games is even more derogatory than our own. It is not surprising, then, that epic games have generally been despised as 'mere decoration', and have often been neglected.

4

The *ludus* is the activity of a child or an animal, not an adult. The difference between boyhood and manhood for Parthenopaeus, for instance, is the difference between games and war. The problems of defining the reality of adult masculinity will recur, most importantly in chapter 5. Of speaking, *ludus* refers to whatever is said without seriousness, to jokes and jests. It is even used of writing poetry which is less than totally serious. The game of poetry and poetry as games will be an important theme throughout this book: the chapter on the wrestling, for instance, reads the match as a metaphor for intertextual competition; the chariot race also evokes ideas about the chariot of song.

The concept also contains ideas of practice and learning: the noun *ludus*, in a way which is completely foreign to the English word 'game', came to refer to schools for children (*ludus litterarum*) and even places of training, like the gladiatorial school.[7] The game in this sense is equated with practice in opposition to doing something for real. The idea of fun or recreation does not always seem to come into it. This crucial difference between practice and reality is the key moment in the discus.

Ludi in the plural, like our 'games', is used primarily to refer to 'a set or festival of public games' (*OLD*), often with an epithet (e.g. *Ludi Romani*, or, for instance, 'Olympic Games'). Although this word is used more strictly for Roman contests held in the circus or theatre (*circenses* or *scaenici*) in opposition to, for instance, gladiatorial *munera*, it was also used to describe festivals of Greek games, including athletics and musical competitions. For instance, Domitian's Capitoline games, at which Statius competed unsuccessfully, are usually referred to as *Ludi Capitolini*.[8] Isidore, writing about the origin of the word, offers a useful retrospective summary:

---

[7] For McDonnell (2003) 243, Plautus' use of *ludus* to mean school (*Rudens* 43) is linguistic borrowing from the Greek σχολή, which naturally refers to both 'leisure' and 'school'. Statius' use of *ludus* to describe his games could be a self-consciously Greek borrowing, like *Siluae*, used to mean 'material', from the Greek ὕλη, another of McDonnell's examples.

[8] Plautus refers to *ludos Olympios* in the *Stichus* (306); other references to the Olympic Games as *ludi*: Plautus *Casina* 759–63; Cicero *De oratore* 3.127; *De natura deorum* 2.6; Pliny *Naturalis historia* 4.15; 7.205; Servius on *Georgics* 3.19 (though he also uses the word *agon*); Velleius Paterculus 1.8.1 (also *ludicrum*); Livy 27.35.3 and 28.7.14 refers to them as a *ludicrum*.

'a *ludus* can be athletic, in the circus, gladiatorial, or in the theatre' (*ludus autem aut gymnicus est, aut circensis, aut gladiatorius, aut scaenicus*, Isidore *Origines* 18.16.3). Thus *ludi*, and Statius' games as *ludi*, combine two aspects of games: they are a public spectacle, a show put on for the entertainment of the audience, and the spectacle itself is sport, a sort of game. They are games and a game, ludic both for audience and competitors.

So much for Roman concepts of *ludi* in general; next, to consider the way that epic poets talk about their games. When Statius refers to his games, he has a variety of names for them. Virgil refers to his games throughout as either *ludi* ('games', *Aeneid* 5.113, 605) or *certamina* ('contests', *Aeneid* 5.545, 695), Silius as *ludi* ('games', 16.579), *certamina* ('contests', 16.312, 457, 527) or *spectacula* ('spectacles', 16.531, 557). Silius' gladiatorial fights are spectacles, and Statius too uses this word of the boxing match (*et erecto timeat spectacula uoto*, 'and each man fears the spectacle with tense prayers', 6.759). These events in particular are spectacular because of their danger: the pleasure of watching games is like the pleasure of reading epic.[9] Statius alone calls his spectacle 'a game' (*ludus*).[10] But what does this imply? *Ludus* has a quite different range of meaning from *ludi*.[11] Perhaps the point is that this is both a moment of play for the epic poet, a dis*play* less serious than the war to come, and also a preparation, a training for heroes and readers in the realities of epic and war. Alternatively, since the second reference is followed (6.5–14) by descriptions of the founding of the other three sets of games on the Greek *periodos* (Olympic, Pythian and Isthmian), perhaps the singular use of *ludus* distinguishes the games from Roman-style festivals and points to their alien status, in a similar way to Livy's description of them as a *ludicrum* (a show, public games). The phrase *Graium ex more decus*, used of Statius' games at the beginning of book 6, ('a traditional Greek celebration', 6.5) certainly emphasises the Greek context and heritage. The interplay between Greek and Roman is

---

[9] In a forthcoming project on *The Epic Gaze*, I shall investigate in more detail the spectacle of epic battle and death, and the particular ways in which epic views its heroes and events.

[10] At the beginning of the Nemean excursus (4.729) and at the beginning of the book of games (6.3).

[11] Virgil uses *ludi* to refer to Greek-style athletic games at *Georgics* 2.381 and at *Aeneid* 5.113.

a particularly fraught Statian issue, and one which will continually return to haunt us, taking centre stage in the boxing. Later on in the games, Statius also uses *ludus* in the singular to refer to one particular event, when Phlegyas of Pisa is preparing for the discus: *hic semper | amori ludus erat* ('This game was always his love', *Thebaid* 6.673–4). The discus is almost the emblem of Greek athletics, part of the pentathlon, and this event in particular is more of a sport than a contest. This is Phlegyas' hobby, in the same way that Tydeus wrestles in his leisure time (*sic otia Martis | degere*, 'thus he spent his leisure from war', *Thebaid* 6.830–31).

The relationship between games and war is particularly important in Statius, who frequently and characteristically describes his games as naked or unarmed battles.[12] Neither Virgil nor Silius uses this term. The most commonly used word for Greek games is *certamina*, which blurs the boundary between contest and fight. But Statius takes this further. When Jupiter is chastising Mars for allowing this huge delay, he underscores the god of war's failure by ironically describing the discus and boxing in warlike terms: *sonat orbe recusso | discus et Oebalii coeunt in proelia caestus* ('The discus sounds with its sphere reverberating and Spartan boxers join battle', 7.20–21). Jupiter brings out the distance between games and war by underlining the similarities: this is the best we can manage, he seems to suggest. I asked you to overthrow the world and only the sphere of the discus is crashing about us; the only battles you can manage are boxing matches.

This lexical survey of the way that Roman epic poets refer to their games brings out the different meanings and functions of epic games. Epic games work against the reality of epic war, but the representation of epic games as games is not uncomplicated. Reality intrudes on the games, and the games become reality. In particular, Statius represents his games as work. He describes them as *labor*, and they can also be an *opus*.[13] Just as poetry can be a game in contrast to the reality of Roman or modern political life, while the body of a poet's writings in Latin as in English can be 'works' (*opera*), so athletics were and are both work and play. The interplay between games and their various realities works both ways: games

---

[12] *Thebaid* 6.18, 249; 7.91.　　[13] *labor*: 6.469, 503, 796, 924–5; *opus*: 6.643, 668.

are always in opposition to and read against war, work, the world, the body; spectators watch competitors; readers read texts. On the other hand, games represent and articulate the realities from which they are marked off; spectators identify with competitors; the circus becomes the cosmos; the reader is within the text.

Prelude

Poetry, as we have seen above, can be 'just a game'. In this section, I explore the poetics of playing and look at the way that Statius suggests that his games are a prelude to serious epic, just as the *Siluae* are a prelude to writing in a serious genre, and as mythological epic is a prelude to writing the serious historical and panegyrical epic of Domitian's great deeds.[14] I want to begin with an example of poetic games from Statius' contemporary, Martial.[15] In the proem to his *Apophoreta*, Martial refuses to write a *Thebaid: uis scribam Thebas Troiamue malasue Mycenas? | 'lude' inquis 'nucibus': perdere nolo nuces.* ('You want me to write about Thebes, Troy or Mycenean tragedies? "Play with nuts!" you say, but I refuse to waste my nuts.' Martial 14.1.11–12.) Martial's interlocutor exhorts him to gamble with nuts rather than writing trifles in the Catullan fashion: don't write nuts, *play* with them. Martial then claims that playing is serious business: he doesn't want to risk losing his trifles. This is set against the background of epic as serious poetry while epigram is play. Perhaps to write an epic is to gamble for stakes too high: writing epic, for Martial, is deep play.

The Virgilian *Culex* uses playing of writing less serious poetry: *lusimus, Octaui, gracili modulante Thalia* ('We have played, Octavius, with slender Thalia directing', *Culex* 1). Statius, in his prose preface to *Siluae* 1, uses the *Culex* as an equivalent of the *Siluae*, a game played before serious poetry: *quid enim [. . .]quoque auctoritatis editionis onerari, quo adhuc pro Thebaide meo timeo?*

[14] Ruurd Nauta in an excellent paper on 'The *Recusatio* in Flavian Poetry', Groningen Colloquium on Flavian Poetry, 2003, covered much of this material, but the emphasis on poetry as a game is my own addition.

[15] For this Martial moment, I thank Sarah Culpeper Stroup in her paper 'Invaluable Collections: The Illusion of Poetic Presence in Martial's *Xenia* and *Apophoreta*' at the Groningen Colloquium on Flavian Poetry, 2003.

sed et Culicem legimus et Batrachomachiam etiam agnoscimus,
nec quisquam est inlustrium poetarum qui non aliquid operibus
suis stilo remissiore praeluserit. ('For why [should they too] be
weighed down with the authority of publication, when I am still
afraid on behalf of my *Thebaid*? But we read the Culex too, and
we even recognise the Batrachomachia, and there isn't a single one
of the famous poets who didn't make some sort of foreplay for his
greater works with a more relaxed pen.' Statius *Siluae 1.Preface.5–
9.*) This makes the Virgilian and Homeric model for the poetic
career override reality, suggesting that lighter genres are inevitably
earlier than heavier ones, even though in this very passage he represents the *Thebaid* as already published. The same word (*praeludo*)
is used in the proem of the *Achilleid* in Statius' bid to postpone
indefinitely the imperial requirement to write an epic in Domitian's
praise (*Achilleid 1.14–20*):

> at tu, quem longe primum stupet Itala uirtus
> Graiaque, cui geminae florent uatumque ducumque
> certatim laurus (olim dolet altera uinci),
> da ueniam ac trepidum patere hoc sudare parumper
> puluere: te longo necdum fidente paratu
> molimur magnusque tibi praeludit Achilles.

> But you, who first above all stupefied both the Italian and Greek
> heroes, for whom the twin wreaths of poet and leader
> flourish in rivalry (already one regrets being conquered),
> pardon me and allow me in my fear to sweat in this dust
> for a little longer: I am not yet confident in my preparations
> to work on you and great Achilles is a prelude to you.

The *Achilleid* is a prelude to an epic on Domitian, a game played
before the real work of historical epic and panegyric. Statius brings
out the idea of writing as a game with the imagery of sweating in
the dust, which refers to the beginning of our epic games, where
the games literally 'foresweat' the war (*praesudare, 6.4*). In *Siluae*
4.4, the poet also uses an image from the beginning of *Thebaid*
6, the image of the ship training for the real sea (*6.19–24*), in a
recusatio for not writing about Domitian: *fluctus an sueta minores |*
nosse ratis nondum Ioniis credenda periclis? ('Should my ship,
accustomed to knowing lesser waves, not yet be trusted to the
dangers of the Ionian?' *Siluae 4.4.99–100.*) The *Siluae* are games

9

to epic's war; mythological epic is equally a game in comparison to the true labour of historical panegyric. Statius always leaves the real writing until later; through the mask of 'just a game' he hides the seriousness of playing.

A very brief history of Roman games

I want now to move to background and historical games. The origins of Roman *ludi* are a prime site for legend and tendentious narrative.[16] Virgil creates a role for Aeneas, Ovid for Romulus.[17] The first *Consualia* is distinguished by its association with the rape of the Sabines.[18] Both ancient and modern historians bring their own agendas to stories told about the history of Roman games.[19] However, what concerns me here is the clear distinction made between the traditional Roman *ludi*, both *scaenici* and *circenses*, and Greek *agones*.[20] The first are always lent the full weight of tradition, presented as originating at the very beginning of the development of Rome, and linked closely to religious festivals. *Ludi* were festivals organised by the state using public money (although the presiding official might supplement this from his own funds), lasting a number of days, performing a religious function and including a number of different types of events. *Ludi scaenici* were dramatic performances and took place in the theatre; *ludi circenses* were primarily chariot racing, which took place in the circus. On the other hand, Greek athletic games are presented as a revolutionary novelty, first occurring in 186 BC, held by M. Fulvius Nobilior as part of the votive games after his victory in the Aetolian war.[21] To start with, they took place as part of other festivals, staged in various different places as a spectacle of the other.[22] Later, quadrennial festivals in the style of the Olympics began to be founded in the

---

[16] See Thuillier (1996a) 37–59; Wiedemann (1992) 1–3 for the relationship between *ludi* and *munera*; Balsdon (1969); Harris (1972).

[17] *Fasti* 2.359–80.   [18] Dionysius of Halicarnassus, 2.30–31.

[19] See Thuillier (1996a) 37–8 on the moral agenda of Roman historians. Thuillier himself has an agenda: to rescue the history of Roman sport from the tyranny of hellenocentrism and to give the Etruscans their proper place in the history of Rome, following his earlier work on Etruscan athletics: Thuillier (1985).

[20] For a clear and useful discussion of this, see Caldelli (1993) 1–52.

[21] See Livy 39.22.2 with Thuillier (1996a) 46–7.   [22] See below, pp. 47–54.

West, such as Augustus' *Actia*, or the *Sebasta* at Naples. These festivals included musical as well as athletic competitions, and in many the musical events were more significant than the athletic.[23] *Munera*, or gladiatorial games, are also shown as developing later (from 264 BC), from funeral celebrations held in the forum. They were originally organised and paid for by relatives of the dead and remained private in provenance until the imperial era, when they fell victim to the general blurring between state and imperial control and finances.[24] If *munera* were symbolic of Romanness in the Greek East, *ludi Graeci* in Rome show the Greekness of Rome.[25] This system of distinctions, then, is similar to Mark Golden's 'discourse of difference in Greek Sport', a way of using sport both to read and to create cultural distinctions.[26] Sport is a key area for constructing cultural identity.[27]

It was only in the time when Statius was writing that we can begin to see a domestication of Greek games. For Nero's attempt at bringing a regular Greek festival within the bounds of Rome died with him, while Domitian's *Capitolia* endured into the fourth century at least.[28] There was also renewed imperial interest in the *Sebasta* in Naples in the time of Vespasian, shown by Titus acting as *agonothete* (master of ceremonies) three times in AD 70, 74 and 78.[29] Domitian's *Capitolia* became part of the *periodos* and was consistently linked with the four original sacred festivals of the Greeks (the Olympian, Pythian, Isthmian and Nemean).[30] The *Capitolia*, probably most important for reading Statius' games,

---

[23] For instance, in the *Demostheneia* at Oenoanda, a festival which is described in a very full inscription, there are sixteen days of musical competitions attracting significant prizes and only one day of gymnastic competitions for citizens with expenses only. For full details, see Wörrle (1988); a useful review and translation of the inscription can be found in Mitchell (1990).

[24] See Wiedemann (1992) 1–3.

[25] 'Ce concours a introduit Rome dans le vie agonistique du monde grec et en a fait une des capitales; la ville jouait alors avec éclat le rôle de πόλις Ἑλληνίς.' Robert (1970) 7.

[26] See Golden (1998) 33–45.

[27] In general see MacClancy (1996); see also specific studies such as Van Nijf (1999) on elite self-presentation in the Greek East; see also König (2000).

[28] See Suetonius *Domitian* 4; Arnold (1960) 247–8; Robert (1970) 7; Thuillier (1996a) 51; Caldelli (1993). Arnold (1960) 248 lists the relevant inscriptions. See Bolton (1948) on Neronia.

[29] Leiwo (1995) 46.   [30] Robert (1970) 8.

considering that he himself competed there,[31] was a triple festival (*triplex*), including musical, equestrian and gymnastic events. From this time onwards, athletics took the heart of Greece, as represented by the *periodos*, into the physical space of the heart of Rome. His reinvention of epic games in the *Thebaid* pays homage to the changed status of games in the Greek style: they were no longer relegated to Greece and self-proclaimedly Greek cities like Naples. Greek athletic games had become Roman too.

Playing with Homer and Virgil

The contest between Greek and Roman is a contest which is played out on a poetic level through the intertextual rivalry of Homer and Virgil. The version of the funeral games preserved in Apollodorus is considerably different: οἱ δὲ ἔθεσαν ἐπ' αὐτῷ τὸν τῶν Νεμέων ἀγῶνα, καὶ ἵππῳ μὲν ἐνίκησεν Ἄδραστος, σταδίῳ δὲ Ἐτέοκλος, πυγμῇ Τυδεύς, ἅλματι καὶ δίσκῳ Ἀμφιάραος, ἀκοντίῳ Λαόδοκος, πάλῃ Πολυνείκης, τόξῳ Παρθενοπαῖος. ('And they set up for him a contest at Nemea, and Adrastus won the horse race, Eteoclus won the running, Tydeus the boxing, Amphiaraus the jump and the discus, Laodocus the javelin, Polynices the wrestling, and Parthenopaeus the archery.' Apollodorus 3.6.4) This version has a horse race instead of a chariot race, the jump as well as the discus; the javelin and the archery are actual competitions, and there is no fight in armour. The names of the Seven are also different, and the events are not distributed one per hero: Amphiaraus wins two. If this version represents the tradition of the *Thebaid* story, it is clear that Statius is more interested in negotiating between Homer and Virgil than in retelling the Theban myths. (Cf. Legras (1905) 79–90). Throughout the book, the analyses of individual events will examine how Statius' games play against both Homer and Virgil; we will also use Silius as a foil to make it more clear what Statius has chosen to do, to look at the give and take between contemporary poets.[32] This section will give a

---

[31] *Siluae* 3.5.28–33.

[32] We cannot judge whether previous versions of the *Thebaid* influenced Statius' games and his poem due to lack of information about these previous versions. Vessey has shown

brief introductory overview, focusing on the role of the chariot race.[33]

But first a very brief summary of the general context of these games. The games in *Aeneid* 5 take place in Sicily, on the occasion of the anniversary of Anchises' death. The Sicilian location speaks of the importance of mythological and historical links between Sicily and Rome.[34] The founding of Acesta in the second half of book 5 enacts integration between Sicilians and Trojans. The chronological setting of the anniversary of Anchises' death is subtly different from the funeral games of Patroclus, and closer to Roman practice, where the festival of the *parentalia* is dedicated to annual remembering of the dead, and where games in memory of the dead were often held a substantial amount of time after their death.[35] Silius follows Virgil closely: Scipio Africanus performs a belated funeral and set of games for his father and uncle when he returns to their place of death in Spain. In Livy 28.21, these are gladiatorial spectacles with athletic contests tacked on, but Silius transforms them into a reworking, and an overt Romanisation, of *Aeneid* 5. The context of the games in the *Thebaid*, however, is distinctly Greek in tone: they are funeral games (even if for the death of a baby, not a hero – a Callimachean celebration of the small) written as an *aetion* of the founding of the Nemean games, set at Nemea.[36] Statius' mythic world of Greece in the *Thebaid* is in a new dimension somewhere between epic and reality, Greece and

that 'on the evidence available there is no viable reason to suppose that Statius utilised Antimachus in his narrative of the funeral games.' Only twenty fragmentary lines remain of the cyclic *Thebaid*, and Vessey concludes that '[i]t is even less likely that he used – or in fact had even read – the "Cyclic" *Thebaid*' (Vessey (1970) 426). See further Vessey (1969). Cf. Ahl (1986) 2815 n. 21; Brown (1994) 1–4.

[33] Vessey (1973) 70 insists that Statius' games are 'exclusively founded on *Iliad* 23 and *Aeneid* 5.' These texts are certainly very important, but, as this book will demonstrate, the games also look to the *Odyssey*, the *Argonautica*, Ovid, Lucan and Seneca, to historical games; they could just as easily have worked with previous versions of the Theban cycle.

[34] See Galinsky (1968).

[35] On the *parentalia* see Beard, North and Price (1998) 31, 50; Weinstock (1971) 291–6; Toynbee (1971) 63–6. Weinstock (p. 89) mentions two instances of Caesar holding games some time after the actual death of the person commemorated: games in memory of his father, who died in 85 BC, held in 65 BC; games in memory of Julia, who died in 54 BC, held in 46 BC. See also Balsdon (1969) on Augustus' games for Drusus, held fourteen years after his death in AD 6.

[36] On the context of the games, see Brown (1994) 30–56.

Rome – it is very difficult to pin down its associations conclusively, but ultimately it does claim a Greek setting.

Statius also returns to a chariot race rather than a ship race, in this doing the same as Silius, so that the opening of book 6 gives the impression that he will reproduce *Iliad* 23. Most importantly, and this point has not been emphasised, Statius' games cover all the events from *Iliad* 23.[37] Virgil has four (ship race, running, boxing, archery) and so does Silius (chariot race, running, gladiatorial fight and javelin). In Statius' games there are seven events (chariot race, running, discus, boxing, wrestling, sword fight and archery) and Homer's eighth event (javelin) appears in a vestigial version. Adrastus is offered two alternative ways of gracing the games with his own achievement: *fundat uel Lyctia cornu | tela rogant, tenui uel nubila transeat hasta.* ('they ask that he might either pour out Lyctian weapons from his bow or cross the clouds with a slender spear', 6.927–8). This means that Statius has all eight Homeric events. Silius is clearly following Virgil, though his return to the final javelin looks to Homer. The first impression from Statius is that he on the other hand bypasses Virgil and returns to a Homeric, pre-Virgilian epic ideal. This in itself can be seen as a mode of authorisation: it is as if Statius is claiming for his games pre-eminence in the art of imitating Homer, finessing Virgil in their epic 'reality'. Statius' games go back to basics, proclaiming their Homeric pedigree. This, however, is only one side of the argument.

Looking closely at the list of Statius' games (see Table 1) makes it clear that imitation of Virgil is at least as high a priority as imitation of the Homeric programme. The running, boxing and archery all occur in the same order as in the *Aeneid*; to bring this about, it was necessary to change the Homeric order. Virgil's games are so set up that they clash directly with the Homeric order, swapping over the running and the boxing.[38] Statius allies himself with Virgil and Romanness in the order of events, but he is mediating between

---

[37] Some scholars have underestimated the Homeric influence on Statius: Willis (1941) describes Statius' games as 'essentially Vergilian' (p. 409). Vessey (1970) corrects the balance. Juhnke (1972) 109 reads the chariot race as much closer to Virgil than Homer, although he goes on to point out the considerable Homeric parallels, and specifically points to the funeral context as Homeric.

[38] Although, as Kytzler (1968) 6–7 points out, Statius keeps to the Homeric order in his combat events.

the two by playing off number and type of events against order and organisation.[39] The contest between Homer and Virgil is part of a larger negotiation in the *Thebaid* between ideas of Greekness and Romanness; while Statius makes his games more Greek, Silius' games are unrelentingly Roman.

Statius is not simply creating a mixture of Homeric and Virgilian elements: the games are a new compound.[40] Traditionally, Statius' claims of inferiority to Virgil and Homer have been taken at face value, ignoring the evidence of what the text actually does.[41] In fact, the games, which have often been called 'derivative', are a prime site for Statius' intimations of superiority.[42] At the beginning of the chariot race, he calls on Apollo for inspiration and suggests that his race will be the best ever (6.296–300):

Primus sudor equis. dic inclyta, Phoebe, regentum
nomina, dic ipsos; neque enim generosior umquam
alipedum conlata acies, ceu praepete cursu
confligant densae uolucres aut litore in uno
Aeolus insanis statuat certamina uentis.

First comes the sweat of horses. Tell, Phoebus, of the famous names
of the drivers, tell of the horses themselves; for never was a more noble column
of wing-footed steeds brought together, as if a thick cloud of birds
contends in a headlong race or Aeolus sets up a struggle
for the insane winds together on one shore.

---

[39] While Statius brings out the clash between Homer and Virgil, Silius irons over the cracks: he replaces Virgil's boxing with gladiatorial fights broadly analogous to the Homeric fight in armour, a way of reading the two orders as compatible.

[40] Vessey (1970) 429 sees Virgilian elements dominating in both chariot race and running.

[41] Most famously, *Thebaid* 12.816–17: *uiue, precor; nec tu diuinam Aeneida tempta,* | *sed longe sequere et uestigia semper adora* ('live, I pray, and don't you challenge the divine Aeneid, but follow far behind and always worship her footsteps'); also the apostrophe to Hopleus and Dymas at 10.445–8, especially: *quamuis mea carmina surgant* | *inferiore lyra* ('although my songs rise from a lower lyre', 445–6). Duff (1964) sees his epilogue as concerning 'above all his worshipful reverence for Virgil, the inspirer of his epic style' (p. 374).

[42] Even Vessey (1970), who champions the games, says: '[a] modern reader may well find the games in *Thebaid* VI one of the least interesting sections of the epic: it is also one of the most obviously derivative.' (p. 426). Duff (1964) has: 'because there were funeral games in Virgil, we must have almost a whole book devoted to the rites and contests in memory of the child Archemorus.' (p. 384). 'And too many of his incidents, in spite of ingenious variation of detail, are but echoes of Vergil. The foot-race and the archery contest at the funeral games of Archemorus ... are perhaps the most marked examples of this unfortunate characteristic.' (Butler (1909) 220–21). On criticism of Statius in general see Ahl (1986) 2804–11.

This makes clear a claim to superiority: these games are not just descendants of the race of Homer and Virgil, they are the culmination of the evolutionary process. But *generosior* makes a claim for the superiority of Statius' horses based on their descent: they are the best because they come after and out of the heritage of their predecessors. And the verbs of gathering and competing (*conlata* and *confligant*) are also verbs of comparison. As they compete with each other, so they should be compared with their predecessors. In the same way, the Flavian epic poets compete with each other for the right to be compared with their predecessors. This incessant competition within the tradition, vertically and horizontally, with the past and with contemporaries, creates a generic framework of extraordinary vibrancy.

The following chapter will show that the chariots are not merely an imitation of the Homeric chariot race, and a repositioning of the Virgilian ship race, but a multiplication of all the races, a structure of repetitions signalled throughout, races within races. Each event has its own intertextual mode: if the chariot race is a structure of repetitions, the running thematises multiplication; the discus stages replacement; the boxing plays with reversal; the wrestling sets up a competition between previous versions; the sword fight displays erasure, and the archery is an exercise in subtraction. Statius self-consciously highlights his own complex games with his models, and we can see different tactics at work in different events. What is more, he is not only playing against the *Iliad* and the *Aeneid*. An alternative stream of epic, running through Apollonius' *Argonautica*, and the *Metamorphoses*, to Valerius Flaccus' Argonautica, flows equally through the *Thebaid*. Lucan, too, is an important forerunner. The complexity of the interplay of his models is always on display; for instance, I read the wrestling match below as a contest between Ovid and Lucan. Reading Statius is a process of extraordinary richness.[43] His famous stance of humility towards his predecessors is matched with a pride in his creations which makes him himself a version of Apollo and his poem the last word in epic.

---

[43] See for example, my discussion of the ekphrasis of the prizes at the end of the chariot race (Lovatt (2002)), where a Homeric object and a Virgilian object form the two prizes, but both are decorated with Ovid.

We have pursued an intertextual reading of Statius' games; intra-textuality is another important aspect. One of the central claims of this book is that epic games are an essential tool for reading epic. *Aeneid* 5 has been read as an *Aeneis in paruo* (a miniature version of the *Aeneid*), and Statius' games are a microcosm of the war in the second half of the *Thebaid*.[44] Kytzler has suggested that one of the organising principles of the structure of Statius' games is the choice of victors (see table 1).[45] Amphiaraus wins the first event and is the first to die; his death is foreshadowed in the event. Adrastus ends the games with an omen of his own survival, alone of all the leaders. Statius brings this structure out in the archery, where Adrastus is asked to take part in the games 'so that victory is not lacking to any one of the number of leaders' (*ne uictoria desit | una ducum numero*, 6.926–7), and even more strongly in the wrestling. In the first lines of the event, Tydeus wishes that he could have entered everything (6.826–30):

> iamdudum uariae laudes et conscia uirtus
> Tydea magnanimum stimulis urgentibus angunt.
> Ille quidem et disco bonus et contendere cursu,
> nec caestu bellare minor, sed corde labores
> ante alios erat uncta pale.

> Now for a long time the varied praises and his conspiratorial manhood
> have been anguishing great-hearted Tydeus with their driving spurs.
> He indeed was good at competing in both the discus and the running,
> nor was he less impressive at fighting with boxing gloves, but
> the anointed wrestling was held above other labours in his heart.

---

[44] Galinsky (1968).

[45] Kytzler's reading of the 'Ordnungsprinzip' of Statius' games (Kytzler (1968) 3–5) suggests four factors in the ordering of Statius' events: reflection of the order of the deaths of the heroes (cf. Legras (1905) 79–90); diminishing numbers of competitors; increasing seriousness of the events (citing Helm (1892) 174); organisation by types of events (races and combat sports are grouped together). It is difficult to know how to interpret the second (and it only works if you count the horses in the chariot race), although I have read this factor in the discus as a play on the difference between the games in the *Iliad* and the *Odyssey*. The third ignores the many elements of the chariot race which make it just as warlike as any other event. The fourth is disturbed by the positioning of the discus, which would surely be grouped with the javelin and archery in a classification of this type. It would be equally possible to characterise the order as evoking the pentathlon: running, discus, wrestling and javelin are all in sequence, only broken by the intrusion of the boxing and the omission of the jump.

Table 1. *Table of structures of games*

Homer: *Iliad* 23	Virgil: *Aeneid* 5	Statius: *Thebaid* 6	Silius Italicus: *Punica* 16	Winners in Statius
Funeral of Patroclus	Rites for Anchises	Funeral of Opheltes	Rites for the two Scipios	
1. Chariot race	1. Ship race	1. Chariot race	1. Chariot race	Amphiaraus
2. Boxing	2. Running	2. Running	2. Running	Parthenopaeus
3. Wrestling		3. Discus		Hippomedon
4. Running	3. Boxing	4. Boxing		Capaneus
		5. Wrestling		Tydeus
5. Fight in armour		6. Fight in armour (see event 3)	3. Gladiatorial fights	Polynices
6. Discus				
7. Archery	4. Archery	7. Archery	4. Javelin	Adrastus
8. Javelin	5. *Lusus Troiae*	(beginning of archery: mention of javelin)	5. Honorific javelin throw	

Statius is playing with his own arrangement of the games. In the *Thebaid*, each hero has his game, as each hero has his aristeia later on in the poem. This is certainly not the case in the *Iliad* where, for instance, Telamonian Ajax draws in both the wrestling and the sword fight, loses the discus, and then comes forward for the javelin.[46] Thus, when Tydeus has *conscia uirtus* and self-consciously chafes against the tight authorial control, on one level, Statius is foregrounding the artificiality of his highly structured games. This strategy is clearly in competition with other organising principles, not least the intertextual concerns we have examined above, and except for Polynices, last competitor and last to die, the other events do not follow the order of the heroes' deaths (Amphiaraus at the end of book 7, Tydeus at the end of book 8, Hippomedon halfway through 9, Parthenopaeus at the end of 9, and Capaneus at the end of 10). But structure is only one way in which the games function as a microcosm of the war, and not by any means the most important one. Like any great poem, every part of the *Thebaid* reflects on, is a *mise en abyme* of, the whole. The games, as a self-standing episode, are a showcase for the interwoven thematic continuity, the intratextuality of the *Thebaid*.

The epic programme

We can think further about the interactions between Greek and Roman in epic games if we also bring in historical spectacles and their multifarious programmes. I want to begin considering the ways that epic poets used real games by looking at the programmes of Homer, Virgil, Statius and Silius and comparing them to the programmes of the Olympic Games and the Roman *ludi circenses*.

The programme of events in the Homeric games was fundamentally different from the Olympic programme, which forms the model for Greek games celebrated at Rome. Two of the Homeric events, discus and javelin, only occur in the Olympic pentathlon. The fight in armour and the archery, both important events in the

---

[46] Odysseus wins the foot race and draws the wrestling; Antilochus enters both races; Diomedes wins the chariot race and draws the sword fight; Epeius wins the boxing but embarrasses himself in the discus; Meriones comes last in the chariot race and the archery, and then comes forward for the javelin.

Iliadic games, do not make it into the Olympics. Various Olympic events (especially the *pankration*) have no precedent in Homer. Given Homer's foundational status in Greek culture, the events from the Homeric games which failed to make it into the ever-expanding Olympic programme (fight in armour and archery) are perhaps more significant than those Olympic events with no Homeric prototype (most importantly the *pankration* – the jump is in the *Odyssey*). We can see from table 2 that Virgil's programme moves as far away from the Olympic model as possible. He has only four events and mediates between his Iliadic model and Roman games: the ship race pays homage to Augustus' Actian games at Nikopolis, and marks a move away from both Homer and the Olympic model.[47] Running and boxing were both events represented by Roman sources as taking place in the *ludi circenses*.[48] The archery is pure Homer, taking on the whole apparatus of tree, dove and cord, but transforming it into something essentially Roman at the very last minute by awarding the prize to Acestes for his display shot, which turns into an omen.

We have seen how Statius mediates between Virgil and Homer in his programme.[49] In the emphasis he places on returning to the epic programme, Statius seems inevitably to move away from contemporary Roman games towards the epic model, more Greek than Roman, more ideal than real. However, the games pull back towards the Roman and the real in other ways. For instance, the chariot race in the *Thebaid* is specifically a four-horse race, unlike the Homeric race.[50] The games and the chariot race begin with what is quite clearly presented as a *pompa*, a procession of divine

---

[47] Briggs (1975) on Virgil's games as Augustan.

[48] Livy 1.35.10 (boxers as well as horses); Cicero *De Legibus* 2.38 (running, boxing, wrestling and chariot races); see Thuillier (1982); Crowther (1983). There is great debate about whether these events, which were part of the *ludi circenses*, were actually athletic as such; we know very little about how they were carried out, or even how often. Even if these events are not viewed as 'athletic', they could still be evoked by the descriptions of epic games. Legras (1905) 238 attributes Statius' presentation of runners in the circus to imitation of Homer. This seems counterintuitive since the athletic space in the *Iliad* certainly was not a circus.

[49] See above p. 12.

[50] *Thebaid* 6.369–70, 501–4. The race in the *Iliad* is a two-horse race, but elsewhere in Homer four-horse races are mentioned: see Mouratidis (1984). On chariot racing at Rome see also: Cameron (1973), Cameron (1976).

Table 2. *Comparison of games*

Homer, *Iliad* 23	Olympics	*Ludi circenses*
1. Two-horse chariot race	Four-horse and two-horse chariot race	Four-horse and two-horse chariot race
2. Boxing	Boxing	Boxing
3. Wrestling	Wrestling	Wrestling
4. Running	Long, 400 m and 200 m running	Running (length unknown)
5. Sword fight	*Pankration*	
6. Discus	Pentathlon (discus, javelin, 200 m, jump, wrestling)	
7. Archery		
8. Javelin	(in pentathlon)	
Odyssey 8.120–30: running, wrestling, jump, discus, boxing.	Other events: horse race, race in armour, competitions for trumpeters and heralds	

Virgil *Aeneid* 5	Statius *Thebaid* 6	Silius Italicus *Punica* 16
1. Ship race	1. Four-horse chariot race	1. Four-horse chariot race
2. Running	2. Running	2. Running
	3. Discus	
3. Boxing	4. Boxing	
	5. Wrestling	
	6. Sword fight	3. Gladiatorial fights
	6.5 Mention of Javelin	4. Javelin
4. Archery	7. Archery	
5. *Lusus Troiae*		5. Honorific javelin throw

and ancestral images, just as the *ludi circenses* did.[51] The epic programme of Statius' games, then, is offset by intruding elements of the Roman and the real. Statius melds these realms together,

---

[51] There is a procession of images of gods and ancestors at 6.268–95 which is clearly set within the context of the games. This *pompa* forms the subject of a separate study, which will be published elsewhere.

bringing Homer into Rome and creating an entirely different mix of the epic and the real, the Greek and Roman from Virgil.[52]

Silius is faced with the distinctly different challenge of taking a set of games which are historical (described in Livy at 28.21) and making them compatible with his epic framework. The solution takes his games in a very different direction from Statius. In Livy, the main part of the games is gladiatorial; in Silius, this becomes the third event of the programme, subordinated to the epic (particularly the Virgilian) model. Yet this gladiatorial event and the honorific javelin throwing significantly change the tone of the games as a whole, turning them into a much more Roman and more military affair than either Statius' or Virgil's games.

The second section of chapter 1 (the chariot race) forms an in-depth discussion of epic games and real games, looking at the games of Virgil, Statius and Silius against the reality of historical games. This is the most historical of the realities at play in the book: chapter 2 investigates the running and thinks about the erotics of *fama*, leading into a discussion of the power of the audience in epic games and war; the third event is the discus, which is read against the reality of the cosmos, teamed up with a wider discussion of heroism and gigantomachy in the *Thebaid*. Ethnicity and national identity is the reality behind the boxing, while the wrestling is played out on the reality of the body. Finally, the fight in armour is matched with the reality of war, while the archery brings us to Adrastus, the producer of the games, and to the reality of power.

---

[52] Legras (1905) 237–8 asks whether Statius was describing the practices of his own time or imitating Homer. He sees the two as mutually exclusive and, on the evidence of the passage, where lots are drawn from a helmet to determine the starting places in the chariot race (6.367; *Iliad* 23.352), concludes that Statius could not have been describing Roman games.

THE CHARIOT RACE

Introduction

This section has three aims: to show how Statius reworks his predecessors in the chariot race, to examine in particular the significance of the Phaethon myth here and for the whole *Thebaid*, and to investigate the poetics of athletics and the chariot race in particular.[1] From the time of Choerilus of Samos in the late fifth century BC, chariots of song have raced each other, and contemporary poets have figured as lagging behind their predecessors in the competition for readers (*SH* 317):

᾿Α μάκαρ, ὅστις ἔην κεῖνον χρόνον ἴδρις ἀοιδῆς,
Μουσάων θεράπων, ὅτ᾿ ἀκήρατος ἦν ἔτι λειμών·
νῦν δ᾿ ὅτε πάντα δέδασται, ἔχουσι δὲ πείρατα τέχναι,
ὕστατοι ὥστε δρόμου καταλειπόμεθ᾿, οὐδέ πηι ἔστι
πάντηι παπταίνοντα νεοζυγὲς ἅρμα πελάσσαι.

Ah, fortunate one, whoever was a skilful singer at that time,
servant of the Muses, when the meadow was still unspoilt;
now that all has been distributed, and the arts have their limits,
we are like latecomers, left behind in the race, and one looks
all around in vain for somewhere to drive a newly-yoked chariot.

In Pindar, athletic competition was already a traditional metaphor for poetry.[2] Poetry competitions ran alongside athletic competitions at the great festivals; Statius himself competed unsuccessfully for the Capitoline crown, though he did win the less important Alban games.[3] He describes his father's poetic victories in terms of the athletic victories of Castor and Pollux (*Siluae* 5.3.138–40):

---

[1] On the agonistic nature of intertextuality, see Hardie (1993) 101–19.
[2] Simpson (1969) 437 n. 1. Poetry as javelin-throwing: *Olympian* 13.89–91; *Pythian* 1.43–5; *Nemean* 7.70–72, 81; 9.55; *Isthmian* 2.35–7. Footrace: *Olympian* 8.54. Boxing: *Olympian* 10.3b–6; *Nemean* 10.20; *Isthmian* 4.19–21. Wrestling: *Nemean* 4.4–5, 93–6; *Nemean* 8.19.
[3] See A. Hardie (2003).

inde frequens pugnae nulloque ingloria sacro
uox tua: non totiens uictorem Castora gyro
nec fratrem caestu uirides plausere Therapnae.

Then your voice was a frequent competitor and lacking in glory
at no festival: green Therapnae did not applaud Castor so often
as victor in the chariot race, nor his brother in the boxing.

Elsewhere in the *Siluae*, Statius represents his own poetry as chariot racing: in 4.7, a key poem for Statius' representation of himself as epic poet in the *Siluae*, for instance (*Siluae* 4.7.1–4, 21–8):

> Iam diu lato spatiata campo
> fortis heroos, Erato, labores
> differ atque ingens opus in minores
>   contrahe gyros,
>
> torpor est nostris sine te Camenis,
> tardius sueto uenit ipse Thymbrae
> rector et primis meus ecce metis
>   haeret Achilles.
>
> quippe te fido monitore nostra
> Thebais multa cruciata lima
> temptat audaci fide Mantuanae
>   gaudia famae.
>
> Brave Erato, now for a long time spread out
> in a broad field, put off heroic
> toils and contract your huge work
>   into smaller laps,
>
> My muses are inert without you,
> the ruler of Thymbra himself comes more slowly
> than usual and look, my Achilles sticks
>   at the first turning-post.
>
> For with you as loyal adviser my
> Thebais, much tortured with the file,
> challenges with daring confidence the joys
>   of Virgilian fame.

Here, both epic and *Siluae* are chariots of song. The image of the *Achilleid* stuck at the first turning-post of the race clearly refers to the poem as a chariot, with the irony that Apollo is described as *rector*, literally driver, and as slower than normal (*tardius sueto*).[4] In the next stanza, it is tempting to read the *temptat* of line 27 as a suggestion that the *Thebaid* is pursuing the *Aeneid* in a chariot race, especially given the idea of pursuit in the *sphragis* to the *Thebaid* (12.816–17). The first four lines, too, can be read as further chariot race imagery.[5] The wide field is that of games as much as battle (*campo* of running course, *Thebaid* 6.594), and in the chariot race Statius describes the business of racing in terms of *gyros*: *dum non cohibente magistro | spargitur in gyros dexterque exerrat Arion* ('while his master was not controlling him, Arion is scattered in circles and wanders out to the right' *Thebaid* 6.443–4). In this image, both epic and *Siluae* are chariots of poetry: the course of the Callimachean *Siluae* is simply more controlled and closer to the mark (and, by implication, epic is a dangerous excess which threatens to run out of control). In the same way, the *Siluae* are described as slim (4.7.9) and more chaste (4.7.12), but it is the *Thebaid* which has been polished in the Catullan manner.[6] Joanne Brown has convincingly shown the strongly Callimachean nature of the *Thebaid*.[7] Here we can see an image of the poet's career as a chariot race, where the huge and uncontrolled laps of epic turn into the tight cornering of the *Siluae*.

It is clear then that Statius associated competition between poets with athletic contests and, throughout his book of athletic games in the *Thebaid*, there is a persistent stream of imagery about the process of writing, reacting to poetry itself, a meta-narrative in which he explores intertextual competitions, and reflects on the role of epic poetry under Domitian.[8]

---

[4] Coleman (1998) 203 points to the pleasing irony of swift-footed Achilles immobilised.

[5] Coleman (1998) 198 suggests that this first stanza refers to epic as horse-racing and lyric as dressage: 'Statius here visualises epic composition not as a sea-voyage but as a gallop around the racetrack, contrasting with the tightly controlled dressage of lyric.' To view both as chariot images is surely simpler, especially given the frequency of poetic chariot imagery and the popularity of chariot racing.

[6] Catullus 1.1: *cui dono lepidum nouum libellum | arida modo pumice expolitum?* ('Who is this charming new book, just now polished with dry pumice, for?') See Coleman (1998) 203 on this Callimachean metaphor.

[7] Brown (1994).

[8] The language of games continually creeps into discussions of intertextuality: Ripoll (1998) 20 suggests that Flavian epic is a product of 'les jeux d'*imitatio* et d'*aemulatio* littéraires.'

Races within races: repetition and deletion

As befits this race which claims to be the greatest ever, Statius has more chariots than either Homer or Virgil, seven to Homer's five and Virgil's four.[9] Silius, following a policy of much closer imitation of Virgil, has four. Statius' contestants are presented in pairs, and the action of the race is similarly divided. First, there is Polynices, paired only with Arion the horse; later, they seem to be racing against each other. Amphiaraus the prophet (and by that right in some sense a figure of the poet as well) is the counterpoint of Admetus, linked by their devotion to Apollo. After Amphiaraus and Admetus comes the positive paradigm, Hypsipyle's sons, the good brothers who love each other. With them in mind, it makes perverse sense that Polynices should be without his other half: for who can that be but his brother? The final pair is Chromis, son of Hercules, and Hippodamus, son of Oenomaus. They are linked by fury and monstrousness: *crudelibus ambo | exuuiis diroque imbuti sanguine currus* ('both chariots are dripping with cruel souvenirs and dread blood', 6.349–50). During the race they will work and race in pairs; at the front, Admetus and Amphiaraus will vie to overtake the randomly lurching Polynices; Euneos will fail to stop Thoas falling; Hippodamus and Chromis will play out a deadly struggle against each other. The race is thus structured as if it were a series of single combats. This is similar to the Homeric race, where Diomedes and Eumelus are the only ones in the running, and Menelaus and Antilochus fight it out for second place after Eumelus' fall. The ship race in Virgil, however, is carefully constructed to give all the ships a share of the drama; Gyas leads from Cloanthus at the beginning; he is passed on the inside and throws his helmsman overboard, which then causes him to be slowed down so much that he is overtaken by Mnestheus, who passed Sergestus when his ship crashed. The final strait sees Cloanthus and Mnestheus neck and neck but, with help from the sea gods, Cloanthus eventually pulls ahead for victory.[10] Thus, we see Mnestheus go from last place to

---

[9] Juhnke (1972) 233.

[10] Silius follows Virgil faithfully in the structure of his race: Cyrnus leads at the beginning, followed by Hiberus, who overtakes. The young driver Durius takes out Atlas with his dangerous driving (like Antilochus in the *Iliad*) and proceeds to overtake Cyrnus until he

almost winning.[11] Virgil's race is most evidently one race: Statius' chariots run several separate races.[12]

Statius' chariot race is a sequence of repetitions. The chariots restart the race (as it were) in the fourth lap: *uixdum coeptus equis labor* ('the toil of the horses has scarcely begun', 469); the wheels clash as if it has happened many times: *rursus* ('again', 454), *iterum* ('again', 455); and when Amphiaraus makes his final push for home, it is as if he is starting again (6.522–4):

> ceu modo carceribus dimissus in arua solutis
> uerberibusque iubas et terga lacessit habenis
> increpitans Caerumque leuem Cygnumque niualem.

> As if just now sent out into the fields when the starting-gates were opened
> he lashes the crests with blows and their backs with the reins,
> shouting at both light Caerus and snowy Cygnus.

As if he is not just repeating his models, but repeating his own race many times over within itself, Statius dramatises the process of repetition in the chariot race.[13]

---

is challenging Hiberus for the lead. But he drops his whip at the last minute (a Homeric touch), and Hiberus pulls home.

[11] This can be read as an example of a Virgilian theme of renewal: from the ashes of Troy the losers come to found the winners of Rome. Von Stosch (1968) 31 compares Virgil's linear narrative with the Homeric and Statian narratives, which fall into two parts.

[12] The structure of the race could well be influenced by the various ways in which the chariot races were run in the circus. As well as ordinary races, there were team races where teams of two, three or four helped each other in the manoeuvring for position which inevitably took place in a race that could last for thirteen laps. The main source for this practice is Sidonius 23.307–427, which gives a vivid description of a team race. See Cameron (1976) 51–3; Harris (1972) 198–205 on Diocles the Red. In the *Thebaid*, Thoas and Euneos set out to help each other, as much as compete against each other. Statius states specifically that their aims are either to win or lose only to each other: *geminis eadem omnia: uultus, | currus, equi, uestes, par et concordia uotis, | uincere uel solo cupiunt a fratre relinqui* ('twins, the same in everything: face, chariot, horses, clothes, equal and in concord in their prayers, they desire either to conquer or to be left behind only by their brother', 6.343–5).

[13] Feldherr (2002) 63–4 points to the ship race as a model of progress in repetition as postulated by Quint (1993) 53, dramatising the redemptive qualities of selective imitation. In Statius' version, however, repetition and the perfect circle lose their redemptive qualities. For instance, Feldherr (63) points to the arrow moving ever closer to its goal as another image of progress. In the *Thebaid*, however, the arrow is the ultimate image of futile repetition and return: the arrow returns into the mouth of the quiver and represents defeat, destruction and the futility of the whole enterprise of the poem (not to mention Oedipus, as Jupiter puts it in book 1, *reuolutus in ortus* ('returning to the beginning', 1.235). On repetition and responses to the *Aeneid*, see Hardie (1993) 14–18. On repetition and intertextuality, see Hinds (1998) 99–122.

As the chariots enter the second lap, Statius writes: *delet sulcos iterata priores | orbita* ('the repeated ruts delete the former furrows', 6.415–16). The conceit is that as the second lap follows in the tracks of the first, inevitably the old tracks themselves are covered up by the new. Read as meta-narrative, it suggests that repetition and imitation entail deletion. Thus when Statius repeats Homer, he replaces Homer in the minds of his readers. The rerun wipes out the previous race as part of its validation. This is a radical rereading of the chariot imagery used by Callimachus, when Apollo warns him to stay away from the paths worn by the chariots of previous poets (Callimachus *Aetia* 1.25–8 Pf.):

πρὸς δέ σε καὶ τόδ᾽ ἄνωγα, τὰ μὴ πατέουσιν ἄμαξαι
τὰ στείβειν, ἑτέρων ἴχνια μὴ καθ᾽ ὁμά
δίφρον ἐλᾶν μηδ᾽ οἷμον ἀνὰ πλατύν, ἀλλὰ κελεύθους
ἀτρίπτους, εἰ καὶ στεινοτέρην ἐλάσεις.

But I command you this: don't tread the path which wagons
    trample, don't drive your chariot on the common ruts
of others nor along a broad road, but on unworn
paths, even though your way is narrower.

Statius' worn path is a place to hide the implications of his story under the authority of previous tracks; it allows him to create new meanings between repetition and deletion.[14]

He even repeats his repetitions. For at the beginning of the race (in one of the most famous lines of the episode) he imitates the notorious Ennian dactylic line of *Aeneid* 8:[15] compare *quadripedante putrem sonitu quatit ungula campum* ('the hooves shook the dusty plain with four-footed sound', *Aeneid* 8.596) with *ante fugam, absentemque ferit grauis ungula campum* ('before the flight, the heavy hoof strikes the absent plain', 6.401). Virgil's line is full of the enthusiasm of young men going off to war as though it was a game; Statius' horses seem to be ready for battle in this race. This repetition is marked by absence. The horses tread a field that is not there, emphasising the futility of both wars and races. This, however, is not the only repetition. At 459 it recurs, this time in a

---

[14] On Statius' Callimachean leanings see Brown (1994) 53–6.
[15] See Henderson (1991) 67 n. 61; Gossage (1969) 88.

section of violent clashes, where he specifically compares the race to an act of war (6.456–9):

> pax nulla fidesque:
> bella geri ferro leuius, bella horrida credas;
> is furor in laudes, trepidant mortemque minantur,
> multaque transuersis praestringitur ungula campis.

There is no peace, no faith:
war, bristling war, would be waged more lightly with iron, you would believe;
such is their madness for praise, they panic and threaten death,
and many hooves are scraped on the cross-wise plains.

The echo of the Sibyl's prophecy in *Aeneid* 6 (*bella, horrida bella*, 'war, bristling war', 6.86) underlines the connections.[16] All wars are repetitions of futile stupidity, as all races are eventually the same; the games in the *Thebaid* are intimately linked to the war ahead, and the *Thebaid* is intimately linked to the *Aeneid*. Statius' races within races reflect, in their structure of multiple repetition, the fragmentation of both models and authorial voice.

The chariot of song

From the time of Pindar, the poet has presented himself as driving the chariot of the Muses.[17] The image of the chariot of song pervades both Greek and Latin poetry.[18] The chariot of song can even be portrayed as taking part in a race. Lucretius asks Calliope to speed him through the last lap (Lucretius 6.92–5):

> tu mihi supremae praescripta ad candida calcis
> currenti spatium praemonstra, callida musa
> Calliope, requies hominum diuumque uoluptas,
> te duce ut insigni capiam cum laude coronam.

---

[16] Von Stosch (1968) 140 n. 7. The anaphora of *bella* occurs in the *Thebaid* four times: 3.355; 3.593; 4.637; 7.797. *Bella horrida* features at 4.601, 6.864, and at *Aeneid* 6.86, 7.41.

[17] Pindar *Pythian* 10.65; *Isthmian* 2.1–5, 7.17–19, 8.61–3; *Olympian* 6.22–5. See: Kenney (1958) 206; Harriott (1969) 63–7; Simpson (1969); Myerowitz (1985) 73–103.

[18] Kenney (1958) 206 citing: Bacchylides *Epinician* 5.176–7; Empedocles fr. 3.5; Callimachus frr. 1.25–8, 195.26–9 Pf.; Columella 10.215–16; Lucretius 6.47, 92–93; Propertius 2.10.2, 3.1.9–14, 3.3.18, 3.9.58; Virgil *Georgics* 2.541–2; Manilius 2.59; Ovid *Ars Amatoria* 1.39–40, 1.264, 2.426, 3.467–8, 3.809–10, *Remedia Amoris* 394, *Fasti* 1.25, 2.360, 4.10, 6.585–6; Juvenal 1.19–20. Cf. Henderson (1970).

Calliope, rest of men and pleasure of gods,
cunning muse, as I run, guide me through that space
to the finishing line of final chalk, written in white beforehand,
so that with you as leader I might take the crown with outstanding praise.

Here, he imagines the last book as the last lap and himself as
poet in the chariot of song, speeding towards the chalk finishing
line and winning the crown of poetic success.[19] The association
with Calliope speaks particularly of his ambitions to attain poetic
immortality as an *epic* poet. In Propertius 4.1, too, the claim to
move away from the frivolous towards the Roman is cast in terms
of a chariot race (Propertius 4.1.69–70):

sacra diesque canam et cognomina prisca locorum:
    has meus ad metas sudet oportet equus.'

I will sing the festivals and the days and the ancient names of places:
my horse ought to sweat for these goals.

The image of the chariot course is satisfyingly double in its implications: the *metae* are turning-points, but Propertius leaves ambivalent which way he is turning, and whether he will turn once or
twice. In the Circus Maximus there are two *metae*, and in the second half of this poem his cheerful confidence that he can leave love
behind for Rome is turned around again by Horos. The traditional
grandeur of the image of the chariot of song is undercut by the
implications of changing back again in the image of the *metae*.[20]
The chariot race, then, can be read metapoetically. Virgil's ship
race too is part of a similar strand of imagery on the ship of song.[21]
It is this image which Statius uses of the *Thebaid* at its close: *et
mea iam longo meruit ratis aequore portum* ('and my ship has now,
after a long time at sea, deserved the port', 12.809).

The significance of poetry for Statius' chariot race in particular
is marked in two ways. First, the eventual winner of the chariot race
is Amphiaraus, a *uates* ('poet/prophet'): he is called *uates* at the
moment of victory: *cessit uictoria uati* ('victory fell to the prophet',

---

[19] Henderson (1970) 740 notes that Lucretius only uses *insignis* in contexts where he refers
to his poetic ambitions.
[20] Propertius 4.2.58 uses the image of the finishing line.
[21] Kenney (1958) 205–6; Myerowitz (1985) 73–103. Kenney holds that it is 'too common
in the poets to be accounted characteristically didactic'.

530).[22] He is a figure of knowledge and prophecy, a follower of Apollo, who knows the plot before it unrolls. Second, and more important, is the involvement of Apollo himself.[23] Apollo first appears at 355, singing poetry to an audience of the Muses, on the mountain sacred to poetry, Parnassus (*Thebaid* 6.358–64):

> nam saepe Iouem Phlegramque suique
> anguis opus fratrumque pius cantarat honores.
> tunc aperit quis fulmen agat, quis sidera ducat
> spiritus, unde animi fluuiis, quae pabula uentis,
> quo fonte immensum uiuat mare, quae uia solis
> praecipitet noctem, quae porrigat, imane tellus
> an media et rursus mundo succincta latenti.

For often he had loyally sung about Jupiter and Phlegra,
his own snake feat and the honours of his brothers.
Then he reveals what spirit drives the thunderbolt and leads
the stars, where the force of the rivers comes from, what is fodder for the
    winds,
from what source the immeasurable sea gains life, which route of the sun
hastens night, which draws it out, whether earth is in the depths
or in the middle, and whether it is surrounded again with a hidden world.

Like Iopas in the *Aeneid* (1.742–6) and Orpheus in the *Argonautica* (1.494–515), Apollo sings a song of the natural world.[24] Statius' Apollo takes it further, however, with the gigantomachy (358–9); in fact, he sets the divine exploits at the beginning of his song, singing dutifully (*pius*) as if commissioned. This is the height of the poetic scale, philosophical epic sung by the god of poetry to the Muses on Parnassus. What is more, when Apollo's instrument is described as a *chelys* ('tortoise'), this looks back to Statius' description of himself in his proem: *tempus erit, cum Pierio tua fortior oestro | facta canam: nunc tendo chelyn; satis arma referre | Aonia* ('there will be a time when braver through the sting of the Pierian gadfly I will sing your deeds: now I stretch out my tortoise; it is enough to tell of Theban weapons', 1.32–4). Apollo represents

---

[22] Also indirectly at 3.450.

[23] On Apollo and poetry in the *Thebaid* see Brown (1994) 40, 169–74.

[24] Venini (1961b) 384; Von Stosch (1968) 118; Vessey (1973) 213–14. The *auidas sorores* ('greedy sisters') in particular are reminiscent of the reaction of the Argonauts to Orpheus' song (1.512–15), where they are reluctant to stop listening, 'charmed by the spell of the song' (θέλκτρον ἀοιδῆς, 1.515); also cf. Dido listening to Aeneas (*Aeneid* 1.748–50).

divine and poetic order, telling of divine contests against destructive monsters, and literally ordering the cosmos in his song. His natural philosophy will return as imagery in Statius' chariot race: the spirit drives (*agat*) the thunderbolt, and leads (*ducat*) the stars; river, wind and storm are images for the speed of the chariots; the path of the sun reminds us of Phaethon. Both Amphiaraus and Apollo are poet figures and the chariot race dramatises the processes of inspiration and poetry at work.

Polynices as Phaethon

Amphiaraus is only second favourite for the chariot race (*spes proxima palmae*, 'next hope for victory', 326). The favourite is Polynices, borrowing Arion, his father-in-law's divine horse.[25] The essential plot of the chariot race revolves around Polynices' failure to control the chariot on loan and Apollo's machinations to secure victory for Amphiaraus. At the beginnning of the race, Adrastus advises Polynices on how to drive the horses, replaying the scene in the *Iliad* where Nestor advises Antilochus (*Iliad* 23.306–48; *Thebaid* 6.316–25).[26] As ever, Statius does not simply repeat: Polynices is not just Antilochus, but also Ovid's Phaethon (*Metamorphoses* 1.747–2.328).[27] We are directed to make the comparison in a simile (6.320–24):

> sic ignea lora
> cum daret et rapido Sol natum imponeret axi,
> gaudentem lacrimans astra insidiosa docebat
> nolentesque teri zonas mediamque polorum
> temperiem:

In the same way, when the Sun gave him the fiery reins,
and put his son on the swift chariot,
lamenting for him as he rejoiced, he taught him about the treacherous stars,
the zones which refuse to be trodden, and the temperate region
in the middle of the poles:

---

[25] On Arion, see Taisne (1994) 333–4. [26] Legras (1905) 85; Vessey (1970) 427.
[27] Vessey (1973) 216. Vessey points out another resemblance, a resemblance to Hippolytus' death as described by Euripides and Seneca. Taisne (1994) 33. Cf. Most (1992) on Seneca's *Hippolytus*.

Verbal reminiscences of Ovid's Phaethon story saturate the description of Polynices as he races, too.[28] Although the links have been well documented by Von Stosch, the implications have not been fully explored.[29] Both stories are structured by the problems of authenticating paternity;[30] both young men threaten and overturn the cosmos.[31] Finally, I will look at what happens when both are read as poet figures.

The story of Phaethon begins with a challenge to his paternity: his peer Epaphus calls him a fool to believe his mother's story that Apollo is his father (*Metamorphoses* 1.750–54).[32] His desire to prove himself his father's son leads to his request to borrow the chariot (*Met.* 2.38–9). He demands the chariot as if it were his inheritance (*Met.* 2.47). It is precisely in the tracks of his father that he must drive (*Met.* 2.133). As he reaches the moment of recognition, when he realises that he will not be able to drive the chariot, he longs to reject the responsibility of divine paternity. Phaethon's tragedy is that he cannot replace his father. In the case of Polynices, it is the other way around. By driving the chariot of Adrastus, Polynices is attempting to abandon his Theban heritage and to become truly the son of his adopted father. When Adrastus allows him to drive the horse, he is emphatically called 'son-in-law' (*genero*, 316); but when the race starts he cannot hide his true paternity from Arion: *senserat adductis alium praesagus Arion | stare ducem loris, dirumque expauerat insons | Oedipodioniden* ('prophetic Arion had realised that another stood as leader and held the reins, and the innocent horse was terrified by the dread son of Oedipus', 6.424–6). The weight of *Oedipodioniden*, taking up half a line, emphasises the inevitability of Polynices' inheritance: he is

---

[28] See Von Stosch (1968) 36–8 on structural similarities between the two stories; 134–5, 145 on verbal reminiscences.

[29] Another tactic, taken by Ahl (1986) 2869, is to link the out-of-control chariot to Plato's image of the chariot of the soul (*Phaedrus* 244–7).

[30] Cf. Ripoll (1998) 34–48 on heredity in the *Thebaid*. He suggests that horizontal succession by contagion replaces vertical succession by 'filiation' (35), that the hereditary, tragic curse of Thebes in the *Thebaid* replaces the ideal of heroic succession which is fundamental to the ethos of epic.

[31] Ahl (1986) 2869 on Polynices and Phaethon. 'The comparison moves beyond the purely equestrian to the cosmic.' Juhnke (1972) 232.

[32] On fathers and sons in epic, see Hardie (1993) 88–119.

dirum by virtue of his paternity.[33] His name continually changes but always relates him to his Theban past.[34] Yet Adrastus always thinks of him in relation to himself: *et socero redit haud speratus Adrasto* ('he returns unhoped for to his father-in-law Adrastus', 512); *at generum famula solatur Achaea*. ('But he consoles his son-in-law with an Achaean servant girl', 549).

For both Phaethon and Polynices, it is not only their own identity which is at stake: their struggle over their paternities draws in the whole world. It has long been agreed that Phaethon's story is a destruction of the world which balances the flood in *Metamorphoses* I with *ecpyrosis* (destruction by fire).[35] The palace of the sun in Ovid's Phaethon story presents the cosmos as an ordered artefact in the shape of the doors made by Vulcan (*Met.* 2.1–18).[36] Apollo's advice to Phaethon presents an ordered version of the cosmos which Phaethon will nearly destroy in its entirety. Polynices overturns the cosmos of the *Thebaid*, too. The circus itself is an ordered representation of the cosmos. The Circus Maximus, with its dolphin lap-counters and obelisk from Heliopolis in Egypt, encompassed not only the empire but the world.[37] The channel of water around the edge of the arena could be read as the ocean encircling the world. The obelisk at the centre represented (and was dedicated to) the sun; the chariots racing around became heavenly bodies. In Statius' circus, the denseness of the imagery draws in the natural world: at the very beginning, the horses are birds or winds, creatures of the air (6.298–300); Arion is the offspring of Neptune,

---

[33] Amphiaraus' horses are the stolen sons of Castor's horse Cyllarus, begotten when his master was far from home: this is another play on the complications of the father–son relationship, the difficulties of authenticating descent. Admetus' horses too are *nec degener illo | de grege. Castaliae stupuit qui sibila cannae | laetus et audito contempsit Apolline pasci* ('not unworthy descendants of that herd which was struck dumb joyfully at the hissing of the Castalian reed and refused to graze once they had heard Apollo', *Theb.* 6.337–9). Thoas and Euneos are, as ever, the opposite paradigm in this game of guess the parent: instead of authenticating themselves through their birth, they prove that their mother tells the truth by being their true mother.

[34] *Labdacides* (451); *Echionides* (467); *exsul Aonius* (504–5); *Thebane* (513). Ripoll (1998) 37–8 studies the epithets used of Polynices and Eteocles.

[35] Otis (1970) 91.

[36] Brown (1987). The chariot race itself is described as if it were an artefact: when Apollo looks down he sees *ingens certaminis instar* ('the huge image of a contest', 369).

[37] Feldherr (1995) 248–9; Zanker (1988) 67–71; Lyle (1984) takes this further. Cf. Henderson (2002) 45: 'The *Circus* stands proud as, more than a representation of Rome as Universe, a massive engine of representation.'

and is inconstant as the sea but simultaneously fiery (*etenim insa-tiatus eundi | ardor et hiberno par inconstantia ponto*, 'for he has an unsatisfied burning to run and his inconstancy equals the winter sea', 305–6); the black and white of Admetus' horses 'resembles day and night' (*noctemque diemque | adsimulant*, 335–6); the spate of similes, as they burst from the starting-gates, encompasses a whole range of natural phenomena (6.405–9: clouds in the sky, winter torrents, spreading fire, falling stars, gathering storms, and mountain streams). At 422–3 the whiplashes are like hail and rain. Into this cosmos, Polynices comes, like Phaethon, a passive but essentially destructive phenomenon. Arion, like the chariot of the sun, runs outside the ordered tracks (6.443–4). When he overtakes Amphiaraus and Admetus again, the inexplicable crash emphasises the destructive force of the chariot out of control and seems to threaten the sky itself: *subit astra fragor, caelumque trem-iscit* ('the crash goes up to the stars, and the heaven trembles', 448).

Polynices is also a version of Phaethon in the wider context of the epic, where his seemingly passive manipulation of the situation drives Argos to war and brings the destruction of the invading army and of Thebes. Jupiter's speech in the council of the gods reads the plot of the *Thebaid* in this way: the war against Thebes is another mechanism aimed at destroying the world, and Jupiter specifically bewails the inefficacy of Phaethon, and claims him as his own tool (*Thebaid* 1.219–21):

> atque adeo tuleram falso rectore solutos
> Solis equos, caelumque rotis errantibus uri,
> et Phaethontea mundum squalere fauilla.

> I had even allowed the horses of the sun to be released
> with a false driver, and the sky to be burned by wandering wheels,
> and the earth to be fouled by Phaethon's ashes.

If Jupiter in Apollo's song is the protector of the cosmos, guaranteeing the proper running of the universe, in the *Thebaid* he is the source of destruction, and Polynices, like Phaethon, is his tool. Adrastus reveals Polynices' destructive power when he forbids him to take part in the fight in armour: *tuque o, quem propter auita | iugera, dilectas cui desolauimus urbes* ('you, on behalf of whom we have abandoned our ancestral acres, deserted our beloved cities', 6.916–17), speaking more truly than perhaps he realises.

Phaethon has also been read as a figure of the poet.[38] Holzberg points out that *fert animus* ('the mind turns me') is used only twice in the *Metamorphoses*, once the first words of the narrator in the proem, and once of Phaethon by his mother (1.775).[39] This, combined with the strong metaphorical associations between the journey of Phaethon and the paths of song, the chariot of the sun and the chariot of song, suggests that the Phaethon story could be read as a model of poetry out of control. If we read Polynices also as a poet figure, then his silence becomes particularly significant. For not only is he passively borne about by Arion without an attempt to control, but he does not even shout out: *solus Echionides errante silentia curru | maesta tenet trepidaque timet se uoce fateri.* ('Only the son of Echion keeps sad silence in his wandering chariot and fears to admit his terror in his voice', 467–8). Throughout the entire episode of the games, Polynices does not speak once. He is a poet figure without a voice.

The fieriness of Phaethon's journey, of the chariot and horses of the sun, seems to spill over into Statius' chariot race. We have read above the description of the horses as they wait to start, which especially brings this out (*ardor, face lumina surgunt, uritur, transfumat*, 6.396–9). As Statius strains at the boundaries of language, their ardour becomes literal flames shooting from their eyes, their anger smoke, as their bits burn. Throughout the race, fire vocabulary describes all the competitors.[40] After Polynices has been shipwrecked, Amphiaraus is assimilated to him: he burns to win (*ardet*, 520) and his desire threatens to burn up the world: *rapit igneus orbes | axis, et effusae longe sparguntur harenae. | dat gemitum tellus et iam tum saeua minatur* ('the fiery axle snatches the wheels and the spread-out sands are scattered far. The savage earth gives a groan and even now threatens', 6.525–7).[41] Poetic inspiration is described in fiery terms by Statius at the beginning of the *Thebaid*: *Pierius menti calor incidit* ('the Pierian heat falls

---

[38] Holzberg (1998) 88–91; Wise (1977).   [39] Holzberg (1998) 89.

[40] *accensum* ('lit up', 428); *incenditur* ('is on fire', 439); *calet* ('is hot', 443); *igneus Aethion* ('fiery Aethion', 465); *flammata sitis* ('flaming thirst', 472); *feruidus* ('boiling', 475).

[41] See Lovatt (2001).

on my mind', 1.3).[42] However, despite the fire of his ambition to win, Amphiaraus is unable to overtake the empty chariot pulled by Arion. This race between the *uates* and the empty chariot rereads the metaphor of the chariots of song in competition with each other. The *uates* is the image of the authorised poet, using song for political ends.[43] One part of Statius' poetic voice tends towards taking on this mantle, while another disavows responsibility for what he creates, representing it as something out of his control, a sort of madness. The *Thebaid* replaces (and deletes) a politically engaged work on Domitian and problematises its own authority in the process.

Apollo provides no safe model of the poet: his creation in the chariot race is essentially a figure of a Fury (6.495–501):[44]

> anguicomam monstri effigiem, saeuissima uisu
> ora, mouet siue ille Erebo seu finxit in astus
> temporis, innumera certe formidine cultum
> tollit in astra nefas. non illud ianitor atrae
> impauidus Lethes, non ipsae horrore sine alto
> Eumenides uidisse queant, turbasset euntes
> Solis equos Martisque iugum.

> He raises an unspeakable thing to the stars, a snake-haired model
> of a monster, with a face most savage to look upon, whether he stirs
>   it up from Erebus
> or created it for moment's cunning plan, it is certainly dressed
> with uncountable fears. The guardian of black Lethe could not
> look on that unpanicked, the Eumenides themselves could not see it
> without deep horror, it would have overthrown the horses of the Sun
> as they travelled and the yoke of Mars.

Statius wonders whether he raises it (*mouet*) or makes it (*finxit*): both words can speak of artistic creation.[45] He raises it to the stars,

---

[42] Vessey (1986) 2968. *Calor* ('heat') is also used at *Siluae* 1 preface 3: *qui mihi subito calore et quadam festinandi voluptate fluxerunt* ('which flowed for me in sudden heat and in a certain pleasure of hurrying') of poetic improvisation – another tactic for disavowing (and hence evoking) seriousness.

[43] Newman (1967). Although Newman claims that *uates* no longer carried this sort of significance in Silver Latin poetry, the concept of the sacred responsibilities of poets was still very much alive in Statius.

[44] Apollo is also the maker of a monster in the story of Coroebus (1.557–668); see Ahl (1986) 2853–4.

[45] Vessey (1970) 427 makes it an example of Statian originality; cf. Vessey (1973) 215–16, which presents it as 'an embodiment of Oedipus' curse'.

like a poet giving immortality through catasterism. This poetic creation makes a hyperbolic claim of superiority over its predecessors: it would terrify Cerberus and the Furies themselves. Once more, we are reminded of Phaethon by the reference to the horses of the sun.

We might sharpen up the political implications of this imagery by reading Polynices as Phaethon through the proem of Lucan's *Bellum Ciuile*. Lucan's proem contains his only direct mention of Nero, praising him as the *telos* of civil war and asking him to choose his celestial role after deification. One of the options he offers is to play Phaethon, but a successful version (Lucan *BC* 1.47–50):

> seu sceptra tenere,
> seu te flammigeros Phoebi conscendere currus,
> telluremque nihil mutato sole timentem
> igne uago lustrare iuuet

> whether it pleases you to hold the sceptre
> or mount the flame-bearing chariot of Phoebus,
> and purify with your wandering flame
> the earth which fears nothing although the sun has changed

Lucan's proem has long been a cause of controversy.[46] How can a poem which is often read as strongly Republican contain sincere praise of the emperor? Ahl, for instance, reads it as satire.[47] I do see these lines as double-edged but not particularly satirical; Stephen Hinds has argued convincingly that Ovid's Phaethon lurks beneath these lines and hints at cosmic dissolution.[48] The adjective *flammigeros* immediately highlights the dangerous nature of the responsibilities of divine power, and although the earth fears nothing, this way of expressing the praise always suggests its opposite. *Igne uago* ('with wandering fire') hardly suggests that Nero's control of the chariot of the sun is secure. From the viewpoint of Statius, Nero's reign led precisely to the political cosmos engulfed in civil war once more, and the equation between Polynices, Phaethon and

---

[46] For a recent analysis see Holmes (1999), who suggests that Lucan's praise of Nero as an exception is heightened by his general hostility to imperial power. See also Fantham (1992) 13–14; Dewar (1994), especially the postscript at 209–11.

[47] Ahl (1976) 47–9.

[48] Hinds (1987) 26–9, which Dewar (1994) 211 suggests is the most promising methodology for a subversive reading of Lucan's proem.

Nero as the causes of cosmic disruption is persuasive. We can take this further, though: Lucan hails Nero as his own poetic inspiration: *tu satis ad uires Romana in carmina dandas* ('you are enough to give strength for Roman song', 66). This statement too is open to a number of readings. Nero as a poet prince is taking on the role of Apollo as inspiration for the poet. We do not need to appeal to Lucan's obvious ambivalence about the gods, here, to see Nero as the emperor appalling enough to make Lucan take the risk of writing a revolutionary poem. But he begins the next section (67–9):

> fert animus causas tantarum expromere rerum,
> inmensumque aperitur opus, quid in arma furentem
> inpulerit populum, quid pacem excusserit orbi.

> My mind moves me to lay out the causes of such great events,
> an immeasurable work opens out, to say what impelled the raging
> people to take up arms, what shook peace out of the world.

Here, Lucan is an Ovid, turning the whole of universal history into civil war and the destruction of Rome, and himself, like Nero, a Phaethon, overturning the cosmos with his poem.[49]

Conclusion

Poet figures and poetry are extremely important for a reading of the chariot race. There is no acceptable face of poetry in this interplay of poetic figures. The image of the poet is fractured, the mirror broken into shards. Polynices as Phaethon, Amphiaraus the *uates* and Apollo are different and competing images of the poet. Yet none of these figures is safe, straightforwardly acceptable and positive. Polynices brings the issue of poetic paternity to the forefront. Is the *Thebaid* the true son of the *Aeneid*? Or must it always be true to its Theban paternity, incestuously breeding with itself? Polynices also threatens the cosmic organisation of both chariot race, poem and world. If poetry can order the cosmos, it can also destroy it. Amphiaraus the *uates* is driven by his desire to win into replicating

---

[49] On Lucan and Ovid, see Wheeler (2002), who reads Lucan's proem as a continuation of the end of the *Metamorphoses*. 'Lucan finds in Ovidian epic cosmological and mythological paradigms of chaos, civil war and horror that anticipate his own worldview' (379).

the madness of the horses and the other competitors. Even Apollo's act of creation is hellish. In Jamie Masters' reading, the voice of the poet Lucan is split: one voice loathes the civil war and the poem; the other strives to repeat it and glories in it.[50] Statius' voice is multiply fractured, but none of the multiple personalities, the poet figures, offers a safe and acceptable option. In the end, although the name of victory is given to the *uates*, the true winner of this chariot race of poetic voices is the empty chariot of song, driven by the fiery madness of Arion.

EPIC GAMES AND REAL GAMES

Statius' games were written against the reality of the rest of the poem, but also against the reality of spectacle in Rome.[51] To understand his games, we need to think not just about intertextuality and intratextuality, but about historical reality, inasmuch as we can reconstruct (or construct) it. Statius' games have often been called 'realistic' in comparison to Virgil's, and thinking about why this is and comparing the ways that they use and represent historical spectacles, bringing Silius in as further control, we can learn much about both.[52] We have already begun to think about the background to Statius' games, both in his epic predecessors and in the panoply of different spectacles and festivals in the Roman world. In this section, I want to ask two things: how real are Statius' games? Are they Greek or Roman? The main problem in answering these questions is how to construct a reality against which to read the texts. We need to know what 'real games' were like, before we can say how real Statius' games were, and we need to know what were the differences between Greek and Roman games, before we can say how Greek or Roman they are. The evidence for ancient games is as complex and incomplete as the evidence for many other areas

---

[50] Masters (1993) passim but especially 1–10.

[51] For a more detailed version of the material in 'Dressed to win' and 'Spectacular spaces', see Lovatt (2004).

[52] Statius is clearly 'a man who had often thrown a discus himself', Harris (1964) 58. Briggs (1975) 283 and Harris (1972) 131 criticise Virgil's lack of realism. Von Stosch (1968) 3 emphasises the reality of the Statian games. Still in 1996 Thuillier is looking to the *Thebaid* for insights into whether riderless horses could win the chariot races, and how exactly the foot race started (Thuillier (1996b).

of ancient history, and one aim of this chapter is methodological:[53] to give some idea of the complexities of the problems and the difficulties of constructing any sort of convincing reality against which to read Statius' games.[54] I want to begin with the much-debated area of athletic nudity at Rome, reading Statius, Virgil and Silius against the ancient and modern debate, which brings out how little we can be sure about. Then we will briefly look at the problem of Greek and Roman in Statius' wrestling. One way of answering the question 'how real?' is to think about realism, and one way of making games realistic is to set them in a solid, physical space which evokes real athletic spaces familiar to readers: the third and final section will investigate how Virgil, Statius and Silius fashion the settings of their games.

Dressed to win?

This section will investigate how Virgil, Statius and Silius deal with the controversial issue of dressing their athletes. Epic athletes begin life with clothes. In the Homeric games, competitors wore a *zoma* (loincloth or pair of shorts).[55] This means that there is a distinct dichotomy between epic games on the one hand, as exemplified by Homer, and Greek games on the other hand, which were carried out in the nude.[56] The evidence for athletic nudity at Rome is scanty, the subject of controversy ancient and modern. Dionysius of Halicarnassus, writing in the first century BC, provides the most convincing evidence of Roman athletes wearing clothes. The general argument of the *Antiquitates Romani* is that Rome was not founded by barbarians but by Greeks. Thus, when, in his description of a *pompa circensis*, he chooses to digress on the subject of athletic apparel (7.72–3), his representation of clothed athletes

---

[53] On the difficulties of reconstructing ancient games, see Golden (1998) 46–73.
[54] Other problems are how to deal with the problems of diachronic change, and how to establish what 'epic convention' is. To deal with the last problem first: with much of the wider epic cycle fragmentary or lost, it is difficult to establish what the norms were for epic games. Willis (1941) has convincingly shown that the Homeric games for Patroclus in *Iliad* 23 were exceptions and not representative. However, Virgil, Statius and Silius were explicitly following and appropriating Homer: for them, Homer was epic convention.
[55] *Iliad* 23.683, 685, 710; *Odyssey* 18.67, 76. See Thuillier (1975).
[56] On Greek athletic nudity: Crowther (1982); McDonnell (1991b); McDonnell (1991a).

works against the overall thrust of his argument. He solves the problem by assimilating the Romans to Homeric Greeks and claiming that the Romans are more true to Greek heritage than the Greeks themselves. This allows Thuillier to argue that athletic nudity was not practised at Rome.[57] Thuillier, coming from a background of work on Etruscan athletics, has the opposite agenda from Dionysius, being keen to differentiate between Romans and Greeks and emphasise the importance of Etruscan influence.[58]

On the other side, we have a different ancient controversy and a different modern perspective. Crowther is the main exponent of the view that athletic nudity was practised in Rome, and argues that Tacitus *Annals* 14.20 allows us to 'know conclusively that athletes were naked at an athletic competition in Rome'.[59] In this passage, Tacitus records reactions to Nero's Greek-style games and, at the height of the condemnation, reports critics as saying: *quid superesse, nisi ut corpora quoque nudent et caestus adsumant easque pugnas pro militia et armis meditentur?* ('What else remains, except that they also bare their bodies and take up the boxing glove and think that those battles replace military service and weapons?'). Tacitus is not here describing athletic nudity, but participating in a long-running debate about Hellenisation and morality. He is particularly arguing against the Roman elite competing in public athletic spectacle. Crowther, coming from a background of work on Greek athletics, concludes that Roman athletes competed in the nude from the first century AD.[60] One other piece of evidence which supports this view is Suetonius' account of Augustus' worries about women watching Greek athletics: at *Augustus* 44.2–3, he portrays Augustus deliberately changing the timing of a display of boxing at the *ludi pontificales* in the theatre, in order to exclude women from watching.

There are various different ways of reconciling these contradictory pieces of evidence. The first and most obvious is change over time: Dionysius is writing in the first century BC, before Augustus' foundation of the *Sebasta* at Naples in AD 2. In the time of Nero, Greek athletics and athletic nudity were still controversial.

---

[57] Thuillier (1975). [58] See Thuillier (1985), or more specifically Thuillier (1980).
[59] Crowther (1980–81). [60] Crowther (1980–81) 121.

By Statius' time, they seem less so. A second possibility is different practices in different contexts. Dionysius is writing about *ludi circenses*, Tacitus about Greek-style games. We know from Ovid *Amores* 3.2 that women watched the circus games along with men, without, it seems, causing undue worry to Augustus. Perhaps runners at the circus games wore 'loincloths', while participants in specifically Greek athletic competitions did not.

Reality in this case is almost impossible to reconstruct. Virgil, Statius and Silius deal with this sensitive subject in very different ways. In none of them is there a specific mention of the *zoma* or *subligaculum*. In Virgil, there is no explicit reference to the nudity of athletes either. Even Euryalus in the running is not specifically described as naked, although the reference to his male beauty might imply it.[61] The boxer Entellus is made to strip off, but the gap remains here between undressed and naked (*Aeneid* 5.421–3):

> haec fatus duplicem ex umeris reiecit amictum
> et magnos membrorum artus, magna ossa lacertosque
> exuit atque ingens media consistit harena.

> When he had said these things, he threw off the double covering from
>   his shoulders
> and revealed the great muscles of his limbs, the huge bones and sinews
> and stood, huge, in the middle of the sand.

Nowhere does Virgil specifically describe an athlete as naked, and nowhere does he refer to a loincloth. Those readers who would expect to see athletes nude are free to read nudity; those who would be outraged are free to supply their own imaginary *subligacula*. Hence, Virgil leaves the issue of nudity open, using ambivalence to negotiate between epic and reality, Greek and Roman.

Silius takes this reticence further than Virgil. As in Virgil's games, there is little opportunity for nakedness; even the boxing has become a collection of gladiatorial battles. The running is the one clearly athletic event to remain (the javelin is reread as a display of hunting and battle skills). There are no references to nakedness

---

[61] *pulchro ueniens in corpore uirtus*, 'manhood arriving in his beautiful body', *Aeneid* 5.344.

in the running, but, like Virgil's, his lingering descriptions of the boys' bodies, though decorous, carry a hint of athletic nudity.[62]

Statius, however, is much more explicit. The first reference to the games to come, at the beginning of book 6, uses nakedness to distinguish games from real battles: *nudasque mouent in proelia uires* ('and stir up naked strength for battles', 6.18) Coming at the beginning of the phrase as it does, the emphasis is on *nudas*, though its implications may still be ambiguous: naked can mean unarmed, and the point is partly that they are fighting without weapons, showing unadorned, uncomplicated physical prowess.[63] However, the boys in the running are all naked (*nuda cohors*, 'naked cohort', 6.595) and Alcidamas the boxer is described twice as *nudus*.[64] Much is made also of the undressing and oiling of the wrestlers (835–6, 847). It is no doubt significant that those whose nakedness is emphasised are young men, and that there is a heavily erotic tone to the descriptions of both Parthenopaeus and Alcidamas. Those who have discussed athletic nudity shy away from the erotic aspects made so obvious by Plato, for one.[65] Alcidamas, in particular, represents the Greek in Statius' games, and when he is first described as naked, his whole troop becomes naked along with him as the epithet slips from one to the other: *nuda de plebe Laconum | prosilit Alcidamas* ('Alcidamas jumps forward from the naked crowd of Spartans', 6.739–40). By choosing to make nudity an explicit part of his games, Statius aligns himself against the epic norm, proclaims the Greekness of at least some of his competitors

---

[62] When Tartessus and Hesperus come forward, they are described as *fulgentes pueri* ('shining boys', 465); Baeticus has 'cheeks sprinkled with the first down' (*aspersus prima lanugine malas*, 468); Eurytus has red hair but a white body (*comam rutilus sed cum fulgore niuali | corporis*, 471–2); the whole group is *primaevi flauentiaque ora decori* ('fair of face and in the first flush of beauty', 486); 'their effort adds to their grace', (*auget pueris labor ipse decorem*, 495); the hair which Hesperus grabs is spread over Theron's 'snowy neck' (*per lactea colla*, 519).

[63] For instance, at *Thebaid* 2.580 *nudo pectore* ('naked breast') means without armour (Mulder (1954) ad versum). However, the repeated emphasis on *nudus* in an athletic context seems deliberately suggestive. Fortgens (1934) 43 points to parallels in the *Siluae*: 3.1.146 (*nudas palaestras*, 'naked palaestras'), 152 (*nudosque uirorum certatus*, 'the naked struggles of heroes'); 5.3.54 (*Graiorum uis nuda uirum*, 'the naked force of Greek heroes').

[64] *nuda de plebe Laconum*, 'from the naked crowd of Spartans', 739; *nudumque in pectora pressit*, 'he presses him naked to his breast', 746.

[65] Except Arieti (1975), whose thesis is that the Greeks exercised in the nude to prove continually their physical and sexual restraint.

and dares to go further than Virgil. What is more, the running, boxing and wrestling, where nudity is closest to the surface, are the three most Roman athletic events, the trio of events included in the *ludi circenses* since time immemorial.

Statius' games are certainly more Greek than Silius' or Virgil's, both in the programme, as we have seen above, and in their costume (or lack of it). There may have been a change in Roman attitudes to athletic nudity in the years intervening between Statius and Virgil; Silius, writing about a self-proclaimedly Roman spectacle, for Roman soldiers, based on a historical account in Livy, makes his games even more conservative than Virgil's, perhaps a reaction against the way Statius enthusiastically embraced Greekness in his spectacle.

Greek and Roman in the wrestling

The tensions and confusions between Greek and Roman elements are continually on display in the negotiations of the games. However, the attempt to draw any firm conclusion about how Greek or Roman they are is continually undermined by the difficulty of saying for sure what is Greek and what is Roman, the need to rely for evidence on other ancient constructions in which cultural identity is also always at stake. Take, for instance, the wrestling. Legras, followed by Vessey, argues that Statius' wrestling match represents Roman and not Greek practices, because when Tydeus is engulfed by the mass of Agylleus at 6.876–85, he goes on fighting despite being on the ground already.[66] Legras claims that this is very different from the Homeric wrestling, where any fall led to a new round. This assumes that Greek wrestling is the same as Homeric wrestling. His argument also assumes that the rules of Greek wrestling and Roman wrestling can be reconstructed securely enough to distinguish between them. When Poliakoff writes about wrestling, he makes no clear distinction between Greek and Roman wrestling.[67] In both, three falls constitute

---

[66] Legras (1905) 89: 'It proves that he is describing Roman wrestling, because Tydeus continues fighting on the ground'; Vessey (1970) 434.
[67] Poliakoff (1987) 23–53.

a victory; it is more difficult to ascertain exactly what a 'fall' is. He shows convincingly from both literary and artistic evidence that touching the back and shoulders on the ground at all constituted a fall.[68] Stretching a man out prone was also counted as a fall: yet the evidence he presents for this brings us back very close to home: *Thebaid* 6.898–904, where Tydeus stretches out Agylleus on his chest and stomach. Ground fighting, although less common in visual depictions of wrestling,[69] was a recognised part of the sport: it was possible, for instance, although difficult, for a wrestler to continue fighting on his knees.[70]

Looking once more at Statius' description of Tydeus overwhelmed, it is very difficult to specify exactly how he was overwhelmed (*Thebaid* 6.876–80):

> instat agens Tydeus fictumque in colla minatus
> crura subit; coeptis non eualuere potiri
> frustratae breuitate manus, uenit arduus ille
> desuper oppressumque ingentis mole ruinae
> condidit.

> Tydeus, driving on, attacks: he threatened a fake attack on Agylleus' neck
> and comes up under his legs; but he was not strong enough to carry out this
> plan
> and his arms were frustrated by their shortness, and the other in his tallness
> came down from above and buried him, crushed
> by a huge mass of falling body.

I read this as describing Agylleus falling forward onto Tydeus: there is no specification of how he is *oppressum* but it seems possible and reasonable that the smaller man forced to his knees under the weight of the larger man could still be described as buried. The problem comes from the extended image of the miner, dead and buried under a hillside, which seems to compare Tydeus to a corpse: difficult to imagine a corpse on his knees. The hyperbolic nature of this image is clear, however: it emphasises the miraculous strength of Tydeus' spirit; it involves Tydeus, like Polynices as Phaethon,

---

[68] Poliakoff (1987) 23–4.   [69] Poliakoff (1987) 33.

[70] Jüthner (1969) 212–13 argues that this passed into idiom: to fall to one's knees is to be in danger rather than to have already been defeated. Herodotus described the city of Chios as thrown to its knees at 6.27 (ἡ ναυμαχίη ὑπολαβοῦσα ἐς γόνυ τὴν πόλιν ἔβαλε, 'The sea-battle threw the city to its knees'). See Poliakoff (1987) 25.

or Hippomedon in the discus, as we will see, in the imagery of hero against the cosmos. He is buried by the mass of the land; he escapes by turning it upside down. If we agree that Agylleus only forces Tydeus to his knees, then there is no need to suggest some disjunction between Greek and Roman rules of wrestling, for which there is no other evidence. This example illustrates how difficult it is to distinguish between Greek and Roman elements in Statius' description of the games, when Statius' descriptions themselves are among the evidence, when there is no simple way of defining what is Greek and what is Roman, when 'Roman' wrestling could be Roman appropriation of Greek wrestling, and when Greek practices change over time and may even be influenced by Roman.

Spectacular spaces

Let us now examine in more detail the different tactics which Virgil, Statius and Silius use when negotiating between epic and reality in the space they create for their games. Epic games take place within an imagined space, an arena whose only limit is the imagination of the poet. By examining the boundaries and fluctuations of this imagined space, we can begin to link epic games with particular contexts and types of spectacle. This project is complicated by the difficulty of assigning real games to real spaces consistently, and the Roman reluctance to create permanent spaces for their games. The *ludi circenses* clearly took place in the circus; the Circus Maximus was the paradigm of this type of venue.[71] Other types of spectacle are not as easily placed. Look, for instance, at the description of the different places in which Augustus staged spectacles according to Suetonius (*Augustus* 43.1–2):[72]

---

[71] On the arrangements of the circus, see Humphrey (1986); Cerutti (1993). Livy 1.35.7–10 presents the Circus Maximus as an unusually early permanent structure.

[72] *Fecitque nonnumquam etiam uicatim ac pluribus scaenis per omnium linguarum histriones, munera non in Foro modo, nec in amphitheatro, sed et in Circo et in Saeptis, et aliquando nihil praeter uenationem edidit; athletas quoque exstructis in campo Martio sedilibus ligneis; ... In Circo aurigas cursoresque et confectores ferarum, et nonnumquam ex nobilissima iuuentute, produxit.* Suetonius is paraphrasing *Res Gestae Diui Augusti* 22–3: he is more interested in keeping in the variety of places than the detailed numbers which grace the *Res Gestae*.

He often held theatrical games in different neighbourhoods and on many stages and with actors speaking in all languages, gladiatorial games not only in the Forum and the amphitheatre, but also in the Circus and the Saepta, and occasionally he produced nothing except a wild beast hunt; he also produced athletes, with wooden seats built on the Campus Martius; ... In the Circus he presented charioteers and runners and hunters of wild animals, and some of those were even of the highest birth.

In this passage, we have gladiatorial games in the widest variety of places: the Forum, amphitheatre, Circus Maximus and Saepta. A special wooden structure in the Campus Martius was built for athletics, but runners also featured in the circus. Chariot races take place only in the circus. In the time of Virgil, then, there was no permanent structure for athletics, but athletics could feature in the programme of the *ludi circenses*.[73]

In the time of Domitian, however, there was a revolution in the spectacular architecture of Rome. The Colosseum, started by Vespasian and inaugurated by Titus, was completed by Domitian, providing a space for gladiatorial games that dominates the urban landscape in its magnificence and sheer size.[74] Domitian was also responsible for building the only permanent stadium in Rome and probably in the west of the Empire. This too has left its mark on the urban landscape of Rome, still visible in the shape of the Piazza Navona.[75] It was built in AD 86 for the *Capitolia*. The permanence of both the festival and the buildings associated with it marks a profound change in Roman attitudes to Greek games.

In what sort of setting do we find the epic games of Virgil, Statius and Silius? I will look for clues about the setting of the games in *Aeneid* 5 and then move on to *Thebaid* 6 and *Punica* 16. The first passage in *Aeneid* 5 describing the setting and the arrival of the audience uses the word *circus* but simultaneously sets the audience on the shore (*litora*) (Virgil *Aeneid* 5.106–113):

> famaque finitimos et clari nomen Acestae
> excierat; laeto complerant litora coetu

---

[73] Suetonius (*Diuus Julius* 39.3) says: *athletae stadio ad tempus exstructo regione Marti campi certauerunt per triduum*, 'athletes competed for three days in a stadium built for the occasion in the area of the Campus Martius').

[74] Coarelli (1980) 183; Coarelli, Gregori, et al. (1999) 161–80.

[75] Thuillier (1996a) 77–80.

uisuri Aeneadas, pars et certare parati.
munera principio ante oculos circoque locantur
in medio, sacri tripodes uiridesque coronae
et palmae pretium uictoribus, armaque et ostro
perfusae uestes, argenti aurique talenta;
et tuba commissos medio canit aggere ludos.

And rumour along with the name of famous Acestes had stirred up
the neighbouring peoples; they filled the seashore with a happy gathering,
about to see the sons of Aeneas, and some were prepared to compete.
First the prizes are placed before the eyes, in the middle
of the circus, sacred tripods and green crowns
and palms as reward for the victors, weapons and cloaks
drenched in purple, talents of silver and gold;
and the trumpet blasts from the middle of a bank that the games should
   begin.

Only after the ship race are we given any more detail about the
space of the games (Virgil *Aeneid* 5.286–90):

Hoc pius Aeneas misso certamine tendit
gramineum in campum, quem collibus undique curuis
cingebant siluae, mediaque in ualle theatri
circus erat; quo se multis cum milibus heros
consessu medium tulit exstructoque resedit.

When this contest had been completed, pious Aeneas heads
for a grassy plain, which woods surrounded on all sides
with curved hills, and there was a circular space for a theatre in the middle
of the valley; the hero took himself there along with many thousands
in a crowd and sat down in the middle on a built-up structure.

The geographical details suggest a primitive Circus Maximus, a
grassy valley set in hills – the word *circus*, though it can also mean
a circle, was far more frequently used of the circus, and particularly
of the Circus Maximus.[76] At the beginning of the *lusus Troiae* Virgil
again describes the space as a circus: *ipse omnem longo decedere
circo | infusum populum et campos iubet esse patentis* ('he himself
ordered the whole people who had poured into the long circus to
go back and let the fields lie open', 551–2). However, it is also a
theatre (288), presenting the games as exotic spectacle rather than

---

[76] *OLD* also gives the meaning as '[a] circular or oval space in which games, esp. chariot
races are held', but all the examples but one of this use come from epic games.

traditional ritual. Greek athletes had been presented in the theatre during the Republic.[77] During the aftermath of the running, the audience is described as *consessum caueae* ('the gathering in the seats of the theatre', 5.340), using the word *cauea* which refers to the seating space in the theatre, and suggests a built structure. However, the structure on which Aeneas sits assimilates Virgil's primitive circus to the Circus Maximus, with its *puluinar*. Humphrey discusses this structure in some detail and suggests that while its primary function was as seating for the gods (in the form of divine images), it later became the royal box for the emperor.[78] While Aeneas sits on a primitive *puluinar*, the other spectators (including Acestes) sit on the grassy bank.[79] Apart from Aeneas, seating in this pre-circus was democratically unsegregated.[80] Aeneas' seating structure puts him above the crowds, separates him from them, a primitive version of the emperor, watching and being watched by the audience.[81]

Entellus, in the boxing, 'stands huge in the middle of the sand': *ingens media consistit harena* (5.423). The word *harena* can either mean simply a sandy place, or more specifically the arena of the amphitheatre, the setting for gladiatorial fights, or equally the part of the circus where races were actually run.[82] Virgil's boxing certainly has affinities with gladiatorial battles: the *caestus* of Eryx spattered with blood and brains (413), and the violent sacrifice of the prize ox (473–84) emphasise the violence of this contest, and

---

[77] Suetonius *Augustus* 44.3 implies that boxing was shown in the theatre. Other examples of athletes shown in the theatre: Pompey presented athletes in his newly built theatre (55 BC; Plutarch *Pompey* 52.4); C. Scribonius Curio showed athletes and gladiators together in a wooden theatre in 53 BC (Pliny *Natural History* 36.24.120).

[78] Humphrey (1986) 78–83. Augustus at *Res gestae* 19 claims that he built this structure himself, but Humphrey argues that there would have been some sort of pre-Augustan wooden structure, which formed the destination of the *pompa*.

[79] *hic grauis Entellum dictis castigat Acestes, | proximus ut uiridante toro consederat herbae*: ('Serious Acestes chastises Entellus with these words, as he sat next to him on the green couch of grass', 5.387–8)

[80] In Livy's vision of Tarquinius' circus, the Circus Maximus came into being with fully segregated seating arrangements for different classes of Romans. Segregated seating in the theatre was introduced earlier and much more comprehensively: Rawson (1991), Wiseman (1987) 79–80; Bollinger (1969). Augustus introduced laws governing seating and other matters such as dress at the *ludi circenses*. During the first century AD, seating regulations at the circus became more complex. See Humphrey (1986) 76–7, 101–2.

[81] Clavel-Lévêque (1984) 152–73.

[82] See Humphrey (1986) 83.

it is no coincidence that Silius replaced boxing in his games with gladiatorial fights.

The imaginary space of Virgil's epic games seems to move from event to event: the ship race is like an extension of the circus, the running is in a theatre as much as a circus, the boxing equivocates between the arenas of the amphitheatre and the circus, and the *lusus Troiae* returns to the circus. Aeneas sits on a wooden structure, while the audience sit on the grassy bank. Only the running, with its theatrical location, is alienated from traditional Roman spectacle; only the archery, with its complete lack of detail about the spatial arrangements, is located entirely in the realm of epic.

Statius' initial description of the setting works similarly to Virgil's.[83] It evokes the contemporary circus, while simultaneously being marked as primitive and different. The circus is a convenient geographical arrangement, rather than a building constructed for the purpose (6.255–60):

> collibus incuruis uiridique obsessa corona
> uallis in amplexu nemorum sedet; hispida circum
> stant iuga, et obiectus geminis umbonibus agger
> campum exire uetat, longo quem tramite planum
> gramineae frontes sinuataque caespite uiuo
> mollia non subitis augent fastigia cliuis.

> A valley besieged by a green ring of curved hills
> sits in the embrace of the woods; rough ridges
> stand around and a rampart thrown in the way with twin mounds
> forbids the field to go out; grassy brows and battlements
> soft with living turf and gentle slopes
> are added to the long and level track.

The phrase *hispida circum | stant iuga* shows how Statius simultaneously distances his reader from the setting, while suggesting familiarity. *[C]ircum* at the end of the line, separated from the verb *stant*, is open to two readings: on the first glance, we have a rough circus; on the second, we have merely ridges that stand *around*. This pun suggests an etymology for the name circus; the rough ridges literally enclose the *circum*, reinforcing the play on the word. This is a flirtation with the idea that the setting both is and is not a

---

[83] Fortgens (1934) 125.

circus.[84] Elsewhere in the games, Statius does describe the setting as a circus.[85] Statius' circus too becomes a theatre when the violence of the discus landing threatens the foundations of the space itself (*theatri*, 715); in the discus drama, the audience are the *cauea* when they persuade Hippomedon to compete (*cauea stimulante*, 'with the audience encouraging him', 654). Only the discus slips briefly into the theatrical, the only event of Statius' games which would have been part of the pentathlon in the Olympic programme and not a separate event.

However, these initial similarities with Virgil's games are deceptive. The space of Statius' games is far more richly endowed with the technical vocabulary of sporting equipment, and in particular the physical accoutrements of the circus. The starting-gates are described at the beginning of the chariot race without using the term *carceres*; the starting line is called the 'line of the boundary' (*liminis ordo*, 6.390) and the horses are 'shut in by one boundary' (*uno margine clausi*, 392); posts and bolts are mentioned (*postes | claustraque*, 398). The actual word *carceres* comes in the comparison of Adrastus' energy at the end to the freshness of chariots just starting the race: *ceu modo carceribus dimissus in arua solutis* ('as if he had just now been sent out into the field, with the starting-gates released', 6.522). The description of the *metae* evokes the circus. For in the *Thebaid*, unlike the *Aeneid* and *Iliad*, there are two turning-posts: *metarum instar erant hinc nudo robore quercus, | olim omnis exuta comas, hinc saxeus umbo | arbiter agricolis;* ('There were two images of turning-posts: the one was oak in its naked strength, once it had been stripped of all its leaves, the other a rocky stub, the referee of farmers', 6.351–3).[86] This was also the case in the Circus Maximus.[87] The *regula* at the start of the

---

[84] The military vocabulary of Virgil's description is multiplied: *obsessa* ('besieged'), *umbonibus* ('bosses'), *agger* ('rampart'), *fastigia* ('battlements'). The landscape seems alive and almost erotic: *uiridi* ('green'), *incuruis* ('curved'), *amplexu* ('embrace'), *sinuata caespite uiuo* ('curved with living turf'), *mollia* ('soft'). The space is a circus, a military camp and a fertile feminine body, simultaneously welcoming and threatening, male and female.

[85] *toto parant descendere circo*, 'they prepare to descend from the whole circus', 620; *non partem exiguam circi transuecta*, 'it crossed no small part of the circus', 702; *ingentem iactu transmittere circum*, 'he sent it across the huge circus with a throw', 932.

[86] Cf. Legras (1905) 237. The length of Statius' chariot race, which continues for at least four laps, suggests the Roman races: the Iliadic chariot race lasted for only one lap.

[87] Thuillier (1996a) 66–8; Humphrey (1986) 174–294.

foot race sounds convincingly like a reference to the bar dropped to begin contemporary races (*ut ruit atque aequum summisit regula limen,* 'as the bar dropped and lowered a level threshold', 593).[88] The description of the finishing line in the foot race as *ostia portae* ('the doorway of the gate', 617) also suggests a built structure. The audience in the chariot race are presented as sitting on seats. When Polynices overtakes Amphiaraus, the audience jump to their feet, baring their seats: *omniaque excusso patuere sedilia uulgo* ('All the seats lie open, with the people shaken off', 6.649). Also different from Virgil is the way that Statius' games seem to take place almost entirely in one space: the text makes clear that the foot race following the chariot race happens in the same place: *uolucres isdem modo tardius aruis | isse uidentur equi* ('the swift horses seem to have gone more slowly just now on the same fields', 6.595–6).

Silius' games, too, seem to take place in a circus fully equipped with all the contemporary accoutrements, and, especially in the chariot race, there is even more emphasis on the audience experience, and more effort put into creating a realistic setting. The funeral takes place on a *campus* ('field', 16.304) but at 312 Scipio moves back to the circus (*inde refert sese circo*). There are starting-gates at 315 (*carceribus nondum reseratis,* 'with the starting gates not yet open') and these even have doors (*fores,* 316). When the race starts, the noise of the bolts opening signals the beginning (*sonuere repagula,* 'the bolts sound', 317). One of the charioteers is even in red (354), and the four competitors may be intended to suggest one from each faction. Here, too, there is continuity between events: the *cauea* is mentioned in the running (472), and in the gladiatorial games (534–5), along with the circus (*circo | innumero fratres, cauea damnante furorem,* 'with the uncountable circus and the audience condemning the brothers and their madness', 534–5). The javelin, too, is 'the last spectacle of the circus' (*spectacula circi | postrema,* 557–8). At 579, the whole is described as *ludi,* clearly funeral games (*ludi funebres*) set in a circus.

While Virgil's events seem to move from space to space, all Statius' and Silius' events seem to take place in the Circus Maximus.[89] The increasing impact of permanent venues for the

[88] Thuillier (1996b) 161.
[89] Legras (1905) 85 presents the circus as the unproblematic location for both sets of games.

staging of spectacles is shown by the change in the balance between portraying the primitive and evoking the contemporary. Statius' and Silius' games are more unavoidably part of contemporary Roman spectacle. Despite the Greekness of Statius' dramatic setting (Nemea) the spectacle of Greek athletics unrolls here in the most traditional and Roman of venues, the Circus Maximus.

Conclusions

Virgil's games are the most separate from reality, elusive in their physical setting, giving few clues about the dress or undress of the competitors, with few links to Greek festivals. Silius is the most concretely Roman, with his emphasis on the physical setting, audience enthusiasms, and on his historical subject-matter, only the running a sop to the Roman habit of going Greek. Statius' games combine Roman and Greek, epic and reality: like Silius, he sets them in the circus, but unlike Silius, he includes the pentathlon. More Greek than Virgil, his athletes are naked, yet he brings out the eroticism of Virgil's running. The reality of Statius' games is a complex and nuanced amalgamation of Greek and Roman spectacles, the epic tradition and contemporary experiences.

2

THE RUNNING

In *Odyssey* 8, Odysseus claims superiority in all events except the running; he is now too old and broken by suffering to compete with the young Phaeacian boys. Here already, the running is the site of self-conscious intertextual irony: for it was the running which Odysseus won in the Iliadic games, when Ajax the son of Oileus tripped in the blood of a sacrifice and fell. From the *Aeneid* onwards, it is an event for boys and becomes a negotiation of masculinity: games as training and playing are essentially boyish; true manhood is necessary for war. To cross the divide between games and war is also to negotiate the transition between boyhood and manhood.

The heroes of the Virgilian race are Nisus and Euryalus, the lovers who later go on to die a futile and tragic death in *Aeneid* 9. Nisus, too, trips, and uses this as a chance to win the race for his beloved Euryalus. Statius' Parthenopaeus has much in common with Nisus and Euryalus.[1] Both Parthenopaeus and Euryalus are beautiful boys, extraordinary among epic heroes for their association with *eros*. The relationship between Nisus and Euryalus is undeniably erotic, as is the description of Parthenopaeus. What is more, Nisus and Euryalus become a demonstration of the power of poetry for Virgil when he apostrophises them after the lovers' death in book 9, and Parthenopaeus is emblematic of the whole poem in the final lines of the *Thebaid*. This section asks: how do these erotic elements fit into the matrix of different ideas about epic heroism? How is Statius' treatment of the problem different from Virgil's? How does the gaze of the audience create and reflect poetic *fama*?

[1] Juhnke (1972) 258.

Intertextual reflections: supplementation

Let us begin by looking at the way Statius self-consciously plays with his intertexts, and particularly the *Aeneid*, in the running.[2] By comparing his treatment with Silius' running race in book 16 of the *Punica*, we can see how Statius brings out the problematic side of Virgil's race. At the beginning of Statius' foot race, the structure of the introductions of the competitors begins by following Virgil: there are a few named heroes and many about whom we know nothing. The difference is that in Virgil it is *fama obscura* ('dark rumour/tradition/fame' *Aeneid* 5.302) which hides the many, but in Statius it is the ignorance of the audience (*multi et, quos uarii tacet ignorantia uulgi*, 'There were many too, whom the ignorance of the varied crowd met in silence', 6.560). Instead, they call for Parthenopaeus: *sed Arcada Parthenopaeum | appellant densique cient uaga murmura circi* ('but they call the Arcadian Parthenopaeus and stir up wandering murmurs in the packed circus', 6.561–2). The internal audience act as if they had been previously choreographed. They are silent about those whom Statius does not mention; they call for Parthenopaeus, from whose viewpoint the race will be run. The audience's silence mirrors the silence of the text; their knowledge is equivalent to poetic tradition. This is especially clear during the ringmaster's introduction of Parthenopaeus, which is saturated with words referring to fame and tradition (6.563–8):

> nota parens cursu; quis Maenaliae Atalantes
> nesciat egregium decus et uestigia cunctis
> indeprensa procis? onerat celeberrima natum
> mater, et ipse procul fama iam notus inermes
> narratur ceruas pedes inter aperta Lycaei
> tollere et emissum cursu deprendere telum.

> His mother is known for her running: who does not know about
> the outstanding glory of Maenalian Atalanta and her footsteps
> overtaken by no suitor? His extremely famous mother burdens
> her son, and he himself, already known by fame from afar, is said to catch

---

[2] See Von Stosch (1968) 41–9 (on structures of foot race), 153–77 (commentary on foot race); 161 for table of correspondences with Virgil.

unarmed stags on foot among the open places of Lycaeus
and to snatch while running a weapon which has been thrown.

Who doesn't know all about Parthenopaeus and Atalanta? Here,
the text seems almost to present an audience made up of the readers of the text magically transported within the frame of fame.
Parthenopaeus is the clear favourite. In contrast, Silius presents
all his competitors as equals: *omnes primaeui flauentiaque ora
decori,* | *omnes ire leues atque omnes uincere digni* ('All were
young, with beautiful faces, all ran lightly, and all were worthy
of winning', *Punica* 16.486–7). He only reveals that Eurytus is
favourite towards the end of the race (*prima coronae* | *spes,* 'first
hope for the crown' 16.505–6).

The tradition of the foot race is one of disputed outcomes. In the
Iliad, Ajax complains that Odysseus had divine help, that Athena
made him slip. Virgil added a new dimension by making the intervention both human and deliberate. For Nisus, like Ajax, falls, but
takes advantage of his fall to give victory to his beloved Euryalus
by tripping Salius. In Statius' version, Parthenopaeus is securely
ahead but his hair, kept long because it is vowed to Diana on his
safe return from the war, is streaming out behind him and Idas,
close behind, uses it to pull him back and win himself. Statius has
overturned the Virgilian version by making Parthenopaeus into the
innocent victim rather than the innocent victor. We care little about
the Virgilian Salius, who is stripped of his victory, despite Aeneas'
consolation prize. Statius' reversal underlines the moral ambiguity
of the Virgilian episode.[3] To deliberately trip someone, even for
the best of motives, goes against the grain of the game.[4] Statius

---

[3] For Kytzler (1968) 11–12, these 'ethical moments' go to the heart of Statius' reworking
of epic.

[4] Farron (1993) 4–7 quotes ancient attitudes to this: Donatus seems to condemn it, and
Cicero uses the analogy of cheating in a foot race to describe how not to behave in the
stadium of life (*De Officiis* 3.42): *Scite Chrysippus, ut multa, 'qui stadium' inquit 'currit,
eniti et contendere debet quam maxime possit ut vincat, supplantare eum quicum certet
aut manu depellere nullo modo debet; sic in vita sibi quemque petere quod pertineat
ad usum non iniquum est, alteri deripere ius non est.'* 'One of Chrysippus' many wise
remarks was this: "The man who runs in the stadium ought to struggle and compete to
the best of his ability in order to win, but in no way should he trip up the man with whom
he is competing or push him out of the way with his hand; so in life it is not unfair for
each to seek for himself what is useful but it is not right to snatch it away from another."'

emphasises the danger in the trick through the violence of the audience response, a threat of civil war within games (6.618–20):

Arcades arma fremunt, armis defendere regem,
ni raptum decus et meriti reddantur honores,
contendunt totoque parant descendere circo.

The Arcadians rage for weapons, and strive to defend their king with weapons,
if the snatched glory and the deserved honours are not returned,
and they are preparing to come down from the whole circus.

Both Adrastus and Statius himself face difficult decisions of how to redo an already very complicated model: in Aeneas' judgement, Virgil has conflated two arguments involving Antilochus from the chariot race in the *Iliad*.[5] First, Antilochus complains when Achilles wants to give his second prize in the chariot race to Eumelus, who was made to crash by divine intervention. Then he, in turn, is the object of a complaint: Menelaus complains that Antilochus cheated by driving dangerously. Achilles gives Eumelus an extra prize, just as Aeneas gives Nisus and Salius extra prizes. Antilochus himself resolves the tensions with Menelaus by apologising. Aeneas never really makes a fair resolution to Nisus' trickery, and although Salius is given a prize, the result is allowed to stand.

Statius' reworking of the judgement is typical both of his style of playing with his models and Adrastus' style of leadership: he is unable to decide, and leaves the outcome ambiguous: *ambiguumque senis cunctatur Adrasti | consilium* ('the old man Adrastus delays in two minds', 6.626–7). It is as if he is looking at the options left to him by his predecessors and is torn between them. His decision 'in the end' (*tandem*) is emphatically none of the above: he decides to restage the race, thereby avoiding any necessity of actually making a decision himself. This rerun dramatises the rest of the race (and the games) as reruns of previous models. It supplements Virgil's running with an opportunity to get it right. It is also an example of Statius going to excess: he gives us not one race, but two. Here, repetition has become a sort of reversal, both correcting and repeating the poetic tradition, both submitting to the power of Virgil and Homer and surreptitiously subverting it.

[5] *Aeneid* 5.348–61; *Iliad* 23.539–64; *Iliad* 23.566–611.

In comparison, Silius takes Statius' version and attempts to make it as unproblematic as possible. His race is more complex: Eurytus is in the lead, closely followed by Hesperus;[6] Theron comes from behind and overtakes Hesperus, who is so angry that he pulls him back by the hair and allows Eurytus to win. There is a technical difficulty with Statius' race that Silius resolves: how would Idas get in front by pulling Parthenopaeus' hair? Surely it would simply slow both of them down? Silius' version makes much more sense: by pulling the hair of one person, he allows another to win. By changing the motivation, Silius also makes this a less complex issue than in Virgil or Statius: Eurytus was winning anyway, and Hesperus is angry at his own defeat, rather than trying to help Eurytus win. There is no question mark over the ultimate victory, and no dispute about the outcome, no need for the excessive repetition.[7] His is a more Roman affair, with Scipio presiding unproblematically over an unproblematic race.

Nisus and Euryalus

Virgil's Nisus and Euryalus episode is one of the most famous and most frequently discussed in the *Aeneid*.[8] The Statian equivalent is usually taken to be the Hopleus and Dymas episode in *Thebaid* 10.[9] However, reading through the games encourages us to see the story of Parthenopaeus, too, in terms of Nisus and Euryalus, and to reread Nisus and Euryalus in the light of the story of Parthenopaeus. This section concentrates on the representation of epic heroism, and argues that the erotics of both stories have been underplayed.[10] Essentially, the death of the beautiful youth is erotic precisely because it is the climax of a successful pursuit of

---

[6] I will examine the intricacies of this interaction further elsewhere.

[7] In this event, Silius certainly seems to be working with Statius' version in mind: the hair is much more strongly integrated into Statius' story, returning at the end of book 9, forming an omen of Parthenopaeus' death.

[8] Key recent work on the subject: Fowler (2000); Horsfall (1995) 170–78 (with bibliography); Hardie (1994) 23–34; Farron (1993) 1–30, 155–64; Potz (1993); Saylor (1990); Makowski (1989); Pavlock (1985); Lee (1979) 77–9, 109–113; Lennox (1977); Duckworth (1967).

[9] Most recently in Markus (1997); cf. Legras (1905) 115–17; Schetter (1960) 43; Kytzler (1969) 209–19; Vessey (1973) 70, 116–17; La Penna (1996).

[10] On the concept of the *Heldenknabe* in Statius, see Schetter (1960) 43–8.

fame.[11] Parthenopaeus, Nisus and Euryalus, and all the other beautiful young men (and occasionally women) who die extravagantly and aesthetically are the ultimate celebrities of epic.

There are two debates about erotics and epic heroism which are important for reading Nisus and Euryalus. First, were they lovers or just friends, and if they were lovers, was their love physical or non-physical? This question goes back to the relationship between Achilles and Patroclus, and puts epic masculinity (and heterosexuality) at stake. In a recent article, Mariscal and Morales set out the evidence for the ancient debate and conclude that the overwhelming consensus was to read Achilles as the *eromenos* ('beloved') of Patroclus.[12] This is an ancient reading of Homer which Dover, among others, rejects.[13] While it may indeed be anachronistic in the case of Homer, the ideology of pederasty was a gesture towards classical Greece for Roman writers.

Erotic and particularly sexual elements have often been repugnant to readers of epic. Those who accept that Virgil's boys are lovers are concerned to make them non-physical. Even Farron, whose entire argument demands that love be taken as foundational to epic ideology, makes this love an abstract emotional quality, erasing the erotic from epic love.[14] In this section, we will explore

---

[11] Vernant (1981) presents the concept of the 'beautiful death' in epic: 'For all time to come it [the beautiful death] elevates the fallen warrior to a state of glory; and the luster of celebrity, this *kleos*, that henceforth surrounds his name and person is the ultimate accolade that represents his greatest accomplishment, the winning of *arete*. Through a beautiful death, excellence no longer has to be continually measured against someone else or to be tested in combat. Rather excellence is actualized all at once and forever after in the deed that puts an end to the hero's life' (51). For him, the beauty of the corpse represents an escape from death and the decay of old age: 'The active, terrifying radiance of the live warrior must be differentiated from the remarkable beauty of his corpse, preserved in a youthfulness that age can no longer mar' (63). Virgil moves away from the Homeric model precisely by making his beautiful boy a lover, and his death a lover's death, by bringing more explicit *eros* into the beauty of epic glory.

[12] See Mariscal and Morales (2003).

[13] Dover (1980) 94 says 'Homer does not portray the mutual affection of Achilles and Patroclus as a homosexual relationship, but it was so interpreted in classical times'. He also points to the tendentiousness of Phaedrus' use of Homer: 'Homer says that Achilles was the younger of the two (*Iliad* 11.786–7), but he does not say *'much* younger'; Phaedrus' addition illustrates how easily (in ancient and modern times alike) the evidence of texts can be bent' (95).

[14] Farron (1993). Makowski (1989) presents a very strong argument that they *must* be viewed as lovers, and Hardie (1994) follows this line, while pointing out the unresolvable issue of how this *eros* functions within Virgil's wider project: 'we need to ask what

the way in which the epic hero could be the object of the erotic gaze, and particularly the homoerotic gaze, of his audience.

The second problem is to explain why the deaths of young virgins in Virgil (both male and female) are eroticised. Fowler's seminal article, 'Vergil on Killing Virgins', addresses this question and convincingly shows that imagery of defloration characterises the deaths of Nisus and Euryalus, Pallas and Turnus.[15] Both of these threads of debate have increased the prominence of erotics in discussions of epic heroism, and extended its reach, and the present section takes this further, arguing that the hero is an erotic object precisely because of his heroism and not in spite of it. I shall refocus this second question to ask why the moment of death in particular is dwelt on with erotic and sensual imagery.[16] Euryalus, as he dies, becomes a flower cut down by a plough, like Catullus' love in Catullus 11, and like the virgin in Catullus 62 reluctant to marry. But the description of his body is also eroticised (*Aeneid* 9.431–7):

> talia dicta dabat, sed uiribus ensis adactus
> transabiit costas et candida pectora rumpit.
> uoluitur Euryalus leto, pulchrosque per artus
> it cruor inque umeros ceruix conlapsa recumbit:
> purpureus ueluti cum flos succisus aratro
> languescit moriens, lassoue papauera collo
> demisere caput pluuia cum forte grauantur.

> But even as he was speaking such words, the sword driven in with
>   all his strength
> pierced his ribs and broke his white chest.
> Euryalus rolls in death and blood flows over his beautiful
> limbs and his neck collapses on his shoulders and sinks:
> just as when a bright flower is cut by the plough
> and languishes dying, or poppies drop down their heads
> on tired necks when by chance they are weighed down by rain.

His chest is white even as the sword is driven through; his limbs are beautiful at the moment that blood covers them. For Fowler,

place a heroic homosexual relationship has in a *Roman* epic; if we reply that it is to be understood as one of the archaic, Graecizing, features of Virgil's depiction of the legendary period that will be superseded in later Roman history, we have to face Virgil's emphatic association of the love of Nisus and Euryalus with the history and power of Rome in the final apostrophe to the dead couple' (33).

[15] Fowler (1987).   [16] Gillis (1983) presents a Freudian reading of *eros* in the *Aeneid*.

STATIUS AND EPIC GAMES

the imagery of defloration increases the pathos of the deaths, by emphasising the youth and innocence of the dead, and by adding an element of horror, making the killings essentially a sexual act. In that explanation, the eroticism is focused on the characters, but surely the eroticism of the description is designed to evoke a response in the reader? Certainly in the foot race, Virgil describes the mutual love of Nisus and Euryalus when he introduces them (5.295–6) but leaves a description of Euryalus' beauty until focusing on its impact on the spectators: *tutatur fauor Euryalum lacrimaeque decorae | gratior et pulchro ueniens in corpore uirtus* ('Popularity protects Euryalus and manhood, arriving in his beautiful body, made more attractive by decent tears', 5.343–4). Here, he is explicitly at the ideal age of pederastic attractiveness, just on the brink of adolescence.

Parthenopaeus and Statius' version of the beautiful boy

Parthenopaeus is introduced in Statius' running in a much more dramatic and erotically charged manner. We have seen how the audience call for him and he finally arrives. He then strips off, revealing his powerful beauty (6.571–3):

> effulsere artus, membrorumque omnis aperta est
> laetitia, insignes umeri, nec pectora nudis
> deteriora genis, latuitque in corpore uultus.

> His limbs shine out, the whole joy of his body
> is revealed, his famous shoulders, his chest no less beautiful
> than his naked cheeks; his face is hidden by the glory of his body.

In Aeschylus' *Septem*, Parthenopaeus is represented as a beautiful boy, but he already has down on his cheeks (Aeschylus *Septem* 533–6):

> τόδ᾽ αὐδᾷ μητρὸς ἐκ ὀρεσκόου
> βλάστημα καλλίπρῳρον, ἀνδρόπαις ἀνήρ·
> στείχει δ᾽ ἴουλος ἄρτι διὰ παρηίδων,
> ὥρας φυούσης, ταρφὺς ἀντέλλουσα θρίξ.

> He says this, son of a mountain mother,
> child with a beautiful face, man-boy man;

62

recently the down creeps across his cheeks,
his youth is blooming and his thick hair stands up.

Aeschylus goes on to say that despite his maidenly name,
Parthenopaeus (one reading of the name might be 'girl-faced')
is fierce and savage (537–8).[17] Statius' Parthenopaeus is somewhat younger: the elements of boyish beauty are not specifically
described, but Statius contrasts him with Idas, who is just passing
into the wrong side of manhood (6.583–7):

> proximus et forma nec multum segnior Idas
> cursibus atque aeuo iuxta prior; attamen illi
> iam tenuem pingues florem induxere palaestrae,
> deserpitque genis nec se lanugo fatetur
> intonsae sub nube comae.

> Next in beauty and not much slower in running
> comes Idas, also next older in age; however, the fertile
> wrestling grounds have already brought on his slender flower,
> and the down creeps on his cheeks but does not confess itself
> under a cloud of unshorn hair.

Statius' Parthenopaeus, unlike Idas, has not yet begun to make the
transition into manhood. He is a *puer* like Euryalus (*pueri*, 5.296).
In the corresponding fracas at the end of each foot race, both boys
have their beauty on their side (*Aen.* 5.343–4, *Theb.* 6.621–3).
Parthenopaeus is even more erotically charged through the image
which describes him as the evening star outshining all other stars
(6.578–82):

> sic ubi tranquillo perlucent sidera ponto
> uibraturque fretis caeli stellantis imago,
> omnia clara nitent, sed clarior omnia supra
> Hesperus exercet radios, quantusque per altum
> aethera, caeruleis tantus monstratur in undis.

---

[17] At 530–31, Aeschylus represents him as honouring his spear more than the gods, a
characteristic which Virgil used for Mezentius, and Statius transferred to Capaneus.
Statius' Parthenopaeus is clearly a pious character, at least in his devotion to Diana. His
shield in book 4 also supports this reading: in Aeschylus, he sports the horrific sphinx
as his emblem; in Statius' catalogue, he has his mother's deeds: *imbelli parma pictus
Calydonia matris | proelia* ('on his unwarlike shield are depicted the Calydonian battles
of his mother', 4.267–8).

In this way, when the stars shine out over a tranquil sea
and the reflection of the starry sky is shaken by the waves,
all shine brightly, but brighter above all
Hesperus sends out his rays, and he is shown as brightly
in the dark blue waves as he is through the deep sky.

This image will be the key to our reading of Parthenopaeus in the
foot race, and we will re-examine it from several different angles.
When Parthenopaeus dies in book 9, he is once more a version of
Euryalus (9.877–83):

at puer infusus sociis in deuia campi
tollitur (heu simplex aetas!) moriensque iacentem
flebat equum; cecidit laxata casside uultus,
aegraque per trepidos expirat gratia uisus,
et prensis concussa comis ter colla quaterque
stare negant, ipsisque nefas lacrimabile Thebis,
ibat purpureus niueo de pectore sanguis.

But the boy is carried by his allies to the pathless parts of the field
laid out (alas naïve in his youth!) and dying he was weeping for his
fallen horse; his face released from its helmet has fallen,
and he breathes out sick grace through his terrified gaze,
and three times they grasp his hair and shake his neck, four times,
it [his head] refuses to stand, and, a crime lamentable for Thebes itself,
bright blood was flowing down his snowy chest.

The flower simile itself is not there, but *purpureus* has transferred
from the flower to his blood, flowing over his white chest. His
head droops like the head of the poppy in the Virgilian image,
and even in death he remains attractive: he has 'sick grace' (*aegra
gratia*). Even without the flower image, links to Euryalus and Pallas
suggest defloration: the contrast of purple and white is reminiscent
of Menelaus' wound in *Iliad* 4 and of Lavinia's blush (*Aeneid*
12.64–9), but the emphasis throughout the passage is on the feel and
look of his dying body.[18] The passage is partly focalised through
those carrying him: *ter quaterque* ('three, four times') mimics their
desperate and repeated efforts to bring him back to life. As if one

---

[18] Dewar (1991) 218–19. He gives Euryalus' death as the primary intertext. Hardie (1983)
182 mentions an 'erotic' element in the laments for *pueri delicati* (pet slave boys) in the
Siluae.

of them, the reader is given a physical intimacy with the dying boy, which, with the imagery of his continued beauty and the beauty of his wound itself, adds up to a heavily eroticised presentation.

Epic stars

Let us now begin to think about the star image and how to read it. Star images can represent epic heroes in two different ways. First, to continue the erotic strand: Hesperus is the evening star, the morning star and the planet Venus.[19] It is associated strongly with love.[20] In Apollonius, Polydeukes is compared to Hesperus, and described as a beautiful boy, downy-cheeked and bright-eyed, just before the boxing match with Amycus (*Argonautica* 2.40–44).[21] Apollonius' Jason, too, is star-like as he goes to bring doomed love to Hypsipyle; not Hesperus, but an unnamed star, gleaming red, which girls gaze at as they fantasise about foreign suitors (Apollonius *Argonautica* 1.774–81). This image clearly brings out the erotic charge of Hesperus, beauty and danger combined. Its magical effects are sinister, even though the girl is only in love with her rightful spouse: Hypsipyle will be abandoned by Jason, but she is only a foreshadowing of the terrible things that will happen when Jason abandons Medea.

There are more sinister ways of reading the star image, too. As well as evoking the beauty of Polydeukes, the imagery of love, it also reminds us of the danger and destructiveness of both heroes and heroism. The star is not just a beautiful object to be looked at; it can also be an omen double-edged in its significance, or even the

[19] See Cuypers (1997) 75. For instance, Cicero at *De natura deorum* 2.53 notes that Lucifer or Hesperus are alternative names for the planet Venus.

[20] For instance, the epigram attributed to Plato by Apuleius (*Apology* 10.8), among others, makes the beloved into the evening star. See Ludwig (1963). Nisbet and Hubbard emphasise the commonness of the image: 'it was a commonplace in encomia, whether erotic, athletic or political, that the person praised surpassed all rivals as the sun, moon, or Lucifer outshone other heavenly bodies.' Nisbet and Hubbard (1970) 163–4. The particular associations of Hesperus, however, and the physical descriptions of the boys' bodies emphatically eroticise this matrix of imagery. Other epigrams from the Greek anthology which describe the boy beloved in these terms are: Meleager 100 (Gow 243, 4528–30); Rhianus 2 (Gow 174, 3204–7); Paton 178, 373.

[21] Von Stosch (1968) 161 links the image with Lucretius 4.212–13.

agent which brings about destruction. In this way, the (physical) star can affect its viewers. The heroic star imagery which originates in the *Iliad* displays this ambivalence. In *Iliad* 22 there are two star similes bringing out the terrifying destructiveness of Achilles: first, at *Iliad* 22.25–31, Priam watches Achilles approaching, bright like the brightest of the stars, like Sirius, which brings plagues and evil to mortals.[22] Later, as he is about to kill Hector, the brightness of his spear is compared to Hesperus, the most beautiful star in heaven (*Iliad* 22.317–20). These two images work together to build the idea that the warrior's glory is as deadly as it is beautiful.[23] The star is often an omen of disease and death. Achilles is compared to both Sirius the bringer of disease and Hesperus the star of love. Yet he is Sirius as he runs across the plain and Hesperus when he is even more dangerously close to the moment of killing, as he poises the spear to throw it.[24]

Apollonius, too, uses star imagery to build up danger in beauty: when Jason meets Medea, he becomes Sirius (Apollonius *Argonautica* 3.956–61):

> αὐτὰρ ὅγ' οὐ μετὰ δηρὸν ἐελδομένη ἐφαάνθη
> ὑψόσ' ἀναθρῴσκων ἅτε Σείριος Ὠκεανοῖο,
> ὃς δή τοι καλὸς μὲν ἀρίζηλός τ' ἐσιδέσθαι
> ἀντέλλει, μήλοισι δ' ἐν ἄσπετον ἧκεν ὀιζύν·
> ὣς ἄρα τῇ καλὸς μὲν ἐπήλυθεν εἰσοράασθαι
> Αἰσονίδης, κάματον δὲ δυσίμερον ὦρσε φαανθείς.

> Soon, however, he appeared to her as she desired
> like Sirius leaping high above the Ocean;
> bright and beautiful to behold

---

[22] Other Iliadic star images for warriors: Diomedes (5.4–7); Hector (11.61–6). See Richardson (1993) 108–9.

[23] Richardson (1993) 138, Moulton (1974) 392–4.

[24] In *Aeneid* 10, when Aeneas arrives on the shore of Latium, he is famously described as vomiting flames from his helmet; but he is also compared in a simile to both a comet and Sirius: *ardet apex capiti cristisque a uertice flamma | funditur et uastos umbo uomit aureus ignis: | non secus ac liquida si quando nocte cometae | sanguinei lugubre rubent, aut Sirius ardor | ille sitim morbosque ferens mortalibus aegris | nascitur et laeuo contristat lumine caelum.* ('The peak of his helmet burns and flame is pouring from the top of the crest, and the golden boss vomits vast flames, not unlike when on a clear night bloody comets glow gloomily red, or when burning Sirius rises, bringing thirst and disease to sick mortals, and makes the sky grim with sinister light.' *Aeneid* 10.270–75). Like Achilles at the beginning of *Iliad* 22, Aeneas the warrior bringing death and destruction is also the star bringing disease and drought to mortals (Harrison (1991) 146–48).

it rises, but it brings unutterable suffering to the flocks.
So the son of Aeson came; to her he was beautiful to behold,
but when he appeared, he stirred up the dire fatigue of passionate longing.

Achilles is deadly with his spear, Jason with his beauty; both
destroy themselves as well as others. Parthenopaeus, an imper-
fect reflection of heroic deadliness, destroys only himself and the
ideals of epic heroism.

In the *Aeneid*, the star image describes Pallas, who is likened to
Lucifer (*Aeneid* 8.589–91):

> qualis ubi Oceani perfusus Lucifer unda,
> quem Venus ante alios astrorum diligit ignis,
> extulit os sacrum caelo tenebrasque resoluit.

> Just like when Lucifer, drenched with the waters of Ocean,
> whom Venus loves above all the other fires of the stars,
> raises his sacred face in heaven and dissolves the shadows.

This strengthens the links between Hesperus and love: here, he is
not the brightest, but the one Venus loves best (and so, like Adonis,
doomed to die youngest). For Putnam, this is evidence of the sexual
tensions in Pallas' relationship with Aeneas, and his death too is
represented in erotic terms.[25] At 11.68–71 he is compared to a
flower plucked by a virgin, another recapitulation of the imagery
from Catullus 62.[26] Parthenopaeus, then, has ambitions to be an
Achilles, would settle for Polydeukes, or perhaps Jason, but is
rather a Pallas or a Euryalus. Parthenopaeus shines out above all
others in the image; he may be the most beautiful hero (his effect
on the audience, as we shall see, is unparalleled), but he is only a
boy and cannot take on the full destructive power of the epic hero.

Eros and the audience

We have seen that Parthenopaeus is presented in an erotic light;
he takes the role of the beloved or *eromenos* in the terminology
of Greek pederasty, like Euryalus, Pallas and Achilles (or even
Turnus). Yet who is his lover? Through whose eyes do we view
Parthenopaeus as an object of love? Nisus is clearly the *erastes*

[25] Putnam (1995) 34.   [26] Fowler (1987) 188.

('lover') of Euryalus; Aeneas should or could be the *erastes* of
Pallas (according to Putnam's reading);[27] those who read Achilles
and Patroclus as lovers usually see Achilles as *eromenos* and Patroclus as *erastes*. In book 10 of the *Thebaid*, when Statius recapitu-
lates the night raid of Nisus and Euryalus, and his noble pair, too,
die heroically and tragically, they are Hopleus and Dymas. These
two are not lovers, but instead the devoted companions of Tydeus
and Parthenopaeus respectively. Dymas takes part in the foot race,
just as Nisus does. He is even described as older, 'slowed down by
his age' (*aeuo tardante*, 6.559). However there is no sign of a close
relationship between them: he is described along with the rest of
the competitors, while Parthenopaeus waits until the last minute
to make his entrance, until the audience are calling out for him.[28]
In the battle of book 9, it is Dorceus who is his companion, not
Dymas. Dymas is not his lover, yet Parthenopaeus is described in
the language of the *eromenos*.

And this is the key: Parthenopaeus is beloved by everyone who
watches; his essential love relationship is with the audience. He
plays the role of scorning his lovers, in both book 6 and book 9
(*ipse tamen formae laudem aspernatur et arcet | mirantes*, 'he
himself, however, scorns praise of his beauty and keeps away
his admirers', 6.574–5; *nec formae sibi laude placet multumque
seueris | asperat ora minis, sed frontis seruat honorem | ira decens*
'he is not pleased by praise of his beauty and he makes his face
harsh with stern threats, but appropriate anger preserves the distinction of his appearance', 9.704–6). Von Stosch, for one, has read
this as a suggestion of flirtation rather than self-consciousness.[29]
The description in book 9 skirts delicately around his motivation,
pointing out that the harsh looks which he puts on only make him
seem more attractive. He is clearly aware of the effect that his
beauty has. He is playing the audience even while he pretends
indifference to it. At the end of the foot race, he uses his grief at
losing to the same effect: *ipse regesta | Parthenopaeus humo uul-
tumque oculosque madentes | obruit, accessit lacrimarum gratia*

---

[27] Putnam (1995).

[28] Kytzler (1969) 217 notes this separation and attributes it to the need to keep Dymas free
from the moral taint of cheating which attaches itself to Nisus.

[29] Von Stosch (1968) 159. See also Schetter (1960) 54.

formae ('Parthenopaeus himself dirties his face and wet eyes with heaps of earth, and adds the grace of tears to his beauty', 6.621–3). His melodramatic frenzy of grief apparently attempts to destroy his beauty, but self-consciously adds to his appeal. And the audience's fury makes sure that he gets the chance to win after all in the rerun.

Even in war, he always has an audience. In the catalogue of book 4, all the nymphs are in love with him (4.254–61):

> quas non ille duces nemorum fluuiisque dicata
> numina, quas magno non abstulit igne Napaeas?
> ipsam, Maenalia puerum cum uidit in umbra,
> Dianam, tenero signantem gramina passu,
> ignouisse ferunt comiti, Dictaeaque tela
> ipsam et Amyclaeas umeris aptasse pharetras.
> prosilit audaci Martis percussus amore,
> arma, tubas audire calens...

> Which leaders of the groves and powers dedicated
> to rivers, which Napaean nymphs did he not steal away with great fire?
> They say that Diana herself, when she saw the boy in the Maenalian
> shade, marking the pasture with his tender step,
> forgave her companion, and fitted the Dictaean weapons
> herself and the Amyclaean quivers to his shoulders.
> But he jumps forward, struck by love of bold Mars,
> burning to hear weapons and trumpets...

The nymphs are all in love with him, and a first reading puts Diana in the same position, in the accusative like the nymphs: not until the *ferunt* is it clear that we are now in an accusative and infinitive construction. But the language of love is applied to Parthenopaeus only to describe his love of war: he is struck (*percussus*) by *amor Martis* and he burns (*calens*) for weapons. This passage is followed by a description of his finery, finishing with this line: *dulce rubens uiridique genas spectabilis aeuo* ('sweetly reddening and perfect to watch, his cheeks in the bloom of youth', 4.274).

He also has an audience during his aristeia in book 9. There is a long richly coloured and sensual description of his armour at 9.685–99.[30] And at 700 he removes his helmet (9.699–703, 706–13):

---

[30] Vessey (1973) 299–300 says only that '[t]his graphic portrait intensifies the pathos of Parthenopaeus' destiny.'

ast ubi pugna
cassis anhela calet, resoluto uertice nudus
exoritur: tunc dulce comae radiisque trementes
dulce nitent uisus et, quas dolet ipse morari,
nondum mutatae rosea lanugine malae.
[. . .] dat sponte locum Thebana iuuentus,
natorum memores, intentaque tela retorquent;
sed premit et saeuas miserantibus ingerit hastas.
illum et Sidoniae iuga per Teumesia Nymphae
bellantem atque ipso sudore et puluere gratum
laudant, et tacito ducunt suspiria uoto.
  talia cernenti mitis subit alta Dianae
corda dolor, fletuque genas uiolata . . .

But when his panting helmet grows hot in the fight,
he rises out naked with his head free: then sweetly shines his hair
and trembling with sunlight, sweetly shines his gaze, and his cheeks,
not yet changed by the rosy down, whose delay he himself grieves.
[. . .] The Theban youth give way of their own accord,
remembering their own sons, and twist back their poised weapons;
but he presses them and wages war with his savage spears on those
  who pity him.
The Sidonian Nymphs on the Teumesian ridges praise him,
as he makes war, attractive in the sweat and dust itself,
and give sighs with silent prayers.
  Grief steals deep into the heart of gentle Diana
as she sees this, and her cheeks are violated by tears . . .

The shining hair and face, even called naked (*nudus*), recall his
description at the beginning of the foot race, as does the emphasis
on the down (*lanugo*), not quite yet growing. Even the Theban
enemies look at him instead of fighting him, and he has an audience
whose interest is undeniably erotic, the Sidonian nymphs. The
emphasis is on the emotional responses of those who watch him –
the Thebans, who think of him as a son, and the nymphs, who make
prayers in sighs. Even Diana is described in the language of love
as *dolor* creeps into her heart, and her cheeks are literally violated
with weeping. At the moment of his death, Parthenopaeus is still
surrounded by an audience, holding him, carrying him, listening
to his every word, his friends (*sociis*, 877).
  Parthenopaeus is always represented as interacting with his audience, as beloved of his audience: these are internal audiences,

audiences in the text. What then of the audience outside the text, the readers? Is there an erotics of reading? An erotics of reading epic? The reader cannot see the body and the beauty of the boy, but can only imagine what it might be like and see its effects on others. There is a tension in reading about the beautiful boy because the generic rules lead the reader to expect that what is beautiful in epic must be destroyed and there is a sort of gratification in the sensuous death scene and the emotional representations of mourning. Yet the reader is not encouraged to identify with the boy but with those watching him: his mother, his patron goddess, his fellow warriors, his lover. He is always other, absent and separate, a spectacle, rather than a person. This is particularly true of Statius' Parthenopaeus: yet there is no response to his final speech and, unlike Euryalus and Pallas, we do not see the reaction of his bereft parent, or even his comrades. At the beginning of book 10, the focus moves immediately to the Thebans and the narrative of the night battle. He is used at the end of the poem to represent the mourning of all the bereaved women, to represent the pointlessness of war, and we as readers must take responsibility for the mourning.

The reflected star

Let us look once more at the star image of 6.578–82 (see above, pp. 63–4) and consider what Statius has added to it. This image makes Parthenopaeus the object of the erotic gaze of his audience.[31] The relationship between the star and his audience is one of mutual power: the star has power over his audience, compelling them to watch him and evoking powerful emotional responses; the audience has power over the star because he owes his status as star to their watching, because their expectations influence his actions. There is one more very significant element to Statius' simile: the stars are all reflected in the sea (6.581–2).[32] This emphasis

---

[31] The idea of the gaze was developed by feminist film theory: in particular, see the 'germinal' article by Laura Mulvey: Mulvey (1975). Introductions to feminist film theory: Penley (1988); Humm (1997); Thornham (1999). In this theory, men look at women, and women become objects.

[32] On reflections in Statius see Taisne (1994) 28–36, although not including this image.

on reflection gives us another way of looking at Parthenopaeus. In his self-absorption, he resembles Ovid's Narcissus.[33] He himself plays the roles of both lover and beloved. In the foot race, Parthenopaeus brings Nisus and Euryalus together in one character. He is both the beautiful boy (Euryalus) and the outstanding runner (Nisus); he is the hero, one of the Seven and yet still a boy carried away by enthusiasm for war; he dies in his full finery, and laments his own death. His relationship with the audience is in a sense a relationship with his own reflection.[34] Parthenopaeus' scorn of his admirers becomes reminiscent of Narcissus' scorn of his admirers (*Metamorphoses* 3.353–5):

> multi illum iuuenes, multae cupiere puellae;
> sed (fuit in tenera tam dura superbia forma)
> nulli illum iuuenes, nullae tetigere puellae.

> Many young men desired him, many girls;
> but (so hard was the pride in his tender beauty)
> no young men touched him, no girls.

Scholars have noted an allusion to Catullus 62 in these lines.[35] Narcissus is like the bride in Catullus, losing her virginity and despised for ever afterwards. Scorning your admirers is both a sign of austere correctness and unattractive self-absorption. Parthenopaeus' reason for scorning his admirers and violently attacking those who hold off their weapons in pity is his longing for manhood, for full-grown masculinity and epic heroism. His beauty does not please him because it is characteristic of his immaturity; his desire is desire for successful manhood, and that desire itself is what brings about his death. There is something narcissistic, then, about epic heroism, concerned with its own reflection, excluding and ignoring the emotions of others. Parthenopaeus is absorbed in his own reflection in the eyes of his audience, so absorbed that he remains unaware of the grief he will cause his mother, even of his

---

[33] On Narcissus, see: Galinsky (1975) 52–60; Brenkman (1976); Stirrup (1976) 97–103; Davis (1983) 84–97; Rosati (1983) 1–50; Knoespel (1985); James (1986) 17–20; Hardie (1988); Hershkowitz (1998a) 177–9. See Von Stosch (1968) 160 on Narcissus and the mirror motif in *Thebaid* 6. The sporting hero can be seen as narcissistic: Connell (1995) 64.

[34] Von Stosch (1968) 173 calls him 'egozentrisch'.

[35] Davis (1983) 85–8, citing Fränkel (1945) 213 n. 31; Frécaut (1972) 119.

unsuitability for war.[36] The irony is that his self-absorption renders his reading of his reflected image fatally flawed. He sees himself as a man; the audience see him as a boy. He imagines fame as an epic hero, where his audience see him as an intruder from the pastoral world of Arcadia. When the nymphs watch him with desire in book 9, he is back in the Ovidian world of hunting and love, the potential victim of a Salmacis, the potential destroyer of an Echo.[37] Even his enemies see him as a son, not as a warrior, while he taunts them as equals. Dryas calls him a boy playing games, and orders him back to Arcadia (9.784–6):

> i, repete Arcadiam mixtusque aequalibus illic,
> dum ferus hic uero desaeuit puluere Mauors,
> proelia lude domi:

> Go, seek Arcadia again and there, mixed with your equals,
> while wild Mars rages here in the true dust,
> play your battles at home.

The transition from boyhood to manhood, from hunting to war, is the transition from games to reality. The dust of battle is real dust, the dust of games only a mimicry. Mars is truly wild and savage; hunting animals (in Arcadia or in the arena) is a game, a preparation for war. Parthenopaeus' self-deception becomes immediately apparent when it lifts at 9.855–6 (*puerque uidetur | et sibi*) and 'he seems a boy even to himself'. In his dying speech, self-absorption and desire for heroic fame has gone. He turns immediately to his 'wretched mother' (*miseram... parentem*, 885) and with the self-awareness typical of Statius' characters, knows about the section earlier in the book (570–636) when she experienced

---

[36] Ripoll (1998) 215 talks about the illusory nature of epic glory in the *Thebaid*. However, he maintains that while the gods are unsuccessful in validating the heroic deaths of their protégés (226), the poet is successful in delivering epic glory for his heroes: 'Stace développe et amplifie un troisième type d'immortalisation des héros dans leurs instants ultimes, qui est le thème de la renommée conférée par la poésie' (233).

[37] Parthenopaeus also shares many epithets with Cupid himself: he is a boy with a bow, called *puer improbe* ('wicked boy', 9.744); his weapons are *saeuus* (e.g. 9.708). At the beginning of Ovid's Apollo and Daphne episode, Apollo makes a claim that the bow is truly a military weapon for men, and insultingly calls Cupid *lasciue puer* ('wanton boy', *Met*. 1.456), but Ovid describes his anger as savage (*saeua Cupidinis ira*, 'the savage anger of Cupid', 1.453). Von Stosch (1968) 170 points out that the description of Parthenopaeus pursued by Idas, especially with his hair streaming out behind him, is reminiscent of Ovid's description of Daphne (*Met* 1.527 ff.).

a premonition of his death (*illa quidem, si uera ferunt praesagia curae,* | *aut somno iam triste nefas aut omine uidit,* 'she indeed, if cares bring true omens, has seen this sad crime already in a dream or through a sign', 886–7). This speech is a bizarre reflection of the erotics of grief: just as love elegy is parasitic on funereal lament, so, as he entrusts the message about his death to Dorceus to give to his mother, he reworks the concerns of erotic poets (9.888–91):[38]

> tu tamen arte pia trepidam suspende diuque
> decipito; neu tu subitus neue arma tenenti
> ueneris, et tandem, cum iam cogere fateri,
> dic:

> You however with dutiful skill keep her in suspense as she fears
>   and for a long time
> deceive her; do not come upon her suddenly or when she is holding
> weapons, and at last, when finally you are forced to confess,
> tell her this:

The same concerns about making the reader receptive to the message are found in love letters (for instance, Ovid *Amores* 1.11.15–20 gives instructions to Nape about how to make Corinna read his letter and reply appropriately).[39] The moment, too, where Parthenopaeus laments that his mother is not there makes literal the worries of love elegists about dying away from their beloved (9.898–9):

> frigidus et nuda iaceo tellure, nec usquam
> tu prope, quae uoltus efflantiaque ora teneres.

> I lie cold on the naked earth, nor are you anywhere
> near, who should hold my head and keep my last breath.

Tibullus at 1.3.5–9 laments first that his mother, then his sister and finally Delia is not with him as he lies dying, before he finishes with *Delia non usquam* ('Delia is not anywhere', 1.3.9). The last kiss,

---

[38] Just as Putnam (1995) argues for quasi-incestuous erotic overtones to the relationship between Aeneas and Pallas, so there is a worrying intensity about the relationship between Atalanta and Parthenopaeus. At 4.317–18 she stops him with her chest as Venus stops Mars at 3.265–7, and as Jocasta attempts to stop Polynices at 7.470–563: all these mothers and peacemakers are fatally undercut in their good intentions by hints of incestuousness.

[39] Also in the relationship between poet and patron. A special case is Ovid *Tristia* 1.1.92–6, where he advises his book to approach Augustus in a circumspect fashion.

and the last breath, are also fantasies of the elegist, for instance at Tibullus 1.1.62 and Propertius 2.13.29.[40] Dewar also points out that *frigidus et nuda iaceo tellure* is modelled on Ovid's description of the hardships of love at *Ars amatoria* 2.238: *frigidus et nuda saepe iacebis humo* ('you will often lie cold on the naked ground'). Parthenopaeus' message to his mother acknowledges not only his boyhood and his inadequacy for war, but also his generic transgression. He says *arma puer rapui* ('I snatched up arms as a boy', 892), self-consciously reworking *arma uirumque cano* ('arms and the man I sing', *Aeneid* 1.1) through both metre and position. He amounted to a character in the *Eclogues* who mistakenly trespassed into the *Aeneid*. His desire for epic *fama* led to his death, just as Nisus' and Euryalus' did. This is why Virgil's apostrophe to Nisus and Euryalus is no mere appendage to the story, but absolutely central to it: the moment of heroic death described by the poet is crystallised, made real and given point because it both creates and equals the ultimate epic *fama*. This too is a factor in the eroticisation of the beautiful death: it is in the moment of death that the epic hero becomes an irresistible celebrity, a star.[41] Fame stimulates, creating a self-conscious frisson for the audience, the readers: this beautiful young man is famous through his death; I make him famous by rereading his death; he died for me to read. Parthenopaeus' love for his reflection in the eyes of his audience has driven him to his death.

The reflected tradition

Once more back to the star image. The fact that Statius' image is a reflection tells us as much about the poet and his relationship to the tradition as it does about Parthenopaeus. The stars shine in the mirror of the calm sea, trembling with the trembling of the water; this reflection is as bright as reality; this Hesperus is as bright reflected as he is in the sky. This makes a play on both the

---

[40] On death in the love elegists, see: Griffin (1985), 142–62; Papanghelis (1986). Dewar (1991) 221 also points to these links.
[41] Vernant (1981).

nature of the simile (a reflection of the main story) and on Statius' relationship with his predecessors, taking the *topos* of Hesperus shining more brightly than all the other stars and reflecting on it as he refracts it. Though the simile makes the claim that the reflected star is as bright as the real star, the fact of reflection is only further highlighted by this claim. The simile also emphasises the medium of the reflection, the sea, and its instability as a mirror. The sea can only reflect the stars when it is calm, but even so the reflection trembles: the threat of storm (so frequently an image for war in the *Thebaid*) is ever-present only just beneath the surface. On a metapoetic level, the instability of the sea is a reminder of the fluidity of tradition, of the way that the star and the hero are reliant on audience and circumstance to ensure their poetic immortality.[42]

Let us go back to the ringmaster's announcement of Parthenopaeus at (6.563–8). This section is saturated with markers of the poetic tradition, as we have seen: who doesn't know about Atalanta? She is *nota* ('known') and *celeberrima* ('most famous'). Yet, as we might expect with such a self-consciously over-the-top flourish, this tradition is not straightforward. Statius is conflating two Atalantas: the devotee of Diana, raped by Meleager, from Maenalia, daughter of Iasus, and the supreme runner, eventually caught by Milanion, daughter of Schoeneus, from Boeotia. The story of Atalanta might even be seen as an *exemplum* of the disputed and uncertain tradition.[43] Apollodorus highlights the dispute (Apollodorus 3.9.2):[44]

---

[42] Fowler sees the Nisus and Euryalus episode as a *mise en abyme*, but Parthenopaeus is even more emblematic for the whole *Thebaid*: he is the warrior whose name is mentioned last, mourning for whom is the last moment in the poem proper, before the final coda. Dällenbach (1989) in his study of *mise en abyme* describes the role of the mirror in works of art as bringing in something from outside, and often reflecting the artist himself.

[43] Propertius' version of the story of Milanion in 1.1 makes Atalanta the daughter of Iasus, locates her in Arcadia and glances sideways at the confusion with the epithet *uelox* (1.1.15) which has been read both as a reference to the foot race and as the natural swiftness of a hunter. See Baker (1990) 22–4 and Fedeli (1980) 71–3.

[44] Ἡσίοδος δὲ καί τινες ἕτεροι τὴν Ἀταλάντην οὐκ Ἰάσου ἀλλὰ Σχοινέως εἶπον, Εὐριπίδης δὲ Μαινάλου, καὶ τὸν γήμαντα αὐτὴν οὐ Μελανίωνα ἀλλὰ Ἱππομένην. ἐγέννησε δὲ ἐκ Μελανίωνος Ἀταλάντη ἢ Ἄρεος Παρθενοπαῖον, ὃς ἐπὶ Θήβας ἐστρατεύσατο.

Hesiod and some others say that Atalanta is not the daughter of Iasus but of Schoeneus, but Euripides says she is the daughter of Maenalus, and she married not Melanion but Hippomenes. And Atalanta had Parthenopaeus, who marched against Thebes, either by Melanion or Ares.

Parthenopaeus could be the child of any of Atalanta and Ares, Atalanta and Milanion (or Hippomenes), and Atalanta and Meleager.[45] Apollodorus has one Atalanta, but Ovid has two.[46] Statius' version leaves plenty of room for ambiguity within itself: he never makes a clear distinction between the two possible sets of attributes of Atalanta. We never find out who Parthenopaeus' father is, as if he really is the offspring of a virgin birth, or because Statius deliberately avoids adjudicating between the competing versions. The heavily loaded references to tradition here are spotlighting a tendentious and ambiguous myth, emphasising the fluidity and subjectivity of tradition itself, and drawing the audience into it. Epic *fama* is equally at the mercy of poet and reader. The way Statius repeats and reverses his models, calling into question their internal logic, the way he plays with his audience demanding self-conscious collusion at the same time as pointing to the fickleness of tradition, the way he evokes simultaneously previous moments which have opposite effects: all these things show that *fama* as a goal is supremely problematic.

Virgil's apostrophe to Nisus and Euryalus links their poetic immortality to the continuing political power of Rome (*Aeneid* 9.446–9):

> Fortunati ambo! si quid mea carmina possunt,
> nulla dies umquam memori uos eximet aeuo,
> dum domus Aeneae Capitoli immobile saxum
> accolet imperiumque pater Romanus habebit.

> Blessed both! If my songs can do anything,
> no day will ever efface you from the remembering age,

---

[45] See *RE*. Hyginus *Fabulae* 70 makes no mention of the variant traditions, and assigns parentage only to Atalanta and Meleager.

[46] *Metamorphoses* 8.260–444 (Calydonian boar hunt) and 10.560–707 (race with Hippomenes). Apollodorus 3.9.2. Those who made Iasus (or Iasion) the father of Atalanta were: Callimachus *Hymn to Artemis* 215; Aelian *Var. Hist.* 13.1; Propertius 1.1.10. Those who favoured Schoeneus were: Diodorus Siculus 4.34.4, 4.65.4; Pausanias 8.35.10; Hyginus *Fabulae* 185; Ovid *Metamorphoses* 10.560–707.

while the house of Aeneas dwells on the immovable rock
of the Capitol and the Roman father holds power.

Virgil's poetry is coextensive with the power of Rome; the eternal
city guarantees the eternal fame of his heroes. Epic fame is intrin-
sically linked to imperial power: Virgil's poetry legitimates the
imperial power of the Augustan house and the rule of the Roman
Empire, just as the emperor and the empire guarantee that Virgil's
poetry will be read. Statius, however, focuses on the problematic
aspects of epic fame and political power. At the end of book 12,
Statius gestures towards the lament for Parthenopaeus but, instead
of making it an emblem of his poetic power, expresses inability to
encompass it (*Thebaid* 12.797–9):

> non ego, centena si quis mea pectora laxet
> uoce deus, tot busta simul uulgique ducumque,
> tot pariter gemitus dignis conatibus aequem:

> I could not, even if some god loosed my breast with hundred-fold voice,
> equal so many simultaneous tombs of soldiers and leaders,
> so much accompanying lamentation, with worthy efforts.

A different recapitulation of Virgil's apostrophe comes after
the battle of Polynices and Eteocles, and turns the desire for
poetic immortality into a *damnatio memoriae* ('an effacement of
memory') (11.574–9):

> ite truces animi funestaque Tartara leto
> polluite et cunctas Erebi consumite poenas!
> uosque malis hominum, Stygiae, iam parcite, diuae;
> omnibus in terris scelus hoc omnique sub aeuo
> uiderit una dies, monstrumque infame futuris
> excidat, et soli memorent haec proelia reges.

> Go fierce souls and pollute deadly Tartarus
> with your death and consume all the punishments of Erebus!
> You, Stygian goddesses, now, spare men from these evils;
> may this day alone in all ages and through all lands
> see this crime, may this unspeakable monstrosity be effaced
> from the future and may kings alone remember this battle.

This demands that epic fame be excised from the memory, and
the pointed reference to kings makes this too a political reference:
as long as there is tyranny and obsession with power, we must

read and digest the tragedy and horror. And desire for epic fame is implicated in the desire for power.

This condemnation of the central aims and ethos of the epic genre is also reflected in the differing representations of lament for the beautiful boys.[47] Euryalus' mother laments his death, demoralises the Trojan troops and is swiftly removed by Ascanius' men. She is a voice which stands out against the predominant ideology of the *Aeneid*.[48] She represents loss and suffering in the face of success, imperial and epic glory. Parthenopaeus' mother, on the other hand, is central to his story: at 4.309–44 she breaks into the catalogue, as if reading the epic herself and only just made aware of Parthenopaeus' intentions to go to war, takes over and trumps his moment of glory. Her premonitions and grief in book 9, too, come before his aristeia so that his failure and death are marked as inevitable. Statius also reads Virgil critically by combining Euryalus and Pallas. Euryalus' death does not contribute anything to the greater good of the Trojan expedition and the Roman Empire to come, while Pallas brings with him allies crucial to Aeneas' success, as well as a deeply symbolic link to the site of Rome itself. Pallas is lamented by Evander, in a way that is legitimated by Aeneas' grief, as a representation of future generations cut off, of political and genealogical tragedy: this is one reading of the significance of the death of virgins. They die before they can have children and guarantee the continued future of their family, like Marcellus in *Aeneid* 6. Parthenopaeus, though, like Euryalus, is lamented by his mother: the hopes of the female side are very different from the hopes of the male. Mothers are concerned with the cost of war and their own suffering when they have no male protectors, not with the long-term political future of their family. In Statius' epic world, there is no long-term political future. Both sides will defeat each other; all will end in destruction; the only point of this war is war itself.

---

[47] See Fantham (1999) 232: 'the grief is greater than the glory. There *is* no glory in this war. These heroes have died for nothing. There is no new liberty, no heroic code of values, to celebrate: there is only a tale of destruction willed by the gods as punishment for humankind.'

[48] See for instance Perkell (1997).

AUDIENCES

Introduction

In a performance, the stage or arena holds a separate world and the audience represent reality. We have seen how Parthenopaeus' relationship with his audience articulates the problems of epic heroism and *fama*. This section will examine the internal audiences of games and war, primarily asking how much power epic audiences have. The audience is an essential element of any set of epic games, in a triangular relationship of power with the master of ceremonies (*editor*) and the competitors. The balance of these power relationships changes from Homer to Virgil and from Virgil to Statius. The role of the audience in games is also distinctly different from the role of the audience in war. Epic presents war, too, as a watched event, a spectacle unfolding in front of an audience. This is especially true of the climactic moments of each epic, the duels between major heroes.[49] In this section, we will examine the portrayal of audiences in the games and compare them with the audiences of duels, asking how much power the audience have in reacting and even intervening, and how that power is presented.[50]

There are two reasons why the audiences of games are especially important: first, historical audiences of spectacles at Rome had power to influence politics. In the late republic, audience reactions at the games (and especially the theatre) were a marker of political power.[51] Cicero scrutinised audience reactions; those whom the audience condemned were in serious trouble.[52] The audience did not simply react to already established political situations but were instrumental in influencing and creating them: a politician hissed

---

[49] This link is made, for instance, by Hardie (1993) 52.

[50] Seneca, too, changed the role of the spectator, and was more interested in observing his audience: see Mader (1997).

[51] On audiences in the republic see: Parker (1999); Bartsch (1994) 71–5; Cameron (1976) 158–60; Yavetz (1969) 21–2. Though these works are mainly concerned with audiences in the theatre, Edmondson (1996) 76–7 points out that the terms of the primary sources are often quite vague in their description of disturbances taking place in a particular context ('at a public spectacle'), and suggests that 'scholars have perhaps been too quick to assume that it took place in the theatre'.

[52] Parker (1999) 168–70, 175–6. For instance, Cicero *Letters to Atticus* 2.19.3; 4.15.6; 10.12a.3; 14.2.

was a politician destroyed. In the *In Pisonem* Cicero challenges Piso to attend Pompey's games of 55 BC (Cicero *In Pisonem* 65):

Give yourself to the people, entrust yourself to the games. Do you fear the hissing? Where is your scholarly detachment? Are you afraid that you will not be acclaimed? Surely philosophers shouldn't care about that either? That hands will be brought against you? For pain is an evil, as you argue: judgement, disgrace, infamy, shame are words and foolishness. But I don't doubt this; he will not dare to go to the games.[53]

Cicero has no doubt that he will not be brave enough to face the hissing.[54] The audience of republican spectacles, at all types of *ludi*, not just the theatre, were powerful to make or break political careers.

In the imperial period, the relationship between the emperor and the audience was equally explosive, but more complex.[55] The numerical superiority of the audience did not guarantee impunity for critics. A famous passage of Josephus shows the tables turned on the audience at chariot races given by Caligula in January AD 41 (Josephus *Jewish Antiquities* 19.24–7). In this passage, the audience demand tax cuts, relying on the power of such public appeals, and the emperor's concern with popularity, but Caligula is so angry that he orders his soldiers to seize those shouting and put them to death. This episode is represented as the event which hardened the resolve of the conspirators to assassinate Caligula. The power of the audience was no longer guaranteed when the audience itself fell under the scrutiny of the emperor. Under Nero, with his transition from audience to performer, the categories of spectator and spectacle became ever more unstable. As Bartsch investigates, imperial writers such as Suetonius show that absolute power radically destabilises categories of watcher and watched: the audience can become the objects of the imperial gaze, required

---

[53] *Da te populo, committe ludis. Sibilum metuis? Vbi sunt uestrae scholae? Ne acclametur times? Ne id quidem curare philosophi. Manus tibi ne adferantur? Dolor enim est malum, ut tu disputas; existimatio, dedecus, infamia, turpitudo uerba atque ineptiae. Sed de hoc non dubito; non audebit accedere ad ludos.*

[54] In *Pro Sestio* 126, he describes the arrival of Appius Claudius at Scipio's gladiatorial games from underneath the stage, attempting to avoid an adverse audience reaction, and receiving an even more virulent hissing for this tactic.

[55] On audiences in the imperial period: Edmondson (1996) 71–2; Wiedemann (1992) 165–9; Veyne (1990) 398–415; Millar (1977) 368–75; Cameron (1976) 157–92; Bollinger (1969); Yavetz (1969) 18–24.

to react in a particular way.[56] Domitian in particular was presented by Tacitus and Pliny as the embodiment of the oppres-
sive gaze.[57] In the *Panegyric*, Pliny rejoices that the audience are
now free to favour whom they choose, whereas under Domitian
the spectators could easily become the spectacle ('Now how free
the enthusiasms of spectators are, how carefree our partisanship!
No one is accused of impiety as they used to be, because they
hated a gladiator; none of the spectators is turned into a spectacle;
no one atones for their wretched pleasures with hook and fire.'
Pliny *Panegyric* 33.3).[58] Tacitus at *Agricola* 45.2 paints a particularly vivid picture of Domitian watching both the punishments
of those he murders and the senatorial audience, noting down
their reactions. In this version of the emperor as master of ceremonies, the audience has become ultimately vulnerable. These
changes in the role of the audience at historical spectacles are
reflected in and negotiated through the changing portrayal of the
epic audience.

Second, the institution of the recitation made literary interpretation essentially a public and audience activity.[59] In the republic, criticism originated with the actor or the author: the audience
merely reacted.[60] Under imperial scrutiny, however, the art of allu-
sive criticism became all the more subtle and paranoid, the more
important it was to hide it.[61] The audience became the locus of
interpretation, of authorisation and legitimation. If the audience
saw a critical innuendo, that was enough for the author to be

---

[56] Bartsch (1994) 1–35. '[I]n those contexts in which there exists a well-defined, self-
conscious audience (as with Nero's stage performances – or modern metatheater), [the-
atricality] entails a reversal of the normal one-way direction of the spectator's gaze, so
that they know themselves watched by the object of their view and respond accordingly
even as the categories of spectacle and spectator lose all stability' (11).

[57] Bartsch (1994) 32–4.

[58] *Iam quam libera spectantium studia, quam securus fauor! Nemini impietas ut sole-
bat obiecta, quod odisset gladiatorem; nemo e spectatore spectaculum factus miseras
uoluptates unco et ignibus expiauit.*

[59] See Bartsch (1994) 80–82. For discussions of the institution of recitation see: Williams
(1978) 303–6; Sherwin-White (1966) 115–16. Fantham (1996) discusses in detail different possibilities for the distribution and reception of literature at Rome (on audiences:
7–11; on Pollio and the origins of recitations: 70–71; on Horace and his audience: 84–
90; on Statius and his audience: 171–2). Alex Hardie emphasises Statius' heritage as a
'Greek professional poet': Hardie (1983) 74–102.

[60] Bartsch (1994) 71–5.

[61] Bartsch (1994) 75–80. See also Fantham (1996) 172–82; Ahl (1984b); Ahl (1984a).

executed.[62] This model of group reading, although not the mode of reading exclusively used in the ancient world, was important enough to create a strong link between audience and reader. Not only the audiences of internal narrators, as persuasively studied by Stephen Wheeler for Ovid's *Metamorphoses*, but also the audiences of internal spectacles can function as narratees.[63] The audiences of games and war portrayed by Homer, Virgil and Statius work as mediators between text and reader, providing a range of responses to events, creating models of reading.[64]

However, just as historical relationships between audience and spectacle, audience and *editor*, became more complex and blurred under the absolute power of the imperial regime, so the internal audiences of imperial epic offer no straightforward model of reading, no simple and effective blueprint for political engagement. In the vortex of meaning created by the power of the emperor, even physical presence is no longer a guarantee of complicity. The portrayal of the audience in Statius' Domitianic epic becomes an opportunity to showcase the problematics of both watching and reading.

Homer: the powerful audience

In the *Iliad*, the audience influences the action of the games. In the fight in armour, the audience demand an end to the fight before anyone is hurt (*Iliad* 23.822–3):

---

[62] According to Suetonius, at least: *Caligula* 27.4 (an Atellan poet burned alive for an ambiguous verse in his play); *Domitian* 10.4 (Helvidius Priscus the younger put to death for an ambiguous reference in the libretto of a stage farce).

[63] Wheeler (1999); on the concept of 'narratee' see Prince (1980); on audience-oriented criticism see: Culler (1980); Suleiman and Crosman (1980); Tompkins (1980).

[64] The idea of epic as spectacle is central to two recent interpretations of Lucan's *Bellum ciuile*. Leigh (1997) 305–6 claims that the point of portraying the aestheticisation of slaughter and death is to disgust the reader into action. Bartsch (1997) 140–41 also sees Lucan as both acting out engagement with his spectacle and causing his readers to do the same. He is writing the 'kind of history that is precisely oriented toward the production of a response . . . our author presents himself as both detached from *and* implicated in his project'. In a discussion of reader-response criticism through history, Tompkins (1980) 203 presents a 'classical' model of audience reaction in which 'language [is] a force acting on the world, rather than a series of signs to be deciphered'. The portrayal of internal audiences, along with all the other methods of persuasion, is designed to create an effect, to influence the action and behaviour of the readers.

καὶ τότε δή ῥ' Αἴαντι περιδείσαντες Ἀχαιοὶ
παυσαμένους ἐκέλευσαν ἀέθλια ἶσ' ἀνελέσθαι.

And then the Achaeans, fearing for Ajax,
ordered that they should stop and be given equal prizes.

This is an emotional reaction to the narrative of the spectacle, fear: this audience acts on its sympathies for the participants. It is the audience who actually 'order' the fight to stop, with no intervention from the master of ceremonies. In the wrestling, the audience intervene in a different manner, by showing their boredom. The wrestlers become aware that the audience are bored by their stalemate and feel compelled to produce an exciting denouement (*Iliad* 23.721–4):

ἀλλ' ὅτε δή ῥ' ἀνίαζον ἐϋκνήμιδας Ἀχαιούς,
δὴ τότε μιν προσέειπε μέγας Τελαμώνιος Αἴας·
"διογενὲς Λαερτιάδη, πολυμήχαν' Ὀδυσσεῦ,
ἤ μ' ἀνάειρ' ἢ ἐγὼ σέ· τὰ δ' αὖ Διὶ πάντα μελήσει."

But when the well-greaved Achaeans grew bored,
then indeed great Ajax son of Telamon addressed him:
'Zeus-born son of Laertes, Odysseus full of tricks,
either you throw me or I will throw you; then Zeus will attend to everything.'

Ajax is very much aware of the feelings and requirements of the audience, though the text hints that Odysseus gains an advantage when the stalemate is broken.[65] At other points in the games, the audience also function as an assembly, ratifying Achilles' decisions. When Achilles wants to give a consolation prize to Eumelus after his crash in the chariot race, he seems to need the audience's assent before acting (*Iliad* 23.534–40). Since the audience applaud or approve his decision (ἐπήνησαν γὰρ Ἀχαιοί), Achilles decides to act.[66] Just after this episode, when Menelaus challenges Antilochus for dangerous driving, he appeals not to Achilles, but to the audience, as if the audience were an assembly or a court: ἀλλ'

---

[65] Though there are latent tensions between the power of Achilles and the power of the audience, the emphasis is on audience power. For instance, after the boredom of the audience causes Ajax to break the stalemate, Achilles steps in to stop the match (*Iliad* 23.733–7) and when the audience has ordered the end of the fight in armour, they demand equal prizes for Ajax and Diomedes, but Achilles responds by awarding the prize to Diomedes (*Iliad* 23.822–5).

[66] Gernet (1955) 16.

ἄγετ', Ἀργείων ἡγήτορες ἠδὲ μέδοντες, | ἐς μέσον ἀμφοτέροισι δικάσσατε ('But come, leaders and lords of the Argives, judge between us both in the middle', *Iliad* 23.573–4). The audience is a powerful force in the Homeric games. In war, audiences come to the forefront most strikingly during duels, and here too they are powerful to influence the action. The watching armies during the duel of Paris and Menelaus in *Iliad* 3 are presented as an audience. Their feeling of excitement and wonder (θάμβος δ' ἔχεν εἰσορόωντας | Τρῶάς θ' ἱπποδάμους καὶ ἐϋκνήμιδας Ἀχαιούς, 'And the horse-taming Trojans and the well-greaved Achaeans were filled with wonder as they watched them', *Iliad* 3.342–3) links this audience to the audience of the fight in armour in the games (θάμβος, 'wonder', *Iliad* 23.815). It is not until after Aphrodite has already whisked Paris away that Athena persuades Pandarus to break the truce with an arrow. Athena's method of travelling down from Olympus causes the same reaction of wonder in the audience. She flashes down like a shooting star, and the armies watch this omen just as they watched the duel, with a repetition of the same lines (*Iliad* 4.79–80). Here, we have one audience intervening to persuade another to intervene as well. For the Homeric divine audiences are highly interventionist.

In *Iliad* 23, the chariot race becomes the playground in which Athena and Apollo work out their rivalry. Apollo knocks the whip out of Diomedes' hands to stop him passing Eumelus, and when Athena notices this, she returns it and takes revenge on Eumelus by breaking his chariot in two (*Iliad* 23.382–400). Although this is not an open manifestation, when Antilochus protests at Achilles' intention to give Eumelus second prize, he points out that Eumelus should have prayed to the gods (23.546–57). Athena intervenes in the foot race, too, and is specifically described as tripping Ajax the son of Oileus, who acknowledges this when he complains that she looks after Odysseus like a coddling mother. Apollo is also presented as influencing the outcome of the archery, answering the prayer of Meriones, but not directly intervening.

In war too, the divine audience in the *Iliad* are ever ready to join in the action of the text, influencing the outcome, if not changing it. *Iliad* 22 is a fine example of the gods as an audience potent to change the outcome of the text. For as Achilles is chasing

Hector around the walls of Troy, the gods are presented as watching the events. Zeus suggests rescuing Hector, but Athena steadfastly refuses (167–81); he then allows her to intervene as she wants (182–5). The description of the divine audience (*Iliad* 22.166–87) comes immediately after the simile in which Achilles' pursuit of Hector is likened to a chariot race (*Iliad* 22.159–66).[67] Here, we see the gods watching and intervening in the duel, just as Pandarus intervened earlier to break the truce, and the audience in the games intervened to stop the fight in armour.[68]

Virgil: the controlled audience

In the *Aeneid*, there is a huge gulf between the audience in the games and the audience of war. The games are a paradigm of the functioning society, a model of control; the war is a demonstration of how that society can break down, how destructive the audience can be when it is out of control.[69] Aeneas, the master of ceremonies, keeps firm control of the proceedings throughout the games. When the action in the boxing threatens to become dangerous, he closes it down (*Aeneid* 5.461–7):

> Tum pater Aeneas procedere longius iras
> et saeuire animis Entellum haud passus acerbis,
> sed finem imposuit pugnae fessumque Dareta
> eripuit mulcens dictis ac talia fatur:
> 'infelix, quae tanta animum dementia cepit?
> non uiris alias conuersaque numina sentis?
> cede deo.' dixitque et proelia uoce diremit.

---

[67] See below, p. 261.

[68] Griffin (1980) 179–204 examines the complexity of the Iliadic representations of the gods as audience: 'The gods look on and delight in the spectacle, but they are not shown as resembling a bloodthirsty audience at a gladiatorial orgy of carnage, but in a complex light. The idea of the divine watcher of whom justice and indignation are expected is sometimes applied to them, but sometimes they resemble the spectators at a sporting event, and sometimes they are the audience of a tragedy' (193).

[69] Inevitably, there is a degree of oversimplification in this schematisation. There are various different ways of reading the two audiences; the dissent might be suppressed in the male world of the games, but is clearly expressed by the excluded women. See Nugent (1992). It is possible to drive a wedge between audience and implied reader in both parts. However, these complications cannot obscure the fundamental differences between the audiences of games and war, and between the audiences of the *Iliad* and the *Aeneid*, the *Aeneid* and the *Thebaid*.

Then father Aeneas did not allow their angers
to go any further nor did he allow Entellus to rage with his bitter courage,
but he imposed an end on the fight and snatched tired Dares
away, soothing him with words and saying such things:
'Unfortunate man, what great madness has captured your mind?
Don't you feel that this strength is other and that the divine powers have
turned against you?
Give in to the god.' He spoke and parted the battle with his voice.

He 'imposes an end on the fight' (*finem imposuit pugnae*) and his
speech is immediately effective. There is no question of consulting
the audience. Similarly, in the prize-giving after the ship race,
Aeneas, like Achilles, decides to give a prize to the shipwrecked
captain, but again it is entirely his own decision, and the audience is
not involved: *Sergestum Aeneas promisso munere donat | seruatam
ob nauem laetus sociosque reductos* ('Aeneas gives Sergestus a
prize as promised because he is happy that he had preserved his
ship and led back his team', *Aeneid* 5.283–4). After the running,
too, in the dispute about Nisus' trick, which as we have seen is
partly modelled on the dispute between Menelaus and Antilochus,
the negotiations are entirely between the competitors and Aeneas.
The audience is not called upon as a court or as witnesses, and
Aeneas emphasises the personal nature of his decisions (*Aeneid*
5.348–50):

> tum pater Aeneas 'uestra' inquit 'munera uobis
> certa manent, pueri, et palmam mouet ordine nemo;
> me liceat casus miserari insontis amici.'

> Then father Aeneas said: 'Boys, your prizes will certainly remain with you,
> and no one will move the victory palm in the order;
> let me be allowed to pity the disaster of an innocent friend.'

Nisus appeals to Aeneas to pity him (*et te lapsorum miseret*, 'and
you pity me for my fall', 354), not to the audience.

We have seen the negative evidence for the lack of audience
power in the games of the *Aeneid*. There is also positive evidence
for the way Virgil portrays the audience in the games as controlled
and united. Feldherr argues not only that the audience on the shore
are united in their response to the events of the ship race, but also
that they identify with the participants in the boats, and that the

readers identify with the internal audiences.[70] Underlying his presentation of the spectacle of the ship race as inclusive and including, transforming the watching Sicilians into Romans, the reading Romans into Augustans, is the assumption that Virgil's audiences are unanimous in their response. This is the ultimate vision of poetic control. Certainly, at the start of the ship race the audience responds in an emphatically unanimous manner (*Aeneid* 5.148–50):

> tum plausu fremituque uirum studiisque fauentum
> consonat omne nemus, uocemque inclusa uolutant
> litora, pulsati colles clamore resultant.

> Then the whole grove sounded together with the applause and noise
> of heroes and partisans in their enthusiasm, and the shut in shores rolled
> with voices, and the hills, struck by shouting, echo.

Not only the audience, but even the whole landscape respond together (*consonat*). When Menoetes is thrown into the water, the description of the audience reaction blurs together the audience on the shore and the audience of the rest of the crew in the ship: *illum et labentem Teucri et risere natantem | et salsos rident reuomentem pectore fluctus* ('The Trojans laugh at him as he falls, as he swims, as he vomits the salty waves from his chest', *Aeneid* 5.181–2). And when Sergestus' ship crashes, the response of his sailors could easily be the response of the audience (and also emphasises the unity of response): *consurgunt nautae et magno clamore morantur* ('The sailors rise up together and delay in a great shout', 5.207).

The audience in the games of the *Aeneid* do not act or intervene; they are not appealed to as judges or witnesses; they are not required to ratify the decisions of the master of ceremonies. They respond to events, and even their response seems choreographed, predetermined, unthreatening. The games in *Aeneid* 5 are a paradigm of successful control. However, the audience of the duel in *Aeneid* 12 act very differently.

The audience are described in detail when the duel is organised. There are the two armies ordered as if they are going to war, and the civilians (*Aeneid* 12.121–5, 129–33):

---

[70] Feldherr (1995). See also Feldherr (1998) for spectacle enacting social transformation.

procedit legio Ausonidum, pilataque plenis
agmina se fundunt portis. hinc Troius omnis
Tyrrhenusque ruit uariis exercitus armis,
haud secus instructi ferro quam si aspera Martis
pugna uocet...
utque dato signo spatia in sua quisque recessit,
defigunt tellure hastas et scuta reclinant,
tum studio effusae matres et uulgus inermum
inualidique senes turris ac tecta domorum
obsedere, alii portis sublimibus astant.

The legion of the Ausonians comes forward, columns with all their weapons
pour themselves out of the gates. Here the whole of Troy
and Tuscany rushes out, an army with varied weapons,
drawn up with their swords not unlike when the harsh
battles of Mars call...
and when the sign had been given and each man went back into his own space,
they fix their spears in the ground and rest on their shields,
then the mothers pour out in their enthusiasm, and the unarmed crowd
and the old men, invalided out, sit down on the towers and the roofs
of the houses, and others stand near the high gates.

This is clearly a watched event. However, this is an audience who will not be satisfied simply to watch. Already in the description the mothers are partisans, like supporters at the chariot races (*studio*). The narrative focuses particularly on the Rutulians and their feelings as they watch Turnus and Aeneas prepare for the duel (*Aeneid* 12.216–21):

At uero Rutulis impar ea pugna uideri
iamdudum et uario misceri pectora motu,
tum magis ut proprius cernunt non uiribus aequos.
adiuuat incessu tacito progressus et aram
suppliciter uenerans demisso lumine Turnus
pubentesque genae et iuuenali in corpore pallor.

But the battle seems truly unequal to the Rutulians,
had done for a long time, and their chests are stirred up by mixed emotions,
now more, when they see the men more closely, not equal in their strength.
This is increased by Turnus marching forward with silent step,
humbly worshipping at the altar with down-turned eyes,
by his adolescent cheeks and the paleness of his young body.

The image of a young and vulnerable Turnus is focalised through his Rutulian supporters. It still takes divine intervention, however, to persuade them to do more than sympathise. Like Athena in the *Iliad*, Juturna manipulates the audience, but, unlike Athena's, her omen is fabricated, deliberately intended to deceive the Rutulians (12.244–6):

> his aliud maius Iuturna adiungit et alto
> dat signum caelo, quo non praesentius ullum
> turbauit mentes Italas monstroque fefellit.
>
> Juturna added something greater to these things and gave
> a sign in the high heaven, and no sign could have disturbed Italian
> minds more effectively and deceived them with its display.

Tolumnius the augur is totally persuaded by Juturna's omen, and the moment in which he throws the spear is the moment in which the narrative and the audience are plunged back into battle and confusion: *simul hoc, simul ingens clamor et omnes | turbati cunei calefactaque corda tumultu* ('At that very moment, then, there was a huge shout, all the ranks were thrown into disorder and their hearts were made hot by the riot', 12.268–9). The audience have taken back the limelight and it will take the majority of book 12 to persuade Turnus to restage the treaty. The results of this audience intervention are disastrous for the Latins: Turnus is still inevitably killed, but added to this is the destruction of the Latin city, the ravaging of its population and the suicide of Amata. And still at the last moment, as Turnus is fatally wounded, there is a link with the games. For the Rutulian audience, watching once more, react in a way that recalls the beginning of the ship race, and the landscape sounding together with the audience: *consurgunt gemitu Rutuli totusque remugit | mons circum et uocem late nemora alta remittunt* ('The Rutulians rise with a groan and the mountain around bellows back and the high groves send back their shout widely', *Aeneid* 12.928–9). The contrast between the two audiences, between games and war, joy and lament, is brought strongly to the forefront.

Another fatally resisting audience in *Aeneid* 12 is Juno: she is the only one of the gods presented as watching the duel like a spectacle. Jupiter is more like a general controlling his troops from a hill. When she asks Juturna to intervene, she claims that

she cannot bear to watch, using similar language to the Rutulians
(*Aeneid* 12.149–51):

> nunc iuuenem imparibus uideo concurrere fatis,
> Parcarumque dies et uis inimica propinquat.
> non pugnam aspicere hanc oculis, non foedera possum.

> Now I see a young man running to meet an unequal fate,
> the day of the Parcae approaches and a hostile force.
> I cannot watch this battle with my eyes, nor this treaty.

However, later on Jupiter finds her watching nevertheless: *Iunonem
interea rex omnipotentis Olympi | adloquitur fulua pugnas de nube
tuentem:* ('Meanwhile the king of omnipotent Olympus addresses
her as she watches the battles from her tawny cloud', *Aeneid*
12.791–2). She shows her desire for close engagement and personal
action at 12.808–12. Already, there is a distinct difference from the
Iliad: now, Jupiter's will and fate seem to be the same thing, and, in
the face of this, Juno is reduced to an agent of irritation and delay,
watching the events unfold from the sidelines rather than mani-
festing herself in her godhead to bring about the outcome that she
desires. In the *Iliad*, the gods all watch the battle together: here,
only Juno watches, and this seems to be an admission of weakness. Only those who do not control the outcome need to watch the
game. Jupiter, then, is more interested in watching the audience,
inasmuch as Juno constitutes an audience, than in watching the
duel itself.

Both the Rutulian audience and Juno are resisting audiences in
Aeneid 12, and both show the relative weakness (and even potential
destructiveness) of the observer. To be watching is not necessarily a position of power; it is also a position of marginality. For
these audiences, it is not possible to break the frame of the action
and take control, only to make futile gestures of intervention. The
imperial figure of Jupiter watches over the watchers and notes
down their responses, punishing those who do not react as they
should. The *Aeneid* presents two models of the power relations
between audience, *editor* and games: one is an idealised presentation of a controlled and harmonious cosmos; the other showcases
the dangerous and destructive potential of audiences who step out
of line.

Audience in Statius and Silius

In both Statius and Silius, the audience are very important, but, as
we shall see, Statius' audience are much more powerful and dangerous than Silius'. The audience in Silius' games are most important
in the chariot race, where he devotes much of the description at
the beginning of the race to the feelings of the audience (*Punica*
16.317–45). He is clearly aiming at a vivid portrayal of the audience experience. The spectator enthusiasm borders on madness
and is described with the language of rage and war.[71] The continual emphasis is on the impotence of the audience: they blur the
boundaries between audience and competitors by leaning forward
like the drivers (*instant praecipites et equos clamore gubernant*,
'they press on headlong and steer the horses with their shouting',
324) but cannot influence the outcome of the race; Silius even gives
the shouts of the audience in direct speech and laments that the ears
of the drivers are deaf (342–4).

From the first, Statius' portrayal of the audience at his games is
complicated: we begin with the heroes watching the audience (or,
since the heroes are part of the audience when not competing, the
audience watching themselves) (6.261–4):

> illic conferti, iam sole rubentibus aruis,
> bellatrix sedere cohors; ibi corpore mixto
> metiri numerum uultusque habitusque suorum
> dulce uiris, tantique iuuat fiducia belli.

> There they gathered, now as the fields were reddening in the sun,
> and the warlike cohort settled; there among the mixed group
> it was sweet for the heroes to measure the number, faces and dress
> of their comrades, and confidence in such a great war pleased them.

They measure the size of their audience and delight in their appearance.[72] At the beginning of the chariot race, the line between
competitors and audience is blurred again (6.410–13):

---

[71] *tollitur in caelum furiali turbine clamor* ('the shouting is raised to the heavens on a
maddened whirlwind', 319); *quatitur certamine circus | spectantum* ('the circus is shaken
by the struggle of those watching', 322–3). The enjambment of this line produces a
surprise for the reader: we would expect it to be the struggle of the competitors, not the
struggle of the spectators; *furit ... furit* ('he rages', 328).

[72] Fortgens (1934) 127–30.

emissos uidere atque agnouere Pelasgi,
et iam rapti oculis, iam caeco puluere mixti
una in nube latent, uultusque umbrante tumultu
uix inter sese clamore et nomine noscunt.

The Pelasgians saw them and recognised them when they had been sent out,
and then they were snatched from their eyes, then they were hidden, mixed
in one cloud of blind dust, and they scarcely recognised each other's
faces in the shadowy chaos by shouts and names.

As the chariots race, they are concealed in a cloud of dust.[73] The
description of the audience blinded by the dust blurs into the competitors themselves blinded by the dust and unable to distinguish
each other in the clamour. The readers, too, are excluded from
this part of the race, as though Statius were one of the audience
blinded by the dust. This is in strong contrast with the ship race
in the *Aeneid*, where the blurring of the lines between audience
and competitors seems to bring the audience closer to the action.
As the sailors on the ships watch the events, the audience seem to
see through their eyes.[74] Virgil's blurring of the boundaries brings
all together in unanimous knowledge, but Statius isolates his spectators even while bringing them together. The dust is like the dust of
battle, causing confusion and blindness, reminding us of the blindness of Oedipus.[75] Lines of sight and power are reversed and confused. There are many versions of the audience in the *Thebaid*, and
this section will demonstrate that while private dissidence remains
possible, the public face of the audience is powerless, passive, dead
or absent.[76]

---

[73] In Silius too, the chariots are concealed by dust (325–7) but this has no effect on the
audience.

[74] 'As Otis shows, by describing the turning post before the start of the race, Vergil presents
his audience with a view of the course in its entirety which replicates the perspective of
a spectator in the elevated stands of the circus. From this position the spectator is not
restricted to watching only a given moment of the race, as the chariots or ships pass his
position, but is constantly aware of the entire course of the race and of each competitor's
position within it.' Feldherr (1995) 246; Otis (1963) 52–3.

[75] The audience can also misinterpret events. In the chariot race, Arion runs fast because
he is attempting to escape his charioteer, but the audience think he is inspired by praise:
Inachidae credunt accensum laudibus; ille | aurigam fugit ('the sons of Inachus believe
that he is lit up by praise; he flees his charioteer', 6.428–9).

[76] Taisne (1994) 42 points out that Statius multiplies the horrified silences found in Virgilian
audiences.

Statius' audiences encourage dissidence and multiple responses. In the discus, the majority reaction to Phlegyas' unfortunate slip is not the only one: *ingemuere omnes, rarisque ea uisa uoluptas* ('They all groan, but there were a few rare moments of pleasure at that sight', 6.697). The groan is an outward sign of a reaction, but Statius suggests that it could be an unreliable sign, that while everyone groaned, not all of them felt the sorrow that the groan suggests. At the end of the running, too, Statius allows a dissident reading of events, while Virgil presents a unanimous viewpoint. Virgil presents descriptions of all the competitors in the impersonal third-person voice of the narrator (*Aeneid* 5.340–47):

> hic totum caueae consessum ingentis et ora
> prima patrum magnis Salius clamoribus implet
> ereptumque dolo reddi sibi poscit honorem.
> tutatur fauor Euryalum lacrimaeque decorae,
> gratior et pulchro ueniens in corpore uirtus.
> adiuuat et magna proclamat uoce Diores,
> qui subiit palmae frustraque ad praemia uenit
> ultima, si primi Salio reddentur honores.

> Then Salius filled the whole seating area of the huge theatre
> and the faces of the elders in the front rows with great shouting.
> He demanded that the honour snatched with a trick should be
>   given back to him.
> Partisanship and decorous tears protect Euryalus,
> and his manhood, the more attractive because it is on the point of
>   arriving in a beautiful body.
> Diores helps and proclaims loudly, Diores,
> who stole away with a place and came to the last prize
> in vain, if the first prize is returned to Salius.

The attitudes of the narrator are equated with the attitudes of the audience and the implied readers: the *clamor* (shouting) of Salius and the *magna uox* (loud voice) of Diores are equally jarring, and the positive description of Euryalus (*decorae, gratior, pulchro, uirtus*) asks that we all join with narrator and Aeneas in favouring him. Statius, however, presents a dissident voice. The Arcadians are raging in support of Parthenopaeus but 'there are some people who like the trick of Idas': *sunt et quis Idae placeat dolus* (6.621). This highlights how tendentious the decision of Aeneas is: he rewards the trickster for fouling. In Homer, Antilochus' trick

94

is much less obviously a foul, forcing Menelaus to move aside out of fear, yet Antilochus immediately owns up and apologises for it. Again, in Statius' games, the dissident voice is a quiet one. The supporters of Parthenopaeus, however, are so violent in their response that they threaten to turn the ordered world of the games into the chaos of civil war (6.618–20). The anaphora of *arma* recalls violent moments in the *Aeneid*.[77] The violence of the audience response climaxes in raging dissonance (*furit undique clamor | dissonus*, 'a cacophonous shouting rages everywhere', 625–6), which is reminiscent of the moment in *Aeneid* 12 when the truce is broken and the armies are plunged back into full battle: *simul hoc, simul ingens clamor et omnes | turbati cunei calefactaque corda tumultu* ('At that very moment there was a huge shouting and all the ranks were thrown into disorder and their hearts grew hot in the riot', *Aeneid* 12.268–9). The audience of Statius' games are not just dissident; they are dangerous. They threaten to break the frame of the games just as the audience of the duel in *Aeneid* 12 broke the truce and brought about their own destruction. The audience of Silius' games also rage in their partisan fanaticism during the chariot race, and Silius emphasises that different people support different horses or charioteers (*Punica* 16.328–32), but the audience gradually disappear from the picture during the race, and there is no hint of their reaction to the result. In the running, too, each shouts for a different runner (382–4) but Silius has removed the disputed outcome, and does not represent the audience response. While giving a sense of the violence and passion of spectators at games, he is careful to make sure that Scipio is in control, and that there is no sense of disorder breaking out in these games within the Roman army.

There is no hint of a divine audience in Silius' games and, whereas in Virgil the winning ship is helped on its way by a push from Portunus, and in Homer Athena and Apollo fight over the outcome, Silius rationalises the Iliadic version: his charioteer drops his whip because of hubris: *ni successu nimio laetoque pauore | proditus elapso foret inter uerba flagello, | forsan sacrasset Zephyro,*

---

[77] *Aeneid* 11.453 (midst of battle), 7.460 (Turnus made mad by Allecto); Von Stosch (1968) 171–2. Also 2.668.

quas uouerat, aras ('if he had not been betrayed by too great success and joyful fear into dropping his whip even while he was
speaking, perhaps he would have dedicated the altars which he
vowed to Zephyrus', *Punica* 16.431–3). The divine audience in
Statius' games are clearly represented by Apollo, watching from
Parnassus. Even as he entertains the gods in his role as ultimate
poet figure, he has at least one eye on the Argive army (6.355–7):

> interea cantu Musarum nobile mulcens
> concilium citharaeque manus insertus Apollo
> Parnasi summo spectabat ab aethere terras.

> Meanwhile Apollo is soothing the noble council
> with the song of the Muses, his hand entwined with his lyre,
> and he was looking down on the earth from the high air of Parnassus.

When he finishes playing, he catches sight of the chariot race
(6.365–70). Both the method of his intervention (6.495–501) and
the results bring the games closer to war. The snake-haired appari-
tion which he calls up to terrorise the horses of Polynices and
wreck his chariot is reminiscent of the *Dirae* who aid Jupiter at
the climax of *Aeneid* 12 (843–68). It not only looks like a Fury,
and possibly comes from the Underworld, but in describing its
terror-inspiring qualities, Statius imagines it terrorising Charon
and the Furies.[78] The result of this hellish intervention, as we have
seen, is the near-death of Polynices (5.513–17). Both the divine
and mortal audiences in the games of the *Thebaid* and their reactions assimilate Statius' games to Virgil's war. They emphasise the
dangers of an audience which intervene, and the dangers of too violent reactions. In war, however, Statius' audiences go beyond this
into a realm where intervening seems no longer to be an option
and, for the divine audience, even watching is too dangerous to
undertake.

The audience of the duel between Polynices and Eteocles in book
11 are similar to Virgil's description in *Aeneid* 12 (11.416–23):[79]

> prominet excelsis uulgus miserabile tectis,
> cuncta madent lacrimis et ab omni plangitur arce.
> hinc questi uixisse senes, hinc pectore nudo

---

[78] See pp. 37–8.   [79] Venini (1970a) xviii.

stant matres paruosque uetant adtendere natos.
ipse quoque Ogygios monstra ad gentilia manes
Tartareus rector porta iubet ire reclusa.
montibus insidunt patriis tristique corona
infecere diem et uinci sua crimina gaudent.

The wretched crowd stand out on the high roofs,
all are wet with tears and lament comes from the whole citadel.
Here the old men complain to have lived, here the mothers stand
with naked breasts and forbid their small children to pay attention.
The Tartarean ruler himself also orders that the doors should be open
so that the Theban dead can attend their family horrors.
They sit on their ancestral mountains and pollute the day
in a sad circle and rejoice that their own crimes are conquered.

This duel is beyond war, not a welcome respite from it, but a perversion of it that is far worse than war itself, and the audience is beyond intervention.[80] Virgil's unarmed crowd (*uulgus inermum*) becomes a wretched crowd (*uulgus miserabile*), weeping all over the grandstands; the old men are not simply invalided out of the war, but long to leave the world itself; the mothers are driven not by excitement but fear – already they have bare breasts, as if taking on prematurely the role of captured women, and they forbid their children to watch.[81] Statius takes this description one further, with a component of his audience that does not even make it into the Virgilian description. This is, after all, a show put on by Hades, and it deserves the audience from hell: the Theban ghosts come to see their own achievements in the world of perversion matched and mastered.[82] The mood of the audience is made quite clear: only the ghosts rejoice in the spectacle.[83] This *nefas* is unwatchable as well as unspeakable.

The audience are entirely passive, so much so that when they replay the moment in *Aeneid* 12 where they could have intervened, when the armies see an omen, the thought and the murmurs are repeated, but the ultimate action is not (11.453–6):

---

[80] On the duel see Ahl (1986) 2883–5.

[81] Venini (1970a) 110–15, esp. 113 on links between the audience in *Thebaid* 11 and *Aeneid* 12.

[82] Cf. Vessey (1973) 162–3: Thebes as an 'earthly mirror of hell'.

[83] The brothers are referred to as *pares* in this passage. See p. 342 for the significance of their presentation as gladiators.

mouet et geminas uenerabile diuum
prodigium turmas, alternaque murmura uoluunt
mussantes: iterare acies, procurrere saepe
impetus et totum miseris opponere bellum.[84]

An omen of the gods worthy of respect stirs
the twin armies, and in turn murmurs swell,
muttering: often there is an impulse for the columns to repeat themselves,
to run forward and to put an entire war in the way of the wretched pair.

Here, the vocabulary of self-conscious repetition finds its way into the reworking of Virgil (*iterare*, 'to repeat'; *saepe*, 'often') and the whole war (*totum bellum*) seems to hold a deep sense of irony: surely this is what the poem has been, a whole war getting in the way of this one duel? But here, there is one crucial difference: this is a delay that does not happen; they receive the omen, mutter and want to act, but they do not. Ultimately, the audience of Statius' duel is entirely passive; they watch the gladiatorial spectacle; they think about intervening but they might as well be dead too, for all the effect they have.

The gods take this audience powerlessness even further; Jupiter is so worried about the effects that the spectacle will have on his divine audience that he forbids them to watch (11.125–35):[85]

'nunc par infandum miserisque incognita terris
pugna subest: auferte oculos! absentibus ausint
ista deis lateantque Iouem; sat funera mensae
Tantaleae et sontes uidisse Lycaonis aras
et festina polo ducentes astra Mycenas.
nunc etiam turbanda dies: mala nubila, tellus,
accipe, secedantque poli: stat parcere mundo
caelitibusque meis; saltem ne uirginis almae
sidera, Ledaei uideant neu talia fratres.'
sic pater omnipotens, uisusque nocentibus aruis
abstulit, et dulci terrae caruere sereno.

'Now an unspeakable pair and a fight unknown before in the wretched
earth comes forward: turn away your eyes! May they venture those things
in the absence of the gods and may they hide from Jove; it is enough to
    have seen
the deaths of the table of Tantalus and the guilty altars of Lycaon

---

[84] Venini (1970a) 121 notes the connection to *Aeneid* 12.216 ff.
[85] Cf. Venini (1970a) 41–4; Vessey (1973) 162.

and Mycenae leading the hurried stars upon the sky.
Now even the day must be thrown into disorder: the evil clouds, the earth
receive them, but let the heavens go into retreat: it is my will to spare the
    firmament
and my heaven-dwelling gods; at least so that the stars of the gentle virgin
and the Ledaean brothers will not see such things.'
So spoke the all-powerful father, and removed his gaze from the guilty
fields and caused the earth to lack his sweet serenity.

The power is now in the spectacle, not in the audience. Yet this
is surely Jupiter's rhetoric, a pretext to evade taking responsibility for the events by refusing to watch them, just as philosophers demeaned the gladiatorial games and publicly trumpeted
their refusal to watch these morally degrading spectacles. This is
a substitute for action.[86] Jupiter in the *Aeneid* has ultimate control
over the course of events, and there is no reason to suppose that
Jupiter in the *Thebaid* has any less control. When he makes the
gods into an absent audience, he is like Tiberius removing himself
from contact with the people in the spectacles by physically removing himself from them and from Rome. The only thing that makes
an audience more powerless than being watched by an emperor is
not being watched by an emperor. If no one watches the audience
reactions, then their reactions can have no meaning.

Conclusion

It is the fantasy of every audience to intervene in the spectacle
before them:[87] Silius' representation of the audience at the chariot
race, who shout at the charioteers and attempt to steer the horses,
vividly brings this out. Audience members identify with the people

---

[86] Griffin (1980) 197–8 points out that the gods in the *Iliad* sometimes turn away from
watching the spectacle of mortal misery, at 13.1–4, for instance, and 11.72–7: 'From God
the All-Knowing Watcher we have thus reached the god who is *not* watching, and who
by not watching defines the position of mortals still more crushingly.' The comparison
between Homer and Statius here is telling: Zeus and the other gods in the *Iliad* turn
away carelessly during slow moments of the narrative; Statius' gods are removed at the
climax of the poem, deliberately and with intent. Jupiter represents the gods as morally
contaminated by the sight, but the action of choosing not to watch is even more clearly
morally questionable.

[87] Hence the current popularity of television programmes which allow the audience to
decide the outcome, like *Big Brother* or *Fame Academy*.

they are watching and vicariously share their experiences: how tempting to go one step further and actually *be* them. Yet audiences who break the frame and intervene become complicit in the spectacle and have to take responsibility for their actions. Audience intervention was part of the institutional apparatus of gladiatorial games, and a recurring theme in epic games and war. Statius has taken this satisfying fantasy and turned it into a nightmare: audience power in the games is grim and terrifying, as is audience impotence in the war. Imperial power threatens to turn the spotlight on the audience, and separation is no longer a guarantee of safety.[88] Statius highlights dissidence in his audiences but this is no easy model for the reader: dissidence could lead to violence, acceptance (or enjoyment) to pollution. On the other hand, refusing to watch at all is equally questionable: for the reader and spectator in Domitianic Rome, there is no comfortable position.

---

[88] To go back to the earlier analogy, how would it change the experience of watching *Big Brother* if the act of voting meant that the television cameras might turn up at your house to interrogate your choice and examine your lifestyle?

3

THE DISCUS

Discus events in epic are not exactly common: with no Virgilian version, the main forerunners for Statius are the *Iliad* (often rather called 'throwing the weight'),[1] Odysseus among the Phaeacians and the death of Hyacinthus in *Metamorphoses* 10.[2] As a non-contact sport, part of the Olympic pentathlon, we might not expect this to be a particularly violent event. However, through an association with the throwing of rocks in battle, it becomes yet another practice for war, and the distinction between practice and reality is very important in Statius' version. Statius makes it even more sinister through dark imagery of magic and destruction. The discus can itself be an image of the world, and here we will begin to think about the hero against the reality of the cosmos, overturning the natural order, competing against divine powers, and the poet following in his footsteps.

Iliad versus *Odyssey*

Statius' discus event plays with and equivocates between his two Homeric models. Replacement is the intertextual mode of choice for this event: Statius investigates Odysseus' gesture of replacement in the games of *Odyssey* 8, and himself replaces both of his models. The games in the *Odyssey* are completely different from Patroclus' funeral games because all sixteen of the competitors are involved in every event: they represent ephebic, intracity games, in which all the young men take part. Statius' discus begins in the world of the *Odyssey*, but, at the moment when Odysseus is

---

[1] Howland (1954) reads the Iliadic event as the shot-put. There is also long-lasting dispute about how the discus was thrown. See Von Stosch (1968) 189–90. For a recent summary, see Langdon (1990).
[2] Von Stosch (1968) 51–64 points to these models; see also commentary 177–93.

mostly strongly evoked, the event mutates into a version of the Iliadic discus.

One message of the discus episode in the *Odyssey* is that Odysseus, with his Iliadic heritage, so far outclasses the Phaeacian boys that they cannot even understand how different he is. After the boys have performed a pentathlon (foot race, wrestling, discus, jump and boxing), they insult Odysseus by calling him a merchant, unfit for athletics. Odysseus proves his heroism with a discus throw and challenges the boys to any athletic event. He purposefully looks back to his athletic prowess at Troy, but declares that he would not want to compete with the previous generation of heroes, like Herakles (*Odyssey* 8.214–25). Odysseus inserts himself into a narrative of declining heroism, where Herakles represents pre-Iliadic greatness, but Odysseus himself is the representative of Iliadic heroism in the *Odyssey*. When Odysseus does finally throw the discus, he marks his superiority to the Phaeacian boys by replacing their normal discus with a much heavier one (*Odyssey* 8.186–8):

> Ἦ ῥα καὶ αὐτῷ φάρει ἀναΐξας λάβε δίσκον
> μείζονα καὶ πάχετον, στιβαρώτερον οὐκ ὀλίγον περ
> ἢ οἵῳ Φαίηκες ἐδίσκεον ἀλλήλοισι.

> He spoke and leaping up with his cloak itself took a bigger
> and thicker discus, heavier by far
> than those which the Phaeacians used with one another.

His throw, then, represents Iliadic heroism outclassing Odyssean heroism, and the gesture of replacement encapsulates the intertextual manoeuvres in this episode.

Statius echoes and plays with this moment of replacement. In the *Thebaid*, the watching heroes assess the size of the challenge when Pterelas brings the discus out: *inspectant taciti expenduntque laborem | Inachidae* ('The sons of Inachus look at it in silence and calculate the work involved', 6.650–51); then, when they see that the lump of bronze is not actually that big, an eager crowd rushes forward (6.651). This creates a situation similar to the Odyssean games, where a large number of people all compete. However, Hippomedon replaces the discus chosen by Adrastus with a heavier one (6.653–9):

et plures agitabat gloria ni se
arduus Hippomedon cauea stimulante tulisset
in medios, lateque ferens sub pectore dextro,
orbem alium: 'hunc potius, iuuenes, qui moenia saxis
frangere, qui Tyrias deiectum uaditis arces,
hunc rapite: ast illud cui non iaculabile dextrae
pondus?'

And glory would have roused many more men if tall
Hippomedon himself, with the audience urging him on,
hadn't brought another discus into the middle, carrying it broadly
on the right side: 'Young men who are going to break down
walls, to throw down the Tyrian citadel, take this one
rather: for who couldn't throw that weight with his right hand?'

The reaction of the other competitors is to back out of the competition (6.660–64). Hippomedon manages to humiliate all his competitors without a throw, and it is as if the arrangement of the competition moves deliberately from the Odyssean to the Iliadic model, from sixteen competitors to four. So Statius replaces the *Odyssey* as true successor of the *Iliad*.

He is also in a sense replacing Virgil: for Virgil reversed *Odyssey* 8 by making Entellus abandon the lethal and terrifying *caestus* of his teacher Eryx in favour of the less impressive Trojan models. Nelis notes that Entellus' speech (*Aeneid* 5.410–20) is partly modelled on Odysseus' first speech of reluctance at *Odyssey* 8.166–85. Entellus, like Odysseus, also looks back to Hercules, who defeated Eryx. So Entellus claims continuity with the pre-Iliadic heroes with whom Odysseus will not compete, and sets the *Aeneid* on a level with the *Iliad*. Statius, then, reworks this gesture and places the discus at the centre again, making his own claim to be closer to Homer than Virgil, Apollonius, or indeed Valerius Flaccus.

If, however, we read this episode through the description of the discus rather than the competitors, it suggests a different metapoetic narrative. The discus in the *Odyssey* is very different from the σόλον in the *Iliad*. The σόλον is a mass of metal, envisaged as a source of iron for agriculture by Achilles as he sets the prize out (*Iliad* 23.831–5). In the *Odyssey*, the discus used is stone, and though bigger than their normal discus it is not portrayed as a lump of metal (*Odyssey* 8.186–90).[3] The event in Statius is called the discus when it is announced (6.646), but the description of Pterelas bringing the weight to be thrown is reminiscent of the *Iliad*; it is a slippery mass of bronze: *it iussus Pterelas, et aenae lubrica massae | pondera uix toto curuatus corpore iuxta | deicit* ('Pterelas goes as ordered and scarcely puts down the slippery weight of the bronze mass next to him with his whole body bent', 6.648–50). When Hippomedon substitutes a heavier one, it is described as *orbem* ('a disk', 656);[4] in his speech, he imagines weights which will break down walls and uses the word *pondus* to describe it (656–9): weapons thrown in war, though, are usually huge masses of stone, not metal. Throughout the rest of the event, it is referred to as a discus (664, 670, 680, 712), except at the moment when Phlegyas drops it and immediately afterwards, when Menestheus takes it up. Then it becomes a weight again (*pondus*, 695; *molis*, 700). Statius here melds together the metal mass of the *Iliad* with the discus of the *Odyssey*. He includes both his models and the gesture of replacement, suggesting that the *Thebaid* replaces both of them.

Practice and reality

The course of the event is not without the usual Statian reversals of expectations: for, as one of the Seven taking part in the event, especially after his dramatic entrance, we would expect Hippomedon to win in an uncomplicated fashion. Instead, there is a practice throw of exceptional quality from another competitor. It is only when Phlegyas comes to make his throw for real that he slips and drops the discus at his own feet. This downfall, coming after twenty

---

[3] Although Harris does his best to assimilate the Homeric mass to the classical discus, by suggesting that ancient smelting techniques might have produced a lump of metal similar in shape to a discus (Harris (1972) 38–9), Gardiner describes the discus thus: 'a circular plate of stone or metal somewhat thicker in the centre than at the circumference.' For pictures of discuses see Gardiner (1955) 156, pl. 112–13.

[4] The word *orbis* equivocates between a disk and a sphere, and also hints towards the discus as *orbis terrarum* ('disk of the world'), like the shield of Achilles. At 7.20–21, when Jupiter complains that Mars has not sufficiently caused destruction in the world because he has allowed games to take the place of war, he uses both words: *sonat orbe recusso | discus*. The ablative absolute enshrines the ambiguity: does it describe the discus rebounding from the ground, or the crash causing the earth to resound?

lines of preparation and build up, including a striking and hyperbolic simile describing the discus as it returns to earth as the moon drawn down from the sky, is deliberately bathetic. Phlegyas takes on the role of Epeius, whose throw inspires the audience's laughter (*Iliad* 23.839–40).[5] Hippomedon, therefore, only wins his event at the expense of someone else's bad luck. This is reminiscent of Ajax, competitor in the Iliadic discus, but in reverse, as Ajax is undermined by his continual failure to win thanks to bad luck.[6]

The contrast between practice and reality maps onto the contrast between games and war. Only in the controlled situation of the games can merit be recognised in spite of luck. In his gesture of replacement, we have already seen Hippomedon reading the discus in terms of war (6.656–9), as the equivalent of large rocks which become weapons in epic battles. Two examples are here particularly significant. At the climax of the *Aeneid*, Turnus attempts to throw a huge rock at Aeneas, but his strength has drained out of him and it falls short (12.896–907). This failed throw essentially leads to his death. At the beginning of the *Thebaid*, there is an example of a successful throw: when Tydeus faces down fifty Thebans, he crushes four beneath a huge rock torn from the cliff (2.559–76).[7] Significantly, Tydeus' rock is described as both a mass (*mole*, 568) like the discus, and a mountain (*montis*, 565) as if he were participating in a gigantomachic battle.[8] War here is the reality against which the games are played out. When Achilles brings out the mass of metal in the Iliadic discus, the reality which he invokes is precisely peacetime society (*Iliad* 23.832–5):

---

[5] Von Stosch (1968) 184 reads the laughter of the Thessalian witch in the image at 685–888 as the reaction of Fortuna to Phlegyas' downfall.

[6] Hippomedon is not the only hero whose heroism is undermined by the nature of his victory. Amphiaraus fails to overtake Arion at the last minute, so his victory is hollow; Parthenopaeus has to run his race twice; Capaneus never finishes his boxing match, and has just been knocked down by his opponent; Polynices loses one event and is not allowed to take part in the other; Adrastus only succeeds in creating a bad omen. Only Tydeus is a *real* winner. Cf. Kytzler (1968) 14, where he reads Hippomedon (third) as one of only two 'unbestrittene, unbezweifelte Sieger', along with Tydeus (third last). He sees this as part of a pattern of ring-composition: Parthenopaeus (second) and Polynices (second last) are most strongly undercut in their victories.

[7] Mulder (1954) 301 cites *Odyssey* 9.481, *Aeneid* 9.569, 10.127 and *Metamorphoses* 14.181 for parallel imagery of mountains used as weapons, bringing us back to Hippomedon as Polyphemus.

[8] In the same passage, he is compared to Briareus fighting against the whole company of gods at 595–601.

εἴ οἱ καὶ μάλα πολλὸν ἀπόπροϑι πίονες ἀγροί,
ἕξει μιν καὶ πέντε περιπλομένους ἐνιαυτοὺς
χρεώμενος· οὐ μὲν γάρ οἱ ἀτεμβόμενός γε σιδήρου
ποιμὴν οὐδ' ἀροτὴρ εἶσ' ἐς πόλιν, ἀλλὰ παρέξει.

Even if his rich fields are very far away,
he will have this and will use it for five turning
years; nor will his shepherd or ploughman, afflicted
by lack of iron, go to the city, but this will supply them.

The prize will be valuable for agriculture after the war. The
Thebaid, however, is entirely taken up with war; just as the prophe-
cies all foretell events within the poem, so the imagery has the
same logic as the twisted world of the poem; there is no glance
outside into a calm and peaceful normality. War draws even closer
with a sinister, threatening simile, comparing the discus to the
shield of Mars (6.665–7):

qualis Bistoniis clipeus Mauortis in aruis
luce mala Pangaea ferit solemque refulgens
territat incussaque dei graue mugit ab hasta.

Just as the shield of Mars in the Bistonian fields
strikes Pangaea with an evil light and terrifies the sun
by shining back and bellows loudly, struck by the spear of the god.

Though ostensibly this simile describes the fear of the competitors
who back off, it is focused on the discus itself, which is terrifying
because it has become a reflection of war. This passage is strongly
reminiscent of the description of Mars at 3.218–26.[9] In particular,
the shield of Mars is again presented as a rival of the sun: *tonat axe
polus clipeique cruenta | lux rubet, et solem longe ferit aemulus
orbis* ('the heavens and the pole thunder and the bloody light of
the shield grows red and the rival disk strikes the sun from afar',
3.225–6). The disk (*orbis*) of the shield is a rival cosmic body,
representing a universe pervaded by war. The discus, through its
shared shape, becomes the world, and, through its destructiveness,
threatens it.

Phlegyas' failure to follow up his practice throw with a successful entrance into reality anticipates Hippomedon's success in the

9 Von Stosch (1968) 180; Taisne (1994) 28–31.

games, which is eventually followed by his failure to make good in the war. The first part of book 9, which contains Hippomedon's aristeia, is particularly rich in Homeric associations, as we will see in the second section of this chapter. In particular, Hippomedon replays Achilles' battle against the river in *Iliad* 21, when he fights the river god Ismenus and fails. In the light of this parallelism, there is added significance in Statius' comment on Phlegyas' failure (6.691–3):

> atque illi extemplo, cui spes infringere dulce
> immodicas, Fortuna uenit. quid numina contra
> tendere fas homini?

> But Fortune, for whom it is sweet to pluck
> immoderate hopes, comes to that man immediately. By what right do men
> hold out against divine powers?

This becomes, then, a comment on and a lament for not only Phlegyas' failure in the discus, but also Hippomedon's death in war, and indeed the entire poem, a narrative of the failure of human heroes in a war, which is instigated and driven on by divine powers.

Measuring up to the task

When Phlegyas makes his first throw, he is described as 'beginning the work': *opus incohat* (698). In this section, I want to investigate the poetics of the discus, approaching it through one of the other (rare) representations of discus-throwing in Latin epic. Ovid's Hyacinthus episode is deeply concerned with issues of writing and commemoration.[10] When Hyacinthus dies, Phoebus names himself the *funeris auctor* ('author of the death', 10.199) and, throughout his lament, poetry and, above all, 'writing' dominate the imagery.[11] Apollo's brief obsession with Hyacinthus leads him to abandon poetry in favour of hunting (*Metamorphoses* 10.170–73):

> nec citharae nec sunt in honore sagittae:
> immemor ipse sui non retia ferre recusat,
> non tenuisse canes, non per iuga montis iniqui
> ire comes, longaque alit adsuetudine flammas.

---

[10] See Wheeler (1999) 55; Tissol (1997) 176–7; Janan (1988) 117–24.
[11] *Met.* 10.198–9, 205–6, 210, 214, 216.

Neither the lyre nor the arrows have their honour:
unmindful of his own ways, he himself refuses not to carry the nets,
not to hold the dogs, not to go as companion along the ridges
of the unequal mountain, and nourishes the flames through long familiarity.

This is expressed in an odd double negative which brings into play the idea of *recusatio* (*recusat*). Hyacinthus' death is the first developed story in the song of Orpheus, and Orpheus himself has refused his normal pursuit, singing cosmological poetry, in favour of erotic poetry (*Metamorphoses* 10.149–54):

> Iovis est mihi saepe potestas
> dicta prius: cecini plectro grauiore Gigantas
> sparsaque Phlegraeis uictricia fulmina campis.
> nunc opus est leuiore lyra, puerosque canamus
> dilectos superis inconcessisque puellas
> ignibus attonitas meruisse libidine poenam.

> The power of Jove has often been told by me before:
> I have sung the Giants with a heavier lyre
> and the victorious thunderbolts scattered on the Phlegraean fields.
> But now a lighter lyre is needed; let us sing of boys
> loved by the gods and girls thunderstruck
> by forbidden fires and deserving punishment for their lust.

Gigantomachy and the victorious power of Jupiter are the weighty subjects which Orpheus (and Ovid) refuses, replacing the heavy lyre with a lighter one. Yet the subject creeps back in when it is the earth herself who actually kills Hyacinthus (*Metamorphoses* 10.182–5):

> protinus inprudens actusque cupidine lusus
> tollere Taenarides orbem properabat, at illum
> dura repercusso subiecit uerbere tellus
> in vultus, Hyacinthe, tuos.

> Immediately, unwisely, and driven by desire for the game
> Taenarides was hurrying forward to lift up the disk, but the hard
> earth threw it back up, striking a blow in return,
> in your face, Hyacinthus.

The giants were the earth's revenge on the gods, and here the hard earth turns Apollo's throw against his beloved. Further, when he is lamenting Hyacinthus' death, the act of singing is described in such a way as to make it the equivalent of the act of killing him: *te lyra pulsa manu, te carmina nostra sonabunt* ('The lyre struck by my hand will sing you, my songs will sing you', 10.205). And Hyacinthus' final metamorphosis turns him into a festival: the Hyacinthia, celebrated annually by the Spartans (217–19).

We have already seen how Apollo leaves his cosmic song to become spectator (and disrupter) of the games. Recent work has investigated the *recusationes* of Statius and his relationship with Muses and emperor.[12] Replacement is also a move in the generic and political play of the *recusatio*; Statius represents himself as writing the *Thebaid* in place of the weightier task of writing about Domitian.[13] Yet here we have seen him suggesting that the *Thebaid* is so weighty that it causes the scale of generic rivalry to collapse. Gigantomachy is inevitably political: by threatening the natural order of Statius' poetic world, his heroes show that the order of Rome is equally unstable. The immoderate love of Apollo for Hyacinthus leads both to his death and to his immortalisation;[14] in the games, the immoderate hopes which Fortune takes pleasure in smashing are those of Phlegyas, but the language is excessive for the situation. Instead, it suggests Caesar and Lucan, Statius and Domitian. In particular, Statius asks *quid numina contra | tendere fas homini?* ('What right has man to compete against divine powers?' 692–3) and the verb *tendere* is the one he uses programmatically of his own poetic ambition when he refuses to write about Domitian (*Thebaid* 1.32–4). Is Domitian stretching himself too far, attempting to take over Olympus, encouraging poets to represent him as Jupiter? Or is Statius the instigator of gigantomachy by challenging Domitian in his role of Jupiter? Or can we separate the political giant-killing from the literary? The discus continues the strand of imagery which maps athletic competition onto poetic competition; it reinforces the ideas in the chariot race of a world out of control, and of poetry that endangers both cosmos and poet.

---

[12] Rosati (2002) and Markus (2003). Both point to the fact that Statius moves away from representing the emperor as inspiration and distances himself from his subject-matter by portraying himself as a passive recipient of the power of the Muses.

[13] See introduction.

[14] Hardie (2002) 64 points out the irony of Apollo, the god of moderation, overwhelmed by his immoderate love of Hyacinthus.

Ovid's discus episode is about death by discus and yet remains a beautiful and touching piece of literature. Yet Statius' discus, which has no explicit violence, has a much more sinister tone than Ovid's aestheticised (and anaesthetised) portrait of the death of Hyacinthus. The imagery of Statius' discus seems particularly Lucanian in its ancestry, reminding us of the blacker paradox for the author of civil war, both entranced and repulsed by his own narrative. The simile of the shield of Mars is not only in a typically Martian setting, but also a typically Lucanian setting. Lucan uses Pangaeus to set the scene for Pharsalia, even to represent it: at 1.679–80 the Bacchic matron's prophecy uses Pangaeus to represent Pharsalia: *uideo Pangaea niuosis | cana iugis latosque Haemi sub rupe Philippos* ('I see Pangaea white with its snowy ridges and broad Philippi under the cliff of Haemus'); and at 7.482 the mountain returns within Pharsalia itself as part of a tangential gigantomachic reference (*Bellum Ciuile* 7.477–84):

>   tunc aethera tendit
> extremique fragor conuexa inrumpit Olympi,
> unde procul nubes, quo nulla tonitrua durant.
> excepit resonis clamorem uallibus Haemus
> Peliacisque dedit rursus geminare cauernis;
> Pindus agit fremitus, Pangaeaque saxa resultant,
> Oetaeaeque gemunt rupes, uocesque furoris
> expauere sui tota tellure relatas.

> Then the crash stretched towards the sky
> and attacked the airy dome of furthest Olympus,
> from which the clouds stay far away, and which no thunder reaches.
> Haemus with its resounding valleys received the shout
> and gave it back again, doubling it in the caves of Pelium;
> Pindus stirred up a roar, and the Pangaean rocks echoed,
> the Oetaean cliffs groaned, and the armies were extremely afraid
> of their own shouts of rage brought back to them by the whole earth.

The sound of the civil war is attacking Olympus; instead of mountains piled on top of each other, the sounds (and the words describing them) pile from mountain to mountain. Olympus may be exempt from bad weather, but it cannot escape from Lucan or from his civil war. This is poetry *as* gigantomachy, attacking the divine with the ultimate *nefas*, speaking the unspeakable, to assail the unassailable.

Statius makes the discus itself threaten to upturn the world. When Hippomedon's discus comes down to earth, it threatens the stability of the earth itself (6.713–15):

> longe super aemula signa
> consedit uiridesque umeros et opaca theatri
> culmina ceu latae tremefecit mole ruinae:

> It landed far beyond the rival marks
> and made the green shoulders and shady tops
> of the theatre tremble as if in a mass of wide ruin.

Here, the open space of Statius' impromptu athletic venue takes on the image of a built arena with seats and roof, and the discus becomes once more a huge mass of rock thrown against the walls of a city, reminiscent of the tower pulled down in *Aeneid* 2 to crush the Greek invaders (2.460–68).[15] For Hippomedon's discus to overcome the *aemula signa* takes a force that is violent and threatening. He moves from replaying Odysseus proving himself among the Phaeacians to representing Polyphemus failing in his attempt to avenge himself (6.716–18):

> quale uaporifera saxum Polyphemus ab Aetna
> lucis egente manu tamen in uestigia puppis
> auditae iuxtaque inimicum exegit Ulixen.

> Just as Polyphemus threw the rock from smoke-bearing Aetna,
> even though his hand was lacking sight, in the tracks of the ship
> he could hear and next to his enemy Odysseus.

Hippomedon here takes on the role of Polyphemus; Statius' reading of the *Odyssey* links Odysseus among the Phaeacians to Polyphemus. Odysseus' discus throw has its own violence; it makes all the Phaeacians throw themselves to the ground in terror (*Odyssey*

---

[15] At 445–6 the Trojans are tearing down their city to use as weapons: *Dardanidae contra turris ac tota domorum | culmina conuellunt;* ('The Trojans in opposition tear down towers and the whole roofs of their houses'). The moment of the tower's impact is described thus: *ea lapsa repente ruinam | cum sonitu trahit et Danaum super agmina late | incidit* ('It fell suddenly and dragged ruin down with a crash and fell widely on the columns of the Greeks', 465–7).

8.190–92). The hero can also become a barbarian, moving from
the suprahuman to the extrahuman, from above to beyond. What is
more, the simile describing Hippomedon's throw is recapitulated
in a gigantomachic variation (6.719–21):

> [sic et Aloidae, cum iam calcaret Olympum
> desuper Ossa rigens, ipsum glaciale ferebant
> Pelion et trepido sperabant iungere caelo.]

> So the Aloidae, when rigid Ossa was already trampling
> above Olympus, carried frozen Pelion itself
> and hoped to join it to the frightened heaven.

These three lines are absent from most manuscripts, including the
oldest, and have been excised for ineptness; they show how one
reader saw gigantomachy as the logical conclusion to the series of
images. This image shows gigantomachy suspended in the moment
of success, and links the discus to Capaneus' assault on the walls
of Thebes.

The (practice) throw of Phlegyas is also linked to the overturning
of the natural world. For Statius stresses the remarkable nature of
the throw by claiming that it moved faster as it went upwards and
slowed down when returning towards earth. He then compares it
in its reluctance to return to earth with the moon drawn down by a
Thessalian witch (6.685–8):

> sic cadit, attonitis quotiens auellitur astris,
> Solis opaca soror; procul auxiliantia gentes
> aera crepant frustraque timent, at Thessala uictrix
> ridet anhelantes audito carmine bigas.

> So the dark sister of the Sun falls, whenever she is torn
> from the thunderstruck stars; far away the tribes
> bash helping bronze and fear in vain, but the conquering Thessalian woman
> laughs at the gasping chariot-horses who have heard her song.

The athlete hurling the discus up in the air becomes the witch
drawing the moon down from the sky, the ultimate symbol of
the overturning of the natural order. This image too represents
poetic competition in microcosm. Statius makes song the source
of the witch's power over the moon and by imagining the chariot of
the moon sets the witch as driver of a chariot, looking back to the
chariot of song. She, however, is competing with the white noise

of superstitious tribes who try to stop her song being heard. This, then, is a competition to make meaning, between those who want to preserve the cosmic order and those who want to destroy it. Destruction wins.[16] The explicit connection to the discus comes through the shape of the moon, as does the link to the shield of Mars, and its rivalry with the sun. But the mood of the simile and its themes bring us back to the dark vision of poetry as civil war and Lucan's Erichtho, the Thessalian witch who overturns life and death, and controls meaning.

The language which Statius uses to describe Phlegyas' throw suggests that this is a competition between man and nature: language of measuring suggests that Phlegyas is competing with the sky itself: *sed caelo dextram metitur* ('but he measures his right hand against the sky', 6.679), suggestive of gigantomachic competition with the cosmos, and reminiscent of Capaneus, whose right hand is his only god.[17] Phlegyas was accustomed to measure the river Alpheus with his discus (*sed alternis Alpheon utrumque solebat | metari ripis*, 'But he was accustomed to measure Alpheus from both banks' 6.674–5), reminding us that Hippomedon will set himself up against the gods in the form of Ismenus and will not measure up.

In his description of the discus, Statius has written a meditation on the difficulties and dangers of attempting to redescribe the world. Whether it is generic boundaries that his poetry threatens, or the political situation in contemporary Rome, or indeed the *diuina Aeneis* (12.816), Statius, like Hippomedon, seems to find that as he pursues his course, unwittingly perhaps, he must take on and fight battles so measureless that he cannot possibly measure up to them. Statius is both the witch transforming and deforming the world order of epic and the desperately scared *gentes* trying to drown her out, the giants threatening the cosmos and Jupiter blasting them with his thunderbolt. In the next section, we will pursue further the battles against the cosmos as Hippomedon and Capaneus struggle to re-enact gigantomachy and impose their own version of reality on the epic world.

---

[16] On witches as poet figures, see O'Higgins (1988); Hardie (1993) 107–9; Masters (1993) 179–215; Lovatt (1999).

[17] *Thebaid* 9.546–50; cf. *Aeneid* 10.773–4. Caiani (1990) 267.

GIGANTOMACHY

The ultimate reality is the world around us, the landscape, the cosmos, the universe. Yet this too is constructed by what we think, say and write, and it is represented and refashioned in both the games and the wider poem of Statius' epic. Philip Hardie has shown how Virgil organises and reorganises his poetic universe and links the order imposed by Roman rule (*imperium*) to the order imposed by the gods on the natural world (*cosmos*).[18] Statius, too, engages with the natural and political order of things;[19] we have already seen how Polynices becomes a figure of Phaethon in the chariot race and threatens to destroy the universe once more, and how the discus showcases heroism which threatens the stability of the landscape and the natural order. How do Statius' heroes engage with the reality of the landscape in the rest of the *Thebaid*?

In the final section of the chapters on 'Gigantomachy in the *Aeneid*' in *Cosmos and Imperium*, Hardie examines the image of Aeneas as Aegaeon at 10.565–70.[20] This comparison of Aeneas to the hundred-hander Aegaeon-Briareus goes against the grain of Hardie's reading of gigantomachy as order preserved and restored by the gods, analogous to order brought out of civil war by Augustus: here, Aeneas is presented as a giant fighting in opposition to Jupiter.[21] This image stimulates some important questions about the myths of gigantomachy and their resonance in Latin epic: the assimilation of gods and giants, their use of similar tactics and the way in which some participants seem to move between sides; all these make the myth of gigantomachy fundamentally ambivalent. Rather than presenting a straightforward image of the victory of order over disorder, gigantomachy can suggest a civil war.[22] This

---

[18] Hardie (1986).

[19] In his exploration of the impact of Virgilian cosmic poetry, Hardie (1986) 382 says of Statius only: 'A cosmic feel also characterizes the mythological epics of Valerius Flaccus and Statius, but without the overt political dimension of the works considered so far.'

[20] Hardie (1986) 154–6.

[21] Tydeus too is Briareus attacking Jupiter at 2.595–601. Mulder (1954) 310 points to a scholiast on *Aeneid* 10.565 (fr. 14, Kinkel), who suggests an Antimachean origin for this version.

[22] Hardie uses both these terms. At the beginning of his first chapter, he refers to '[t]he simple outline of the myth of Gigantomachy, the opposition between forces of order and disorder' (85) and in the concluding section of his second he carefully distances himself

section examines these issues further and investigates how imagery of gigantomachy and titanomachy often relates to poetic competition in Statius. The difference between the two wars is fundamentally one of legitimate or illegitimate succession, one successful and therefore legitimised, the other about failure and presented as illegitimate. The pursuit of this line of metapoetic imagery brings to the foreground the tensions about literary succession especially prevalent in Statius. What is Statius' poetics of gigantomachy?

The section begins with an investigation of the way gigantomachy is used by Latin poets and follows the use of gigantomachic imagery as Capaneus and Hippomedon take their turns to fight the reality of the epic landscape in books 9 and 10 of the *Thebaid*.

Mythic confusion and civil war

Gigantomachy is doubly unstable for early imperial Latin writers because there are two ways in which the boundaries become blurred. First, gigantomachy, the battle of the Olympian gods and the giants, is part of a group of myths which also includes the titanomachy, the battle between the gods and their predecessors, the titans, and typhonomachy, the battle between Zeus and the monster Typhon, and the attempt of Otus and Ephialtes to attack heaven by piling up mountains.[23] The boundaries between these myths are often blurred by the writers who use them. Second, there are two very different models of the nature of war at work in these myths. The first of these models is that of the war of succession between equal or similar enemies; the second is the destruction of monsters by a saviour. The titanomachy is a straightforward war along the first lines; the typhonomachy fits very easily into the second model. Gigantomachy, however, is somewhere between the two, and can be represented in either way. The giants are sons of Earth like the titans, but can be presented as monstrous in their size and physical shape (they are represented in later antiquity as having snake

from the idea that the war in Latium is a civil war: 'Alternatively, an approach is made through the idea that the war in Latium is an image of *civil* war, in which guilt adheres to both sides' (155).

[23] Key works on gigantomachy: Mayer (1887); Vian (1952); Fontenrose (1959).

tails rather than legs). In the version preserved by Apollodorus, the wars of the titans and giants are linked by the motivation of Earth: she gives birth to the giants so that they can take revenge on the Olympian gods for the destruction of the titans.[24] This makes gigantomachy part of the story of titanomachy.

Augustan poets are notorious for confusing the myths of gigantomachy, titanomachy and typhonomachy.[25] Since these myths seem to activate different images of war, it is important to examine *how* poets use them and confuse them. Is it really a case of 'indifference', or is the blurring of boundaries inevitably loaded? There is a problem about establishing a normative version of the myth against which to compare the various fluid versions used or created by poets. Hesiod is an authority only for the titanomachy – he does not write the gigantomachy.[26] This gives us a canonical version of one side of the myth which allows some comparison. Apollodorus' version of the gigantomachy is a much less secure control, but presents at least one coherent narrative of all the myths.[27] One answer to this problem is that Augustan poets do not seem to confuse the narrative indiscriminately, but either pile up the myths together, or equivocate between them. This in itself seems to suggest an awareness of their manipulation of tradition. In *Odes* 3.4, Horace uses gigantomachy to praise Augustus' *uis temperata* (moderate force); he piles up titans, giants, hundred-handers and Typhon against an Augustan Jupiter, carefully segregating him from any hints of monstrosity. In *Amores* 2.1.11–18, Ovid uses gigantomachy to represent the epic he refuses to write, and creates a virtuosic muddle of the various myths:[28] *centimanus*

---

[24] Apollodorus 1.6.1: Γῆ δὲ περὶ τιτάνων ἀγανακτοῦσα γεννᾷ Γίγαντας ἐξ Οὐρανοῦ . 'And Earth bore the giants from Uranus, angry about the Titans.'

[25] Vian (1952) 173 refers to the confusion in Virgil, Horace, Propertius, Ovid and Seneca as 'indiscutable'. Hardie (1986) 85 uses 'gigantomachy' to refer to the whole group of myths 'especially where ancient indifference to the distinction is plain'. Cf. Ripoll (1998) 340 n. 135.

[26] Hesiod *Theogony* 116–59 (birth of Titans, Cyclopes and Hundred-handers); 617–735 (account of titanomachy).

[27] Apollodorus 1.2.1 (titanomachy); 1.6.1 (gigantomachy); 1.7.4 (Aloidae).

[28] Other *recusationes* which seem to confuse the myths include: Prop. 2.1.19–39 (Propertius seems to be juxtaposing the titans and the giants as alternative subjects, rather than confusing them); Prop. 3.9.47–38 (only *Coeum* is out of place in the gigantic context – but Vian (1952) 175 points out that Coeus and Iapetus are the only Hesiodic titans who regularly participate in the gigantomachy). *Ciris* at 29–34 adds Typhon to a gigantic

Gyes ('hundred-handed Gyas') fought in Hesiod's version of the titanomachy on the side of Jupiter; the description of Earth avenging herself recalls the motivation for the gigantomachy which Apollodorus describes; the mountains come from the entirely separate giant myth of Ephialtes and Otus (*Odyssey* 11.305–20).[29] Lucan uses gigantomachy as a metaphor for civil war in his prologue. If this was what we had to go through to reach the rule of Nero, then it was all worth it (*Bellum Ciuile* 1.33–9; 44–5):

> Quod si non aliam uenturo fata Neroni
> inuenere uiam magnoque aeterna parantur
> regna deis caelumque suo seruire Tonanti
> non nisi saeuorum potuit post bella gigantum,
> iam nihil, o superi, querimur; scelera ista nefasque
> hac mercede placent; diros Pharsalia campos
> inpleat et Poeni saturentur sanguine manes...
> multum Roma tamen debet ciuilibus armis,
> quod tibi res acta est.

> But if the fates could find no other way for the coming
> of Nero and if eternal reigns are prepared by the gods
> at great cost and the heavens could not serve the Thunderer
> except after the war of the savage giants,
> then we complain about nothing, O gods; even those crimes and blasphemies
> are pleasing for that reward; may (the) Pharsalia fill
> its dreadful fields and satisfy the ghost of the Carthaginian with blood...
> nevertheless Rome owes much to civil war,
> because it was all done for you.

Here, Lucan makes gigantomachy the equivalent of civil war and Jupiter the equivalent of Nero (*seruire* is especially pointed when we might expect Jupiter to be saving (*seruare*) the heaven instead of heaven serving Jupiter).[30] The language of money (*parantur*, *mercede*, *debet*) seems to ask whether we can quantify the horror of war while casting suspicion over the motives for both wars. The echo of Jupiter's speech in *Aeneid* 10 (*fata uiam inuenient*, 'the fates will find a way', *Aeneid* 10.113) rereads the *Aeneid* as

context and presents him as climbing a stepladder of mountains to Olympus; issues of authorship and dating make it difficult to draw many conclusions from this. See Lyne (1978) 114–15.

[29] On gigantomachy as most prestigious of epic subject matter: Innes (1979) 166–68.

[30] Cf. *Bellum Ciuile* 7.144–50, comparison of preparations for Pharsalia to preparations for the battle of Phlegra.

yet another civil war, only slightly twisting Virgil's trajectory of history towards Nero instead of Augustus. Statius too reads gigantomachy as civil war with a passing allusion to it in *Siluae* 5.3: *talia dum celebras, subitam ciuilis Erinys | Tarpeio de monte facem Phlegraeaque mouit | proelia.* ('While you celebrate such things, civil strife brandishes its sudden torch on the Tarpeian mountain and stirs up Phlegraean battles.' *Siluae* 5.3.195–7) Phlegra was the battlefield of gigantomachy, so this epithet presents the Tarpeian hill as Olympus and in combination with *ciuilis* marks the battles as civil conflicts. This poem is a lament for his father and in this section he celebrates his poetic achievements: a poem about the civil wars of AD 69. No surprise, then, that he should describe the civil war in terms reminiscent of the highest epic themes: *mouere* also suggests poetry – it is as if the Fury is writing the war as a gigantomachy. Shortly afterwards, he presents himself as following in his father's footsteps to the Muses and gaining admission to the sacred state of poetry with his father's name: poetic succession is clearly an important concern of this poem, establishing Statius senior as a serious successor in the grand tradition of epic, and Statius himself as his rightful and legitimate poetic heir.

Gigantomachy is about challenging the accepted and acceptable: there is tension between the different stories in the group and how they can be arranged, narrated and used, a civil war of myth; gigantomachy is the highest and most inflated theme of epic: there is tension about what epic should be, how and whether poets should write it, a civil war of genre; gigantomachy is political capital, what patrons might expect from poets, the ultimate elevation of the here and now to the level of the mythic (and the ultimate bathos): tensions too about how it relates to the political, whether it is a metaphor for civil war or a simple demonstration of the victory of order over chaos, a civil war between poetry and politics.

We will now look at the two 'gigantic' heroes of the *Thebaid*, Hippomedon and Capaneus, as they fight against the gods and the natural world, beginning with Hippomedon's battle with the river Ismenus in book 9.

Hippomedon: the reluctant giant

In a spate of ferocious grief for Tydeus, Hippomedon re-enacts Achilles' battle with the river god from *Iliad* 21.[31] The model of gigantomachy is used by characters in the text, by Hippomedon himself and his opponents, not by the narrator, in an attempt to construct polarities for their own ends. There are two very different Hippomedons in the river battle: as presented by his enemies, he is a monstrous, swollen figure of horror; as presented by his own speech, he is a dignified hero doing what he must, unaware of the forces against him and overwhelmed by destructive divine and natural forces. The speeches enact a struggle over the imagery of gigantomachy: both Hippomedon and Ismenus attempt to force each other into the role of giant.

Hippomedon was characterised as a giant in earlier versions of the story. At 6.654, Hippomedon is introduced as *arduus Hippomedon* ('high Hippomedon') and this epithet is repeated at his first appearance in book 9 (91). At that moment, Statius describes him in a simile as a rock standing against a mass of water (*Thebaid* 9.91–4):

> ceu fluctibus obuia rupes,
> cui neque de caelo metus et fracta aequora cedunt,
> stat cunctis immota minis, fugit ipse rigentem
> pontus et ex alto miserae nouere carinae.

> Just as cliffs stand in the way of waves,
> a cliff which does not have fear of anything from heaven and the
>   seas fall back broken,
> it stands unmoved by all threats, and the sea itself flees
> its solidity and the wretched ships recognise it from the deep.

Dewar, in his commentary, links both of these descriptions with Hippomedon's presentation in the tragedians as a gigantic figure.[32] In Aeschylus' *Septem*, the messenger's description of Hippomedon

---

[31] Klinnert (1970) 88–99; Juhnke (1972) 24–43; Vessey (1973) 294–8.
[32] Dewar (1991) 75–6. 'The tragedians portray him as a giant of terrifying stature' (76). Dewar points out that *arduus* as an epithet, all but one time in the *Thebaid*, is used of Hippomedon and Atlas (1.98) and is reminiscent of Virgil's description of Typhoeus (*Aeneid* 8.299).

begins with his great size (σχῆμα καὶ μέγας τύπος, 'shape and great form', *Septem* 488) and then describes the emblem on his shield as a great image of Typhon, breathing fire (491–6). In Euripides' *Phoenissae* he is explicitly called a giant (ὡς γαῦρος, ὡς φοβερὸς εἰσιδεῖν, | γίγαντι γηγενέται προσόμοιος, 'how haughty, how terrifying to look at, like an Earthborn giant', 126–7). The image of the rock recalls Virgil's Mezentius (*Aeneid* 10.693–6):[33]

> (uelut rupes uastum quae prodit in aequor,
> obuia uentorum furiis expostaque ponto,
> uim cunctam atque minas perfert caelique marisque
> ipsa immota manens)

> (Just like a cliff which juts forward into the vast ocean,
> in the way of the furies of the winds and exposed to the deep,
> and bears all the violence and threats of the sky and sea
> while remaining motionless itself.)

Mezentius, too, is a gigantic figure, compared in size to the giant Orion at *Aeneid* 10.763–8; notoriously, he is the *contemptor diuum* ('scorner of the gods', *Aeneid* 7.648; 8.7), like Capaneus; this simile links Hippomedon to Capaneus and both to gigantomachy.[34]

However, epithet and simile can bite both ways. The only other instance of *arduus* comes in this very fight, and it is used of Ismenus (9.418). Mezentius in this simile in the *Aeneid* seems at his most sympathetic, fighting one against many, about to witness the death of his son and choose to sacrifice himself.[35] Moreover, the simile comes to Statius via Ovid: one of the similes which links the wrestling match between Hercules and Achelous with the wrestling match between Jason and the bulls is the comparison of Achelous and Jason to rocks attacked by masses of water (*Metamorphoses* 9.40–41; *Argonautica* 3.1293–5). In Ovid, however, it is Achelous,

---

[33] 'This simile is a close imitation of Virg. *Aen.* 10.693 ff.' Dewar (1991) 76. See also Klinnert (1970) 100–102; Von Moisy (1971) 62–5; Tanner (1986) 3030; Caiani (1990) 262. Other elements reinforce this link: both have a conversation with a horse (*Aeneid* 10.860–69; *Thebaid* 9.204–19); both are characterised by their *pietas* towards the dead. See Caiani (1990) 262–3.

[34] On the links between Capaneus and Mezentius see Legras (1905) 216; Venini (1961b) 389; Snijder (1968): *ad versum* 3.602; Klinnert (1970) 18; Caiani (1990) 266–9. Both call on their right hands as gods: *Aeneid* 10.773–4; *Thebaid* 9.546–50. See Dominik (1994b) 100.

[35] On Mezentius, see Lee (1979) 88–93; Gotoff (1984); Harrison (1991) 274–5.

the river god, who is compared to the rock and Hercules to the mass of water. But there is a connection rather with Hercules here. When Statius makes a new invocation, he refers to Hippomedon's aristeia as *labor* (9.315–18):

> nunc age, quis tumidis magnum inclinauerit undis
> Hippomedonta labor, cur ipse excitus in arma
> Ismenos, doctae nosse indulgete sorores:
> uestrum opus ire retro et senium depellere famae.

> Now come, allow me to know, learned sisters,
> what toil laid great Hippomedon low in the swollen waters,
> why Ismenus himself was stirred up to war:
> it is your task to go backwards and push away decline from fame.

And when Crenaeus taunts Hippomedon, he specifically denies that the hero can claim the role of Hercules: *non haec fecunda ueneno | Lerna, nec Herculeis haustae serpentibus undae* ('This is not Lerna, fertile with poison, nor are these the waters drunk by the Herculean snakes', 9.340–41). Hippomedon joins the ranks of the heroes in the *Thebaid* competing to play the role of Hercules. Once more, the contest is to assign the roles of monster and monster-slayer: which is which? To take this further, anxieties about poetic succession come to the fore here: Hippomedon is attempting to succeed Achilles, and Statius is asking for the Muses' help in going backwards to the source of epic. Yet the wording of his invocation recalls Lucan 4.812: *a quibus omne aeui senium sua fama repellit* ('from which its own fame pushes all decline of age away.')[36] This moment comes from Lucan's anti-memorialisation of Curio at the end of book 4, after his defeat at the hands of the Africans, the reverse of empire: these are events which look after their own fame. Lucan might like to silence them, but they tell themselves.

The rhetoric of gigantomachy

The speeches of Crenaeus' mother, her friend and the river Ismenus all paint Hippomedon as the most monstrous of heroes. Crenaeus' mother presents Hippomedon in this way (9.393–5):

[36] Dewar (1991) 120.

ecce furit iactatque tuo se in gurgite maior
Hippomedon, illum ripaeque undaeque tremescunt,
illius impulsu nostrum bibit unda cruorem.

Behold Hippomedon raging and boasting that he is greater than you
in your flood, and the banks and waves trembling at him,
the waters drinking our blood because of the attack of that man.

A nymph points him out as if he were a murderer rather than a
warrior: *Nympharum docet una patrem monstratque cruentum |
auctorem* ('one of the nymphs tells the father and points out the
bloody author of the deed' 9.417–18). Finally, Ismenus draws a
striking contrast between Crenaeus' innocence and Hippomedon's
ghastly joy in the victory: *at tu, qui tumidus spoliis et sanguine
gaudes | insontis pueri*, ('but you, who rejoice swollen in your
spoils and the blood of an innocent boy', 9.442–3). This Hippomedon is a boastful, bloody and joyful murderer, who has deliberately
chosen to attack the river and kill his relatives.

Sometimes the narratorial voice supports this presentation, especially in the reactions of the landscape to Hippomedon's aristeia.
When Hippomedon first seizes Tydeus' horse, he is described as a
centaur: *semifer aeria talis Centaurus ab Ossa | desilit in ualles:
ipsum nemora alta tremescunt, | campus equum.* ('in this way the
half-beast centaur jumps down from airy Ossa into the valleys: the
deep groves tremble at the man and the plain at the horse.' 9.220–
22). Throughout the battle, the landscape reacts with terror: at
228–9, the river is stupefied by the warriors; at 257, the stream is
afraid of both Hippomedon and Hypseus; at 347–8, the waves, the
woods and the banks are shocked and grieved by Crenaeus' death.
Thunderbolt imagery applied to Tydeus' horse makes Hippomedon
both monster-slayer and monster: at 9.218, the speed and ferocity of the horse is equivalent to a thunderbolt (*fulmine*), putting
Hippomedon in the place of Jupiter using the thunderbolt as a
weapon. At 286, however, the death of the horse becomes a thunderbolt used against him, as if the combination of horse and
Hippomedon (already a centaur) were a giant struck down by
Jupiter.

However, especially in comparison with Achilles, Hippomedon
is neither boastful, joyful nor even especially brutal. The beginning

of book 21 of the *Iliad* finds Achilles at his most horrifyingly brutal, refusing to spare Lycaon, taking twelve captives to sacrifice at the pyre of Patroclus and rejoicing in the fates of those eaten by fishes. He fights alongside the river until Scamander asks him to stop killing people in the river: only then does he actually jump into the river (*Iliad* 21.233–4). Hippomedon, on the other hand, does not actively choose to fight the river: he simply follows the battle into the river (230–35). He is not the only hero there: Hypseus is also killing people in the river. While Achilles is directly challenged by the river and chooses to defy him, Hippomedon is unaware of his divine opponent until it is too late. Even after he has killed Crenaeus, the river does not address him, but instead addresses Jupiter about him, and Statius makes it clear that Hippomedon was not privy to this exchange because he is portrayed as shocked by the sudden flood: *Hippomedon... miratur creuisse uadum seseque minorem* ('Hippomedon is amazed that the flood increases and that he is smaller', 9.457–8). Nor is he boastful over the death of Crenaeus: he specifically says nothing either in response to the boy's taunt or after his death (*nihil ille*, 'he says nothing', 343). He does not seek him out to murder him in an unequal fight: instead, it is Crenaeus who 'was rejoicing' in the fighting (*gaudebat*, 319), is overconfident on his home territory and in his beautiful armour (typical of boys about to die in battle, like Atys and Parthenopaeus), and makes a rash attack on Hippomedon: *tunc audax pariter telis et uoce proterua* ('then equally bold with his weapons and fierce voice', 9.339).[37] Hippomedon's only 'boast' before the river attacks him is over a man he spares, not over a man he kills (9.294–301).[38] On the other hand, the language of boasting, swelling and madness is used by the narrator about the river himself, even if in its literal physical manifestation, when the river attacks Hippomedon: *furentibus* ('raging', 446); *tumidi* ('swollen', 459); *iactat* ('tosses, boasts', 462); *ouans* ('exulting',

---

[37] In comparison, Tydeus taunts the body of Atys by not even deigning to take his spoils (8.588–91).

[38] His only battle taunt comes after the river has attacked him and follows the pattern of many Argive taunts against the Thebans, accusing the river of slavery to the womanly Bacchus (9.476–80). This is Hippomedon struggling to control the fight with the river, to push it back into the normal paradigms of the battle between Argive and Theban heroes, and it is this taunt that brings about his downfall.

488).[39] When the river attacks him, it uses the trunk of an oak tree (9.483–5) as a weapon, just like a giant. In Hippomedon's version of the fight, the river is not a flood but a storm. The river is overturning the cosmos, not him. Consider the speech, in which he asks Mars to rescue him from dying ignobly by drowning, which looks to Achilles in *Iliad* 21 (9.506–10):

> exclamat: 'fluuione (pudet!), Mars inclute, merges
> hanc animam, segnesque lacus et stagna subibo
> ceu pecoris custos, subiti torrentis iniquis
> interceptus aquis? adeone occumbere ferro
> non merui?'

He shouts out: 'For shame, renowned Mars, will you drown this soul in a river, will I go under these sluggish lakes and pools like a shepherd, caught in the unfair waters of a sudden torrent? Have I not deserved to fall by iron at least?'

This is primarily a reworking of *Iliad* 21.273–83:

> "Ζεῦ πάτερ, ὡς οὔ τίς με θεῶν ἐλεεινὸν ὑπέστη
> ἐκ ποταμοῖο σαῶσαι· ἔπειτα δὲ καί τι πάθοιμι.
> [...]
> ὥς μ' ὄφελ' Ἕκτωρ κτεῖναι, ὃς ἐνθάδε γ' ἔτραφ' ἄριστος·
> τῶ κ' ἀγαθὸς μὲν ἔπεφν', ἀγαθὸν δέ κεν ἐξενάριξε·
> νῦν δέ με λευγαλέῳ θανάτῳ εἵμαρτο ἁλῶναι
> ἐρχθέντ' ἐν μεγάλῳ ποταμῷ, ὡς παῖδα συφορβόν,
> ὅν ῥά τ' ἔναυλος ἀποέρσῃ χειμῶνι περῶντα." (*Iliad* 21.273–4, 279–83)

'Father Zeus, why does none of the gods pity me and undertake to save me from the river? Then may I suffer even that!
[...]
I wish that Hector had killed me, who is best of those brought up here; then a brave man would have killed, and he would have killed a brave man. But now it has been decreed by fate that I should be taken by miserable death trapped in a great river, like a boy swineherd, whom a torrent had washed away, as he crossed in winter.'

Hippomedon and Achilles share the image of the pastoral boy swept away by a vastly superior natural force; Statius brings out

---

[39] A metaliterary reading of this episode is also suggested by the Callimachean association of the swollen river with swollen epic song (Brown (1994) 19–20): Hippomedon is then overcome by the sheer hyperbolical force of epic itself.

the implications of this image more clearly with the epithet *iniquis* (unfair). But the death is unfair for different reasons: it is unfair to Achilles because he had expected to die, as his mother had prophesied, by the arrows of Apollo; for Hippomedon, it is an unfair death because it is sudden and he has not deliberately provoked it. The contrast between drowning and dying in battle evoked by *fluuione (pudet!)* (506) also recalls *Aeneid* 1.94–101:[40]

> 'O terque quaterque beati,
> quis ante ora patrum Troiae sub moenibus altis
> contigit oppetere! O Danaum fortissime gentis
> Tydide, mene Iliacis occumbere campis
> non potuisse tuaque animam hanc effundere dextra
> saeuus ubi Aeacidae telo iacet Hector, ubi ingens
> Sarpedon, ubi tot Simois correpta sub undis
> scuta uirum galeasque et fortia corpora uoluit?'

> O three times, four times blessed,
> you who succeeded in falling before the faces of your fathers
> and under the high walls of Troy! O son of Tydeus, bravest
> of the Danaan tribe, why couldn't you savagely make me bite the dust
> on the Trojan plain and pour out this soul by your right
> hand, where Hector lies, dead by the weapon of Achilles, where huge
> Sarpedon lies, where the Simois snatched so many shields and helmets
> of men and their brave bodies and rolls them beneath its waves?'

Aeneas here clearly looks back to Achilles' speech, especially when he dwells on the dead in the river. Hippomedon's *hanc animam* follows Aeneas, reading Aeneas' speech as a version of Achilles'. To die in the river is the heroic equivalent of drowning at sea, and the language in which Statius' flood is described is saturated with imagery of storms at sea. For instance (9.459–61):[41]

---

[40] And, through it, *Odyssey* 5.299–312. Dewar (1991) 155; Dominik (1994b) 252–3. Another inheritor of this tradition is Lucan's Caesar in the storm (5.504–677), where it is almost as if Caesar has called up the storm deliberately as a challenge to the gods: when he *is* eventually driven back to the shore, this is a reassertion of divine control and the natural order.

[41] Also: *non secus aequoreo...salo* ('no differently from the marine swell', 462–3); *nigrante...aestu | spumeus* ('foamy in a black tide', 464–5). The death of Cretheus, a sailor called *contemptor profundi* ('scorner of the deep'), contrasts his success at surviving sea storms with his death in the river, suggesting that there is an equivalence between the two (9.306–10). He is even called *naufragus* ('shipwreck', 310).

hinc atque hinc tumidi fluctus animosaque surgit
tempestas instar pelagi, cum Pliadas haurit
aut nigrum trepidis impingit Oriona nautis.

On this side and that the swollen waves and a wind-blown
storm rise up, the image of the sea when it drains the Pliades
or dashes black Orion against the panicking sailors.

Even the Theban weapons which keep him away from the bank
seem to be part of the storm: *grandine ferri* ('a hail of iron', 488).
When the river subsides and Hippomedon's body emerges from
the water, he is compared to a cliff re-emerging after a storm
(9.522–5):

illius exangues umeri et perfossa patescunt
pectora: ceu uentis alte cum elata resedit
tempestas, surgunt scopuli quaesitaque nautis
terra, et ab infestis descendunt aequora saxis.

His bloodless shoulders and furrowed chest
re-emerge: just as when a storm, raised high by the winds,
has settled down again, and the cliffs rise up and land sought
by sailors, and the sea climbs down from the hostile rocks.

This simile reinforces the image of Hippomedon as rock earlier
in the passage; both cliffs and sea are personified, and here the
rocks are hostile, moving away from passive resistance. The attitude of the sailors has changed, however: before, the rock was a
threat; now, the rock represents land and safety. By standing up
to the chaotic violence of the natural world (and the gods in the
Thebaid) Hippomedon is also a champion of those overwhelmed
by the storm of war. The way in which Juno engineers the end
of the flood in the *Thebaid* also links the river battle to the storm
passage in *Aeneid* 1: unlike Hera in the *Iliad*, who calls on Hep-
haestus to scorch the river into submission with his flames, Juno
implores Jupiter for help, and he stops it with a nod: *non spernit
coniugis aequas | ille preces, leuiterque oculos ad moenia Cadmi |
rettulit, et uiso sederunt flumina nutu* ('He does not scorn the
fair prayers of his wife, and lightly brings back his eyes to the
walls of Cadmus, and the waves settled when they had seen his

nod', 9.519–21).[42] Hardie has shown how the storm in *Aeneid* 1 can be read as essentially gigantomachic: the winds are like giants imprisoned under their mountains; they threaten the ordering of the cosmos; gigantomachy has been allegorised as a storm.[43] So, by turning Hippomedon's fight with Ismenus into a version of the storm in *Aeneid* 1, the narrator implicitly undermines the identification of Hippomedon as giant and river as challenged god. Instead, the imagery suggests that the hyperbolic violence of the storm is what threatens the cosmos, not Hippomedon's fighting. Hardie also points to the word *turbidus* as a gigantomachic storm word, which is used to describe scorner of the gods Mezentius at *Aeneid* 10.763, immediately before he is compared to the gigantic Orion. This is the word which characterises Ismenus as he makes his final attack on Hippomedon (482).

The imagery of the fight itself would seem to provide support for Hippomedon's version in the narratorial voice. In the imagery of *Iliad* 20 and 21, Achilles is portrayed as a fire. At 20.490–92 he is a forest fire and at 21.12–14 the Trojans are like locusts caught up in a forest fire. This imagery clearly puts him in opposition to the river as a similarly elemental and destructive natural force. In Aeschylus' *Septem*, the image of Typhon on Hippomedon's shield is above all characterised by his fieriness: Typhon traditionally belched flame in his battle against the gods. It would thus make sense for Hippomedon to retain this association with fire in his battle against the river.[44] However, Statius is clear: he is not a fire, but a rock, not actively opposing the river but passively holding

---

[42] The irony, of course, is that here Juno is begging Jupiter to stop the storm, rather than malevolently engineering its beginning as in the *Aeneid*. See Feeney (1991) 343 on the transformation of Juno in the *Thebaid*. This makes the reference to *Aeneid* 1 all the more pointed.

[43] Hardie (1986) 90–97.

[44] Other imagery from the Iliadic description of Achilles makes it into the text, such as the image of Achilles as a dolphin frightening the fish: *Iliad* 21.22–4; *Thebaid* 9.242–7. At the end of this simile in the *Thebaid*, the dolphin abandons the fish to race with ships (*uisis malit certare carinis*, 247). This hints both at the futility of Hippomedon's attempt to compete with the gods and at his attitude to battle. The dolphin, like the hero, may be bigger than those he terrorises, but he is essentially more similar to them than to the ships with which he longs to compete. This moment also encapsulates the tension between play and reality: for the ships, the competition with the dolphin is a game, but for the fish it is a matter of deadly reality.

his ground against it.[45] He is not a destructive force raging against the cosmos but a solid force for stability, standing against the overwhelming destructiveness of the natural and the divine. By sheer sleight of hand, the river god has become the giant attacking the order of the cosmos, Hippomedon merely a victim of its disintegration.

A thread of imagery which links and contrasts Hippomedon to Turnus also plays a part in this assimilation and confusion. The image of Typhoeus which adorns the shield of Hippomedon in the *Septem* is adopted by Virgil for Turnus' shield.[46] Hippomedon in the *Thebaid*, however, has the image of the Danaids on his shield (4.132–5), corresponding to the image on the sword-belt of Pallas.[47] Turnus, unlike Hippomedon, as I have shown above, does rejoice in the slaying of Pallas: *quo nunc Turnus ouat spolio gaudetque potitus* ('Turnus now exults in this spoil and rejoices that he has acquired it', *Aeneid* 10.500). Hippomedon therefore takes on aspects of both Turnus and Pallas, underlining the way Virgil assimilates them as well as contrasting them, and becomes in the end the victim of violent natural forces, rather than a representation of them.

Capaneus: gigantic poetics

The majority of gigantomachic imagery in the *Thebaid* clusters around Capaneus, and it is through this cluster that I will examine the presentation of poetic competition as gigantomachy and show how Capaneus and Jupiter are assimilated through the confusion of the myths.

Gigantomachy and poetry are closely linked in Ovid as well as Statius. In the first poetic contest between gods and mortals in the *Metamorphoses*, the contest between the Pierides and the Muses, gigantomachy is the issue over which they fight. The Pierides use the myth to present the gods as cowards, metamorphosing to escape Typhoeus (5.319–31); the Muses counter with a

---

[45] As well as the rock imagery, he is also a city withstanding siege engines: 9.144–7; at 490 he is *obsessus*, besieged like a city.

[46] *Aeneid* 7.783–8; see Hardie (1986) 118–19.

[47] *Aeneid* 10.496–9; see Conte (1986) 185–95; Lyne (1990) 324–5.

presentation of Typhoeus buried under Sicily, threatening destruction of the cosmos with his earthquakes (5.346–61). The Pierides are described by the Muses as giving the giants false honour (*falsoque in honore gigantas ponit*, 'she places the giants in false honour' 5.319–20). Gigantomachy is not just the subject-matter over which they compete; it mirrors the act of competing. For Ovid, representing the gods inevitably challenges them. In Statius, the matrix of gigantomachy and poetry, challenging the gods, challenging tradition and the political situation, converges on the figure of Capaneus.[48]

Capaneus' section of the catalogue in book 4 exemplifies the way these themes come together.[49] The description begins with Capaneus' extraordinary stature, which suggests already that he despises the war (*despectans*, 'looking down on', 165). He has already been compared to cyclopes and Centaurs (3.604–5), emphasising the monstrous nature of his size.[50] His body figuratively becomes landscape itself: *laterum tractus spatiosaque pectora* ('the region of his flanks and his spacious chest', 173). This foreshadows the way his body is represented during his fall from the walls. As they watch him struck by the thunderbolt, both armies are terrified that his body will crush them: *cedunt acies, et terror utrimque | quo ruat, ardenti feriat quas corpore turmas.* ('The columns give way, and there is terror on each side about where he might fall and what squadrons he might strike with his burning body.' 10.930–31) His armour strengthens the gigantic image:[51] the most prominent feature (deliberately more prominent than in Euripides *Phoenissae*, where the giant is only on the shield) is a giant on his helmet (175–6);[52] his spear is an entire tree (176–7), reminiscent of the trees torn up by Enceladus in *Odes* 3.4.55; even the bronze covering of

---

[48] Ripoll (1998) 344: 'Capanée représente dans l'épopée le héros titanesque par excellence.' Capeneus is also gigantic in tragedy: Aeschylus *Septem* 444; Sophocles *Antigone* 127; Euripides *Phoenissae* 1172. Cf. Klinnert (1970) 11–78; Vessey (1973) 123; Caiani (1990); Frings (1991) 10–16. On images of Gigantomachy in the *Thebaid* see: Taisne (1994) 121–4.

[49] On the catalogue as an instance of *aemulatio*, see Kytzler (1969) 219–30; cf. Vessey (1973) 196–205; Legras (1905) 51–5.

[50] Snijder (1968) 238; cf. Vessey (1973) 157, who reads barbarism, strength and impiety from these comparisons.

[51] Cf. Harrison (1992).

[52] *Phoenissae* 1130–31. Hill (1983) 85; cf. Vessey (1973) 200.

his shield is described in the language of gigantic battle: it is a mass thrown on (*iniectu molis aenae*, 167).

The idea of poetic challenge to the gods is introduced by the story of Thamyris, whom Capaneus' people lament (4.181–6):[53]

> quos Helos et Pteleon. Getico quos flebile uati
> Dorion; hic fretus doctas anteire canendo
> Aonidas mutos Thamyris damnatus in annos
> ore simul citharaque (quis obuia numina temnat?)
> conticuit praeceps, qui non certamina Phoebi
> nosset et inlustres Satyro pendente Celaenas.

> Those whom Helos and Pteleon nourish. and Dorion which weeps for the
>   Getic bard;
> this Thamyris confident that he could surpass the learned Muses
> in singing was condemned to silent years
> and suddenly he fell silent both with mouth and lyre
> (who can scorn divine powers face to face?). who did not know about
> the struggles of Phoebus and the Celaenae made famous by the hanging satyr.

Thamyris challenged the Muses at singing and, as a punishment for his challenge, was silenced. This is a poetic challenge to the gods, compared by Statius to the story of Marsyas. Thamyris is silenced, not flayed: yet the phrase *conticuit praeceps* ('he fell silent head-long') suggests that he falls silent like someone falling from a great height, like a giant thrown down from Olympus to the Underworld. The question *quis obuia numina temnat?* ('who can scorn divine powers face to face?') reminds us of Capaneus' attitude to the gods, foreshadows his death and looks back to Hippomedon in the discus (*quid numina contra | tendere fas homini?* 'By what right do men compete against divine powers?' 6.692–3). It also suggests political doublespeak. Lucan was silenced because he dared to compete with Nero, because his poetry dared to compete with imperial versions of the civil war.[54] This passage opens the way to a reading of Capaneus as a poet challenging the authority of those who control meaning, challenging the authority of the poetic tradition (represented by the Muses) in such a way as to have a political effect. When Capaneus puts himself in opposition to Amphiaraus in their

---

53 Vessey (1973) 200 ignores the poetic element of Thamyris' challenge.
54 *Tacebis* ('you will be silent', 104) is the emphatic final word of Calliope's lament for Lucan in *Siluae* 2.7.

argument in book 3, he calls himself *augur* (3.668) and takes over
the role of the prophet.[55] Capaneus and Thamyris are linked by
more than proximity: Capaneus is a bizarre and unexpected poet
figure.

Capaneus as giant

Capaneus is the archetypal figure of the giant in the *Thebaid*. When
Capaneus first enters the text, the stirring up of war is compared to
Enceladus stirring the mountains in an earthquake as he turns over
(3.593–7):[56]

> it clamor ad auras,
> quantus Tyrrheni gemitus salis, aut ubi temptat
> Enceladus mutare latus: super igneus antris
> mons tonat, exundant apices fluctusque Pelorus
> contrahit, et sperat tellus abrupta reuerti.

The shouting goes up to the breezes,
as great as the groans of the Tyrrhenian sea, or when
Enceladus tries to change sides: the fiery mountain
thunders above him in its caves, the peaks overflow and Pelorus
draws in its waves and the sundered land hopes to return.

Immediately after this image, Capaneus bursts into the poem. From
the start, he is associated with the giant who represents both landscape and earthquake, the natural order and its upheaval. The most
explicit gigantic reference to Capaneus compares his assault on
the walls of Thebes to the Aloidae piling Pelion on Ossa (10.848–
52):[57]

> dicit, et alterno captiua in moenia gressu
> surgit ouans: quales mediis in nubibus aether
> uidit Aloidas, cum cresceret impia tellus
> despectura deos nec adhuc inmane ueniret
> Pelion et trepidum iam tangeret Ossa Tonantem.

He speaks and rises exulting with alternate step
onto the captive walls: just as the aether saw the Aloidae
in the middle of the clouds, when impious earth was growing

---

[55] On this confrontation see Snijder (1968) 235–9; Klinnert (1970) 11–21; Vessey (1973)
157–9 (reading Capaneus as philosopher rather than poet); Frings (1991) 10–16.
[56] Vessey (1973) 157.   [57] Williams (1972) 128.

and about to look down on the gods and immense Pelion was still to come
and Ossa was already touching the frightened Thunderer.

Here, the story of the Aloidae is frozen at the moment of their greatest success, as if about to conquer: Jupiter is frightened (though
calling him Thunderer reminds us what he is about to do), and the
lines of visual power are in the process of being reversed.[58] The
aether is still gazing at Capaneus, but the earth is about to look
down on the gods (as Capaneus looked down on the war in book 4)
and mountains are about to touch even Jupiter. Heaven and earth
are reversed, and the order of the cosmos disrupted.

Capaneus is compared to the giants yet again after his assault on
Thebes and fall at the thunderbolt of Jupiter at 11.7–8: *gratantur
superi, Phlegrae ceu fessus anhelet | proelia et Encelado fumantem
impresserit Aetnen.* ('The gods rejoice with him, just as if he was
panting, tired after the battles of Phlegra, and had pressed down
smoking Aetna on Enceladus.') Most vivid, however, is the final
image of the body of Capaneus as the body of Tityos, raping the
landscape with its very presence (11.12–17):[59]

quantus Apollineae temerator matris Auerno
tenditur; ipsae horrent, si quando pectore ab alto
emergunt uolucres immensaque membra iacentis
spectant, dum miserae crescunt in pabula fibrae:
sic grauat iniectus terras hostiliaque urit
arua et anhelantem caelesti sulphure campum.

He is stretched out and his body is as great as the assaulter of Apollo's mother
in Avernus; the birds themselves are horrified, if ever they emerge from his deep
chest and watch the immense limbs of Tityos as he lies there,
while the wretched entrails grow to feed them:
thus, thrown on, he weighs down the lands and burns the hostile
fields and the panting plain with heavenly sulphur.

Statius reverses the normal structure of horror and gaze here: we
do not look down on the horror of Tityos' entrails eaten by birds,
instead we look from the point of view of the birds at the horror of

---

[58] Goff (1988) 50 notes a similar moment of poise in the gigantomachic imagery on the
tent in Euripides' *Ion*.
[59] Cf. Vessey (1973) 123 comparing Euripides' *Phoenissae* 1185–6: Capaneus as Ixion.

the body which defies nature in its size. The battle is now between Capaneus' body as landscape and the landscape itself as he burns it and leaves the plain panting, as Jupiter was panting on his return from Phlegra. Capaneus is linked back to Enceladus, reversing the structure of that, too: rather than Aetna thrown on the giant, the giant is thrown on the landscape. *Iniectus* also looks backs to his armour in the catalogue. The chain of imagery throughout the representation of Capaneus makes his assault on Thebes a cosmic disturbance, yet assimilates hero and giant to the landscape he is assaulting, so that it becomes once more a civil war of imagery. To attempt to escape the bounds of epic heroism, to drive heroic epic into gigantomachy, rends the ground of the epic itself, threatens the landscape of the poem, becoming too large and too heavy for the world of the poem to contain it.

Assimilating Capaneus and Jupiter

These images present Capaneus fairly straightforwardly as a giant attacking the gods, but other images seem to confuse and conflate Capaneus and Jupiter, giants and gods, using the civil war of myth to problematise any simple identification of gigantomachy with the victory of order over chaos. First, there is the episode of the sacred snake in book 5. While Hypsipyle has been helping the Argives find water and telling them her story, the baby Opheltes, whom she was looking after, has been accidentally killed by a large snake sacred to Jupiter. Who but Capaneus should immediately take revenge? As he fights the snake, he presents himself first as carrying out a deliberate act of sacrilege and then as a giant-killer, assimilating himself to Jupiter (5.565–70):

> 'at non mea uulnera,' clamat
> et trabe fraxinea Capaneus subit obuius, 'umquam
> effugies, seu tu pauidi ferus incola luci,
> siue deis, utinamque deis, concessa uoluptas,
> non si consertum super haec mihi membra Giganta
> subueheres.'

> 'But you will never flee my wounds,' shouts Capaneus
> and goes after it with the trunk of an ash tree, 'whether

you are the wild inhabitant of a panicked grove,
whether you are a pleasure granted to the gods (I wish to the gods!),
not even if you bring a giant to fight against me, joined
above these limbs.'

The killing of the snake is an act of sacrilege against Jupiter; the idea of the snake as potentially a giant's leg is a self-conscious sideswipe at the complexity of the poetic and artistic tradition of portraying giants, which also puts Capaneus into the position of Jupiter. Jupiter is almost tempted to turn him back into a giant by thunderbolting him forthwith: but, like the Jupiter of Ovid *Amores* 2.1, he only picks up his thunderbolt, failing to actually hurl it.[60] He saves Capaneus for a 'more serious' (*grauiora*, 585) thunderbolt.[61] It is as if Statius here is enacting a *recusatio* of epic within his epic, as we have already seen in the discus. When Capaneus does mount the walls, Statius asks for an inspiration that is more than epic in order to write about him (*maior amentia*, 'greater madness,' 10.830).[62]

In the games, too, Capaneus is both gigantic and Jovian.[63] At 6.753–55 he is Tityos, but a Tityos miraculously standing (6.753–5):[64]

hic, quantum Stygiis Tityos consurgat ab aruis,
si toruae patiantur aues, tanta undique pandit
membrorum spatia et tantis ferus ossibus extat.

This one, as big as Tityos would be when he rose from the Stygian fields,
if the fierce birds allowed it, so big everywhere [Capaneus] opens out
the spaces of his limbs and he stands out wild with his great bones.

Capaneus is both giant and landscape again, looking back to books 3 and 4, with his spacious limbs and his gigantic body, and looking forward to the image of his body as Tityos in the Underworld. In this case, he is a Tityos improbably allowed to stand up, escaping

---

[60] Cf. Vessey (1973) 188.

[61] Though it is Menoeceus whom Creon accuses of planning things more weighty than war in book 10: *quae bello grauiora paras?* (10.691). This may also play with an echo of Jupiter in the Semele episode of Ovid's *Metamorphoses*, when Jupiter tries to spare Semele by using only his lighter (*leuius*) thunderbolt (3.305). This is in direct contrast to the thunderbolt with which he destroyed Typhoeus (3.303).

[62] See Lovatt (2001). Cf. Vessey (1973) 222.

[63] Ripoll (1998) 344 presents him as regressing to *feritas* in the boxing.

[64] Cf. Vessey (1973) 223.

briefly from his punishment; *consurgat* looks forward to Capaneus climbing the walls (*surgit ouans*, 'he rises exulting' 10.849) just before the simile of the Aloidae. But just before this image, his fists have been described as *fulmineas... manus* (6.750).[65] He is both giant and thunderbolt in the games.

In book 10, Capaneus again makes a claim to play Jupiter when he tries to claim the lightning for himself as the storm begins: *'his' ait 'in Thebas, his iam decet ignibus uti, | hinc renouare faces lassamque accendere quercum.'* ('These' he said 'are the fires it is right to use against Thebes, these, to renew this torch and light up this tired oak.' 10.925–6) When the moment of the more serious thunderbolt comes, Jupiter himself recalls the gigantomachy: *'quaenam spes hominum tumidae post proelia Phlegrae?'* ('What hope is there for men after the battles of swollen Phlegra?' 10.909) This clearly aligns Capaneus with the giants. However, in the passage that follows, Statius applies the image of gigantomachy in an ambiguous way: it comes directly after a description of Jupiter stirring up the heavens and seems to refer to that (10.913–17):

ipsa dato nondum caelestis regia signo
sponte tonat, coeunt ipsae sine flamine nubes
accurruntque imbres: Stygias rupisse catenas
Iapetum aut uictam supera ad conuexa leuari
Inarimen Aetnamue putes.

The heavenly palace itself thunders of its own accord, even though the sign
has not yet been given, and the clouds themselves come together without wind
and the rainstorms run together: you would think that either Iapetus
had broken his Stygian chains or that conquered Inarime or Aetna
had been lifted to the steep heavens.

The second-person address formulation ('you would think') of this image leaves its import deliberately vague, and it works in two ways. On the wider level of context, this refers in general to the fear of the gods and the need for Jupiter's response: the gods are so afraid, you would think it was gigantomachy all over again. But on a more immediate level, the parallel is between the disturbance in the heavens and the disturbance in the earth caused by the earthquake of the escaping Titans and the dislocation of mountains by giants.

---

[65] Cf. Vessey (1973) 222 'a foreshadowing'.

Jupiter's storms have the same effect on the cosmos as the efforts of his enemies. The fact that this storm has arisen spontaneously, without Jupiter's conscious assent, is reminiscent of *Aeneid* 1 and the storm, which Hardie has shown to be full of the imagery of gigantomachy. The image of gigantomachy disturbing the order of the cosmos is transferred from Capaneus onto Jupiter himself, and this makes sense of one of the wider problems in the Capaneus episode. How can one man climbing a city wall constitute a threat to the heavens and the entire organisation of the universe? Answer: if he evokes a response which in its extremity is gigantic and destructive.

Capaneus as poet figure

We have already see Capaneus acting as a poet figure, and there are moments in the text when he seems to be attacking poetry itself. When Capaneus is climbing up on the walls, he scorns them as the product of mere poetry (10.873–7):

> 'humilesne Amphionis arces,
> pro pudor, hi faciles, carmenque imbelle secuti,
> hi, mentita diu Thebarum fabula, muri?
> et quidnam egregium prosternere moenia molli
> structa lyra?'

'Are these low citadels the walls of Amphion,
for shame, these easy walls, which followed unwarlike song,
these walls, long the subject of the lying myths of Thebes?
What is outstanding about laying low fortifications built
by a soft lyre?

Here, Capaneus' paradoxical relationship with epic poetry is revealed: he both scorns poetry as unwarlike and assumes that any walls built by poetry must be easily conquered, and yet in the same breath accuses the legends of lying because the walls do not live up to their legendary status.[66] His attempt on the gods is also an attempt to rise above and beyond the confines of epic heroism. Mortal battles are tedious to him, as they are to Jupiter.[67] By taking

---

[66] See Lovatt (2001). On the textual problems, see Williams (1972) 129–30.
[67] *iam sordent terrena uiro taedetque profundae | caedis* ('now earthly things grow shabby to the hero and he grows bored of the endless slaughter', 10.837); cf. *taedet saeuire*

on the role of the giants attacking heaven, he is rising above heroic epic in generic terms: as we have seen, gigantomachy was the height of epic subjects. When Statius describes his death at the beginning of book 11, he has achieved poetic fame as both hero and giant.[68] Though his *uirtus* was unequal to the task he has set himself (*iniquae*, 11.1), he is described as *magnanimus* ('great-hearted'), the epithet of great heroes in the *Thebaid*.[69] His flaming fall to earth 'marks the walls' of Thebes (*signauit muros*, 11.4): his death brings him back down to the level of purely heroic achievement, to be memorialised in poetry, but not to escape its confines.[70] Yet his attempt to go beyond the hero's lot has scarred the landscape and the walls of Thebes. As he lies dead, he still clutches a fragment of tower (*complexus fragmina turris | toruus adhuc uisu*, 'embracing a broken piece of tower still fierce of face', 11.9–10): he has not given up his destructive impact on the landscape. His poetic fame is ensured: *memorandaque facta relinquens | gentibus atque ipsi non inlaudata Tonanti* ('leaving behind deeds which deserve to be remembered by the races of men and not unpraised by the Thunderer himself', 11.10–11). Yet it is Jupiter who takes on the role of the poet as he sets the world to rights after his own storm (*componit dextra uictor concussa plagarum | Iuppiter*, 'Jupiter the victor composes the convulsed heavens with his right hand', 11.5–6).

Capaneus is both a poet figure and a challenger of the power of poetry, just as Jupiter both cuts the poet down to size and takes on the role of poet constructing the universe. We have seen how Capaneus and Jupiter are assimilated. Politically, this makes the distinction between legitimised and illegitimate authority extremely difficult to maintain. Is Capaneus a freedom fighter or a terrorist? Is

---

corusco | fulmine ('[Jupiter] grows bored of raging with the glittering thunderbolt', 1.216–17).

[68] On this passage, see Venini (1970a) 3–9.

[69] Used eighteen times in the *Thebaid*, to designate particular heroism: Vessey (1970) 435 n. 1. Cf. Caiani (1990) 269 n. 16, where she points out that it is used of Mezentius in the *Aeneid*.

[70] Whether Capaneus succeeds in achieving heroic immortality is disputed. Klinnert (1970) 133 claims Capaneus as a hero of humanism and independence from the gods; Dominik (1994a) 33 describes him as 'a victim rather than a hero'; Ripoll (1998) 347 tentatively suggests a measure of success: 'c'est en quelque sorte le poète lui-même qui rend un hommage relatif à la *uirtus* archaïque de héros homériques fourvoyés dans l'univers du *bellum impium*.'

Jupiter a monstrous tyrant or an efficient ruler? In terms of poetics, the poet collaborates with the tyrant in defining the ordered political universe but simultaneously challenges and attacks the operations of power. Poetic succession is central to claims of poetic authority. By representing himself as the rightful heir to Homer, Virgil successfully established his poetic (and political) authority. Statius is not simply representing himself as the Domitianic Virgil: he is suggesting that succession (and success) does not legitimise power. By taking the side of the giants and showing how giants and gods are often interchangeable, he undermines epic poetry's power in constructing the universe. The poetics of gigantomachy lay bare the civil war at the heart of epic poetics: the epic poet is both giant and Jupiter, Capaneus and Domitian.

Conclusion: Capaneus, Hippomedon and gigantomachy

Let us return to the imagery of rocks and water. Alcidamas and Capaneus in the boxing of *Thebaid* 6 are compared to a mass of water fighting against a rock (6.777–9):

> ut praeceps cumulo salit unda minantes
> in scopulos et fracta redit: sic ille furentem
> circuit expugnans;

> As a wave jumps headlong in a heap against the threatening
> cliffs and returns broken: so he circles around his raging
> enemy, storming him.

Alcidamas is the water and Capaneus is the rock. We have seen above how Hippomedon is compared to a rock (9.91–4), looking back to Capaneus in the games and forward to his eventual failure to stand up to a literal river.[71] Whereas ships are at the mercy of the sea, and can conceivably fall foul of the rock itself, this version of the image presents a rock that successfully stands up to natural forces, remaining whole, unmoved and stiff, a representation of successful (if passive) heroism. Most importantly, the rock fears nothing from heaven, on the face of it a reference to storm and rain, but also a reminder that Hippomedon should fear the gods, that

[71] Taisne (1994) 147.

his destruction will come from heaven. Ultimately, both Capaneus and Hippomedon will fight against the landscape and the gods and attempt to impose their own version of reality. But reality will overcome them. Their heroic excesses will lead to self-destruction rather than escape from the limitations of the human, mortal body.

Throughout the first half of book 9, the civil war of gigantomachic imagery is waged over and upon the helpless body of Hippomedon. Ultimately, neither the mortal hero nor his immortal opponent is free from the tainting image of the giant: both parties in the fight are threatening the order of the cosmos with their fighting. The story of Capaneus illustrates how gigantomachic imagery can be used to construct powerful polarities and also to undermine those polarities. In the case of Hippomedon, we see the characters in the text actually doing this. Statius highlights the complexity and ambivalence of the gigantomachic tradition and underlines how it is used in a tendentious way to construct simplistic polarities. At the same time, especially in the figure of Capaneus, we can read Statius' own poetic ambitions as a (traditional) form of gigantomachy, attacking the order of the poetic cosmos.

4

THE BOXING

Introduction

The epic boxing match is characterised by a structure of sudden narrative reversals. Boxing is about literally knocking your opponent over. This study of the tradition of epic boxing matches from Homer to Statius will show that reversal is the key to both the structure of the individual match and the structure of intertextual negotiation. In a recent *tour de force*, Damien Nelis has used Virgil's boxing match as a showcase of the way Virgil reads Homer through Apollonius.[1] I shall respond by arguing that Statius is equally subtle and even more complex in his reworking of his predecessors. If the chariot race shows a self-conscious manipulation of the mode of repetition, the boxing reflects on reversal as an intertextual trope as well as a narrative device. This chapter takes these moves beyond metapoetics, however, by looking at issues of national identity in Statius' boxing match, also at stake in the Virgilian match. Nationality and civilisation are at the forefront of epic portrayals of boxers, and reversals of the narrative structures of boxing matches can be mapped onto reversals in the presentation of Greek and Roman culture, civilisation and barbarism.

Statius' boxing match comes at the end of a long sequence. The fight between Irus and Odysseus in *Odyssey* 18 and that of Amycus and Polydeukes in book 2 of Apollonius' *Argonautica* both reverse the match between Epeius and Euryalus in the *Iliad*. Similarly, both Valerius Flaccus (*Argonautica* 4.199–343) and Statius are rivals in their reworking of Virgil.[2] In all of these matches, a champion issues a challenge in supreme confidence, and expectations are aroused.

[1] Nelis (2001) 8–21.
[2] On Statius' boxing, see Von Stosch (1968) 65–74, 194–214; Kytzler (1968) 7.

The *Iliad*

In the Iliadic boxing match, this champion, Epeius, declares that his skill in boxing is not matched by his skill in war (*Iliad* 23.669–71). He is no warrior or hero, and his skills as an athlete are not the skills of war. Yet despite being a sport bound by rules, boxing remains violent and in many ways barbaric. As if to counteract his earlier admission, Epeius concludes his challenge with a gruesome description of the physical damage he will do to his opponent: ἀντικρὺ χρόα τε ῥήξω σύν τ᾽ ὀστέ᾽ ἀράξω ('I will break his flesh and shatter his bones', *Iliad* 23.673). Boxing may be different from war but for Epeius it is just as serious and as dangerous.[3] Thus, Epeius sets up an expectation of how dangerous and deadly his boxing match will be, and this expectation is fulfilled when he knocks down Euryalus, who is indeed carried off by his friends: αἷμα παχὺ πτύοντα, κάρη βάλλονθ᾽ ἑτέρωσε· ('spitting thick blood, with his head lolling.' *Iliad* 23.697) Boxing is marked as closer to war and more dangerous than most other events; however, it is still distinct from war. Epeius can be good at boxing but no hero on the battlefield, and there is never any question of him attempting to kill Euryalus: Epeius' barbarism stops at the end of the match. He even helps Euryalus up in an amicable fashion.[4]

The *Odyssey*

The boxing match between Odysseus and Irus in *Odyssey* 18 is clearly in dialogue with the Iliadic match and enacts a reversal of the outcome, representing in microcosm the way that the *Odyssey* plays with the *Iliad*. For Irus is like Epeius in many respects, champion on his own ground, defending his territory against the threatened incursion of another beggar. While Irus is big but not strong (18.3–4), Epeius is good at boxing but not at war. Odysseus in comparison seems old and effete; he tries to use words to defuse the

---

[3] Poliakoff (1987) 68, 85–8 points out that boxing was a highly dangerous sport in the reality of games in the ancient world. Thuillier (1996a) 114 on the popularity of Roman boxing (Terence, *Hecyra* 33–6; Horace *Epistles* 2.1.183–6).

[4] αὐτὰρ μεγάθυμος Ἐπειὸς | χερσὶ λαβὼν ὤρθωσε ('but great-hearted Epeius took him and pulled him up with his hands', *Iliad* 23.694–5)

situation, and when pressed into fighting negotiates to safeguard himself against audience retaliation (51–65). When he reveals his true physique, it terrifies Irus. At this point, the suitors have become aware of the spectacle, a source of pleasure for them (τερπωλὴν, 37), and force the reluctant Irus to fight. The reader then takes Odysseus' point of view as he wonders how badly to hurt Irus and decides to conceal his true strength from the suitors (90–94) so that the outcome is never at issue for us. The challenger was always going to reverse the straightforward win of the defending champion in *Iliad* 23, and he does so, with the details ironically recalling the Iliadic fight (97–9). In opposition to the *Iliad*, where Epeius helps Euryalus up and his friends in the audience carry him out, the suitors, unaware of the way the fight foreshadows their own fate, fall about laughing, and it is left to Odysseus himself to drag out Irus by the feet.

Apollonius

On the first level of fight structure, the boxing match between Amycus and Polydeukes in book 2 of the *Argonautica* also reverses the Iliadic prototype.[5] Amycus is the as yet undefeated champion; Polydeukes takes him on; the fight itself is longer, and when Amycus goes for the big punch and misses, Polydeukes deals him a fatal blow. Thus, as Nelis points out, both the *Odyssey* and the *Argonautica* turn the tables on their champions and reverse the outcome of the Iliadic match.[6] What is more, Apollonius is also playing with the *Odyssey*. Polydeukes is a young man (Apollonius, *Argonautica* 2.43–4):

> τοῖος ἔην Διὸς υἱός, ἔτι χνοάοντας ἰούλους
> ἀντέλλων, ἔτι φαιδρὸς ἐν ὄμμασιν.

> Such was the son of Zeus, the bloom of his first down
> still growing, his eyes still bright.

---

[5] Though not strictly a game, the influence of this boxing match on Virgil and his successors, and its close relationship with the Homeric boxing match argue strongly for its inclusion in the pattern of reversals (see Knight (1995) 62–72). See pages 279–80 for the pattern of fragmented games in Apollonius.

[6] Nelis (2001) 12.

This is a contrast to Odysseus' apparent age and squalor. However, Polydeukes is also the son of Zeus, and almost a god himself. Amycus, too, is more than a simple champion; he is a monster, deliberately barbaric in his rejection of the code of hospitality, the Cyclops of the *Argonautica* (*Argonautica* 2.38–40):

ἀλλ' ὁ μὲν ἢ ὀλοοῖο Τυφωέος, ἠὲ καὶ αὐτῆς
Γαίης εἶναι ἔικτο πέλωρ τέκος, οἷα πάροιθεν
χωομένη Διὶ τίκτεν·

The one was like the son of terrifying Typhoeus, or even a monster, one of
the children Gaia herself once bore when she was
angry with Zeus.

To quote Nelis: '[t]his is a victory for skill over sheer power, youth over maturity, good over evil, Greek over barbarian.'[7] This complication of the roles which the combatants are playing in the fight creates contrasting expectations: on the Homeric model, we would be expecting the champion to triumph, but on the gigantomachic model, the divine must inevitably crush the monstrous.

On the second level, that of the expectations of violence in the fight, Apollonius provides us with an extreme against which to measure his successors. The fight in the *Odyssey* is not part of an athletic contest, but becomes a parody of the Iliadic games, with Antinous taking on the role of Achilles and offering goats' bellies as prizes (*Odyssey* 18.43–9). When Odysseus reflects about how much to hurt Irus, the narrative toys with the idea of turning this into a fatal encounter. These fights are only partly games; Amycus' habitual use of boxing to kill strangers is a violation of the nature of athletic games as well as the rules of hospitality.[8] Amycus' own perversion of the rules and the polarised nature of conflicts between the divine and the monstrous both make it necessary that the outcome should be final, extreme and fatal. Polydeukes' defeat of Amycus leads to full-scale war with the Bebrycians. This is a demonstration of boxing as war. It is ironic, however, that it is Polydeukes, the crusader for civilization, who should make a kill,

---

[7] Nelis (2001) 18.

[8] Zissos (2003) reads Valerius Flaccus' version as a gladiatorial fight; boxing, however, was a sport quite distinct from gladiatorial fights, not always embedded in the Greek athletic contest, but also presented in the circus games, for instance, and admired by Augustus in the form of street fighting (Suetonius, *Augustus* 45.2).

not his barbarian opponent. This passage complicates the issue of violence in games, and opens a space for further exploration of games and their relation to war in its imitators.

Virgil

The boxing in the games in *Aeneid* 5 begins much in the manner of the Homeric boxing with a champion who seems to be irresistible. However, Dares does not issue a challenge like Epeius, Irus and Amycus, but simply by the act of revealing his shoulders and reputation he almost succeeds in walking off with the prize uncontested (*Aeneid* 5.376–9). This sets him up as a version of Odysseus, whose physique, enhanced by Athena, terrifies Irus; later, however, Entellus will take over this role with a closer reminiscence of the moment of revelation. Virgil draws out the suspense far longer than Homer: Dares actually demands the prize, and the crowd is roaring for it to be given to him, before Acestes persuades Entellus to take up the fight. This is a reversal in itself, for the challenger to be shamed into fighting. It is also a new twist on the Odyssean version, putting Entellus in the position of both Odysseus in book 8, where the young Phaeacians shame him into competing, and Irus in book 18, where the audience force him to compete, bringing out the intratextual links between the two. What is more, Entellus is the outside chance not because he is young, like Polydeukes, or unknown, like Euryalus, but because he is old, as Odysseus appears to be in *Odyssey* 18 and claims to be in *Odyssey* 8, and his experience actually *is* outweighed by his immobility. Virgil reverses the play on the youth and desirability of Polydeukes in Apollonius by making his hero an old man. In another reverse, it is Dares who wants to back out, after he sees the huge *caestus* once used by Entellus' teacher Eryx in a fight with Hercules. As Nelis points out, the way that Virgil plays with his models is so complex that no single straightforward pattern wins out: contestants compete with each other to take on the role of victor in the previous matches. 'There is no complete identification between Virgil's characters and any single model, whether Homeric or Apollonian.'[9]

[9] Nelis (2001) 16.

The issue of nationality and conflict between two cultures is also important in Virgil's boxing match.[10] When he introduces Dares, Virgil describes him in this way (*Aeneid* 5.370–74):

> solus qui Paridem solitus contendere contra,
> idemque ad tumulum quo maximus occubat Hector
> uictorem Buten immani corpore, qui se
> Bebrycia ueniens Amyci de gente ferebat,
> perculit et fulua moribundum extendit harena.

> the man who alone was accustomed to compete against Paris,
> and, at the same tomb where great Hector lies,
> he struck down the victor Butes with his huge body, who
> came and presented himself as from the Bebrycian tribe
> of Amycus, and laid him out dying on the tawny sand.

This spectacular description puts Dares firmly into a Homeric and Apollonian epic context: he sparred with Paris and beat a descendant of Amycus to death. Dares is certainly from the world of Greek epic: the Trojans within the *Aeneid* can be seen to represent the Greek epic world from which the Roman nation is to escape, and from which it is also to be forged, just as Virgil's *Aeneid* is both based upon and intent on surpassing both the *Iliad* and the *Argonautica*. To take this further, Euryalus in the *Iliad* had defeated all the Cadmeans in the games for Oedipus (*Iliad* 23.679–80); Virgil then substitutes a Bebrycian for the Cadmeans.[11] Following the metapoetic narrative, he is putting himself in relation to Apollonius, as Homer stands in relation to the *Thebaid*. Virgil's Italian victor will defeat the Trojan who had already defeated Apollonius' Bebrycian, just as Homer's Epeius will defeat Euryalus, victor in the Theban games.

Dares is also part of the violence of Apollonius' boxing match, although *moribundum* ('dying') holds back from the finality of death itself. Entellus, on the other hand, is a Sicilian, taught by the Sicilian god Eryx. He represents one version of the Italian side of Romanness, embodying the paradoxical nature of the Italians in

---

[10] Nelis' only comment on this point: 'In *Aeneid* 5 age wins over youth, strength over skill, the honest if hot-headed Entellus over the boastful Dares, the Sicilian over the Trojan', 18.

[11] As Nelis (2001) 14 points out.

the *Aeneid*.[12] Yet there is at least one version of the myth where Entellus was a Trojan, not an Italian.[13] Nationality and the tensions between Trojan and Italian are key issues for any reading of Virgil's boxing match.

Finally, the time comes in the fight for the big punch, as attempted successfully by Epeius and unsuccessfully by Amycus; in this case, however, it comes not from the champion, but from the challenger; Entellus attempts a blow from above, misses and falls to the ground (5.443–8). Thus far, the challenger follows in the pattern of Apollonius' champion. Yet rather than have him killed as he falls, Virgil reverses the outcome: for his friend helps him up (following the pattern of the defeated challenger in Homer) but he is fired with rage by his fall (5.453–4) and piles blow upon blow on Dares, so dangerously that Aeneas stops the fight and declares him winner.

At this point, it would seem that Virgil has re-reversed Apollonius' upheaval of the expectations of violence and game boundaries instituted by the *Iliadic* boxing match. A strong authority figure has intervened in the escalation of violence beyond the bounds of games and stopped the fight before it became war.[14] Yet, as one might expect, it is not that simple. Entellus' rage is not appeased merely by being declared winner of the fight. His prize is an ox,

---

[12] There are (at least) two models of the ideal primitive at play in Virgil's presentation of the Italians in the *Aeneid*: first, a pastoral golden age type of primitivism by which the Trojans can be figured as corrupting the innocent Italians and dragging them forward from the age of Saturn to the age of Jupiter (see Thomas (1982) 93–107); secondly, the *duritia* traditionally displayed by the barbarian enemies of Rome and part of the Roman self-presentation of their own decline (see Horsfall (1990) 306–7). These two models play against each other in the ambivalent situation where the Italians must be both the enemy and the ancestors. What is more, Virgil destabilises categorisations of 'Italian', and manipulates the image of the war as a replay of the Trojan war to further undermine the opposition between the two sides. It is a problem, in the analysis of Toll (1997) of Virgil's project as 'Making Roman-ness', that Romanness in the *Aeneid* is so complex and unstable. However, self-presentation is always made from a bricolage of the other and will inevitably contain fractures, contradictions and inconsistencies. On Italians in the *Aeneid*, see also: Moorton (1989); Saunders (1927); Warde-Fowler (1918).

[13] Feldherr (2002) 6. *sane sciendum, hunc secundum Hyginum, qui de familiis Troianis scripsit, unum Troianorum fuisse, de quo Vergilius mutat historiam.* ('of course it ought to be known, and this is according to Hyginus, who wrote about Trojan families, that he was one of the Trojans, about whom Vergil changes the story', Servius *ad. Aen.* 5.389); see also Williams (1960) 121.

[14] Nelis (2001) stops here in his reading of the fight, as his description of Entellus as 'honest if hot-headed' (18) shows.

and in a terrifying gesture he sacrifices it in substitution for the life of Dares to his god-teacher Eryx, killing the ox with one blow. In his article on the boxing, Andrew Feldherr sees the concept of sacrifice as the key to understanding the fight, and suggests that this moment provides a tool for reading the entire epic.[15] He sees the sacrifice as a pious and redemptive act, and draws a parallel between Entellus and Aeneas at the end of the poem. It is clearly true that the substitution of the ox for Dares makes the act of brutality less barbarous, but surely there is no substitution in book 12? What is more, Entellus' act of sacrifice cannot be read as simply pious. For it looks back to Amycus as he prepares for the big blow which is to fail and cause his death, where he is compared to a man about to sacrifice an ox (*Argonautica* 2.90–92):

> ἔνθα δ᾽ ἔπειτ᾽ Ἄμυκος μὲν ἐπ᾽ ἀκροτάτοισιν ἀερθείς
> βουτύπος οἷα, πόδεσσι τανύσσατο, κὰδ δὲ βαρεῖαν
> χεῖρ᾽ ἐπὶ οἷ πελέμιξεν·
>
> Then Amycus stretched himself up on the tips of his toes
> like a man slaughtering an ox, and smashed his heavy
> hand down on him.

Thus, the challenger Entellus is assimilated to the violent and monstrous champion Amycus, reminding us of the more negative side of the primitive.[16] By smashing the skull of the ox, Entellus is declaring a desire to have killed his opponent; his anger has transformed him from a sympathetic to a terrifying figure, from a successful Euryalus to a successful Amycus. Entellus, like Cacus and Turnus, represents Italian resistance to the values of the Greek epic world. Far from creating a unified national identity in the *Aeneid*, Virgil presents a variety of dissenting voices. He uses the complexity of his negotiations with his models to represent the moral

---

[15] Feldherr (2002). Cf. Hardie (1993) 51–2 on sacrifice and games in the *Aeneid*.

[16] Furthermore, Entellus' teacher, Eryx, died in a fight with Hercules (*Aeneid* 5.411). Since Hercules in the *Aeneid* appears frequently in the role of bringer of civilisation as well as being one model for both Aeneas and Augustus, this places Eryx in the same category as Cacus, a native Italian barbarian rebelling against the influx of Greek and 'civilising' forces. However, the assimilation of Hercules and Cacus in book 8 problematises any simple dichotomy between civilisation and barbarism; see Morgan (1998). Galinsky (1990) 293–4 reads Herakles as the symbol of Greek national identity.

complexity of his epic, and the violent inversion of them to show his own victory as an epic poet over his predecessors.

Valerius Flaccus

When Valerius restages the boxing match between Amycus and Pollux, he plays with Virgil as much as Apollonius.[17] The basics of the plot stay the same but by adding to it he changes the dynamic of the whole fight. For instance, the beginning of the episode looks back through the *Aeneid* to the Cyclops episode of the *Odyssey* by introducing a figure called Dymas, who warns the Argonauts about Amycus just as Achaemenides in *Aeneid* 3 warns Aeneas and his men about the Cyclops.[18] Valerius plays with the fear, reluctance and enthusiasm about fighting in his models for the fight, and creates a repeated series of reversals as the Argonauts first hear about Amycus, see his *caestus* and the remains of his former victims, meet him and receive his challenge. When Amycus actually arrives and issues the challenge, Virgil's running comes to the surface (4.222–6):

> talia dicta dabat, cum protinus asper Iason
> et simul Aeacidae simul et Calydonis alumni
> Nelidesque Idasque prior quae maxima surgunt
> nomina; sed nudo steterat iam pectore Pollux.
> tum pauor et gelidus defixit Castora sanguis;

> He spoke such words and straight away harsh Jason,
> the sons of Aeacus, simultaneously with the offspring of Calydon
> and the son of Neleus, and even earlier Idas, whose names are great,
> rose up; but already Pollux had stood up with naked breast.
> Then fear fixed Castor and his blood froze.

Far from a reluctance to compete, the Argonauts are now like eager competitors at the beginning of an athletic event, specifically echoing the beginning of Virgil's running, where Salius and Patron come forward simultaneously (*simul et*, *Aeneid* 5.298); Valerius doubles

---

[17] On Valerius' boxing match, Hershkowitz (1998b) 78–91 lays the groundwork; Zissos (2003) explores its gladiatorial links.
[18] Hershkowitz (1998b) 78–9.

this with *et simul . . . simul et* (4.223). Where Virgil has an unnamed multitude which fame has forgotten, Valerius' competitors have *maxima nomina* – perhaps implying that their prowess might not live up to their reputations. What is more, Virgil's competitors come forward in careful order: *Nisus et Euryalus primi* ('Nisus and Euryalus first', 294) then Diores (*quos deinde secutus . . . Diores*, 'Then Diores followed them', 296–7), then two Trinacrians (*tum duo Trinacrii iuuenes*, 300), last of all the nameless throng (*multi praeterea*, 'many moreover', 302). Valerius reverses this process, with each competitor arriving earlier than the last. Jason gets up straight away (*protinus*); the next two are simultaneous; Idas is even earlier (*prior*), and Pollux had stood up before any of them.

If this process assimilates the fight to Virgil's most straightforwardly athletic event, however, the simile which follows does the opposite. Castor is afraid and watches Pollux as the epic narrator watches Achilles chasing Hector at *Iliad* 22.160–64: this is no game but a deadly serious epic battle (4.227–31):

> nam nec ad Elei pugnam uidet ora parentis
> nec sonat Oebalius caueae fauor aut iuga nota
> Taygeti, lauitur patrios ubi uictor ad amnes,
> nec pretium sonipes aut sacrae taurus harenae,
> praemia sed manes reclusaque ianua leti.

> For he does not watch a fight before the face of his Olympian father
> nor do the cheers of the Spartan fans resound in the theatre or on the
>   well-known
> ridge of Taygetus, where the victor is washed in his ancestral stream,
> nor is the prize of the sacred sand a loud-hoofed horse or a bull,
> but the booty is a ghost and the open door of death.

The arena here is specifically not a gladiatorial arena but an athletic one, and the prize of a bull looks back to Virgil's prize bull in *Aeneid* 5; the simile draws a particularly strong contrast with Spartan athletics and the audience on the stands – even though the Argonauts are an involved and important audience. This simile is focalised through Castor's fear for his brother, like Priam's and Hecuba's fear for Hector, and the imagery follows from Amycus' challenge, where he sarcastically suggests that there is a prize to be won: *prima manu cui dona feram? mox omnibus idem | ibit honos.*

('To whom will I give the first prize with my hand? Soon the same honour will come to all', 4.216–7) The honour and the prize alike are death; he will use his hand to inflict it.[19] This, too, reverses Virgil: while Entellus turns his athletic prize into death and sacrifice at the end, Amycus refers to this displacement with loaded sarcasm at the beginning. Valerius Flaccus has brought out the dark side of sacrifice in his version; for Amycus treats his murders as sacrifices to Neptune: *ea Neptuno trux ipse parenti | sacrifici pro rupe iugi media aequora supra | torquet agens;* ('The fierce man himself takes them and hurls them down from the craggy ridge into the middle of the sea as a sacrifice to his father Neptune', 4.109–11).

The build-up to the fight is still not over, however; Valerius doubles and trebles the moments of confrontation, creating further suspense as we wait for the killer blow. Amycus issues yet another challenge to Pollux (4.240–43) and displays his physique (4.243–6):

> nec plura moratus
> ingentes umeros spatiosaque pectoris ossa
> protulit horrendosque toris informibus artus.
> deficiunt uisu Minyae, miratur et ipse
> Tyndarides;

> Delaying no longer, he proffers his huge shoulders
> and the spacious bones of his chest
> and the terrifying limbs with their deformed muscles.
> The Minyae are unable to cope with the sight, and Pollux himself
> is full of wonder.

Valerius draws attention to the way he has strung out the preparations with the comment *nec plura moratus* ('having delayed no further') and adds to this with a self-conscious reference below to the suspense of the internal audience: *hinc illinc dubiis intenta silentia votis* ('on this side and that silence is stretched out in

---

[19] As the fight goes on, Valerius reminds us that this is boxing as war by comparing the rest break to a break in war: *respirant ambo paulumque reponunt | brachia; ceu Lapithas aut Paeonas aequore in ipso | cum refovet fixaque silet Gradivus in hasta.* ('Both breathe and set aside their fists for a little; just as Mars revives the Lapiths and the Paeonians on the plain itself and is silent leaning on his spear', 4.279–81).

doubtful prayers', 257).[20] In the *Odyssey* and the *Aeneid*, this is the time for the champion to feel worried and want to back out: Valerius has reversed the situation by giving the moment of revelation back to the champion; he now displaces the fear onto the watching Minyae, and Pollux is allowed only neutral admiration, although he is implicitly included in the wish of the Argonauts that Hercules was still there to take his place. In the early stages of the fight, though, Pollux is portrayed as fearful: *uigil metu* ('watchful with fear', 265) and, in the simile of a ship in a storm, the helmsman is panicky as well as skilful (*trepidi quam sola magistri | cura tenet*, 'a ship which only the care of its panicked master holds safe', 269–70). Pollux is skilful in evading the fight: *Pollux sic prouidus ictus | seruat et Oebalia dubium caput eripit arte.* ('So Pollux prudently pulls his punches and snatches away his doubtful head with Spartan skill', 271–2) and this, too, suggests fear as well as skill.

Just as Valerius draws out the build-up in order to create repeated reversals, he equally prolongs the fight itself so that he toys with the ultimate reversal of the knockout again and again without actually ever using it. After Pollux's defensive wariness at the beginning of the fight, he gradually begins to attack (*paulatim*, 274). Then, as in Apollonius, they take a brief break (279–81); in Virgil the only break came after Dares floored Entellus. The next move is a feint with the right by Pollux, followed by a strong left which leaves Amycus 'raging and dazed by the unexpected deceit' (*illum insperata turbatum fraude furentemque*, 293). This passes over Dares' success in toppling Entellus in the *Aeneid*, without making it

---

[20] This moment gives some grounds for wondering about Valerius' reading of the response of the audience in the boxing match of *Aeneid* 5. It gives a sense of there being two sides, one supporting Amycus and one Pollux, and different prayers from each; but in fact, in opposition to Apollonius' version, Amycus' subjects do not support him. While his subjects bring him victims (107–9), his *caestus* are sacred through fear (186) and his own people watch him with fear: *quem nec sua turba tuendo | it taciti secura metus* ('not even his own crowd go about free of silent fear of him as they look', 200–201). At the end of the fight, the Bebrycians flee (315–16) rather than fighting to avenge him. So the comment about audience prayers is deliberately ambiguous: are they doubtful because they do not know what the outcome will be? Or because they do not know who to support? Does the *hinc illinc* emphasise contrast between the two factions or surprising similarity of feeling? And, reading back through this to Virgil, are the Sicilians and the Trojans shouting for the same person or a different one? Is Virgil's implied audience unanimity as problematic as Valerius' implied lack of unanimity?

the decisive moment. Now Amycus attacks in an uncontrolled rage, like Entellus, but Pollux makes this the opportunity for another attempted knockout which also fails (4.299–303):

> hos inter Pollux subit et trucis ultro
> aduolat ora uiri: nec spes effecta, sed ambae
> in pectus cecidere manus. hoc saeuior ille
> ecce iterum uacuas agit inconsulta per auras
> brachia.

Pollux slipped between his fists and flew at the face of the man of his own accord: but his hope was not fulfilled and both his hands fell against his chest. He, made even more savage by this, – look! – again drives his arms without intent through the empty air.

At each stage, Amycus becomes more and more exaggeratedly out of control, and the signal *ecce iterum* self-consciously points out Valerius' repetition of the key moment of Virgil's fight. Finally, Pollux topples him (304–5), rains down punches (305–7) and covers him with blood (308–9). The fatal blow eventually falls on a man already down and mostly out (309–11). Pollux finishes the fight by standing over him and boasting jubilantly (311–14). This change to the structure of the fight also changes the level of violence, both by allowing space for much more vivid and detailed description of the injuries, but also by making the kill deliberate and cold-blooded. Apollonius' Polydeukes is defending himself when he strikes the single blow which kills Amycus. Valerius' Pollux, like Aeneas at the end of the *Aeneid*, waits until his opponent is clearly down and beaten and kills him with chilling coolness. Valerius even lingers over his quasi-medical description of the precise placing of the death-blow: *uitalia donec | uincula, qua primo ceruix committitur artu, | soluit dextra grauis.* ('The heavy right hand undoes that life-giving link, where the neck first joins the shoulder.' 309–11). Perhaps we should imagine Aeneas, too, vaunting over the dead body of Turnus.

In a final twist, however, Valerius gives us victory celebrations which situate Pollux once more as an athletic victor. The Argonauts raise his arms in victory (*fessasque attollere palmas*, 326) and acclaim him (4.327–9):

'salue uera Iouis, uera o Iouis' undique 'proles'
ingeminant, 'o magnanimis memoranda palaestris
Taygeta et primi felix labor ille magistri!'

'Hail, truly of Jove, O true offspring of Jove,' they say again and again
everywhere, 'O Taygetus, worthy of renown for its great-hearted
wrestling schools and that fortunate toil of his first teacher!'

It is his Spartan athletic education that allows him to prove his
divine parentage. Castor tops this off by garlanding him with laurel
(333–4) and last of all, during the celebratory banquet, he is praised
by his fellow Argonauts and by, presumably, Orpheus: *toto mox
tempore mensae | laetus ouat nunc laude uirum nunc uatis honoro |
carmine* ('soon during the whole time of the feast, he rejoices
happily now in the praise of the heroes and now in the honouring
song of the bard', 341–3), like a Pindaric victor at the moment of
receiving his victory ode.

Valerius Flaccus is self-consciously aware of his place in the
tradition of epic boxing matches, and creates a new version of
the fight between Amycus and Pollux that outdoes both Virgil
and Apollonius. He reverses Virgil in many respects, and draws
out the fight into a series of complex repetitions. The tensions
between athletics and war are continually brought to the forefront,
and both Pollux and Amycus are darker and more violent than their
predecessors.

Statius

Statius' version draws energetically on the whole tradition to create
his own reflections and reversals, going back through Valerius to
Apollonius, and through Virgil to Homer. We have the athletic
frame once more, and Capaneus opens with a challenge again;[21]
despite his hugeness, he chooses not to rely on his purely visual
impressiveness (*immanis cerni immanisque timeri*, 'huge to see,
huge to be feared' 6.731) to discourage competition.[22] From the
start, he intends violence; he asks for a Theban opponent so that
the violence will not be civil war (6.735–7):[23]

---

[21] On challenges in the games, see Dominik (1994b) 178–9.
[22] On Capaneus as similar to Epeius: Legras (1905) 88–9; Vessey (1970) 432.
[23] Cf. Vessey (1970) 433 'The irony... is only too apparent.'

> atque utinam potius de stirpe ueniret
> aemulus Aonia, quem fas demittere leto,
> nec mea crudelis ciuili sanguine uirtus.

And I wish that a rival might rather come from
the Theban race, whom it would be right to send down in death,
so that my courage would not be stained by civil blood.

This raises our expectations of the likely level of violence in the fight to come.[24] He has also added another factor to the confusion of boundaries between war and games: if the games are held by one side in a war, then any potential intrusion of war into the games is a potential intrusion of civil war into the war.[25] Games inevitably mean fighting between friends. This comment is particularly ironic in the context of the *Thebaid*, where the status of the war is particularly indeterminate: inspired by brother against brother, it seems truly *plus quam ciuilia* ('more than civil'), yet Creon's refusal to bury Polynices seems to be a last-ditch attempt to force the war into the category of foreign. Is it really any more 'civil' war for Capaneus to kill a Spartan than to kill a Theban?[26]

So far, we seem to be going back to the Iliadic roots: but Alcidamas, Capaneus' opponent, brings us back into the world of the *Argonautica*. He is a young Spartan, trained by Pollux himself, inheriting the skills and the role from his teacher, as Entellus inherited his *caestus* from his teacher Eryx. And Statius here reverses Valerius and Virgil by dispensing with the reluctance altogether (*Thebaid* 6.739–42):

---

[24] Also, it links Capaneus with Lucan's Scaeva, an exemplum of *uirtus* made foul in civil war: *pronus ad omne nefas et qui nesciret in armis | quam magnum uirtus crimen ciuilibus esset* ('he had a leaning towards all crime and who did not know how great a crime courage is in civil war', 6.147–8).

[25] Horace in *Epistles* 1.18 uses the cover of a game, in this case a mock re-enactment of Actium by young Lollius and his brother, to undermine covertly the official rhetorical stance that placed Actium outside the category of civil war: *partitur lintris exercitus, Actia pugna | te duce per pueros hostili more refertur, | aduersarius est frater, lacus Hadria, donec | alterutrum uelox Victoria fronde coronet.* ('the armies are shared out between boats, and the battle of Actium is brought back with you as leader by boys in hostile fashion, and his brother is the enemy, the lake is the Adriatic, until swift Victory crowns one or the other with a garland', Horace *Epistles* 1.18.61–4). See Bowditch (1994).

[26] This leads on to the problem of the status of the Theban war: is it or is it not a civil war? Ahl (1986) 2812–16 asserts that it is. On the Theban war viewed as civil war in Roman literature: Ripoll (1998) 213; Jal (1963) 402–7.

tandem insperatus nuda de plebe Laconum
prosilit Alcidamas, mirantur Dorica regum
agmina; sed socii fretum Polluce magistro
norant et sacras inter creuisse palaestras.

At last and unexpected Alcidamas jumped forward from the naked crowd
of Spartans and the Doric column of the kings
were amazed; but his allies knew that he was confident in his teacher
Pollux and that he grew up among the sacred wrestling grounds.

His jump forwards shows his eagerness; while the Argive army as a
whole is confused, his friends know their Valerius and are confident
that teacher and *palaestra* will stand him in good stead.[27] The
tandem plays with our expectations: in fact, Statius does not delay,
and Alcidamas is not really unexpected. Alcidamas is Spartan, like
Pollux, and there is the same emphasis on his native skill; however,
Valerius' Pollux is not a pederastic icon like Apollonius'. His face is
twice described as starry (*sidereus*, 4.190, 331) but this seems more
to point to the fact that he will become a star, while in Apollonius
he is described as like a star in an image reminiscent of pederastic
epigram, as we have seen in chapter 2 (Apollonius *Argonautica*
2.40–42):

ὁ δ᾽ οὐρανίῳ ἀτάλαντος
ἀστέρι Τυνδαρίδης, οὗπερ κάλλισται ἔασιν
ἑσπερίην διὰ νύκτα φαεινομένου ἀμαρυγαί.

But the other, of the line of Tyndareus, was like that star in the heavens
whose sparkling rays are brightest as it rises
through the darkness of evening.

In Statius, the description of Alcidamas suggests that he has a
pederastic relationship with his teacher (6.743–6):

ipse deus posuitque manus et bracchia finxit –
materiae suadebat amor; – tunc saepe locauit
comminus, et simili stantem miratus in ira
sustulit exultans nudumque ad pectora pressit.

The god himself placed his hands and moulded his arms –
love of his material persuaded him – then often he placed him

---

[27] Statius has taken the two elements from Valerius' acclamation at the end of the fight and
put them at the beginning.

at close quarters, and amazed at him as he stood in matching anger
lifted him up, exulting in him and pressed him naked to his chest.

This sensuous passage emphasises the erotics of pedagogy, reading boxing as lovemaking.[28] Pollux sculpts the physique of his
pupil, and literally makes Alcidamas, creating his body: the athletic trainer as Pygmalion. Like Polydeukes in Apollonius, he is
an icon of the desirable young man, but ironically takes the role of
beloved, putting Pollux instead in the role of lover. It seems counterintuitive that a boxer should be presented as a beautiful young
man, the object of erotic attention: boxers were usually presented
in art as ugly and disfigured (or perhaps ennobled) by injury.[29]
What is more, Capaneus clearly directs an insult at Alcidamas at
the end of the match which implies both a pederastic relationship
with Pollux and strong disapproval of it (6.819–22):

> 'liceat! non has ego puluere crasso
> atque cruore genas, meruit quibus iste fauorem
> semiuir, infodiam mittamque informe sepulcro
> corpus et Oebalio donem lugere magistro?'

> Let me be! Why can't I stain those cheeks with thick dust
> and gore, by which that half-man earned
> that favour, and send his misshapen body
> to the grave and give his Spartan master grief?

Nationality is part of the insult: the implication must be (at least
in part) that to be Spartan is to practise pederasty. Roman attitudes to pederasty were ambivalent. While Williams has convincingly shown that Romans were not hostile to 'homosexuality' as
a whole, his claim that pederasty, or sexual relationships between
freeborn men and boys, was neither seen as something particularly Greek nor particularly discouraged among Roman men is far

---

[28] *Comminus* can be used of 'copulation' as well as fighting: Lewis and Short cite Lucretius
4.1051, which is part of a general 'love as wound' metaphor.

[29] See Poliakoff (1987) on representations of boxers with cauliflower ears. The boxer
Melancomas was represented as very beautiful and was alleged to have had a relationship with the emperor Titus. See Dio Chrysostom *Orations* 28, 29; Themistius *Oration*
10; König (2000). However, he had a special technique of keeping his opponents at
arm's length so that they did not hit him, which made him a somewhat unique boxer.
Pindar does not write many odes for boxers; *Olympian* 7 to Diagoras of Rhodes represents him as someone who deserves respect rather than someone beautiful. The boy
boxer Hagesidamus in *Olympian* 10 is represented as a beautiful boy and compared to
Ganymede.

from convincing.[30] His own evidence for the way Roman thought connected Greek athletics and the gymnasia with pederastic relationships seems sufficient to me to show that pederasty was marked as Greek. Walters makes a strong case for the deep ambivalence felt by Romans towards sexual relationships with freeborn youths who would shortly become men in their own right.[31] Capaneus here takes the extreme view: the relationship between Pollux and Alcidamas has disqualified Alcidamas from any claim to the status of *uir* (high-status mature man), reducing him to a *semiuir*.

This fight has been read as one of skill versus force.[32] In this fight, however, skill and cunning are consistently presented as attributes of Alcidamas' Greekness: *providus astu | et patria uigil arte Lacon* ('the Spartan, foresightful in his cunning and alert in his ancestral skill', 769–70) is a particularly convincing example of this. The imagery and structure of the fight follow the Argonautic tradition and Statius corrects Valerius by going back to Apollonius. Apollonius contrasts Amycus and Polydeukes by juxtaposing two images: the monstrous image of Typhoeus with Polydeukes as star. Valerius takes only the monstrous side, and consciously outdoes Apollonius by making Amycus a version of Typhoeus himself, rather than a son of Typhoeus, and by making him scornful of the opposing gods (*Argonautica* 4.236–8):[33]

non aliter iam regna poli, iam capta Typhoeus
astra ferens Bacchum ante acies primamque deorum
Pallada et oppositos doluit sibi uirginis angues.

Not otherwise did Typhoeus, claiming that the kingdom of heaven and the stars
were already captured, grieve that Bacchus at the head of the column
and Pallas first of the gods and a girl's snakes stood against him.

Valerius' Amycus is more than just a giant; he is a giant for whom gigantomachy is not enough, for whom the ultimate enemy, the gods and the cosmos itself, is a disappointment. Statius, however, goes back to Apollonius: the image of the gigantic and monstrous

---

[30] Williams (1999) 62–95. See also Cantarella (1992) 97–186.
[31] See Walters (1997) or, for a fuller treatment, Walters (1993).
[32] Kytzler (1968) 7; Von Stosch (1968) 65–74, 194–214; Alcidamas is 'ethically' superior (72). Vessey (1970) 433 characterises it as a fight between *furor* and *prudentia*.
[33] Vessey (1970) 434 links the image only to other gigantomachic imagery describing Capaneus. See above, chapter 3.

Tityos is set in close opposition to the description of the boyish Alcidamas (emphasised by *hic...hic*).

We can also see Valerius and Statius engaging with the same image from Apollonius' fight in the different ways they deal with his sea image.[34] Amycus attacks Polydeukes like a wave attacking a ship (Apollonius *Argonautica* 2.70–73):

> ἅτε κῦμα θαλάσσης
> τρηχὺ θοὴν ἐπὶ νῆα κορύσσεται, ἡ δ' ὑπὸ τυτθόν
> ἰδρείῃ πυκινοῖο κυβερνητῆρος ἀλύσκει
> ἱεμένου φορέεσθαι ἔσω τοίχοιο κλύδωνος

> like a jagged wave of the sea which rears up against a swift ship
> and the ship barely survives through the skill of the clever helmsman,
> and the wave surges, breaking over the deck

In Valerius, the simile is written from the point of view of the ship and the helmsman, and the wave becomes a sea maddened by winds (Valerius Flaccus *Argonautica* 4.268–71):

> spumanti qualis in alto
> Pliade capta ratis, trepidi quam sola magistri
> cura tenet, rabidum uentis certantibus aequor
> intemerata secat:

> Just as a ship on the foaming deep, captured by the Pleiads,
> which the care of the panicked helmsman alone holds safe,
> cuts unharmed the sea maddened by struggling winds:

In Statius, only the wave remains, and the ship is replaced by a rock (Statius *Thebaid* 6.777–9):

> ut praeceps cumulo salit unda minantes
> in scopulos et fracta redit, sic ille furentem
> circumit expugnans;

> As a wave jumps headlong in a heap at threatening
> cliffs and returns broken, so he goes around him
> as he rages, storming him.

In Apollonius, the wave represents Amycus almost overwhelming the vulnerable yet skilful Polydeukes with his power, like a force of nature. In Valerius, the focus is on the skill and emotion of Pollux

---

[34] See Hunter (1989). Vessey (1970) 434 also links this to a simile describing Capaneus at 10.864–9 as a river destroying a bridge.

rather than the force of Amycus. Statius reverses the simile by making Alcidamas the wave, taking the battle to the static rock of Capaneus. He adapts the emotion of the simile to the more complex situation of his fight: while the sympathy in both Apollonius and Valerius is clearly with the ship and against Amycus, neither wave nor rock has the upper hand, and both are forces of nature. What is more, Statius is also looking to the rock simile from Apollonius' fight between Jason and the bulls (3.1293–5) which we examine below (p. 277). Here, Jason is a rock standing up to the bulls as a storm; once more, Statius' version has reversed the roles by making the wave rather than the rock the focus of the action. In this way, he goes back to Apollonius and links the boxing match to Jason's quasi-athletic feats in book 3, as well as inverting the way the imagery is used.[35]

The ship image, however, returns at the break, where Valerius has used the image of Mars refreshing fighting armies. Statius instead has rowers breaking off briefly from their task (*Thebaid* 6.799–801):

> sic ubi longa uagos lassarunt aequora nautas
> et signum de puppe datum, posuere parumper
> bracchia: uix requies, iam uox citat altera remos.

> Thus when the long sea has exhausted wandering sailors
> and the signal is given from the poop, they rest their arms
> for a little: but rest is scarce, now another shout calls for oars.

Again the image moves away from war and violent competition; here, the two fighters are imagined as rowers on the same boat, co-operating in their journey. Rather than setting remorseless violent sea against pathetic helpless boat, both fighters are natural forces, and both rowers on the sea.[36] Thus, Statius makes both his boxers sympathetic in their way and, despite suggesting that Capaneus

---

[35] Statius also alludes to another image from Apollonius' match, going one further than Valerius. Capaneus is also a wounded lion or tiger (*non leo, non iaculo tantum indignata recepto | tigris*, 'no lion, no tiger was so outraged at a javelin's wound', 787–8), like Amycus as a lion hemmed in by hunters (*Argonautica* 2.26–9).

[36] Both fighters are tired, too (796–8), whereas in Valerius Amycus is exhausted while Pollux remains fresh (275–9), transferred by Statius instead to the wrestling match (872–5).

has an unfair advantage (*iniustis uiribus*, 774), this is a much more even match.

However, after all this negotiation with Valerius and Apollonius the dénouement is pure Virgil: Capaneus attempts a knockout blow, which Alcidamas evades; as he falls, Alcidamas strikes him and Capaneus rises up in such a towering rage that Adrastus calls an immediate end to the fight.[37] If we read Virgil as I have done above with Entellus as the challenger, then this is a clear reversal.[38] In the *Aeneid*, it is Dares who is asked to give up in the face of Entellus' rage, while in the *Thebaid* it is Capaneus who is dragged out of the ring, fuming and foaming at the mouth. Whereas the emphasis in the *Aeneid* is on submitting gracefully to the unbendable will of the gods, it is the *nefas* of civil war, and human madness that terrifies Adrastus, breaking up his words into a frenzy of repetition and imperatives, with gasping elisions. Tydeus and Hippomedon are only just able to restrain the hero and as they drag him away, cursing the Spartan, and fully aware that the satisfaction of victory has been taken away from him, the Spartans laugh at him.[39]

Statius uses the clash of the two traditions, Virgil and the *Argonautica*, to radically destabilise the outcome of the match. For following the Virgilian model, Capaneus, in the role of Entellus, is the true winner, deprived of a clear victory by the intervention of the master of ceremonies. But how do we know this is the model that the match would have followed if Adrastus had not stepped

---

[37] Legras (1905) 88–9; Vessey (1970) 432.

[38] See Feldherr (2002) 6 n. 14 citing Nelis (2001) 13–21 on another model of the way that successive boxing matches play with the audience's awareness of the tradition, one of blurring the distinctions between winner and loser, of confusing the allocation of roles from previous matches. So Dares in the *Aeneid* can be seen to replay both the roles of winner and loser from the Iliadic boxing match: he is like Epeius in proclaiming a challenge, and like Euryalus in basing his expectations of victory on an earlier victory (*Iliad* 23.679–80). In the same way, he takes on both roles from the Apollonian boxing match: his previous victim was a Bebrycian, and his youth assimilates him to Polydeukes; his role as challenger assimilates him to Amycus. Entellus in the same way plays the roles of both a previous loser and a previous winner: he produces horrific and terrifying boxing gloves like Amycus (*Argonautica* 2.51–4), yet his age and the shock of the revelation of his strength echo Odysseus in his boxing match with Iros (*Odyssey* 18.66–74). Statius introduces another kind of blurring, by blurring the outcome of the match itself. Capaneus and Alcidamas take on distinct roles, but neither gains a decisive victory.

[39] Capaneus is called *heros* (*Theb.* 6.817) even as he pushes the laurels of victory and the prize away in his bloodlust. Von Stosch (1968) 73 sees the boxing as 'the fight with two victors', but in a boxing match two victors equals no *real* victor: Capaneus' victory is fatally undercut.

in? For if we swap traditions, Alcidamas, pale at his own success (*euentuque impalluit ipse secundo, Theb.* 6.805), becomes a Pollux (*territus ipse etiam atque ingentis conscius ausi*, 'terrified himself and aware of his huge daring', *Arg.* 4.295) and Capaneus, knocked down and enraged, becomes an Amycus,[40] particularly in his final taunt, which recalls Amycus' second challenge (Valerius *Argonautica* 240–42):

> 'quisquis es, infelix celera puer; haut tibi pulchrae
> manserit hoc ultra frontis decus oraue matri
> nota feres.'

> 'Whoever you are, hurry up, doomed youth; the glory
> of a beautiful brow will not remain for you nor will you take back
> to your mother the face she knew.'

By this model, perhaps Capaneus in his maddened rage would not have killed Alcidamas as Adrastus fears, but might instead have been fatally knocked out by his more skilled opponent. By stopping the match just before the match of *Aeneid* 5, in which Entellus is already beating Dares to a pulp, Statius both overturns the expectation of violence set up at the beginning of the match and refuses to allow his reader to make a final decision about which is his number one model, the *Argonautica* or the *Aeneid*.

Narratives of Greekness and Romanness

These reversals and the narratives of nationality which are implicated in them suggest different ways of reading the boxing match as an interaction of Greek and Roman culture and national identities. The boxing match in the *Iliad* is purely a Greek affair. Polydeukes, however, is an emblematically Greek hero, defeating the barbarian monster.[41] Nationality becomes far more problematic and disputed with Virgil: Entellus is Italian (though not securely so) and also

---

[40] Although he is also a Pollux, confusingly enough, just before the fight stops when the blood is trickling down his forehead (*Theb.* 6.782–3); after the match, Pollux' celebration is marred only by a wound on his forehead (*Arg.* 4.330–32). Their reactions are very different, however: Pollux wipes it off with his glove, unafraid, while for Capaneus it is the final insult that makes him mad. However, his concern with audience reactions (*Theb.* 6.784–5) is a characteristic of Amycus (*Arg.* 4.297–8).
[41] Hunter (1993) 28–9.

the barbarian;[42] however, he is characterised as the noble barbarian, committing an act of sacrifice rather than an act of murder. Dares is part of the world of Homer and Apollonius, and therefore his defeat by Entellus can symbolise the overcoming of Greek epic (and synecdochically the whole of Greek culture) by Virgil's Roman poem. However, he is not Greek; he is Trojan, and thus the result of the boxing match corresponds to Jupiter's representation to Juno that the Italian element will take the upper hand in the fusion of colonising Trojans and native Latins into the Roman stock. One could read the *lusus Troiae* as suggesting the opposite, along with Aeneas' speech at the beginning of book 5: that in the end the Trojans will control the form of Rome, and that what is important to Aeneas will be important to Rome.[43] The contesting claims of Troy and Italy about the precise ingredients of Romanness can, and should, be left unresolved. The *Aeneid* problematises Romanness by presenting a fragmented Italy at war with itself and with the outsiders. This is a strong reversal of the representation of Greek civilisation overcoming barbarity in Apollonius, and of the homogeneity of the *Iliad*. Valerius also turns the rhetoric of his match around: his Pollux, as we have seen, is much more violent, less a civilising force than Polydeukes. The match rather becomes a fratricidal war, between the son of Zeus and the son of Neptune, rereading gigantomachy as a version of civil war.[44]

Alcidamas is throughout characterised by his Greekness (and specifically as a Spartan).[45] When he enters the scene, he springs out 'from the naked troop of Spartans' (*nuda de plebe Laconum,*

---

[42] See above on the blurring of Entellus' nationality. Feldherr (2002) 67–8 also points out that the negotiations over choice of *caestus* result in each giving up his national identity with his weapons.

[43] See pp. 172–6, Greek and Roman.

[44] Hershkowitz (1998b) 84 points to this but does not make the connection with civil war. Before the fight, he shows us Neptune mourning over the pre-ordained outcome; in his challenge, Amycus says: *Neptuni en Domus atque egomet Neptunia proles* ('Behold the house of Neptune and I myself am the offspring of Neptune', Val. Flacc. *Arg.* 4.209) and also: *aliis rex Iuppiter oris* ('Jupiter is king on other shores', 219). The combatants are described as: *Iovis et Neptunia proles* ('offspring of Jupiter and Neptune') at 256.

[45] Von Stosch (1968) 197 suggests that this links him more thoroughly to Polydeukes. Sparta was one model for Roman military hardihood: Horsfall (1990) 306–8; Rawson (1969) 94–115. This leads to some ambivalence as to which of the two competitors takes the role of Romanness: however, the way that Alcidamas is characterised as Spartan in the boxing is through his skill and cunning, not through his militarism and hardness, so that Spartan here seems more to mean Greek.

739); during the fight, he is described as more learned (*doctior*, 765); we have already noted *providus astu | et patria uigil arte Lacon* ('the Spartan, foresightful in his cunning and alert in his ancestral skill', 769–70); *callidus* ('clever', 782); *motu Spartanus acuto* ('the Spartan with his swift movement', 792) and *non tamen immemor artis* ('nevertheless not unmindful of his skill', 794). At the end, Adrastus refers to him as *Lacona* ('Spartan', 812), Capaneus says he will send his body back to his Spartan master (*Oebalio magistro*, 822) and he is *alumnum Taygeti* ('the offspring of Taygetus', 824–5). His skill is characterised as specific to his nationality: he is fast, alert and clever. Possibly this emphasis on skill shades over into wiliness; is he too reliant on skill to make up for deficiencies in strength? Pollux, too, is Spartan, skilful and evasive, but the emphasis on his divine origins distances him from national identity. Capaneus, however, is not characterised by his nationality: in fact, it is easy to forget that he is Greek. His predecessors are Amycus and Entellus, which means in the logic of the epic boxing match that he must play the role of barbarian. He is modelled extensively on the character of Mezentius in the *Aeneid*, both in his negative aspect as *contemptor deorum* ('scorner of the gods') and also in his positive aspect as a representative of heroism and *duritia* ('hardness') among the Italians.[46] His *amor Martis* ('love of war') – in book 3, he is a strong proponent of military action – and his refusal to use trickery in war at all (*ipse haud dignatus in hostem | ire dolo*, 'he himself thought it unworthy to go against the enemy with a trick', 10.258–9) embody Roman values. At least in part he must play the Roman to Alcidamas' Greek: for he is familiar within the epic, a hero to whom we have already been introduced several times, one of the Seven whose fates we will follow throughout the poem. Alcidamas is very much the outsider, appearing as he does from within a tight group of his compatriots. Inasmuch as the Roman audience is encouraged to identify with the heroes who are the focus of the poem, so far must Capaneus become an avatar of Romanness. On the other hand, he himself represents the fight as a sort of civil war when he hopes that he will not kill his opponent

---

[46] We have already noted how Hippomedon is linked to Mezentius through the rock simile of *Aeneid* 10.693–6. Hershkowitz (1998b) 84–5 assimilates Amycus to Mezentius; Capaneus has a much stronger claim to this role, however. See Caiani (1990).

and wishes for a proper foreign enemy. If Spartans can also be seen as proto-Romans, then both contenders have a claim on Romanness, and the fight becomes another staging of civil war. On the other hand, when Capaneus calls Alcidamas *semiuir* ('half-man', 821) he mobilises the rhetoric of orientalising effeminacy, typified by the speech of Numanus Remulus at *Aeneid* 9.598–620.[47] Turnus uses this word against Aeneas at 12.99 (*semiuiri Phrygis*, the 'Phrygian half-man'), as does Iarbas at 4.215 (*et nunc ille Paris cum semiuiro comitatu*, 'and now that Paris with his entourage of half-men'). This rhetoric links the oppressed categories of female and barbarian in opposition to Roman manliness. By calling Alcidamas a *semiuir* and accusing him of taking the passive role in sex, Capaneus both questions his masculinity and locates him as an essentially un-Roman figure. Romanness and masculinity are so intimately linked that by losing one you lose the other. We can begin to see from this analysis the problems of constructing nationality in the multifaceted world of the *Thebaid*.

It is striking that although Alcidamas is the outsider, he inspires considerable sympathy in the internal audience: *quem uinci haud quisquam saeuo neque sanguine tingi | malit, et erecto timeat spectacula uoto* ('no one preferred that he should be conquered or stained with savage blood, and each fears the spectacle with intent prayers', 758–9), and when he finally knocks Capaneus down the crowd roars: *clamorem Inachidae, quantum non litora, tollunt, | non nemora* ('the sons of Inachus raised a shout unmatched by shores and woods', 806–7). Capaneus' strength, on the other hand, is described as *iniustis uiribus* ('unjust strength', 774). This is a much more unequal match in terms of size and strength than Virgil's, more reminiscent of the way that the Rutulians in *Aeneid* 12 see the fight between Turnus and Aeneas. Alcidamas is *paulo ante puer* ('a boy only recently', 756) as well as smaller, less experienced and not the son of a god.

If Capaneus' representation or at least part-representation of Romanness is accepted, then, on the model of Dares and Entellus as foreshadowing the Italian war, possible narratives of a contest

---

[47] See Hardie (1994) 14–18, 188–98; Horsfall (1990) 312–13; Dickie (1985); Thomas (1982) 98–100.

between Greek and Roman emerge from this fight. For Capaneus is well aware that the *semiuir* Alcidamas has undermined his own *uirtus* by wounding him in such a bathetic manner and using his own brute force against him. Likewise, there was an awareness among cultured Romans that despite their military conquest of Greece, Greek culture had to some extent conquered Roman culture. Hellenising was seen as a sign of moral decline, as well as cultural status. Who has really won the fight? Capaneus is given the palms and prizes, but this is a persuasive rhetorical move, for the Spartans laugh at his threats (*minas risere Lacones*, 825). This laughter carries heavy irony, as he himself had laughed at Alcidamas when he first stepped forward: *indignatur Capaneus ridetque* ('Capaneus is outraged and laughs', 747).[48] His own laughter has been turned against him. We are left with an unresolved contest between brute force and trickery, between Greek and Roman, between a boy whose secure gender identity is called into question and an excessively masculine man.

NATIONAL IDENTITY

Introduction

The issue of Greek and Romanness is especially important in the work of Statius, highlighted by his self-presentation in the *Siluae*. His links with Naples and his portrayal of the career of his father place him at the interstices of Greek and Roman culture.[49] In his lament for his father (*Siluae* 5.3), Statius describes his father's poetic and pedagogical achievements. His strong affiliation to Greek culture is emphatically displayed. He competed in poetic *agones* not only in Naples and the surrounding area but also in Greece itself;[50] he taught sophisticated Hellenistic poetry as

---

[48] Vessey (1970) 434 links this laughter to Jupiter's at 10.907.
[49] See Hardie (1983) 2–29.
[50] *sin pronum uicisse domi: quid Achaea mereri | praemia nunc ramis Phoebi nunc gramine Lernae | nunc Athamantea protectum tempora pinu* ('but if it was easy to conquer at home, what was it to deserve Greek prizes, covering your temples now with the branches of Phoebus, now with the grass of Lerna, now with the Athamantean pine?' *Siluae* 5.3.141–3).

well as the classical foundation stones of Greek culture.[51] He probably wrote in Latin as well as Greek: he is described as translating
Homer. It seems likely that his poems on Roman subject-matter,
such as the civil war of AD 69 and the eruption of Vesuvius, might
have been in Latin. Statius' tribute to his father, written in Latin
but paying homage to Greek culture, shows the interdependence
of Greek and Roman culture already at this early stage.[52]

When Statius wrote a poem for his wife, persuading her to move
with him back to his birthplace at Naples, he praised Naples as a
mixture of Roman and Greek (*Siluae* 3.5.93–4):

> quid laudem litus libertatemque Menandri,
> quam Romanus honos et Graia licentia miscent?
>
> Why should I praise the shore and the freedom of Menander,
> which mixes Roman honour with Greek freedom of choice?

This poem demonstrates that Statius is keen to present himself
as a product of Naples, an offspring of the union of Greek and
Roman. Magna Graecia as a whole lost much of its Greek flavour
after the Roman conquest.[53] However, Naples was one exception,
where official municipal inscriptions continued in Greek, despite
widespread use of Roman names and personal inscriptions in Latin
among the elite.[54] Two explanations for this phenomenon have
been suggested: on the one hand, Costabile sees the Greek elite as
adopting the Roman *tria nomina* as a political act of allegiance.[55]
Lomas, on the other hand, diagnoses a 'revival of Hellenism among
the elite during the first and early second centuries AD'; she stresses

---

[51] McNelis (2002) argues that Statius senior's curriculum of more obscure Greek authors
provided cultural capital for his aristocratic students, who went on to achieve political
success.

[52] By the time of Apuleius, such interdependence is well documented: although Apuleius
wrote in Latin, he claimed to speak Greek at home and to write to his family in Greek. In
Apology 87, he complains about the poor Greek of a letter alleged to have been written
by him and argues that he writes Greek too well to have written the letter. In 98, he
chastises Pudens for speaking Punic, only a little Greek that he had picked up from his
mother, and no Latin at all.

[53] See Lomas (1993) 174–87. The amount of evidence is not large for all areas, but for
instance: 'In many cities, Greek inscriptions disappear, or persist in very small numbers.
With the exception of Tarentum and Locri, however, these cities are ones from which
we have comparatively small amounts of evidence of any sort.'

[54] Kaimio (1979) 72. See also Lomas (1993) 175–6. Other exceptions were Rhegium and
Velia.

[55] Costabile (1978).

that 'this Hellenism is a cultural construct, not something which is consequent upon ethnicity.'[56] We have, then, on the one hand, Greeks pretending to be Romans, and, on the other, Romans pretending to be Greeks. The elite of Naples occupied an idiosyncratic position in the interstices of Greek and Roman culture, and possessed the ability to manipulate their self-presentation in either direction, as the situation required. Yet what is particularly striking in this phenomenon is that it was advantageous to seem Greek. There was a 'high status accorded to cities with a demonstrably Greek past and Greek culture'.[57] What is more, Kaimio's examination of the relationship between the Latin and Greek languages pinpoints Greek as primarily the language of culture.[58] All this suggests that there was much to gain for Statius in aligning himself with the Greek side of Roman literature.

Yet he did not write in Greek; he wrote in Latin, and the majority of his surviving work is in that most Roman of genres, epic. It seems clear to me that just as the Hellenising tendency at Naples was embraced by Romans and for Romans in order to present Naples as a city of leisure and culture, so Statius wrote his epic of Greek myth for a Roman audience. The Greek flavour of his language, his Greek subject-matter and his own 'Greek' origins all added up to a Latinity which claimed sophistication through affiliation to Greekness. Naples and the Neapolitan Statius were as much Romano-Greek as Greco-Roman.

Games and sport are an important part of national identity: in modern times, the 'national sport' is a concept frequently aired in the public forum by the English press (often in lament for decline). Chariot racing and gladiatorial games form a large part of the modern popular conception of what it is to be Roman. In ancient Greece, too, recent research has shown how important athletics and athletic festivals are in the construction of social and regional identities.[59] Epic games participate in this arena, forming and being influenced by the very real problems and issues at the heart of the negotiation of identity. In this section, I shall investigate the problems of national identity in the *Thebaid*. Statius is a poet between

---

[56] Lomas (1993) 181.   [57] Lomas (1993) 183.   [58] Kaimio (1979) 323.
[59] See, for instance, Golden (1998); Van Nijf (1999); König (2000).

Greece and Rome, yet the story of the Seven against Thebes has long been read as mythological irrelevance, unrelated to Rome and Romanness.[60] Both sides in the fratricidal war are Greek, and the events took place long before the founding of Rome. Nevertheless, the *Thebaid* presents itself as an epic destined for the education of Roman citizens, following in the footsteps of that uncontroversially 'national' epic the *Aeneid*. How does Statius engage with issues of national identity; how do his tactics compare with Virgil's, and most especially, how do both authors use epic games for this purpose? Who should a Roman reading the *Thebaid* identify with? Is the *Thebaid* a very Roman civil war? These are the wider questions that I will address in this exploration of the play of identities in the *Thebaid*.

Let us begin with the *Aeneid*. Kate Toll has recently argued that the obsession with Augustanism (whether pro- or anti-) in the *Aeneid* misrepresents the main thrust of Virgil's project: to forge an identity for the vast mass of Roman citizens in Italy who had only recently gained citizenship after the Social Wars.[61] However, Virgil's representation of Romanness is characterised by complexity and fragmentation.[62] Trojans and Italians each form part of Jupiter's ultimate recipe for Romanness; they are defined in contrast to each other and to Greeks and Carthaginians. Yet it is never quite clear who is Italian, Greek or Trojan. Different groups represent themselves differently to different people and in different situations, and the narratorial descriptions of practices and values are equally slippery. The use of the figure of Dardanus is a case in point:[63] when Latinus receives the Trojans and greets them with a view to establishing connections with them, he stresses

---

[60] So Ogilvie as late as 1980 says that 'The *Thebaid* cannot be said to be *about* anything.' (Ogilvie (1980) 292). More considered, and more damning, is Vessey's conclusion in the *Cambridge History of Classical Literature* that 'The *Thebaid* is not a Roman epic, it has no national or patriotic motive.' (Vessey (1982) 572). The *Thebaid* certainly contrasts strongly with the epics of Silius and Valerius Flaccus; the *Punica* deals with Roman subject-matter and explicitly links it to the later history of Rome; Valerius Flaccus refers his epic of myth frequently to Roman practices and ideas. The *Thebaid*, however, rarely looks outside the claustrophobic *limes* of its own catastrophe.

[61] Toll (1997); see also Miles (1999) 240–45, who suggests that there was also a degree of continuity between the Social Wars and the civil wars, through regional support for different leaders.

[62] For useful recent introductions to this topic, see Zetzel (1997) and Miles (1999).

[63] See Miles (1999) 332 n. 8; Anderson (2002).

their descent from Dardanus (calling them *Dardanidae* at 7.195), who, according to *fama*, was born in Latium (*Aeneid* 7.205–11).[64] The emphasis on *fama* and memory points to the provisionality of the story, which Latinus chooses to endorse for his current purposes, while also giving it the distance and respectability of tradition.[65] Ilioneus in response also looks to Dardanus' Italian origins (7.239–42);[66] the narrative of immigration becomes a narrative of returning home. Dardanus works as justification alongside the will of the gods and fate. Aeneas, however, rolls out quite a different story about the origins of Dardanus to create a link with Evander (*Aeneid* 8.134–42):

> Dardanus, Iliacae primus pater urbis et auctor,
> Electra, ut Grai perhibent, Atlantide cretus,
> aduehitur Teucros; Electram maximus Atlas
> edidit, aetherios umero qui sustinet orbis.
> uobis Mercurius pater est, quem candida Maia
> Cyllenae gelido conceptum uertice fudit;
> at Maiam, auditis si quicquam credimus, Atlas,
> idem Atlas generat caeli qui sidera tollit.
> sic genus amborum scindit se sanguine ab uno.

> Dardanus, first and founding father of the Trojan city,
> born, as the Greeks say, from Electra daughter of Atlas,
> came to the Trojan land; great Atlas was the father
> of Electra, who holds up the heavenly spheres on his shoulder.

---

[64] *atque equidem memini (fama est obscurior annis)* | *Auruncos ita ferre senes, his ortus ut agris* | *Dardanus Idaeas Phrygiae penetrarit ad urbes* | *Threiciamque Samum, quae nunc Samothracia fertur.* | *hinc illum Corythi Tyrrhena ab sede profectum* | *aurea nunc solio stellantis regia caeli* | *accipit et numerum diuorum altaribus auget* ('and indeed I remember (the story has grown darker through the years) that the Auruncan old men report it thus, that Dardanus, born in these fields, reached the Idaean cities of Phrygia and Thracian Samos, which is now called Samothrace. From here, from his Tyrrhenian seat of Corythus, he set out and now the golden palace of the starry heaven receives him with a throne and he increases the number of the gods with his altars', *Aeneid* 7.205–11).

[65] It might also suggest an intratextual memory of the prophecy of the Penates to Aeneas back on Crete in the course of the aimless wanderings of book 3: *hae nobis propriae sedes, hinc Dardanus ortus* | *Iasiusque pater, genus a quo principe nostrum* ('this is our own home, in which Dardanus and father Iasius were born, from whom our race was sprung', 3.167–8); the prophecy also mentions Corythus (170).

[66] *sed nos fata deum uestras exquirere terras* | *imperiis egere suis. hinc Dardanus ortus,* | *huc repetit iussisque ingentibus urget Apollo* | *Tyrrhenum ad Thybrim et fontis uada sacra Numici* ('but the divine fates drove us by their orders to seek out your lands. Here Dardanus was born, and he drives us back here, and Apollo impels us with his huge commands to the Tyrrhenian Tiber and the sacred shallows of the spring Numicus', 7.239–42).

Mercury is your father, whom white Maia bore
conceived on the cold summit of Cyllene;
but Atlas, if we believe anything that has been heard, that same Atlas
fathered Maia, Atlas who bears the stars of heaven.
So both our races divide themselves from one blood.

This version privileges Greek descent over Italian birthplace; it is told by the Greeks (according to Aeneas) and forms a link with the Arcadians of Evander (who, like many of the inhabitants of Virgil's Italy, are recent immigrants). Again, the speaker marks his story with Alexandrian footnotes (*ut Grai perhibent*, 'as the Greeks say'; *auditis si quicquam credimus*, 'if we believe anything that has been heard') and the complexity of his manoeuvres points to a self-conscious awareness of his own tendentious rhetoric.

Stories about descent and ancestry form an important part of the process of establishing identity, as do names which call attention to these stories. Virgil offers his Roman readers a way of forming their own identity through the story of Aeneas, just as Aeneas offers Evander the story of Dardanus. Statius, too, uses names and epithets to reflect on identity, heredity and ethnicity, and we will examine this in more detail later. Let us turn for the moment to the games and the different ways in which identity is constructed and contested in *Aeneid* 5.

Constructing identity in Virgil's games

The games of *Aeneid* 5 have long been read as evidence of Virgil's Augustan programme.[67] However, they are also rich in negotiations of Roman identity. The games as a ritual look forward to the founding of a new nation which will be foreshadowed in the founding of Acesta for the Trojans who stay behind in Sicily at the end of book 5. Aeneas' speech specifically points to their recurrence as a ritual in the city to be: *atque haec me sacra quotannis | urbe uelit posita templis sibi ferre dicatis* ('and when the city has been set up and the temples dedicated, may he be willing to accept these rites which I will offer to him every year', 5.59–60). The representation

---

[67] Briggs (1975), see also Cairns (1989).

of the past is linked to the present, and aetiology is a way of constructing identity. Aeneas' rituals for his father, including funeral games, are the forerunners of Roman rituals and form a link to the present which defines him as Roman and celebrates Romanness. The Trojan past is emphatically linked to the Roman present by the captains of the ships in the ship race and the ritual of the *lusus Troiae*. In the ship race, Mnestheus is introduced as the ancestor of the *gens Memmia*, Sergestus of the *gens Sergia* and Cloanthus of the *gens Cluentia* (5.116–23):

> uelocem Mnestheus agit acri remige Pristim,
> mox Italus Mnestheus, genus a quo nomine Memmi,
> [. . .]
> Sergestusque, domus tenet a quo Sergia nomen,
> Centauro inuehitur magna, Scyllaque Cloanthus
> caerulea, genus unde tibi, Romane Cluenti.

> Mnestheus drives the swift Pristis with keen oarsmen,
> soon to be Italian Mnestheus, from whose name came the race of Memmius,
> [. . .]
> and Sergestus sails in the great Centaur, from whom the Sergian
> house keeps its name, and Cloanthus sails in the sky-blue
> Scylla, from whom came your race, Roman Cluentius.

Each name is marked as the origin of a Roman name; the Trojan Mnestheus is first transformed into an Italian (*mox Italus*) and then into the ancestor of the Memmii. With Cloanthus, the second-person address to a generalised Cluentius, along with the adjective *Romanus*, makes the connection even more specific and personal, looking forward to the climactic moment of *Aeneid* 6 where *Romane memento*, famously laying out the mission of the Roman nation, and at the heart of the *Aeneid*'s construction of Roman identity, comes in the same metrical position. The names of the characters competing in the games are names that link them to the Roman present: names that will become founding cornerstones of Roman history.[68] Their leadership (or lack of it) holds lessons for Roman character, as many have read it.

[68] O'Hara (1996) 108–9 'This kind of naming of people and cities makes etymological aetiology a part of the *Aeneid*'s central concerns, for the poem itself is at the heart an *aetion* for the Roman state and people . . . in its interest in aetiology the *Aeneid* is simultaneously most Roman and most Alexandrian.' On aetiology of the names of Roman *gentes*, 159–60.

The description of the *lusus Troiae*, however, is even more compelling in its self-conscious reflection on the negotiation of Roman identity through games, and we will look at it in rather more detail. The *lusus Troiae* comes at the end of Virgil's games, a spectacle to follow the contests with co-operative display, just as the dancing comes at the end of the games in the *Odyssey*. The young Trojans, led by Ascanius, perform a display of choreographed riding and military skills. Augustus' fondness for this ritual, which he revived, until the injury of one participant led to its curtailment, has marked it as an Augustan moment in the games, a clear reference to Augustan practices. But Virgil represents it rather as a Roman moment, the establishment of a continuity of past and present. To take an Augustan practice and represent it as an emblem of Romanness is clearly a loaded statement; but let us first see how the description works. The three squadrons of boys are commanded, like the ships, by significantly named leaders (*Aeneid* 5.563–76):

> una acies iuuenum, ducit quam paruus ouantem
> nomen aui referens Priamus, tua clara, Polite,
> progenies, auctura Italos; quem Thracius albis
> portat equus bicolor maculis, uestigia primi
> alba pedis frontemque ostentans arduus albam.
> alter Atys, genus unde Atii duxere Latini,
> paruus Atys pueroque puer dilectus Iulo.
> extremus formaque ante omnis pulcher Iulus
> Sidonio est inuectus equo, quem candida Dido
> esse sui dederat monimentum et pignus amoris.
> cetera Trinacriis pubes senioris Acestae
> fertur equis.
> excipiunt plausu pauidos gaudentque tuentes
> Dardanidae, ueterumque agnoscunt ora parentum.

> One column of the youths, which small Priam led as they rejoiced,
> bearing the name of his grandfather, your bright offspring,
> Polites, destined to increase the Italian nation; a Thracian horse,
> piebald with white patches, bore him, displaying the white marks
> of his front foot and on high his white forehead.
> The second Atys led, from whom the Latin Atii were descended,
> small Atys, loved as a boy by the boy Iulus.
> Finally, Iulus, beautiful above all in looks,
> was carried by a Carthaginian horse, which white Dido
> had given to him as a reminder and token of love.

The rest of the young men were carried on the Sicilian horses
   of Acestes.
The sons of Dardanus received them in their trepidation with applause
   and rejoiced as they watched, and recognised the faces of ancient ancestors.

The leader of the first column, Priam, carries his Trojan heritage
strongly in his name, yet, like Mnestheus, Virgil emphasises that
he will become Italian (*auctura Italos*). Atys, like Mnestheus,
Sergestus and Cloanthus, bears a name which marks him as the
ancestor of a Roman *gens*, the family of Augustus' mother, Atia.[69]
The text leaves unstated the same comment on Ascanius, but
twice refers to him by his aetiologically significant name Iulus,
founder of the Julian *gens*, both emphatically at the end of con-
secutive lines. Again the audience are *Dardanidae* bringing out
the crossover between Trojan and Italian identities. It is not clear
whether *Dardanidae* includes both Trojans and Sicilians in the
audience or is designed to exclude the Sicilian element: Acestes
is Trojan but his followers do not seem to be; Dardanus can be
an image of how the Trojans were Italian in the first place; however, the following phrase (*ueterumque agnoscunt ora parentum*,
'and they recognised the faces of ancient ancestors') suggests that
the text marks out those who knew the parents and ancestors of
the boys. *Dardanidae*, here, then, seems to be used to mark the
Trojans out from the Sicilian part of the audience. The recognition of the boys as a link with the past by the internal audience
plays against the way the text asks its Roman readers to recognise
them as a link with the future, the present of the Augustan reader-
ship. The way that Virgil moves from *Italos* to *Latini* to *Romane
Cluenti* (5.123) also suggests an equivocation between Italians,
Latins and Romans, which fits in well with the idea that the *Aeneid*
is at least partly designed to create an identity for all Italians as
Romans.
   The description of the display itself, and in particular the two
similes of the labyrinth (588–91) and dolphins (594–5), make a
pointed contrast with the Phaeacian games in *Odyssey* 8, which
also end in a display from the boys, but a display of dancing, rather
than warlike skills. The language of the description of the *lusus*

[69] O'Hara (1996) 163.

Troiae moves back and forth between dancing and war (*Aeneid* 5.580–82):

> olli discurrere pares atque agmina terni
> diductis soluere choris, rursusque uocati
> conuertere uias infestaque tela tulere.

> They ran apart in equal groups and three columns
> separate into divided choruses, and called back again
> they turn their paths and charge with hostile weapons.

The description of the columns as choruses is juxtaposed with the image of a battle charge; in the same way, the two similes which both evoke the complexity and playfulness of dance are sandwiched between lines of densely military language (*Aeneid* 5.592–5):

> haud alio Teucrum nati uestigia cursu
> impediunt texuntque fugas et proelia ludo,
> delphinum similes qui per maria umida nando
> Carpathium Libycumque secant.

> Not otherwise do the sons of the Trojans entwine their footsteps
> in their path and weave flight and battle in play,
> like dolphins who cut the wet Carpathian and Libyan
> seas with their swimming.

While the Phaeacian boys are first humiliated by Odysseus' superior strength and then presented as masters of the fundamentally unwarlike skills of dance, the Trojan boys use their play and dance to mimic war and learn military skills. This constructs a Roman ideal to set against the otherness of the Phaeacians.

The passage ends with a particularly strong moment of linking, from Trojan to Alban to Roman, by both practice and naming (*Aeneid* 5.596–602):

> hunc morem cursus atque haec certamina primus
> Ascanius, Longam muris cum cingeret Albam,
> rettulit et priscos docuit celebrare Latinos,
> quo puer ipse modo, secum quo Troia pubes;
> Albani docuere suos; hinc maxima porro
> accepit Roma et patrium seruauit honorem;
> Troiaque nunc pueri, Troianum dicitur agmen.

> Ascanius first, when he was surrounding Alba Longa with walls,
> brought back this custom of movement and this contest,

and taught the ancient Latins to practise it frequently,
in the way which he himself did as a boy and the Trojan youth with him.
The Albans taught their descendants; and from this in the future
great Rome inherited it and preserved the honour of their ancestors;
Now the boys are called 'Troy', and the column is called 'Trojan'.

Again, the act of founding is linked with the passing on of traditions
and the setting up of ritual; games and walls a city make. The
Trojan name and identity is passed through Latins and Albans to
Rome, validating an Augustan practice by extrapolating it into the
past, and suggesting self-reflexively that its original purpose was
to honour ancestors.

Statius' games are also a new foundation, but they are an *aetion*
for one of the major festivals of the Greek *periodos*, the Nemean
games. At the beginning of book 6, he places them in the context
of the origins of the other games in the *periodos*: first the Olympic
Games (5–7), then the Pythian (8–9), and finally the Isthmian
(10–14). This is a pan-Hellenic festival, a celebration of Greekness.
Yet there is a Roman flavour to the way he describes the festivals of the *periodos*: the first competitor at the Olympics is *pius
Alcides*, putting Herakles into the shoes of Aeneas; the Pythian
games are recast as games celebrating success in war: *proxima
uipereo celebratur libera nexu | Phocis, Apollineae bellum puerile
pharetrae* ('next Phocis freed from the grip of the viper is celebrated, the childhood war of Apollo's bow', 6.8–9); the Isthmian
games, like those of the *Aeneid*, mark the anniversary of a death. It
is as if Rome is appropriating the culture of *Graecia capta*; not surprising, perhaps, given that the Capitoline games, and Augustus'
Actian games, had made a large part of the contemporary *periodos*
Roman territory.[70]

[70] This version of the interaction of Greek and Roman culture, where Romans appropriate
Greek culture for the purpose of establishing their own cultural as well as political
ascendancy over it, is persuasively set out by Erich Gruen. Particularly interesting for
the purposes of this study is the use of games as part of this process. Gruen points to
the games which Aemilius Paullus held at Amphipolis in 167 BC (Polybius 30.14; Livy
45.32.8–11; Plutarch *Aem. Paul.* 28.3–5 with Gruen (1993) 247–8). Livy represents this
drawing up of the festival as an act of generalship parallel to victory in battle: *uulgo dictum
ipsius ferebant et conuiuium instruere et ludos parare eiusdem esse, qui uincere bello
sciret* ('his saying was commonly reported that to draw up a banquet and prepare games
was easy for the man who knew how to conquer in war', Livy 45.32.11). The next logical

Statius and audience loyalties

Games also become an arena for defining national identity through audiences and their reactions. By watching and cheering for your fellow-countryman, you reinforce your own national identity. The audience of Statius' games, like Virgil's, incorporate two groups: those involved in the expedition, and those from the cities around (6.1–3). However, Statius' expedition is much more Iliadic than Virgil's. It is an army composed of allies from various parts of Greece going against a single city and their allies. We will examine below the composition of the Argive army, as portrayed in Statius' catalogue and represented in his battle narrative. Statius' audience, then, as we shall see, are a complex gathering from different cities and regions, and they display their loyalties accordingly.

Feldherr has traced how the various audiences of the ship race in the *Aeneid* are drawn into the frame of the action, all incorporated into one enthusiasm for Rome's ancestors.[71] In opposition to this unanimity is Statius' running, where the competitors are supported by their compatriots: Idas is cheered by the young men of Pisa and Elis (*excipiunt plausu Pisaea iuuentus | Eleaeque manus*, 'the youth of Pisa and the Elean bands receive him with applause', 6.555–6); it is the Arcadians who protest when Parthenopaeus is fouled (*Arcades arma fremunt*, 'the Arcadians rage for their weapons', 618). When Parthenopaeus prays to Diana to aid him in his rerun, he worries about disgracing Arcadia: *ne, quaeso, sinas hoc omine Thebas | ire nec Arcadiae tantum meruisse pudorem* ('don't, I beg, allow me to go to Thebes with this bad omen, or to have won such great shame for Arcadia', 636–7). We have seen above how Statius' boxing has a strong focus on the divided loyalties of the Argive army. In other events, the origins of different competitors in different cities are highlighted; in the discus, competitors are listed by city (*Thebaid* 6.651–3):

---

step for the appropriation of Greek games was taken by Anicius, who brought Greek games to Rome. 'There they would not only exhibit their wares to a Roman audience but would be conspicuously manipulated by the *imperator* in a stunning display of Roman power to exploit Hellenic culture.' Gruen (1993) 248.
[71] Feldherr (1995).

mox turba ruunt, duo gentis Achaeae,
tres Ephyreiadae, Pisa satus unus, Acarnan
septimus;

Soon a crowd rushes forward, two of the Achaean race,
three from Ephyre, one offspring of Pisa, the seventh an
Acarnanian.

Phlegyas is referred to as a Pisan at 668 (*Pisaeus Phlegyas*) and in
the sword fight the two combatants are mentioned by city (*Thebaid*
6.912–13):

iamque aderant instructi armis Epidaurius Agreus
et nondum fatis Dircaeus agentibus exul.

And now they are present drawn up with their weapons: Agreus from Epidaurus
and the Theban exile not yet driven by the fates.

All this works to represent the games as a Pan-Hellenic event, an
important festival like the Olympic or Capitoline games, where the
whole civilised world gathers to compete, and to assimilate Statius'
Argive army to the Iliadic army.

Taking sides: nationality and identification in the *Thebaid*

Just as games are an occasion for the formation and reinforcement
of identity in the audience by supporting competitors, so in narrative, and especially in the game of epic, identification with the
protagonists is an opportunity for readers to renegotiate their own
sense of self. The text engages with these reading possibilities and
in this section I address the question of identification and national
identity in the *Thebaid*. How would a Roman audience have read
(or heard) the *Thebaid*? Who would they have identified with,
and with what effect? How does the text encourage or discourage
sympathy and identification with its characters? Clearly, there are
methodological difficulties in studying audiences who are silent
and long gone; this section is inevitably speculative and relies on
the model reader constructed by the text, rather than the varied and
heterogeneous actual readers of contemporary Rome and the later
reception of Statius. But there is much to be learnt from at least a

brief bout with these thorny and complex issues, and I hope that this beginning will provoke further arguments.

Statius has radically transformed the Theban war. In Aeschylus' *Septem*, for instance, we follow the Thebans as they defend themselves against the invading army of Argos, and sympathise with their desire to protect their city. In Statius' version of the story, the audience is encouraged to identify with both sides and, if anything, more with the Argives. Eteocles is represented as a tyrant and Polynices as a weak, manipulative but basically sympathetic character. This is not the place to deal with all aspects of identification and sympathy in the *Thebaid*. Rather, I will focus on the way that the two armies are represented in terms of the rhetoric of nationality and think about how a Roman audience might have engaged with this. I want to look at two different aspects: first, the way Statius chooses to name the two sides, and how that influences their representation; second, the make-up of the two armies, and how that is represented in the catalogue of the Argives in book 4 and the *teichoscopy* (viewing from the walls) of book 7.

The name game

Virgil uses epithets to think about the construction of identity in the *Aeneid*.[72] Statius is notorious for his circumlocutions around names, for the sheer number and variety of his epithets. How does he use the power of epithets in the *Thebaid* to construct identities for his armies and the possibilities of identification for his readers?

By far the most common epithets for the Thebans and the Argives are just that: words derived from Thebes, either in Greek or Latin form, singular or plural, or from Argos.[73] However, Statius uses many other epithets for his two conflicting armies, each of which tells a story about the origins and identity of the army and suggests ways of reading the poem. Epithets for the Thebans look to the history of Thebes and rivers close to Thebes. *Dircaeus*, referring to the spring Dirce, *Ismenius* and *Asopius*, referring to the rivers

---

[72] Anderson (2002).
[73] For instance: *Thebae* (6.14); *Thebane* (6.513); *Thebes* (9.255 with Dewar's note); *Thebe* (10.594). For Argos: *Argos* (6.15); *Argolidum matrum* (6.138); *Argolicus* (6.732); *Argiua* (10.475); *Argis* (10.730).

Ismenus and Asopus, link Thebes to its surrounding landscape. These three are not especially common.[74] The epithets *Ogygius* and *Aonius* are both used quite frequently,[75] and look back to the inhabitants of Thebes before it was conquered by Cadmus; Ogygus was the legendary king of the Ectenes, according to Pausanias, and the Aones were a native Boeotian people.[76] Even more common, however, are epithets that remind us of the story of Cadmus, his father Agenor and his origins in Tyre or metonymically Sidon.[77] All of these epithets emphasise the distinctiveness of Theban identity; the last category, in particular *Tyrius* and *Sidonius*, make the Thebans intriguingly non-Greek and link them to Virgil's Carthaginians. *Tyrius* is by far the most common adjective for Carthaginian in *Aeneid* 1 and 4, followed by Sidonian.[78] Thebans, then, in many respects, form an 'other' category, which fits with the use of Thebes as a symbolic 'other' for Athens in Athenian tragedy, as analysed by Zeitlin.[79]

The epithets used for the Argives show quite a different pattern. Their descent from the river Inachus is the most common aspect of Argive identity to be emphasised, along with the heritage of Pelops, occasionally Tantalus and the locality of Lerna. However, the majority of epithets equate the Argives to a pan-Hellenic Greek force: they are called *Danai*, *Pelasgi*, *Graii*, *Achaei* and *Achiui*, all of which are more usually used in Latin poetry to refer to the Greeks as a whole.[80] Ἀχαιοί and Δαναοί are the epithets most often used in Homer to refer to the Greek army. The Argives then are represented as the whole of Greece and in particular as a different version of the Greeks in the *Iliad*, while Thebes, as a distinct city

---

[74] *Dircaeus*: fifteen times; *Ismenius*: eight times; *Asopius*: four times. Twice, Boeotia is mentioned.

[75] 27 and 43 times respectively in the *Thebaid*.

[76] On Ogygus: Paus. 9.5.1 with Dewar (1991) 207. On the Aones: Paus. 9.5.1 and Strabo 9.2.3 with Dewar (1991) 57–8.

[77] Tyrian is the most common epithet after Theban; Cadmus' name occurs thirty-nine times, Sidonian occurs twenty-four times, and Agenor is mentioned twelve times.

[78] *Karthago* is used as frequently as a noun; *Poeni* only occurs three times in *Aeneid* 1 and once in *Aeneid* 4.

[79] Zeitlin (1990).

[80] Dewar (1991) comments as much on both *Danai* (9.141: 'in verse the word is usually applied to the Greeks in general but in the *Thebaid* always refers to the Argives') and *Pelasgis* (9.12: 'In Roman poetry "Pelasgi" normally means "Greeks" but here "Argives"').

whose foreign origins are emphasised, takes on, to a certain extent, the role of Troy. Later, we will see how the rhetoric of foreignness and effeminacy which is used against the Trojans in the *Aeneid* is also used against the Thebans in the *Thebaid*. Let us now look in a little more detail at the catalogues and their representations of the Argives and the Thebans.

Cataloguing peoples

Helen Asquith has examined the Argive catalogue of *Thebaid* 4 at length and shown that Statius uses the symbolic and cultural resonances of the places mentioned to create a picture of Greece that 'attempts to represent all the principal features known to the readers, yet at the same time to acknowledge what might be expected of the Heroic age.'[81] Like the games, the catalogue mediates between historical Greece and Homeric Greece, putting history and battle sites next to places that have disappeared since their moment of glory in the Homeric poems. There is an important difference between the Argive army as described in the catalogue (4.32–309) and the Theban army as described in the *teichoscopy* (7.243–373). The Theban army comes entirely from the area close to Thebes, while the Argives cover the whole of the Peloponnese, as well as Calydon and Thebes.[82] The Thebans are represented as essentially homogenous, while the Argives are a complex mixture of peoples from different regions. When Antigone looks out from the walls of Thebes in book 7 and asks her elderly companion Phorbas to tell her about the defenders of Thebes, she begins by worrying that the Thebans will not be able to stand up to the Argives (*Thebaid* 7.247–9):

> 'spesne obstatura Pelasgis
> haec uexilla, pater? Pelopis descendere totas
> audimus gentes:'

> 'Is there hope that this column will be able
> to stand up to the Pelasgians, father? We heard that all the peoples
> of Pelops are coming down on us.'

---

[81] Asquith (2001) 44.
[82] See Asquith (2001) map before 44. Mozley (1928) also points out that 'all these towns are in Boeotia.' 152 n. *b*.

In these few lines, we are given some idea of the complexity of the representation: the Argives are clearly a bigger army; they are all the races of Pelops (presumably suggesting that they come from the Peloponnese). This suggests a unity of sorts, reflected in their completeness (*totas*). However, they are peoples in the plural (*gentes*), which suggests the fragmented tribes within the whole. When Eteocles addresses the Theban forces at the end of the section, he calls them *Aoniae populi* ('Aonian peoples,' 388) and he appeals to their kings (*reges*, 375). But when he talks about their race, it is in the singular: *urbem socia de gente subistis | tutari* ('You have come from an allied race to protect the city,' 381–2). This is reflected in Phorbas' description, where the individual cities and geographical features such as mountains and rivers provide different types of warriors, but there are no larger regional conglomerations.[83]

The Argive catalogue in book 4, on the other hand, is much more extensive both in size and coverage of the Greek landscape; each of the Seven has a contingent, although their territories overlap and interpenetrate.[84] In the first section, Adrastus' army, the text draws attention to the heterogeneity of the troops even within this group (*Thebaid* 4.63–7):[85]

> haec manus Adrastum numero ter mille secuti
> exultant; pars gaesa manu, pars robora flammis
> indurata diu (non unus namque maniplis
> mos neque sanguis) habent, teretes pars uertere fundas
> adsueti uacuoque diem praecingere gyro.

[83] The troops from around Parnassus have a shared link to Apollo (351–3): *omnibus inmixtas cono super aspice laurus | armaque uel Tityon uel Delon habentia, uel quas | hic deus innumera laxauit caede pharetras* ('Look at the entwined bay on all above their helmets, and they have on their weapons either Tityos or Delos, or the quivers which the god himself emptied in uncountable slaughter').

[84] Asquith points out the wide spread of Hippomedon's, Polynices' and Amphiaraus' troops: 'Hippomedon has these far-flung towns in common with Polynices, and to a lesser extent with Amphiaraus. In each case, the suggestion is that the leader is drawing his troops from all over the Peloponnese. One function of the catalogue was to express the scale of the conflict through the extent of the land involved: what the catalogue does most simply is to express the idea that "the whole of the Peloponnese went to war"' (Asquith (2001) 62).

[85] In the catalogue of *Aeneid* 7, the men from Praeneste are similarly described but without the explicit narratorial comment on their heterogeneity: *pars maxima glandes | liventis plumbi spargit, pars spicula gestat | bina manu* ('the greatest part scatter shot made of grey lead, others carry two javelins in their hands,' *Aeneid* 7.686–8). See Parkes (2002) 104–8.

This band, three thousand in number, follow Adrastus
and rejoice; some have pikes in their hands, some have wood
long hardened in the flames (for there is neither one custom nor one
blood among the troops), some are accustomed to whirl smooth
slings and surround the daylight with an empty circle.

In contrast to this, Tydeus' Aetolians (*Aetolis urbibus*, 'from Aetolian cities,' 101) have a coherent and strongly presented regional
identity: *omnibus aeratae propugnant pectora crates, | pilaque
saeua manu; patrius stat casside Mauors* ('Bronze shields defend
the chests of all and savage javelins are in their hands; ancestral
Mars stands on their helmets' 110–11). All have the same accoutrements, and Mars is described as ancestral.

Amphiaraus' troops come from two distinct areas, and I want to
look at them in some detail: first come the Spartans, directly after
the description of Amphiaraus and his betrayal by his wife; they
are followed by the Pisans; the two parts are linked by reference to
athletics, and this entry in the catalogue looks forward strongly to
the games and to the last heroic stand of Alcidamas and the Spartans
in book 10 of the *Thebaid*. The description of Amphiaraus begins
with his horses: *Taenariis hic celsus equis, quam dispare coetu |
Cyllarus ignaro generarat Castore prolem, | quassat humum* ('He
is high on Taenarian horses, the offspring which Cyllarus fathered
in unequal union without the knowledge of Castor, and shakes the
ground' 4.214–16). This points us forward to the chariot race and
his eventual descent to the Underworld, complete with chariot, as
if he is driving through the poem. The description of Amphiaraus
in the chariot race begins with him high on his horses (*Thebaid*
6.326–9):

Oebalios sublimis agit, spes proxima palmae,
Amphiaraus equos; tua furto lapsa propago,
Cyllare, dum Scythici diuersus ad ostia Ponti
Castor Amyclaeas remo permutat habenas.

High up, Amphiaraus, next favourite for victory,
drives Oebalian horses; your offspring, Cyllarus,
taken by theft, while Castor was diverted to the mouth of Scythian
Pontus and changed his Amyclaean reins for the oar.

The idea of the stolen horses looks back to Diomedes in the chariot race of *Iliad* 23 and the horses taken from Aeneas, as well as contributing to the theme of degeneration, of illicit succession and distorted inheritance, which parallels the *confusa domus* of Oedipus, and comes to a climax in the games with Tydeus wrestling Agylleus for the privilege of following in the footsteps of Hercules.[86] But as the Spartan horses give Amphiaraus a link with Castor, no matter how unorthodox, and Alcidamas was taught to box by Pollux (6.741, *Polluce magistro*), so the Spartans in the catalogue are taught by a god (4.228–33):

> deus ipse uiros in puluere crudo
> Arcas alit nudaeque modos uirtutis et iras
> ingenerat; uigor inde animis et mortis honorae
> dulce sacrum. gaudent natorum fata parentes
> hortanturque mori, deflet iamque omnis ephebum
> turba, coronato contenta est funere mater.

> The Arcadian god himself nourishes the heroes
> in the bloody dust and implants the ways and angers of naked
> manhood; from there comes vigour of spirit and the sweet rite
> of honoured death. The parents rejoice at the fates of their children
> and cheer them on to die, and now the whole crowd weeps
> for a young man but the mother is happy with a garlanded corpse.

The identity of the Spartans is formed by their enthusiasm for athletics and war, the way they link the two together. The Arcadian god is Mercury, in his guise of civilising force, the bringer of athletics (Horace *Odes* 1.10.1–4):

> Mercuri, facunde nepos Atlantis,
> qui feros cultus hominum recentum
> uoce formasti catus et decorae
> more palaestrae

> Mercury, eloquent descendent of Atlas,
> clever one, who shaped the wild society
> of recent men with his voice and the custom
> of the glorious wrestling ground.

---

[86] Parkes (2002) 228 points to precedents for the 'covert breeding' at *Iliad* 5.265ff. and *Aeneid* 7.280ff.

Here, athletics and Greek culture are the beginning of civilisation, valorised by the particularly Roman term *decus*; Statius' Spartans, too, look back to Horace's *dulce et decorum* tag (*Odes* 3.2.13) with their sweet honour of death.[87] Wrestling shades over into war in the *puluere crudo* (bloody dust), and *nuda uirtus* speaks equally of the peculiar Spartan enthusiasm for nakedness in athletics (even, as far as Propertius was concerned, extending to mixed exercise of naked men and women) and of their extreme courage in war.[88] Propertius 3.14 twists the Roman idealisation of Spartan military hardiness by juxtaposing it with a rant on the decline of Roman morality (3.13) and making the naked exercise of Spartan women a chance for men to watch lasciviously and for lovers to go unchaperoned. This comes back in a new form in Statius with the eroticisation of Alcidamas' training in *Thebaid* 6. Where Mercury shapes society, Pollux shapes the limbs of his protégé: *ipse deus posuitque manus et bracchia finxit | (materiae suadebat amor)* ('the god himself set his hands and fashioned his arms (love of his material encouraged him)', 6.743–4). War shades into athletics, too, at 231–3, where Spartan anecdotes of maternal ferocity are replayed as parents watching their children's sporting success, rejoicing in their deaths and encouraging them to die. Death in battle becomes the athletic garland of victory.

Amphiaraus' troops from Elis and Pisa continue the athletic theme, although Statius suppresses the Olympics in favour of the founding myth of Oenomaus, his man-eating horses and the chariot race in which Pelops defeated him (*Thebaid* 4.241–5):

> curribus innumeris late putria arua lacessunt
> et bellis armenta domant: ea gloria genti
> infando de more et fractis durat ab usque
> axibus Oenomai; strident spumantia morsu
> uincula, et effossas niueus rigat imber harenas.

> They shake the crumbling fields widely with uncountable chariots
> and tame the herds for war: that glory of their people
> endures from the unspeakable practices and broken axles

---

[87] Parkes (2002) 240 comments on the 'startling use of *sacrum*' and points to Horace.
[88] Parkes (2002) 238: 'Statius repeatedly figures athletics as a version of and prelude to war'.

of Oenomaus; the foaming bits shriek with
biting and the snowy shower wets the dug up sand.

Chariot racing and horse breeding defines them as a people; the flip
side is the heritage of Oenomaus, which shows through in the violence of the language. The massed chariots disturb the landscape
itself, as Amphiaraus will 'cause' the earthquake.[89] In the chariot
race, Amphiaraus is kept from inheriting the atrocities of Oenomaus; this instead is displaced onto Hippodamus, son of Oenomaus, who is almost eaten by his own horses.

So the Spartans are defined by athletics and the Pisans by chariot
racing but both groups are given a macabre and morbid twist,
emphasising how games intersect with war. When Alcidamas has
his final moment of fame in book 10, athletics again form the
backdrop for this Spartan last stand (*Theb.* 10.494–507):

> solas dum tardius artat Echion
> Ogygias, audax animis Spartana iuuentus   495
> inrupit, caesique ruunt in limine primo
> incola Taygeti Panopeus rigidique natator
> Oebalus Eurotae; tuque, o spectate palaestris
> omnibus et nuper Nemeaeo in puluere felix,
> Alcidama, primis quem caestibus ipse ligarat   500
> Tyndarides, nitidi moriens conuexa magistri
> respicis: auerso pariter deus occidit astro.
> te nemus Oebalium, te lubrica ripa Lacaenae
> uirginis et falso gurges cantatus olori
> flebit, Amyclaeis Triuiae lugebere Nymphis,   505
> et quae te leges praeceptaque fortia belli
> erudiit genetrix, nimium didicisse queretur.

While Echion closes the Ogygian gate alone
too slowly, the Spartan youth, bold in spirit,
break in, and cut down as they rush over the front of the threshold
are Panopeus the inhabitant of Taygetus and Oebalus the swimmer
of the frozen Eurotas; you, watched in all the gymnasia
and recently lucky in the Nemean dust,
Alcidamas, whose first boxing gloves were bound

---

[89] Parkes (2002) 245 says only that *lacesso* underlines the warlike character of the Pisans,
although she does make a link between *quassat humum* (216) and his eventual fate:
'Amphiaraus' chariot-driving is consistently portrayed in terms of violence towards the
earth' (229).

by the son of Tyndareus himself, you look back as you die at your
master
shining in the vault: the god falls too, with his star turned away.
For you the Oebalian grove will weep, for you the slippery bank
of the Spartan virgin, and the torrent sung by the false
swan, you will be lamented by the Amyclaean Nymphs of Diana
and the mother who educated you in the laws and brave
precepts of war will cry that you learnt too well.

The Spartans are called ephebes in book 4, and here Alcidamas
falls literally on the threshold of manhood; Alcidamas was a sympathetic spectacle for the audience in book 6, and here Statius
adds an audience of Nymphs and a regretful Spartan mother to
his version of Virgil's lamenting landscape from the catalogue in
Aeneid 7.[90] He emphasises Alcidamas as athletic spectacle and
object of Pollux' pederastic love. Not only does Alcidamas look
up to his catasterised lover as he dies, but the star himself turns
away his face, presumably in grief. The Spartans are identified by
their military prowess: they are Roman in their boldness and patri-
otism; swimming in frozen rivers was also an attribute of hard,
primitive Italy.[91]

In the complex and ever-changing discourse of Roman
Hellenism, Sparta was a key element.[92] Roman writers (and Greeks
writing about Rome) were keen to identify Rome as 'exactly like
Sparta only better'.[93] Valerius Maximus uses the Spartans as models of frugality and military courage, and claims that they came
closest to the gravity of early Rome: *proxima maiorum nostro-
rum grauitati Spartana ciuitas* ('the Spartan state, closest to our
ancestors in gravity', Valerius Maximus 2.6.1).[94] Seneca uses the

[90] *te nemus Angitiae, uitrea te Fucinus unda, | te liquidi fleuere lacus.* ('The Angitian grove lamented you, the glassy waters of Fucinus, and the limpid lake.' *Aeneid* 7.759–60) made famous by Parry (1966).
[91] Not in Virgil's catalogue, but in the ethnographical diatribe of Numanus Remulus in *Aeneid* 9: *durum a stirpe genus natos ad flumina primum | deferimus saeuoque gelu duramus et undis* ('a race hardy by descent, we bring down our children first of all to the rivers and harden them in the fiercely chilly waters' *Aeneid* 9.603–4).
[92] Rawson (1969) 99–115.
[93] Rawson (1969). Rawson traces the comparison with Spartan political institutions in particular through Cato, Polybius, Cicero and Dionysius.
[94] He singles out the warlike abilities of the Spartans ahead of the peacetime skills of the Athenians: *Egregios uirtutis bellicae spiritus Lacedaemoniorum prudentissimi pacis moribus Athenienses subsequuntur* ('Next to the noble spirit of warlike valour of the

Spartans as moral exemplars: a captured boy who dashed his brains out rather than perform servile actions (*Epistulae morales* 77.14); the Spartans at Thermopylae are the equivalent of an unnamed Roman *dux* and his men in not fearing death (*Epistulae morales* 82.20–22). The collection of rhetorical exercises on whether or not to retreat at Thermopylae made by Seneca the Elder at *Suasoriae* 2 shows how important the Spartan ideal was in Roman education. Spartans can be used as exemplars of Roman virtues; they are available as models of Romanness before the fact. Yet they are also extreme examples of the alienness of Greekness: Romans adopt the idea of Sparta in order to claim their own superiority; courage in war should be imitated, pederastic relationships should not. Women should bring up warlike children but should not exercise naked or dance in public.[95] Statius' Spartans exemplify both sides of this: their last stand in book 10 looks back to Turnus' *aristeia* at the end of *Aeneid* 9; their hard, primitive upbringing mirrors the rigours of Virgil's idealised early Italy as ancestor of Roman hardness. Yet he also focuses on athletics and pederasty, emblematic of Spartan Greekness. Alcidamas is skilled, but does his cleverness shade over into the wiliness of the negative side of Roman images of Greeks? Too much cleverness and not enough strength? Roman readers of Statius might have simultaneously sympathised with Alcidamas and found him a representation of the Greek 'other'.

Hall of mirrors

If in a small way the brief image of the Spartans in Statius' catalogue and games can form a reflection of Romanness at least in part, what about other groups in the *Thebaid*? We have seen that

Lacedaemonians come the Athenians, greatly expert in the ways of peace', 2.6.3). Cicero, in the *Pro Flacco*, puts the two states the other way around: *Adsunt Athenienses, unde humanitas, doctrina, religio, fruges, iura, leges ortae atque in omnis terras distributae putantur; [. . .] Adsunt Lacedaemonii, cuius ciuitatis spectata ac nobilitata uirtus non solum natura corroborata uerum etiam disciplina putatur;* ('There are present men from Athens, from where civilisation, learning, religion, crops, rights, and laws are thought to have originated and been distributed to all lands; [. . .] There are present Lacedaemonians, the tested and noble manliness of whose state is thought to have been strengthened not only by nature but also by discipline.' Cicero *Pro Flacco* 62–3).

95 Rawson (1969) 108.

the Argives play the role of the Iliadic Greeks to the Theban version of the Trojans. The war in the second half of the *Thebaid* also plays constantly with Virgil's war between Italians and Trojans. Let us look now at the way that Parthenopaeus mobilises the rhetoric of foreignness and effeminacy against the Thebans.[96] Amphion accuses him of being a boy in a man's game, and tells him to go back to hunting in Arcadia; he responds thus (*Thebaid* 9.790–800):

'sera etiam in Thebas, quarum hic exercitus, arma
profero; quisnam adeo puer, ut bellare recuset
talibus? Arcadiae stirpem et fera semina gentis,
non Thebana uides: non me sub nocte silenti
Thyias Echionio genetrix famulata Lyaeo
edidit, haud umquam deformes uertice mitras
induimus turpemque manu iactauimus hastam.
protinus astrictos didici reptare per amnes
horrendasque domos magnarum intrare ferarum
et – quid plura loquar? ferrum mea semper et arcus
mater habet, uestri feriunt caua tympana patres.'

'I bring these weapons against Thebes, whose army this is,
even too late; for who is such a boy that he would refuse to fight
such people? You see the root of Arcadia and fierce seed of a tribe
not Theban: I was not brought forth in the silent night
by a Thyiad mother enslaved to Echionian Bacchus;
I have never worn the disgraceful bonnet
on my head or brandished the shameful spear in my hand.
I learnt to crawl immediately on frozen rivers
and to go into the terrifying lairs of great wild beasts
and – why speak further? My mother always has a sword
and bow, your fathers batter hollow drums.'

---

[96] Compare Hippomedon at *Theb.* 9.476–80 questioning the manhood of the river Ismenus:

sic etiam increpitans: 'unde haec, Ismene, repente
ira tibi? quoue has traxisti gurgite uires,
imbelli famulate deo solumque cruorem
femineis experte choris, cum Bacchica mugit
buxus et insanae maculant trieterida matres?'

So ranting: 'Where has this sudden anger of yours come from,
Ismenus? Or from what pool have you drawn this strength,
slave of an unwarlike god and used to blood
only in women's dances, when the Bacchic box wood
bellows and the mad mothers stain the triennial festival?'

Statius here reworks the confrontation between Numanus Remulus and Ascanius, in which Numanus taunts the Trojans for being Phrygian women (*O uere Phrygiae neque enim Phryges*, 'O truly Phrygian women, not Phrygian men,' *Aeneid* 9.617); Ascanius answers the taunt with a single fatal bowshot, and Apollo congratulates him on becoming a man. In Statius' version, Parthenopaeus is accused of not being man enough and turns the rhetoric of manhood on his accuser, representing the Thebans in very similar terms to the Trojans while his Arcadian upbringing mirrors the idealised early Italian *duritia* (hardness) of Remulus and Camilla. Where Remulus taunts the Trojans for being women not men, Parthenopaeus emphatically contrasts his mother (at the beginning of the line) with their fathers (at the end). The gender reversal is on his side but he uses it to undermine their masculinity: my mother is more of a man than your fathers. His Arcadian roots replay Remulus' *durum a stirpe genus* ('a race hard from the roots'); Parthenopaeus takes it one further with the river endurance: while the Italians swim in icy waters as children, Parthenopaeus learnt to crawl on a frozen river. The *quid plura loquar* self-consciously cuts off the repetition of Remulus' rhetoric; Parthenopaeus has heard it all before, and so have we. The Theban worship of Bacchus replaces the Trojan worship of the Great Mother but both have their effeminate headgear (*mitrae, Aeneid* 9.616) and their drums (*tympana*, 619). Other elements of Remulus' speech, the dancing (*choreis*, 615) and the boxwood (*buxus*, 619) find their way into Hippomedon's taunt of Ismenus. In both cases, the taunt is shown to be empty rhetoric, much more emphatically in Virgil, with the immediate death of Remulus, while Parthenopaeus lives on for another hundred lines. This episode when read against Virgil shows Statius once again confounding the issues, bringing out the complexity of Virgil's almost civil war. In the *Aeneid*, we sympathised with the boy and his coming of age and despised Remulus; in Statius, we and the internal audience sympathise with Parthenopaeus – and with Amphion, whose speech expresses the sympathy that even the Thebans feel for him, despite his urgent desire to be taken seriously as a warrior.

There is no simple way of reading the identities of the Thebans and the Argives. In some senses, the Thebans are like the Trojans or the Carthaginians: the wild excesses of the tragic past suggest we can afford to take Parthenopaeus' accusations a little more seriously than Numanus'. On the other hand, Theban origins in the fratricide of the *spartae*, the men grown from the dragon's teeth, mirror Rome's origins in the fratricide of Romulus and Remus; the contorted familial chaos of the house of Oedipus would be worryingly familiar to those obsessed with imperial succession. Inasmuch as the *Thebaid* is a story about Thebes destroying itself, Thebes is Lucan's Rome. Yet the *Thebaid* is also a story about a conquering army that fails to conquer, an expedition to foreign parts that ends in chaotic retreat. The story is multivalent, and the inclusiveness of the Argive army allows different regional voices to splinter any idea of a united Greece. Identity and identification in the *Thebaid* are equally problematic; this war is more than civil in more than one sense.

5

THE WRESTLING

Introduction

We have seen how ancient poets use chariot racing and other sports to represent poetic competition. In modern critical literature, too, competition can be figured as a sporting contest. On the first page of Harold Bloom's seminal discussion of poetic competition, *Anxiety of Influence*, he uses the metaphor of wrestling: 'My concern is only with strong poets, major figures with the persistence to wrestle with their strong precursors, even to the death.' In this chapter, we will look closely at Statius' wrestling match and unpick its representations of intertextual competition. For the match offers itself as a textual and intertextual metaphor: the bodies of the competitors can be read as the bodies of poetic texts; the theme of paternal inheritance is a poetic anxiety as much as a heroic one; but, above all, the clear allusions to wrestling matches in Ovid and Lucan, and through them back to a tradition which includes Virgil, Apollonius and Homer, create an ever more complex process of reading the match, in which Statius is truly wrestling with tradition.

The challenge is to decide how to understand the significance of this metaphor. A wrestling match is an aggressive competition between two contestants; it is dichotomy in action. Critics are drawn to dichotomies as ways of articulating literary history. We can read Latin epic of the first century AD through many different dichotomies: Ovid versus Virgil; love versus war; innovation versus tradition; Callimachean versus epic. But if we agree that Statius' wrestling match can be read as a metapoetic narrative, which conflict is it representing, and which dichotomy is it displaying? And where is Statius in this?

Tydeus the Iliadic hero

Tydeus is the paradigmatic hero of Statius' wrestling match. At 6.826–30, the narrator comments that Tydeus was good at all the events and could have entered anything. These comments invite us to contrast the tight structure of Statius' games with the *Iliad*, where, for instance, Telamonian Ajax draws in both the wrestling and the sword fight, loses the discus, and then comes forward for the javelin.[1] Thus, when Tydeus' *conscia uirtus* self-consciously chafes against the tight authorial control, Statius is linking Tydeus with the multi-talented Iliadic heroes, proclaiming Tydeus' status as most Homeric (and most heroic) of the heroes.[2]

Tydeus enters the *Iliad* portrayed as an exemplary hero for his son Diomedes: at 4.365–421, Agamemnon accuses Diomedes of cowardice and degeneracy, of failure to live up to his father, and even his patron Athena mirrors this accusation at 5.800–813. Tydeus is specifically pre-Homeric, and shows Statius playing with the two time-lines in the *Thebaid*, the narrative of the myths, which places him earlier than Homer, as Homer's predecessor, and the narrative of intertextual competition, in which Tydeus is the son of Diomedes. Ironically, Tydeus, too, is worried about the problems of living up to his ancestry.[3] Throughout the *Thebaid*, we can see his inheritance: the issue of what it is to be a hero, of over-boldness, transgression of the barrier between mortal and divine, draws on the problems of Diomedes as he goes beyond the instructions of Athena and attacks Apollo. Like Diomedes, Tydeus is a great advocate of war, continually speaking out in favour of it.[4] In the catalogue of heroes in the proem, he comes first, the answer to the poet's question: *quem prius heroum, Clio, dabis?* ('who

---

[1] Odysseus wins the foot race and draws the wrestling; Antilochus enters both races; Diomedes wins the chariot race and draws the sword fight; Epeius wins the boxing but embarrasses himself in the discus; Meriones comes last in the chariot race and the archery and then comes forward for the javelin.

[2] Ripoll (1998) 314, 320 on Tydeus and his *conscia uirtus*. In the *Aeneid*, the phrase is used of Entellus (5.455), Turnus (12.668) and Mezentius (10.872); Ripoll contrasts Coroebus (who has *conscia uirtus* at 1.644) as an 'héros idéal' (320), whose heroism and *uirtus* is directed by *pietas* and consequently has moral value, rather than being an end in itself.

[3] His taunt to Polynices at 1.461–5 displays this simultaneous confidence in and worry about living up to his heroic lineage. Ripoll (1998) 24.

[4] *Thebaid* 3.336–44; 7.534–63; *Iliad* 9.32–49; 14.109–34.

will you give me first of the heroes, Clio?' 1.41). He is the pre-eminent warrior, the favourite of Athena, the hero who achieves the feat of single-handedly killing the battalion of Thebans sent to ambush him on his way back from Thebes, who would have received immortality from Athena if he had not fallen foul at the last minute of his life by chewing the head of his enemy.[5] In short, Tydeus is a symbol of the hero and has special significance for an understanding of Statius' negotiations with the epic genre. He is a heroic hero who parades his Homeric roots, an Iliadic not an Odyssean hero, a hero of war not love, a traditional rather than an innovative hero. But can this reading of Tydeus in the *Thebaid* survive the complex intertextual layers of the wrestling match?

Setting up the intertexts

Statius gives extremely strong signals that his wrestling should be read against Ovid's Hercules and Achelous episode.[6] To begin with, Tydeus has learnt his wrestling techniques 'around the shores of Achelous' (*Acheloia circum | litora*, 6.832–3) and though Statius only says that he has been taught by a god (*felicesque deo mon-strante palaestras*, 'with a god coaching in the blessed wrestling grounds', 6.833), it seems likely that this god was Achelous him-self.[7] Agylleus' Herculean descent puts him naturally into the role of Hercules. What is more, two of the similes in Statius' wrestling match have counterparts in the Ovidian episode. The bull simile at 6.864–7 echoes Ovid's bull simile at 9.46–9. So, too, the buried miner under the mountain at 880–85 recalls Achelous' complaint (56) that Hercules' weight on his back was like the weight of a mountain. Ovid's wrestling match is clearly an important intertext. The importance of the *Metamorphoses* for reading the *Thebaid* has long been underestimated: if we divide epics into the Ovidian and the Virgilian, the *Thebaid* always falls into the latter group. Hinds has suggested that the *Achilleid* is Statius' Ovidian epic, but this

---

[5] Becoming a bestial version of Hercules: Vessey (1970) 438; Ripoll (1998) 336–9.
[6] Ripoll (1998) 144 points out that the whole episode of the games is placed under the patronage of *pius Alcides*.
[7] Though Brown (1994) 37–8 and Vessey (1970) 435 assume that it was Hercules. This ambivalence is appropriate, given that Tydeus moves between the two roles.

needs to be taken further.[8] By giving the *Metamorphoses* their due in the *Thebaid*, we are left wondering how secure after all is the distinction between the Ovidian and the Virgilian.

An equally important intertext, however, is Lucan's description of the wrestling match of Hercules and Antaeus in book 4 of the *Bellum Ciuile*. Lucan is also a very important predecessor: in *Silvae* 2.7, Statius writes a poem of praise of the dead poet on the anniversary of his birth and ranks him above all other epic poets, even Virgil. Their shared subject-matter (civil war), the shared reluctance to perpetuate the war, along with the narrative that Jamie Masters, writing about Lucan, has termed the 'split voice', their shared characterisation as 'Silver' epic, all of these things bring Lucan and Statius very close together.[9] The clearest signal pointing to Lucan's wrestling match is the closing image of Agylleus and Tydeus as Hercules and Antaeus (6.893–6):

> Herculeis pressum sic fama lacertis
> terrigenam sudasse Libyn, cum fraude reperta
> raptus in excelsum, nec iam spes ulla cadendi,
> nec licet extrema matrem contingere planta.

> Thus *fama* tells that the earth-born Libyan, squeezed
> by the arms of Hercules, sweated, when he was snatched on high,
> after his deceit had been discovered, and there was no longer any
>   hope of falling,
> nor was he allowed to touch his mother with even the tip of his toes.

This is reinforced by the earlier moment, where Agylleus seems to be surreptitiously touching the earth for support, already taking on the role of Antaeus: *ac furtim rapta sustentat pectora terra* ('and he supports his chest furtively on the stolen earth', 6.875). The language of the two wrestling matches has much in common. Both Antaeus and Agylleus show the same signs of defeat: 'Antaeus' state of exhaustion is betrayed by frequent breaths and cold sweat': (*quod creber anhelitus illi | prodidit et gelidus fesso de corpore sudor*, BC 4.622–3); Agylleus is also gasping for breath, and his sweat pours off him like a river: *flatibus alternis aegroque effetus*

---

[8] Alison Keith's forthcoming work on Ovid's Theban narrative in the *Thebaid* will greatly redress this imbalance, but there remains much to be done on this complex relationship.
[9] See further Lovatt (1999).

hiatu | exuit ingestas fluuio sudoris harenas ('with heaving breath, worn out with sick gasps, he stripped off the caked sand in a river of sweat', *Thebaid* 6.873–4).[10] On the other hand, Tydeus' continued strength and toughness are more like Antaeus when he has been rejuvenated by contact with the earth. There is verbal similarity in the descriptions of the actual fighting, too, but as before it is hard to point to any one moment which replays another exactly. The words and ideas are woven together from Hercules' and Antaeus' first hold (4.617–19), Antaeus' first fall (4.626–9) and Hercules' final victory (4.649–50), and combined in Tydeus' first hold (6.860–63) and moment of triumph (6.889–90).

Both Ovid's wrestling match between Hercules and Achelous and Lucan's between Hercules and Antaeus, then, are signposted as important intertexts for Statius' wrestling. Yet these two matches also pull us back into a wider tradition of fights; we need to understand both Ovid's and Lucan's matches in relation to both their immediate contexts and the traditions with which they too are wrestling before we can attempt to understand the significance of this for reading Statius. Let us go back, then, and start from Hercules and Achelous.

Hercules and Achelous

Naturally, Ovid's wrestling match has metapoetic concerns. It is narrated by Achelous himself; when Theseus asks for the story, he underlines the irony of telling the story of his own defeat – glancing at Aeneas in *Aeneid* 2 (*Metamorphoses* 9.4–7):

> triste petis munus. quis enim sua proelia uictus
> commemorare uelit? referam tamen ordine, nec tam
> turpe fuit uinci, quam contendisse decorum est,
> magnaque dat nobis tantus solacia uictor.

> You seek a sad gift. For who wants to commemorate
> his own defeat in battle? Nevertheless, I will tell all in order;
> it was not so shameful to be conquered, as it is a distinction
> to have competed, and the stature of the victor gives great comfort to me.

---

[10] Here, too, Statius is outdoing and overdoing his predecessors; two phrases rather than one describe Agylleus' breathing; he is not merely out of breath, but almost gasping his last; the straightforward cold sweat has become a hyperbolic river.

Before they wrestle, Achelous begins a verbal *agon* (9.16–26) in which Hercules refuses to compete: *melior mihi dextera lingua:* | *dummodo pugnando superem, tu uince loquendo* ('my right hand is better than my tongue: as long as I conquer in a fight, you can win in speaking', 9.29–30). Achelous thus suggests that the wrestling match stands in for a battle of words, a battle which could have reversed the result of the wrestling.[11]

Galinsky has read the wrestling as an Ovidian reworking of the battle between Turnus and Aeneas.[12] Hercules (following on from *Aeneid* 8) in his role as civiliser is a predecessor for both Aeneas and Augustus; Achelous, then, becomes a version of Turnus. The most striking similarity comes in the bull simile (*Metamorphoses* 9.46–9):

> non aliter uidi fortes concurrere tauros,
> cum, pretium pugnae, toto nitidissima saltu
> expetitur coniunx: spectant armenta pauentque
> nescia, quem maneat tanti uictoria regni.

> In the same way I have seen brave bulls engage in battle,
> when a spouse is desired as the prize of the fight,
> the loveliest in the whole pasture: the ignorant herd watch
> and fear, wondering whom victory will give such a great reign.

Compare the above passage with *Aeneid* 12.716–22:

> cum duo conuersis inimica in proelia tauri
> frontibus incurrunt, pauidi cessere magistri,
> stat pecus omne metu mutum, mussantque iuuencae
> quis nemori imperitet, quem tota armenta sequantur;
> illi inter sese multa ui uulnera miscent
> cornuaque obnixi infigunt et sanguine largo
> colla armosque lauant, gemitu nemus omne remugit.

> When two bulls attack, locking horns in hostile
> battle, and the panic-stricken herdsmen retreat,
> and the whole herd stands silent with fear, and the heifers murmur,
> wondering who will rule the grove, whom the whole herd will follow,

---

[11] In opposition to the battle of words between Odysseus and Ajax in book 13, where a real fight might have reversed the result of the verbal agon.
[12] Galinsky (1972) 95–8 sees the relationship as one of banalisation and deflation.

and they share out wounds with much force and, struggling hard,
they fix their horns into each other and wash necks and shoulders
with generous blood, and the whole grove bellows back with groans.

The emphasis in both versions of the simile is on the herd waiting for the outcome, waiting to find out who will be their ruler.
This is strikingly inappropriate in the Ovidian version, where the
wrestling match is presented as simply and straightforwardly about
Deianira.[13] There is no great reign at stake. However, the *Aeneid*
is more easily read as essentially a fight over the love of a woman.
This simile also goes back to Virgil's description in *Georgics* 3 of
the effects of love on bulls (209–241), which ends with the famous
tag: *amor omnibus idem* ('love is the same for all', 244). The bulls
in the *Georgics* are inspired by love to fight, and they forget about
the realities of bovine life (216–17); love leads to defeat, dishonour
and exile.[14] In *Aeneid* 12, Lavinia has receded into the background;
Turnus and Aeneas fight for power, glory and revenge. Yet epic is
always open to readings which place love at the centre of all wars.[15]
In the interior proem of *Aeneid* 7, Virgil calls on Erato, the muse
of love poetry, to inspire his description of the war (37–44).[16] This
echoes Apollonius' interior proem of *Argonautica* 3, which does
lead into the love story of Medea. Ovid's wrestling match rereads
the *Aeneid* as essentially a love poem.[17] It is not a parody of epic,
but a reading which brings the alternative stream of epic into the
foreground and reclassifies the *Aeneid* as part of that stream: love
is more important than war.

The wrestling match between Hercules and Achelous also
looks back to the *Argonautica*, most noticeably through the rock
metaphor, which we have come across above (p. 159). Jason is

---

[13] The opening lines of Sophocles *Trachiniae* take Deianira's point of view while watching
the conflict; the emphasis is soundly on her emotions, with little detail of the wrestling
match itself (perhaps a traditional male representation of the female gaze).

[14] Hershkowitz (1994) follows this trail as she analyses bull similes in the whole *Thebaid*.
See also Hardie (1993) 23.

[15] For instance, Ovid *Heroides* 1, 3; *Amores* 2.12.17–22.

[16] Kyriakidis (1994) maintains that this invocation is more about the relationship between
the poet and the Muses than about love and war, and is reluctant to read the *Aeneid* as a
poem of love.

[17] *Metamorphoses* 9.27 echoes a line from the confrontation of Aeneas and Dido (*Aeneid*
4.362), reinforcing this reading.

compared to a rocky reef withstanding the blast of the waves as the bulls charge him (*Argonautica* 3.1293–5):

> αὐτὰρ ὁ τούσγε,
> εὖ διαβάς, ἐπιόντας, ἅτε σπιλὰς εἰν ἁλὶ πέτρη
> μίμνεν ἀπειρεσίῃσι δονεύμενα κύματ' ἀέλλαις.

But he, setting his feet well apart, withstands them attacking
just like a rocky reef in the sea withstands the waves
stirred up by endless storms.

This is transferred to Achelous, withstanding the furious attack of Hercules (*Metamorphoses* 9.40–41):

> haud secus ac moles, magno quam murmure fluctus
> oppugnat; manet illa, suoque est pondere tuta.

No differently does a rock stand against the waves with their great
roar; he remains, and is safe in his own weight.

Ovid's description of Hercules wrestling Achelous in bull form is also reminiscent of Jason actually bringing the bulls physically under the yoke (*Argonautica* 3.1306–9):

> καί ῥ' ὅγε δεξιτεροῖο βοὸς κέρας ἄκρον ἐρύσσας
> εἷλκεν ἐπικρατέως παντὶ σθένει, ὄφρα πελάσσῃ
> ζεύγλῃ χαλκείῃ, τὸν δ' ἐν χθονὶ κάββαλεν ὀκλάξ,
> ῥίμφα ποδὶ κρούσας πόδα χάλκεον.

And he took hold of the tip of the horn of the right-hand bull,
dragging it down forcefully with all his strength, and brought it near
to the bronze yoke, and threw it down to the ground in a squat,
striking its bronze foot swiftly with his foot.

See (*Metamorphoses* 9.82–4):

> induit ille toris a laeua parte lacertos
> admissumque trahens sequitur, depressaque dura
> cornua figit humo, meque alta sternit harena.

He put his arms around my muscles from the left,
and when I had been allowed to run, he followed dragging,
and pushed my horns down and stuck them in the hard earth,
and laid me out on the deep sand.

Ovid's Hercules, then, takes on the role of Apollonius' Jason. Herakles is an important figure in the *Argonautica*: he has been read as a paradigm of heroism; he defeats the entire crew put together in a rowing endurance contest (1.1153–71); after they accidentally leave him behind searching for Hylas, they frequently despair that they will not be able to succeed without him. Most importantly, he provides a contrast for Jason: Jason is a new type of hero, whose skills lie in the area of love as much as in the area of war.[18] When they have to choose a leader, Herakles is the obvious choice, but he resigns in favour of Jason (1.336–47). Jason and Herakles can be read as opposite paradigms of heroism; in their contrast, they dramatise the contrast between the alternative streams of epic.

Apollonius' *Argonautica* has no set-piece epic games as such; however, the Homeric events are scattered throughout the text in tangential versions. Apollonius depicts the chariot race of Pelops and Oenomaus in the ekphrasis of the cloak (1.752–8) which Jason wears to seduce Hypsipyle; then comes the boxing match between Amycus and Polydeukes at 2.1–153. The pursuit of the Harpies by Zetes and Calais can be seen as a race: the simile of the hunting dogs breathing on the necks of their prey (2.278–83) is reminiscent of Odysseus breathing on Ajax's neck at *Iliad* 23.763–6. In the same way, Jason's feats in book 3 can be read as two more Homeric games. The taming of the bulls is presented as a wrestling match, and the hurling of the weight is represented by the huge rock which Jason throws in among the Earthborn: at 3.1366, the boulder is a σόλος ('mass' – also used of the discus in *Iliad* 23). Aeetes and the Argonauts going to watch Jason's feat with the bulls are compared to the audience of games. Aeetes is described as being like Poseidon going in his chariot to the Isthmian games at 3.1240–45. The Argonauts are also an audience going to games (ἀέθλων), and the distance between the coast and the site of the contest is described by reference to a chariot race at funeral games.[19] This

---

[18] The nature of Jason's heroism is a focus of scholarship: Lawall (1966); Beye (1969). For a masterly summary of the different trends, see Hunter (1988). Other recent work on the subject: Clauss (1993); Hunter (1993) 8–35; DeForest (1994) 47–69; Pietsch (1999) 99–151. Hunter (1988) links the presentation of Jason with the novelty of Apollonius' approach to epic: 'If Jason sometimes resembles the great heroes of Homer and sometimes wears a quite different aspect, it is because of Apollonius' constant concern with the experimental, with testing the limits and the possibilities of the epic form and with exploring what it has seemed to take for granted.'

[19] Jason's feats are described as ἀέθλοι, as are Hercules' labours; heroic achievements have a semantic link to athletic achievements.

fragmentation of the narrative and ritual of epic, this stark decon-
struction of epic games, carries a strong metaliterary claim to be
writing a new sort of epic, an alternative, Alexandrian statement
of difference from Homer. When Ovid brings Apollonius into his
equally fragmented, revolutionary epic narrative, in the contest of
a wrestling match, but not epic games as such, he both reads Apollonius as his predecessor and authorises his own alternative version
of epic.

Hercules and Antaeus

Let us now turn to Lucan's wrestling match, and examine the context and significance of Hercules and Antaeus in the *Bellum Ciuile*
and its games with epic tradition. Lucan's Hercules and Antaeus
episode is an excursus from the main narrative, a story told by
an anonymous peasant to Caesar's legate, Curio.[20] Curio lands in
Africa near to the site of Zama, the battle in which Scipio Africanus
defeated Hannibal at the end of the second Punic war. This was
a pivotal point for Rome and empire: the moment when Rome
became a world power. After hearing the story of Hercules and
Antaeus, Curio fights Varus, his Pompeian opposition, and wins.
However, he is then beaten in turn by Juba, represented by Lucan
not as a Pompeian but as an African, descendant of Jugurtha and
Hannibal. This moment of Roman defeat foreshadows the battle
of Thapsus, in which two Roman armies, each commanded by a
Scipio, murder each other. It is an inversion of Scipio's success, an
African revenge for Roman imperial conquest, or so Lucan sug-
gests (*BC* 4.788–90):

> excitet inuisas dirae Carthaginis umbras
> inferiis Fortuna nouis, ferat ista cruentus
> Hannibal et Poeni tam dira piacula manes.

> Let Fortune rouse the hostile shades of grim Carthage
> with new sacrifices, let bloody Hannibal
> and the Carthaginian shades accept such a grim atonement.

[20] Ahl (1976) 82–115 devotes a grim chapter to Curio's adventures in Africa, entitled *Sangre
y arena*, which reads the blood and sand in the African desert as a sort of gladiatorial
arena in which the soldiers of the civil war are gladiators and human sacrifices to the
dead.

The destruction of Carthage and the Carthaginians is paid for by the civil war, by Rome destroying herself. Ahl reads this episode against the backdrop of *Aeneid* 8.[21] In wide terms, Curio becomes a sort of anti-Aeneas, venturing to Africa, like Aeneas going upriver to Evander's city, hearing a tale of Hercules, fighting a battle. As Ahl puts it: 'Curio is in almost every respect the complete opposite of Aeneas, a shrivelled and degraded caricature of the Roman spirit.'[22] If the *Aeneid* is fundamentally a narrative of the foundation of Roman *imperium*, Lucan writes its destruction, and as Aeneas founds the Roman empire by proxy, so Curio destroys it. In this wider context, the story of Hercules and Antaeus corresponds to the story of Hercules and Cacus.

The narrative frame of the story itself can also be read against the *Aeneid*. As Ahl points out, this story is told not by a refugee king like Evander but by a *rudis incola*, an unnamed peasant, representative of the oral traditions of the land (4.591–2):

> nominis antiqui cupientem noscere causas
> cognita per multos docuit rudis incola patres:

> A crude peasant taught Curio, desiring to know the causes
> of the ancient name, what was known through many generations of fathers.

The juxtaposition of *docuit* with *rudis* brings out the irony of the illiterate teaching the Roman high command about Roman history. The authority of tradition is not linked to the authority of kingship but the anonymity of myth. The narrator and the narratee have no obvious connection with each other, and little clear connection with the story. In the *Aeneid*, the narrative reason for the Hercules and Cacus episode is to explain the origins of the festival of Hercules which Evander and his people are celebrating. The praise of Hercules is a very concrete reason for telling the story, a strong link between frame and story. Thematically, too, Hercules' conquest of the bestial Cacus has a strong link with the main narrative threads of the *Aeneid*. For instance, Galinsky presents Hercules as a version of both Aeneas and Augustus, a civilising force bringing peace to the world.[23] This association can also work the other way. Hercules

---

[21] Ahl (1976) following Thompson and Bruère (1970) 167–72.
[22] Ahl (1976) 93–4.   [23] Galinsky (1990).

is assimilated to Cacus, portrayed as violent and bestial and terrifying in a similar way.[24] The 'pessimists' would then link this ambivalence to Aeneas and Augustus, assimilating them to their enemies.

It is difficult to see Lucan's Hercules and Antaeus episode itself in the same way. As a reason for the narrative, the aetiology and play on naming seem weak: why does Curio not know where he is? Surely he must be aware of both the mythical and historical associations of his landing point? The reader is drawn to look for parallels with the wider text, and must try to find a way of linking Hercules and Antaeus, Hannibal and Scipio, Juba and Curio. Bruère and Thompson want to read Curio as a version of Antaeus and Hannibal, defeated on African soil.[25] This makes the African (and Pompeian) Juba the true inheritor of Rome. Ahl finds this unsatisfactory: Curio is the Roman against barbarians Hannibal and Antaeus; although he is defeated, he is the Roman defeated by the African. 'In the case of Hercules and Scipio, the "right" side wins. But in Juba's case, victory has gone to the "wrong" side.'[26] Lucan's own story, the narrative present, is a story forever disrupted and wrong. The great paradigms from myth and history are there as anti-exempla, to bring out the full unreadability of civil war.

Going further than Ovid and Lucan

Statius takes on these traditions and overcomes them; he represents himself as the ultimate innovator, beating Ovid and Lucan at their own game. He continually overtakes and exceeds the Ovidian wrestling. Going back to the bull similes, let us look at Statius' version (*Thebaid* 6.864–7):

> non sic ductores gemini gregis horrida tauri
> bella mouent; medio coniunx stat candida prato
> uictorem expectans, rumpunt obnixa furentes
> pectora, subdit amor stimulos et uulnera sanat:

---

[24] See Morgan (1998) for a complex and multifaceted reading of the episode, which makes many twists and turns.

[25] Thompson and Bruère (1970) 167–72.   [26] Ahl (1976) 102.

Not so intensely do twin bulls, leaders of the herd,
stir up terrible war; the white spouse stands in the middle
    of the meadow
waiting for the victor and raging they burst their struggling
chests, love applies spurs and heals their wounds:

The first two lines of Statius' reworking are extraordinarily Ovid-ian. Ovid uses the word *coniunx* ('spouse', 9.48) to describe the female audience in a way which makes concrete the link between Virgil's simile and Aeneas' and Turnus' fight for Lavinia; Statius recognises the importance of the word by repeating it. Ovid puts the adjective *nitidissima* ('extremely bright', 9.47) describing the *coniunx* literally inside the *toto saltu* ('whole pasture'); the pasture both contains the *coniunx* and at the same time she represents it. Winning her is equivalent to winning the land. Statius echoes this trick of word order and comments on it by making it more elab-orate and obvious: *medio coniunx stat candida prato* ('the white spouse stands in the middle of the meadow'). This is a descrip-tion of Ovid's word order, which takes it further with *stat* dead in the middle, surrounded by the *coniunx* and her epithet, in turn surrounded by the meadow and its epithet. Statius' method of intro-ducing his simile also makes a claim to surpass Ovid: *non sic* ('not thus') is in the same position as *non aliter* ('not otherwise') but means exactly the opposite; while Ovid uses a formula to mark the comparison, Statius claims that narrative reality exceeds the capacity of this simile to convey it. There is a peculiarly Statian twist to the description of the bulls as *ductores gemini* ('twin lead-ers') which hints at the fratricide to come, and the phrase *horrida bella mouent* recalls *Aeneid* 7 and the internal proem: *dicam hor-rida bella* (41); *maius opus moueo* (44). The third and fourth lines of Statius' simile, however, are far more Virgilian, looking back, as it were, through the *Metamorphoses* to its Virgilian models: *uictorem expectans* ('waiting for a victor') summarises the next two lines of Ovid's simile, which stops there – but Statius goes on, as in *Aeneid* 12, to describe the carnage of the fight, echo-ing Virgil with *obnixa*. He then goes back one stage further still, through to the *Georgics* and the description of bulls fighting, which is the model for the simile in *Aeneid* 12:[27] *subdit amor stimulos et uulnera sanat* echoes *caeci stimulos amoris* (*Georgics* 3.210), bringing out a paradoxical sense in which love is blind because it makes the combatants unaware of the pain of the wounds it causes. This self-conscious display of intertextual virtuosity is still not enough for Statius. He adds a further twist to this well-used simile by making his wrestlers metamorphose into boars and bears as well (6.868–9):

> fulmineo sic dente sues, sic hispida turpes
> proelia uillosis ineunt complexibus ursi.

> In the same way boars with teeth like lightning flashes
> and ugly bears enter their bristling battles with
> shaggy embraces.

Where Ovid rereads Virgil by putting love back into the motivations for his fight, Statius comments again by emphasising the stimulus of love when here there really is not even an ostensible love interest in the fight. In this simile, we can see Statius weaving together the different strands of intertextual influence and simultaneously portraying himself as the pinnacle of this long series of achievements. He wrestles with tradition, but far from being buried under its weight, he lifts it high and throws it to the ground.

In the simile of the miner buried under the mountain, Statius exceeds both Ovid and Lucan. Achelous makes the simple statement that Hercules' weight was like a mountain on his back (*inposito pressus mihi monte uidebar*, 'I seemed to be pressed down by a mountain on top of me', *Metamorphoses* 9.55). When Hercules is about to lift up Antaeus, he demands that if Antaeus falls, he should only fall on Hercules himself, so that he does not touch the ground: *huc, Antaee, cades* ('you will fall here, Antaeus', Lucan 4.649). Statius takes the plot situation from Lucan (Agylleus

---

[27] In particular, *Georgics* 3.220–23 are the precursors of *Aeneid* 12.720–22: *illi alternantes multa ui proelia miscent | uulneribus crebris; lauit ater corpora sanguis, | uersaque in obnixos urgentur cornua uasto | cum gemitu; reboant siluaeque et longus Olympus.* ('Alternately they mix battle and frequent wounds with much force; black blood washes their bodies, and they drive in their horns, turned on the struggle with a vast groan; the woods and tall Olympus echo it back.' *Georgics* 3.220–23)

falls on Tydeus) and the imagery from Ovid, making it literal and inflating it so hyperbolically that it is difficult to see how Tydeus does manage to escape (6.880–85):

> haud aliter collis scrutator Hiberi,
> cum subiit longeque diem uitamque reliquit,
> si tremuit suspensus agger subitumque fragorem
> rupta dedit tellus, latet intus monte soluto
> obrutus, ac penitus fractum obtritumque cadauer
> indignantem animam propriis non reddidit astris.

> Not otherwise does the miner of the Spanish hills,
> when he goes underground and left far behind both day and life,
> if the hanging rampart has trembled and the broken earth
> has given a sudden crash, he hides inside, overwhelmed
> by the mountain released, and deep inside his broken and crushed
> corpse does not give back his indignant soul to the stars where it belongs.

This jarring image, which blurs rather than clarifies the workings of the wrestling match, as we have seen above (p. 46), is the realisation of possibilities in Ovid and Lucan, and the hyperbolic culmination of the idea of a wrestling match with the earth.

A metapoetic narrative?

Statius' wrestling match dramatises a contest over paternity. Agylleus attempts to prove that he can live up to his physical descent from Hercules, while Tydeus is a rival for this inheritance. He follows in the footsteps of Hercules: Athena is his patron, and at the end of his aristeia she sets out to bring him immortality: *iamque inflexo Tritonia patre | uenerat et misero decus immortale ferebat* ('and now Tritonia had come, when she had persuaded her father, and was bringing immortal glory to the wretched man', 8.758–9). Throughout the wrestling, Agylleus emphatically fails to live up to Hercules.[28] He is introduced as someone who boasts of his lineage;

---

[28] There is another son of Hercules in the games, Chromis, in the chariot race: *alter satus Hercule magno* (346); *Herculeum Chromin* (464); *Tirynthius heros* (489). Chromis does live up to his father when he overtakes Hippodamus: *uiribus Herculeis et toto robore patris* (480) but he gives up his chance of winning when he stops to save Hippodamus from being eaten by his horses. At the end, it is Amphiaraus who then takes the role of Hercules when he receives as his prize a drinking bowl that had belonged to Hercules

he equals Hercules in physical size, but he does not have the hardness or strength of his father. Most dramatically, Tydeus becomes a Hercules figure in his moment of victory, and Agylleus is relegated to the role of Antaeus. Tydeus, by winning the wrestling, supplants Agylleus in his position as 'son of Hercules'. This seems to be a strong claim on Statius' part to subsume and surpass all his predecessors: Tydeus begins as Achelous and ends by taking the role of Hercules as well. He fuses his models into one paradigm of heroism.

The lavish physical descriptions of the wrestlers have poetic connotations. Agylleus is huge but lacking in strength (6.836–42):

> leuat ardua contra
> membra Cleonaeae stirpis iactator Agylleus,
> Herculea nec mole minor, sic grandibus alte
> insurgens umeris hominem super improbus exit.
> sed non ille rigor patriumque in corpore robur;
> luxuriant artus, effusaque sanguine laxo
> membra natant

> Agylleus, who boasts about his Cleonaean roots,
> lifts his tall frame against him,
> not less in mass than Hercules, rising so loftily
> with his huge shoulders, he stands out monstrous above men.
> But he does not have the stiffness and strength of his father in his body;
> his limbs run riot, and his sprawling appendages swim with excess blood.

His size is not an advantage to him because it is badly utilised: he is so unfit that he weighs himself down. He is excessive, but his excess does not translate itself into power. Tydeus, on the other hand, is tightly constructed and heavy within his small size: *quamquam ipse uideri | exiguus grauia ossa tamen nodisque lacerti | difficiles* ('Although he himself seems scanty, nevertheless his bones are heavy and his arms knot tough with muscle', 6.843–5). Throughout the fight, the emphasis is on the competing bodies of the wrestlers. Tydeus remains unaffected by the physical labours: he remains as hard as ever (870–72):

(6.531–9). At 2.613–28, Tydeus fights (and kills) another Chromis, who claims a Herculean role by wearing a lion skin and carrying a club (618–19). Mulder (1954) 318 calls this Chromis an 'alterum Herculem'. Vessey (1970) 437 makes another link to his aristeia in 2: lifting Agylleus at 890–91 is like lifting the huge rock 2.561–4.

uis eadem Oenidae; nec sole aut puluere fessa
membra labant, riget arta cutis durisque laborum
castigataque toris.

Tydeus has the same force; his limbs do not slip,
tired by sun or dust; his skin, taut and trim with the hard
muscles of toil, is stiff.

However, Agylleus is coming to pieces (872–5):

> contra non integer ille
> flatibus alternis aegroque effetus hiatu
> exuit ingestas fluuio sudoris harenas
> ac furtim rapta sustentat pectora terra.

He, on the other hand, is no longer whole;
worn out with panting breaths and sick gasps,
he sheds the caked sand in a river of sweat
and supports his chest on the furtively grabbed earth.

The plot of the fight is determined by their contrasting physiques.
At the beginning, Tydeus forces Agylleus to destroy his height
advantage by bending over (851–3):

> iam tunc astu deducit in aequum
> callidus et celsum procuruat Agyllea Tydeus,
> summissus tergo et genibus uicinus harenae.

Now crafty Tydeus in his cunning draws himself down on the level,
with his back bent down and his knees next to the sand,
and makes high Agylleus bend forward.

Later, Tydeus' shortness foils his attempt to grab Agylleus' legs:
frustratae brevitate manus ('his arms were frustrated by their shortness' 878), and the hugeness of Agylleus' body becomes a weapon
as it crushes him with its weight.

Texts and bodies were linked in ancient literary criticism. For
instance, Seneca (*Epistulae Morales* 114) condemns Maecenas'
literary style in terms of gender, physical style, mannerisms of
dress and deportment.[29] Masculinity is a quality of texts as much
and in the same way as it is a quality of posture, physiognomy, dress
and gait. Maecenas is accused by Seneca of *mollitia* ('softness'),

---

[29] Graver (1998) 607 *Non oratio eius aeque soluta est quam ipse discinctus?* (Seneca
Epistulae Morales 114.4). Cf. Seneca *Controuersiae* 6–10; Persius *Satires* 1.

precisely the quality which characterises Agylleus' physique.[30] Agylleus' excessiveness is also a quality of effeminate style, as is his looseness; whereas Tydeus is tightly constructed and whole. Graver summarises the 'metaphoric pattern which associates the term "masculine" with writing which is tightly structured, well integrated and consistent.'[31]

Further, *corpus* spans both the physical body of the author and the metaphorical body of his works. Farrell has shown that this double usage was not a dead metaphor but one that extended itself into bodily metaphors in wider discussions of poetic works, most famously in Horace's description of the rearranged words of epic as *disiecti membra poetae* ('the limbs of a poet torn apart', *Sat.* 1.4.62).[32] Thinking of poetry in terms of a physical body corresponds with the presentation of literary style as posture and gait. The bodies of our wrestlers, then, on which the drama of the wrestling match is played out, can be read as the poetic bodies of texts or characterisations of literary style.

Who is this fight between, then? The moment of the mining image fits well with a reading of the match as a fight between the *Metamorphoses* and the *Aeneid*. The physical descriptions throughout the course of the fight are resonant of these two very different narrative structures: the tightly constructed, serious, spirited *Aeneid* fights the overblown, luxuriant, loose *Metamorphoses*. Statius traces the limitations of both: while Ovid does not last (Agylleus is too unfit), Virgil is too limited (Tydeus' arms are too short). This then makes sense of the crux of the match, where the sheer mass of the *Metamorphoses* is overcome purely by the keenness of the spirit of the *Aeneid*. Alternatively, to move away from

---

[30] Graver (1998) 612–13. Agylleus is *mollis* in contrast to Tydeus' *duritia*.
[31] Graver (1998) 620.
[32] Farrell (1999) 130–31. Other ancient uses of this metaphor include: Cicero, *Letter to Quintus* 2.13; Suetonius *Vita Horatii*; Ulpian *Digest* 32.52; Ausonius *Epistles* 10.29. See also Most (1992) 407–8; Svenbro (1984). *Caput, corpus, lumen, membrum,* and *pes* all are used to conceptualise the text. *Forma* then must surely also refer to the arrangement of words as much as the arrangement of body parts. Most reads the Neronian fascination with amputation in terms of Seneca's amputated style, but refuses to be pinned down to any further conclusion. The idea of the 'split voice' seems peculiarly appropriate in this context: perhaps mutilation, fragmentation and suicide are more at issue here than amputation. Not only did critics see poetry as a body, but poets saw poetry as a body that can destroy itself.

the dichotomy of Ovidianism versus Virgilianism, perhaps this should rather be a fight between the two obvious intertexts, Ovid and Lucan, a fight over who is the true inheritor of Virgil, or perhaps who is the most effective anti-Aeneid. The physical descriptions of Tydeus fit Lucan's abbreviated text even better; both competitors, then, have Hercules/Virgil as the forefather/model who achieved the apotheosis of lasting literary success.

So specific an allegorical interpretation has its attractions, but a more general opposition between styles or ideas must be more plausible. The contest over paternity could be read in terms of innovation and tradition. The literal birthright of Agylleus, along with his weight and size, would make him into a plausible repre-sentation of literary tradition. Tydeus, on the other hand, stealing his paternal role model, small, tight and clever in his tactics, is a version of poetic innovation, successfully appropriating prede-cessors into a bizarre new relationship. The irony of this reading, of course, is that the *Thebaid* has often been read as the most traditional of epics (although I hope one by-product of this book will be to show the manifold and varied ways in which Statius innovates and self-consciously plays with tradition and his place in it).

Beyond metapoetics: the reality of earth

There is something hollow about metapoetic narratives as an end in themselves.[33] I want to leave behind that level of reading now, and bring together themes of land, earth and conquest which char-acterise this whole series of wrestling matches, starting with the match which lies behind both Ovid and Lucan: Hercules and Cacus.

Both the wrestling matches of Ovid and Lucan have been read against the fight between Hercules and Cacus; the participation of Hercules makes this move almost inevitable. But can the fight between Hercules and Cacus be read as a wrestling match? Not

---

[33] Thompson and Bruère (1970) 169 deny that there is any further significance to Lucan's wrestling match: 'A desire to out-Ovid Ovid appears to be the sole purpose of Lucan's pastiche ... Similarly, no evocative significance need be attached to Lucan's use of Virgil's short account of the actual seizure of Cacus by Hercules.'

simply and straightforwardly: the main problem is that they do not actually meet until right at the end of the story. When Cacus realises how terrifying Hercules is in his anger, he hides in his cave and fortifies it with rocks. Only after tearing the landscape itself apart can Hercules finally make contact with his opponent. When he does, the fight is over immediately (*Aeneid* 8.259–61):

> hic Cacum in tenebris incendia uana uomentem
> corripit in nodum complexus, et angit inhaerens
> elisos oculos et siccum sanguine guttur.

> Here he snatched Cacus, vomiting vain fires in the shadows,
> in the knot of his embrace, and sticking to him, throttled him
> until his eyes were forced out and his throat was dry of blood.

This fight in a moment, however, is described in terms of a miniature wrestling match: the final moments of Statius' match share its vocabulary. After escaping from under him, Tydeus sticks to Agylleus' back: *tergo necopinus inhaeret* ('he sticks to his back unexpectedly', 6.888) and Agylleus is unable to escape from his knotty grip: *premens euadere nodos | nequiquam...parantem* ('pressing him as he tries in vain to escape from his grasp', 6.890–91).[34] Wrestling monsters (or people) to death is a common Herculean motif.[35] Inasmuch as this is a fight, it is a wrestling match. We could take it further, however, and read the rest of his feat too as a sort of wrestling match. For the extraordinary achievement of Hercules is to wrestle with the mountain itself in which Cacus is hiding.

When Evander begins the story, it starts from the landscape (*Aeneid* 8.190–92):

---

[34] Thompson and Bruère (1970) 169 point to echoes of the same words in Lucan's wrestling, at 632 (*Herculeosque nouo laxauit corpore nodos*) and 648 (*haerebis pressis intra mea pectora membris*).

[35] In Virgil, he kills Eryx in a boxing match, but Apollodorus makes it a wrestling match. On the way back from acquiring the cattle of Geryon, he loses a bull: εὑρὼν δὲ ἐν ταῖς τοῦ Ἔρυκος ἀγέλαις, λέγοντος οὐ δώσειν ἂν μὴ παλαίσας αὐτοῦ περιγένηται, τρὶς περιγενόμενος κατὰ τὴν πάλην ἀπέκτεινε. ('Finding the bull in the herds of Eryx, when the king refused to give it to him unless Herakles should beat him at wrestling, he threw him three times and killed him during the wrestling.' Apollodorus *Bibliotheca* 2.5.10) In other wrestling matches recorded by Apollodorus, Herakles kills Polygonus and Telegonus (2.5.9) and Menoetes son of Ceuthonymus (2.5.12).

iam primum saxis suspensam hanc aspice rupem
disiectae procul ut moles desertaque montis
stat domus et scopuli ingentem traxere ruinam.

Now straightaway look at this cliff hung from rocks,
how far away the house stands, a deserted mass
of torn apart mountain, and the crags have dragged down a huge ruin.

The physical remnants of the fight are displayed in the mountain;
the ruin of Cacus is identified with the ruin of his landscape. In the
wrestling in *Iliad* 23, the wrestlers themselves, propped against
each other in a mutually unmoving grasp, are compared to a house
(*Iliad* 23.710–13):

ζωσαμένω δ᾽ἄρα τώ γε βάτην ἐς μέσσον ἀγῶνα,
ἀγκὰς δ᾽ἀλλήλων λαβέτην χερσὶ στιβαρῆσιν
ὡς ὅτ᾽ἀμείβοντες, τούς τε κλυτὸς ἤραρε τέκτων,
δώματος ὑψηλοῖο, βίας ἀνέμων ἀλεείνων.

And the two of them went into the middle, girded for the contest,
and they grasped each other in an embrace with their strong hands,
just as when planks alternate, which a famous builder fitted together,
of a high house, avoiding the forces of the winds.

Cacus' rocky lair is a craftsman's work as well as his house (*domus*,
8.192): he blocks the entrance with a rock like a door (*Aeneid*
8.225–7):

ut sese inclusit ruptisque immane catenis
deiecit saxum, ferro quod et arte paterna
pendebat, fultosque emuniit obice postis

Having broken the chains, he threw down a huge rock
to shut himself in, which used to hang there by iron
and his paternal skill, and fortified the supported doorposts with a barricade.

Statius' wrestlers, in a moment of stalemate at the beginning of
the fight, are similarly architectural: *interdumque diu pendent per
mutua fulti | bracchia* ('meanwhile for a long time they hang, sup-
ported by each other's arms', *Thebaid* 6.862–3). When Hercules
attacks this obstacle, he is defeated three times and ends in stalemate (*Aeneid* 8.230–32):

> ter totum feruidus ira
> lustrat Auentini montem, ter saxea temptat
> limina nequiquam, ter fessus ualle resedit.

Three times, seething with anger, he scrutinises the whole
mountain of the Aventine; three times he attacks the rocky threshold
in vain; three times, exhausted, he sits back down in the valley.

In the *Iliad*, three bouts end in stalemate: Odysseus throws Ajax,
both come down together and Achilles stops the match in the third
round. In Ovid, Hercules wrestles Achelous in three different forms
and beats him in each, as god, snake and bull. In Lucan, there are
also three rounds: the first fall comes at 4.626–9, the second at 640–
42 and the third (and fatal) round, in which Hercules squeezes
Antaeus to death in mid-air, at 649–53. Just as in the wrestling
match with Antaeus, Virgil's Hercules uses some lateral thinking
to break the stalemate, tearing open the mountain from its peak
(*Aeneid* 8.236–9):

> hanc, ut prona iugo laeuum incumbebat ad amnem,
> dexter in aduersum nitens concussit et imis
> auulsam soluit radicibus, inde repente
> impulit;

This peak, as it leaned forward from the ridge towards the stream on the
left, his right hand shook, struggling against it, and loosed
it, torn up from its very roots, and from there suddenly
pushed it over.

The response from the landscape is one of terror: *impulsu quo max-
imus intonat aether, | dissultant ripae refluitque exterritus amnis*
('at which attack, the great aether thunders, the banks of the river
jump apart and the stream itself flows backwards, terrified', 8.239–
40). This is destruction on a cosmic scale, underlined by the simile
which follows, describing Cacus and his cave revealed to the world
as like the dead and the Underworld terrified when they are opened
up to daylight.[36] Hercules, then, wrestles with a (hellish) landscape
of Italy and literally turns it upside down.

The other wrestling matches, too, can be read as wrestling with
landscape. Although Achelous does not fight Hercules as a river,

---

[36] Statius will make this image reality in books 8 and 9 when Amphiaraus is swallowed by
the earthquake.

he is part of the landscape as well as a god. Lucan makes much of Antaeus as offspring of the earth (4.593–7):

> nondum post genitos Tellus effeta gigantas
> terribilem Libycis partum concepit in antris.
> nec tam iusta fuit genetricis gloria Typhon
> aut Tityos Briareusque ferox; caeloque pepercit,
> quod non Phlegraeis Antaeum sustulit aruis.

> After the birth of the giants, Earth, not yet worn out,
> conceived a terrifying birth in the Libyan caves.
> Nor was Typhon or Tityos or fierce Briareus so
> justly a glory for their mother; she spared the sky,
> because she did not raise up Antaeus on the Phlegraean fields.

Antaeus is earthborn, like the giants and monsters destroyed by the gods. He is a monster emerging from Libyan caves, but specifically held back from the cosmic disorder and destruction of gigantomachy. Again in 598–600, the personification of earth as parent is at the fore (4.598–600):

> hoc quoque tam uastas cumulauit munere uires
> Terra sui fetus, quod, cum tetigere parentem,
> iam defecta uigent renouato robore membra.

> The earth also heaped this gift on top of the vast strength
> of her offspring, that, when they touched their parent,
> immediately their failing limbs flourish with renewed robustness.

The language describing the gift (*uastas cumulauit uires*, 'she piled up vast strength') suggests a continuity between the earth and her offspring, that she heaps more strength onto his vastness, like mountain piled on mountain. The link between Antaeus and earth becomes more and more pronounced, until he seems to be draining the earth of its power (4.643–4):

> quisquis inest terris in fessos spiritus artus
> egeritur, tellusque uiro luctante laborat.

> Whatever breath there is in the earth is drawn out
> into his tired limbs, and the earth labours with the struggling hero.

Hercules is competing with the earth, not just Antaeus: *conflixere pares, Telluris uiribus ille, | ille suis* ('they competed as equals, one with the strength of the earth, the other with his own strength',

4.636–7). Juno, the divine audience watching the spectacle, makes a connection between this match and Hercules' brief spell as a mountain (4.637–9):

> numquam saevae sperare nouercae
> plus licuit; uidet exhaustos sudoribus artus
> cervicemque uiri, siccam cum ferret Olympum.

Never was it allowed for the savage stepmother to hope more:
she sees limbs and neck of the hero drained with sweat;
even bearing Olympus it was dry.

This passage equates Hercules' battle with the earth with his feat of taking on the role of Atlas and carrying the weight of the heavens. And this is worse. It is a truly cosmic battle.

In all three contests, when Hercules the conquering hero takes on a native monster, he seems to be wrestling with the landscape itself. Another Herculean wrestling match, as told by Diodorus Siculus, brings out these themes even more explicitly. This version of Hercules' contest with Eryx in Sicily makes it a wrestling match, and a charter myth to explain Greek colonisation in Sicily (Diodorus Siculus 4.23.2–3):[37]

As Herakles drew near to the region of Eryx, Eryx, the son of Aphrodite and Boutas, who ruled the land at that time, challenged him to a wrestling match. A penalty came with the match, and Eryx put up his land while Hercules wagered his cattle. At first Eryx was angry because the cattle were worth much less than the land. But Herakles explained that if he lost them he would lose his immortality and so Eryx agreed to the terms. They wrestled and he was beaten and lost the land. And Herakles put the land in the care of the natives, agreeing that they should take its fruits until one of his descendants should appear and ask for it back, which actually happened.

This story brings out into the open and simplifies the theme of man versus land, native versus coloniser, which runs through the stories of Hercules and Cacus, Hercules and Achelous, Hercules and Antaeus, and which forms the background for Statius' conquest of literary territory in the match between Tydeus and Agylleus.

Love and war, and the alternative streams of epic, are also brought together in this landscape. Wrestling was a euphemism

---

[37] See Malkin (1994) 203–18 on this story and the expedition of Dorieus.

for sex.[38] And sexual potency is also at stake in these wrestling matches. This is clearest in the fight between Hercules and Achelous, where the denouement of the fight is not the death of Achelous but his mutilation. Hercules tears off his horn, depriving him of his sexual union with Deianira and transferring the potential of his fertility to the horn itself, which becomes the *cornucopia*. When Antaeus is rejuvenated by contact with the earth, his transformation is described in terms reminiscent of sexual potency (4.629–32):

> rapit arida tellus
> sudorem: calido complentur sanguine uenae,
> intumuere tori, totosque induruit artus
> Herculeosque nouo laxauit corpore nodos.

The dry earth snatches his sweat: his veins are filled with warm blood and his muscles swell, all his limbs harden and loosen the Herculean knots with new body.

The exchange of liquids, the warm blood, the swelling and hardening, all suggest a sort of sexualised potency.

In Statius, Agylleus' defeat is presented in terms of sexual humiliation. Agylleus is feminised as he is forced into the passive role. The language describing him is reminiscent of Ovidian sexual language.[39] When he is exhausted by the fight he is literally *effetus*, 'worn out by childbearing'. The description of Tydeus' final victorious grapple has the potential for double meaning (6.889–93):

> mox latus et firmo celer implicat ilia nexu,
> poplitibus genua inde premens euadere nodos
> nequiquam et lateri dextram insertare parantem

---

[38] See Adams (1982):157. Thanks to Rebecca Rosewarne for pointing out the sexual overtones of the physical descriptions.

[39] When Agylleus first rises to fight he 'lifts his tall limbs' (*levat ardua membra*, 836–7) in words reminiscent of the lover in the *Remedia amoris* becoming aroused again after a long night (*levat membra*, 'he lifts his member' 205). See Adams (1982): 46 n. 5 for *membrum* as a synonym for penis. The physical description of Agylleus as *effusaque sanguine laxo | membra natant* ('his spread out limbs swim with loose blood' 841–2) echoes Ovid's biggest sexual boast: *laxe ponere membra* (*Amores* 2.10.18). In the same place, Ovid lays claim to the sexual energy of a Tydeus: size is not everything: *sufficiam – graciles, non sunt sine uiribus artus; | pondere, non neruis corpora nostra carent | et lateri dabit in uires alimenta uoluptas.* ('I will be enough – my limbs are slender but not without strength; my body lacks weight, not muscles, and pleasure will feed strength to my flanks.' *Amores* 2.10.23–5)

improbus, horrendum uisu ac mirabile pondus,
sustulit.

Soon his swift body winds his groin in a firm embrace,
pressing his knees with his own knees, as he attempts to escape
his grip in vain, and the wicked man raised him up, as he was preparing
to insert his right hand in his side, terrifying to see the unbelievable weight.

The humiliation of Agylleus is presented in sexual terms.[40] He
suffers from *pudor* when he cannot fight back and he leaves shameful traces on the ground (6.901–4):

deficit obsessus soloque pudore repugnat.
tandem pectus humi pronamque extensus in aluum
sternitur, ac longo maestus post tempore surgit,
turpia signata linquens uestigia terra.

Besieged, he fails and fights with shame alone.
At last he is laid out, his chest stretched out, forward on his belly,
and sadly he rises after a long time,
leaving behind shameful traces on the marked earth.

Agylleus is wrestling not only for his right to succeed his father,
but even for his right to be a man at all. Love and war are two sides
of conquest: the ability to control the fruits of the land is mirrored
by the ability to control the production of offspring. Aeneas and
Turnus fight both for Italy and Lavinia; Ovid removes the land
from his narrative of love and heroism; Lucan removes love from
his narrative of the conquest of land and the son of the earth. But
in both the imagery remains.

In Statius, every category is fatally confused. Polynices has
gained his territory with his wife: but nevertheless he comes back
to his native land as a foreign conqueror and seeks once more the
love of his mother. As Hercules and Cacus, Aeneas and Turnus,
are mirrored in each other, and as Lucan's civil war heroes can
only destroy each other, Tydeus gains neither land nor immortality. He deconstructs the fight itself in the most literal way possible:
he eats his enemy, becoming monster and animal instead of god
and hero. As he lies dying, it is not him but Capaneus who is

---

[40] Latin often presented humiliation in sexual terms, with the powerful man sodomis-
ing or irrumating the powerless. The classic example is Catullus 16 (with Richlin
(1983):144–56).

compared to Hercules, when he brings the head of Melanippus to his friend: *qualis ab Arcadio rediit Tirynthius antro | captiuumque suem clamantibus intulit Argis.* ('just as Hercules returned from the Arcadian cave and carried the captive boar to the applauding Argives', 8.749–50). Tydeus, who has been the most successful imitator of Hercules the civiliser, who appropriated his lineage in the wrestling, is now presented with the head of his enemy in the guise of a boar, his own symbol throughout the poem, as if presented with his own head.

BODIES

Introduction

We have read the bodies of Tydeus and Agylleus as textual bodies and pursued sexual imagery in the wrestling. In this section, I want to explore the construction of epic masculinity through descriptions of bodies in both games and war. 'Gender studies' has put an inevitable emphasis on women.[41] However, one major lesson which feminist theory has taught is that masculinity or manliness is not the 'normal' state from which women deviate. Masculinity is constructed and negotiated, often in opposition to femininity, but also within a system of differences among men, differences of class, age and race.[42] Alison Keith's study of gender in Latin epic has shown that epic is central to the process of educating Romans in the practices of masculinity, and Statius, too, sees his epic as destined for education: *Itala iam studio discit memoratque iuuentus* ('now Italian young people learn and recite you with enthusiasm', 12.815).[43] Here, I want to focus on the fissures in ancient constructions of masculinity (or masculinities, as Bob Connell puts it in his

---

[41] On Men's Studies, see: Brod (1987); Kimmel (1987); Gilmore (1990); Connell (1995); Berger, Wallis and Watson (1995); Segal (1997); Bowker (1998). Treatments of masculinity within classics include: Gleason (1995); Foxhall and Salmon (1998a); Foxhall and Salmon (1998b); Walters (1993); Walters (1997).

[42] See especially Connell (1995).

[43] Keith (2000) 8–95. 'Epic poetry was supremely valorised as a literary form centred on the principle of elite male identity (*uirtus*) in the ancient Roman educational system, where the masculine focus of the genre was both mirrored and magnified.'

seminal sociological study of Australian manhood), the ways in which Statius explores and problematises heroic masculinity.[44] Bodies have long fascinated scholars and artists alike.[45] The body is a reality which seems indisputably real: we all have bodies, readers and writers alike, and are all driven by the needs of our bodies. Yet the body is also a symbol, the site of ideas and the seat of identity.[46] The body exists in the imaginary realm, too, and through the body the imaginary can be made to seem more real. For athletes in particular, the body is the guarantee of success and the limit of victory.[47] In war, even more so, victory is determined by pain.[48] Statius' use of bodies, the imagery that coalesces around bodies in games and war, is a fundamental starting point for thinking about the nature of masculinity, and heroic masculinity in particular, in the *Thebaid*. Both games and war are tales of bodies, narratives inscribed on and through the limbs of those who take part. The body of the athlete and the body of the hero are both bodies pushed to their limits (and sometimes beyond). This section will examine the imagery which characterises defeated and victorious bodies in both games and war. It will show how this imagery relates to gender categories, and how Statius constructs, explores and problematises epic masculinities.

Attributes of masculinity

I want to begin by looking at ways of characterising the masculine body (often in opposition to the feminine body) in other ancient writers. Ancient thought is often characterised by polar oppositions.[49] Masculinity and femininity are associated with oppositions displayed in various physical qualities. For instance, medical

---

[44] Connell (1995).

[45] See Turner (1984); recent classical studies include: Montserrat (1998); Wyke (1998); Porter (1999). On the body in Virgil see Heuzé (1985).

[46] See for instance Heuzé (1985) 1: 'the real body, simple, evident, there before you, is an illusion.'

[47] The work of Michael Messner on sport and masculinity is particularly useful; see Messner (1987a, 1987b, 1992).

[48] Scarry (1985) argues that war is a competition in pain; she explores the particular nature of pain, war and torture.

[49] See for instance Lloyd (1966).

writers discussing how babies of both sexes are conceived present a view of the different characteristics of male and female bodies.[50] Temperature is very important in this conceptualisation, as well as moisture: a woman is more fertile because she is moister, and she is more likely to conceive a boy if her womb is hotter. Galen suggests that women were thought of as colder: 'The female is more ineffectual than the male for this main reason, that it is colder' (Galen, *De Usu Partium* 14.6).[51] Quintilian (*Inst.* 11.3.28) discusses why it is that the male voice is weak in the transition from boyhood to adolescence and concludes that it is not on account of heat, but fluidity. In this case, it is not the distinction between male and female that is at issue, but the distinction between man and boy. However, there is more than just the opposition of hot, dry male and cold, wet female.[52] Varro (*De Re Rustica* 1.41.4), discusses the greater fertility of the moist female over the dry male, and takes as given that the female is looser (*laxiora*):[53] 'thus the fig, the Phoenician apple and the vine, on account of their feminine softness, are prone to growing' (*itaque ficus, malus punica et uitis propter femineam mollitiam ad crescendum prona*). The female is wet, loose and soft; the male is dry, tight and hard.

Another way of characterising the masculine in Roman thought is wholeness, or impenetrability. Walters sees this as the primary measure of a *uir*: the body of a freeborn Roman citizen in good standing is impenetrable, both sexually and in the context of violence and beatings.[54] For Walters, 'bodily integrity' is not only the primary, but the only, measure of the man. In my view, it is one

---

[50] Corbeill (1997) 108, in his discussion of the invective of sexual deviance, shows that it is most likely that this tradition of the warm, dry male and the cold, moist female, represented in the Roman period by Galen, Aretaeus, and (he argues) Varro, goes back through the Late Republican times to the works of Empedocles.

[51] ἔστι δὲ τὸ 9ῆλυ τοῦ ἄρρενος ἀτελέστερον ἑνὶ μὲν καὶ πρώτῳ λόγῳ, διότι ψυχρότερον (Kuhn (1964) 158). Also 162: οὔκουν 9αυμαστὸν οὐδὲν, εἴ τὸ 9ῆλυ τοῦ ἄρρενος εἰς τοσοῦτον ἀτελέστερον, εἰς ὅσον ψυχρότερον. '[Women's] lack of heat made them more soft, more liquid, more clammy-cold, altogether more formless than were men.' (Brown (1988) 10.)

[52] Brown (1988) 10 cites Aretaeus (2.5) thus: 'For it is the semen, when possessed of vitality, which makes us men, hot, well-braced in limbs, heavy, well-voiced, spirited, strong to think and act.' This adds the qualities of heaviness, strength and 'well-braced-ness' (quite possibly equivalent to stiffness).

[53] Corbeill (1997) 108.

[54] Walters (1997) 30 'social status was characterized on the basis of perceived bodily integrity and freedom, or the lack of it, from invasion from the outside'.

of a cluster of attributes which the Roman man strove to maintain. Walters sees the *uir* primarily in opposition to the slave, making the scars of the soldier problematic, since they would seem to indicate a slavish lack of integrity.[55] However, if manhood is seen as a complex of attributes, taking the upper hand in a number of oppositions (between man and boy, man and beast, man and woman as well as man and slave), then the loss of one, such as wholeness, might be overlooked through reference to the others. Thus, Tydeus is proud of his battle scars, so proud that he displays them at the end of the wrestling (6.905–10). He can demonstrate his scars because it is the end of the wrestling match and he has won, validating his manhood. If he had lost, the spectators might have said that his wounds have destroyed his *uirtus*. But since he won both the battle and the wrestling, his scars are a matter of pride, showing that he can overcome his penetration by the weapons of the enemy by the sheer force of his strength, energy and vitality.

Masculinity, then, is constructed at least partly through bodily qualities. Men are whole, hot, tight, hard, dry and stiff; women are fragmented, cold, loose, soft, moist and flaccid. In the following sections, we will see how these physical qualities characterise the victorious and defeated bodies of Statius' heroes in both games and war.

The athlete's body

Athletics is a drama of the body; success and failure are literally signified by bodily attributes. When Alcidamas, in the boxing, marks Capaneus with a blow that draws blood, it is not the blow itself but the significance of it that angers Capaneus (6.780–88). It is the shame of the stains, the marks which the audience can see but he cannot, that sends Capaneus into a frenzy. The text emphasises the importance of the signification of the athlete's body with the repeated *signa*: *designat*(782); *signantur* (783). The clearest set of signs of victory and defeat in Statius' games are

---

[55] '[T]he scars from a soldier's wounds are conceptually placed as the polar opposite of scars from a servile beating. They are his mark of manhood, the signifier, permanently inscribed on his body, of his social status as a full man.' (Walters (1997) 40)

written on the bodies of the wrestlers.[56] I have analysed these passages already, but now I draw out the oppositions of bodily victory and defeat. Agylleus carries with him in his very physique the signs of his own defeat, even before the fight starts, and Tydeus is already marked as victor (6.841–6). The text endorses Tydeus' reading of Agylleus' body, contrasting the *rigor* (stiffness) and *robur* (strength) of Hercules with the excess, fluidity and looseness of his son (*luxuriant artus, effusaque sanguine laxo | membra natant*, 'his limbs run riot, and his sprawling appendages swim with excess blood' 6.841–2), implying that Tydeus, with his heavy bones and inflexible joints, has that *rigor* and *robur* which his opponent lacks. Inflexible (*difficilis*) here is the opposite of easily manipulable (*facilis*); it seems that it is masculine to keep one's shape, to be whole, hard, inflexible, upright and unbending, while to be easily forced out of shape is to be female. The imagery describing Agylleus emphasises moisture: he is literally poured out and swimming with blood. This image of fluidity helps to characterise his looseness. His size is also transformed into a grotesque image of unmasculine fertility by the verb *luxuriant*, whose primary meaning according to the *OLD* is of excessive growth in plants; it is used secondarily of bodily swelling. In the passage of Varro cited above, excessive growth in plants run riot is linked with feminine looseness and moisture. In this way, Statius characterises Agylleus' vast size as growth gone mad, and Tydeus' compactness as masculine tightness.

As the fight progresses, the oppositions continue to dominate. At 6.870–75, Agylleus is clearly exhausted (*contra non integer ille | flatibus alternis aegroque effetus hiatu*, 'he on the other hand was not in one piece, worn out with panting breaths and sick gasps', 872–3), while Tydeus maintains his energy and force (*uis eadem Oenidae*, 'the son of Oeneus has the same force', 870). The first and last phrases in this passage make clear the states of the two contestants, without recourse to the imagery of the victorious or defeated body: it is clear from *uis eadem Oenidae* that Tydeus is the positive half of the opposition, and from the image of Agylleus

---

[56] 'The virtue of all-in wrestling is that it is the spectacle of excess ... It is therefore in the body of the wrestler that we find the first key to the contest.' (Barthes (1993) 15–7).

supporting his body on the earth that Agylleus has taken on all the negative qualities of defeated athlete. 'Tight' is the primary meaning of *arta* (871) applied to Tydeus' skin, which is also stiff (*riget*, 871). His muscles are hard (*duris... toris*, 871–2), while Agylleus is both *non integer* (not whole, 872) and sick (*aegroque hiatu*, 873). Tydeus is characterised as lacking the fluidity of defeat when his limbs are described as not flagging (*nec... labant*, 870–71); the river of sweat coming off Agylleus (*fluuio sudoris*, 874) looks back to the stream of blood (*tepido riuo*, 783) flowing down Capaneus' forehead as a signifier of defeat.[57] The bodies of the wrestlers, then, both determine the course of the fight and display the marks of its outcome. We have seen how Tydeus sexually humiliates Agylleus; his lack of masculine bodily control leads to domination by other men.

In the discus, Phlegyas' body is read by the audience as a promise of masculine prowess (6.668–70):

> Pisaeus Phlegyas opus incohat et simul omnes
> abstulit in se oculos: ea uiso corpore uirtus
> promissa.

> Pisaean Phlegyas begins the work and immediately stole
> all eyes onto himself: in the sight of his body, such manhood
> is promised.

However, his throw does not live up to the promise of either his practice throw or his body; Hippomedon, on the other hand, is marked out as a true winner by his rigidity (6.707–10):

> erigit adsuetum dextrae gestamen, et alte
> sustentans rigidumque latus fortesque lacertos
> consulit ac uasto contorquet turbine, et ipse
> prosequitur.

> He holds up the usual discus in his right hand, and lifting it high,
> takes care that his side is stiff and his arms are strong
> and hurls it with a huge spin, and follows it through
> himself.

It is this rigidity that marks Hippomedon out from the other competitors: strength alone is not enough. Phlegyas' strength is a

---

[57] The fluidity of weeping becomes a form of emasculation: Brown (1988) 79.

fluid strength, a gathering of blood (*collecto sanguine*, 680);[58] his unfortunate slip occurs just when he is at his most curved: *iam ceruix conuersa, et iam latus omne redibat* ('now his neck is bent back and his whole side comes back', 694).

The boxing is also another important moment in the games for the negotiation of masculinity and of the limits of the body. I want to reread the boxing briefly in the light of the imagery we have been examining above. At the beginning of the fight, Adrastus announces it as a display of masculinity: *haec bellis et ferro proxima uirtus* ('this is masculinity second only to war and weapons', 730). Capaneus' boast, too, ends on the key word *uirtus* (737). The description of the fight begins with Capaneus standing, a solid and unchallenged hero: the placing of *constitit* emphatically at the beginning of the line is significant, as we will see further below (p. 228).[59] Both boxers begin with their bodies held tall and their hands upright: *fulmineas alte suspensi corpora plantis | erexere manus* ('their bodies are poised high above their feet and they raise their lightning hands', 750–51). Alcidamas, only just out of boyhood (*paulo ante puer*, 756), is redeemed not by bodily qualities, but by mental agility. He remains whole (*integer*, 772) through cunning and skill. The vigour of his talent (*uigor ingenio*, 775) even allows him to overshadow Capaneus (*intratque et obumbrat et alte | adsilit*, 'he gets inside his guard, overshadows him and jumps high at him'). He uses Capaneus' fear of his *rigida arma* ('rigid weapons' 780) to achieve first blood. The fragility of his resistance, however, is made clear when Capaneus, seething (*feruidus*, 788) in his rage, forces him onto his back (*in terga supinat*, 789). As the fight continues, both show signs of exhaustion and defeat (6.796–8):

> et iam utrumque labor suspiriaque aegra fatigant:
> tardius ille premit, nec iam hic absistere uelox,
> defectique ambo genibus pariterque quierunt.

> And now toil and sick gasping tires out both men:
> this one attacks more slowly, nor is the other as swift to escape now,
> and both are exhausted in the knees and rest equally.

---

[58] Cf. 2.561 with Mulder (1954) 301.   [59] 2.585 of Tydeus.

In this passage, both are sick and slow, and their damaged knees are no longer able to maintain uprightness. The fight is so balanced, Capaneus' body against Alcidamas' mind, that both fighters seem equally defeated.

If the body shows signs of victory and defeat, these signs can be manipulated as a sort of deception. Here, Alcidamas is shown voluntarily presenting himself in a posture of defeat in order to gain an advantage. For when Capaneus rushes him, Alcidamas ducks out of the way (6.802–5):

> ecce iterum immodice uenientem eludit et exit
> sponte ruens mersusque umeris: effunditur ille
> in caput, adsurgentem alio puer improbus ictu
> perculit euentuque impalluit ipse secundo.

> Look, he escapes him again, as he rushes in immoderately, and gets out of
>   the way
> by collapsing of his own free will and plunging his shoulders: Capaneus is
>   poured
> onto his head, and the wicked boy struck him as he was rising,
> another blow, and grew pale himself at the favourable outcome.

By failing to stand up to Capaneus, by faking the signs of defeat, Alcidamas turns the fight around, turning the vocabulary of defeat against Capaneus as he is literally poured (*effunditur*) headlong onto the ground. As Capaneus loses his hold on his masculinity, Statius goes further than he had done before, now specifically calling Alcidamas a boy (*puer improbus*, wicked boy) and showing him clearly afraid (*impalluit*) of his own success.[60] It is this incident which makes Capaneus so angry that Adrastus immediately calls an end to the fight, even though he is still described as unbroken (*nil frangitur heros*, 'the hero is not broken at all', 817). And it is this that leads him to call Alcidamas a half-man (*semiuir*, 6.821). To be knocked over by a boy, put into the position of defeat by a bodily deceit, strikes at the heart of Capaneus' *uirtus*. It is no surprise, then, that he abuses Alcidamas with the language of

---

[60] *Puer improbus* is the quintessential epithet of Parthenopaeus in his *aristeia*, as he uses his divine weapons indiscriminately and kills men who pity him as a son. At 10.744, the narrator calls him *puer improbe*. Yet Alcidamas' fear at his own success makes him more similar to Arruns, who kills Camilla at *Aeneid* 11.806–8, and Melanippus, the killer of Tydeus, who hopes that he will be able to hide at *Thebaid* 8.717–20.

sexual deviance, calling his masculinity into question precisely to combat the threat to his own masculinity that his humiliation has created.

The boxing, then, is an exploration of the competition between body and mind to form and uphold masculinity. Capaneus' superior bodily strength and size is no guarantee that he will not be humiliated by skill and agility. This also shows how masculinity is defined not solely against femininity but also against the incomplete masculinity of boyhood, and sexuality defined as passive and therefore deviant. In the boxing, wrestling and the discus, then, bodies and bodily attributes both determine and display the course of victory and defeat. The bodily attributes of masculinity are the signs of a successful athlete. The victorious athlete is tight, solid, hard, upright, straight, hot, stiff and whole; the defeated athlete is loose, fluid, soft, supine, bent, cold, flexible and fragmented. In the rest of this chapter, I want to use these signs to explore Statius' testing of masculinity and the bodies of heroes in war. I shall pursue Tydeus, as he fights against his body's limits in his two aristeias in books 2 and 8, and Agylleus, who takes part in the night raid of book 10. Finally, I turn to investigate the heroic body in death, and ask whether there is such a thing as positive masculinity and heroism in the *Thebaid*.

The body at war: following Tydeus and Agylleus

Tydeus has two aristeias, in both of which he becomes one against a multitude, replaying the Scaeva episode from Lucan's *Bellum Ciuile*; Agylleus, on the other hand, is involved with the night raid of book 10, which has been read as the least heroic heroism, perverting the ways of epic. Tydeus is continually represented as held back by the limits of his body. In book 1, when he and Polynices fight, his masculinity is too big for his body: *maior in exiguo regnabat corpore uirtus* ('a greater manhood reigned in his small body', 1.417). His first aristeia takes place in the valley of the Sphinx, when he is returning from his embassy to Eteocles.[61] He

---

[61] Vessey (1973) 146–7 'The narrative of Tydeus' battle against this assailant need not be analysed in depth [...] there was a competition to invent more hideous forms of death [...] It is a characteristic of Statius' art which, however repellent, has to be accepted.'

is ambushed by fifty men, and his first reaction is to retreat up the hillside and attack them with the landscape itself. As he hurls a rock down, we see him acting the hero, despite his retreat: using his whole strength (*toto sanguine*, 'with all his blood', 561); holding up and lifting the rock (*sustinet*, 562; *erexit*, 563). The enemy are broken and unable to hold themselves up: *simul ora uirum, simul arma manusque | fractaque commixto sederunt pectora ferro* ('at the same time the faces of the men, the weapons, the hands and the chests collapse, broken and mixed in with the weapons', 2.566–7). When he sees the signs of failure on the enemy, he gains the courage to stand firm himself: *ut subitis exterrita fatis | agmina turbatam uidit laxare cateruam* ('when he saw the column terrified by the sudden deaths and the crowd disturbed grow loose', 576–7) he jumps down from the cliffs and stands against them (2.580–85):

> mox in plana libens, nudo ne pectore tela
> inciderent, saltu praeceps defertur et orbem,
> quem procul oppresso uidit Therone uolutum,
> corripuit, tergoque et uertice tegmina nota
> saeptus et hostili propugnans pectora parma
> constitit.

> Soon, so that weapons might not fall on his naked chest, he jumped down
> headlong onto the plain, willingly, and snatched up
> the shield which he saw roll far away when Theron had been crushed,
> and hedged in by his well-known boar skin on back and head
> and defending his chest with an enemy shield
> he took his stand.

The long movement of the sentence, with all its various motions, ends emphatically on *constitit*. Tydeus has consolidated his position, and is now back in the posture of a hero. Just after he defiantly refuses to spare the suppliant Menoetes, finishing: *ite sub umbras, o timidi paucique!* ('Go to the Underworld, o cowards and too few!'), his body forces him to stop, with all the attributes of defeat (2.668–74):

> ast tamen illi
> membra negant, lassusque ferit praecordia sanguis.
> iam sublata manus cassos defertur in ictus,
> tardatique gradus, clipeum nec sustinet umbo
> mutatum spoliis; gelidus cadit imber anhelo

pectore, tum crines ardentiaque ora cruentis
roribus et taetra morientum aspergine manant.

But nevertheless his limbs deny him, and his exhausted blood beats against
his heart. Now his raised hands fall in vain blows,
his step is slowed, and the boss cannot hold up the shield
weighed down with spoils; a cold shower falls from his gasping
chest; his hair and his burning face are wet with bloody dew
and the foul spray of dying men.

This is the warrior as athlete, pushed to the limits of his bodily
endurance in fighting, mirroring the dying men he himself has
killed.[62] He is unable to lift his hands and keep his shield up; he
is swamped with blood and sweat. Tydeus here is defeated by his
own body (*membra negant*, 'his limbs deny him', 669), and his own
blood beats him as he can no longer strike others. Paradoxically,
at the moment when Tydeus has proved beyond doubt his super-
masculinity, his true heroism, by taking on fifty men single-handed,
he is assimilated to the defeated and dead. In taking his body to
the extreme edge of achievement, he is in danger of destroying it.
Immediately after this passage, there is a simile, comparing him to
a lion gorged on sheep (2.675–81):

> ut leo, qui campis longe custode fugato
> Massylas depastus oues, ubi sanguine multo
> luxuriata fames ceruixque et tabe grauatae
> consedere iubae, mediis in caedibus adstat
> aeger, hians uictusque cibis; nec iam amplius irae
> crudescunt: tantum uacuis ferit aera malis
> molliaque eiecta delambit uellera lingua.

> Just as a lion who has grazed on Massylian sheep, when the guard
> has fled far from the fields, when hunger has run riot with much
> blood and his neck and his mane droop, weighed down
> with gore, and he stands sick in the middle of the slaughter,
> gaping and conquered by food; no longer does his anger
> grow more fully fierce: he only beats the air with his empty jaws
> and licks out the soft fleece with his tongue hanging out.

---

[62] Hershkowitz (1998a) 254–5 uses this passage as part of her pattern of madness in the
Thebaid: increased madness leads to exhaustion and lassitude. I have argued elsewhere
that there is more than one pattern of madness in the *Thebaid*. See Lovatt (2001). However, this imagery of exhaustion and defeat describing heroes in moments of victory is
certainly characteristic of Statius.

Here, the same imagery carries over from the description of Tydeus into the description of the lion. The blood and gore cause his mane to lose its uprightness. He is sick and gasping with exhaustion. What is more, these lines seem specifically to echo the description of Agylleus' body in the wrestling: hunger has run riot (*luxuriata*), just as Agylleus' body is grown to excess; *sanguine multo* is in the same metrical position as *sanguine laxo* (6.841), and Agylleus too is sick and gasping (*aegroque... hiatu* 6.873). In victory, Tydeus suffers from the same excess that marks Agylleus out for defeat.

In book 8, Tydeus' body ultimately reaches and passes its limits. His aristeia is the mirror image of the feats of book 2, in which he again takes on the Theban masses. This time, however, his body asserts its limits in a more terminal way and as he lies dying, he condemns it as a deserter: *odi artus fragilemque hunc corporis usum | desertorem animi* ('I hate my limbs and this body, fragile, of little use, deserter of my soul', 8.738–39).

The night raid

Agylleus' opportunity for an aristeia is the night raid in book 10.[63] Juno arranges with the god Somnus to subdue the Thebans who are left guarding the Argive camp in drunken sleep, so that they can be slaughtered.[64] Thiodamas, the replacement for Amphiaraus, leads the raid, along with his two captains, Actor and Agylleus. Throughout the raid, the enemy are saturated with imagery of defeat. Their first view of the enemy is as booty lying on the ground: *et protinus*

---

[63] On the night raid as *aemulatio* with both Virgil and Homer: Kytzler (1969) 209–19; Juhnke (1972) 143–4. See also Vessey (1973) 303–7; Williams (1972) xx–xxi, 66; Snijder (1968) 12.

[64] Intertexts include the Doloneia in the *Iliad*, the sack of Troy in *Aeneid* 2 and the raid of Nisus and Euryalus in *Aeneid* 9. Vessey (1973) 304 adds Ovid's Ceyx and Alcyone episode (*Metamorphoses* 11.583–649). The slaughter among the banqueting tables is also reminiscent of the battle of the Lapiths and the Centaurs. Constraints of space prevent me from taking these intertexts properly into account: a useful direction for future research would be to test the ideas here by comparison with other texts, to see to what extent the paradox of heroic masculinity is one common to all ancient epic, or to what extent there is a distinctively Statian take on it.

ingens | praeda solo ceu iam exanimes multoque peracti | ense iacent ('and immediately the huge booty is lying on the ground as if already lifeless and driven through by many swords', 10.264–6). Words of slipping, lying and leaning dominate: *explicitum* ('spread out', 277); *remissis* ('slack', 277); *inlapsum* ('slipped down', 278); *iacentes* ('lying', 279); *adclines* ('leaning against', 280). Wine and blood form one liquid signifying destruction, and the powers of speech and movement are denied them. The poet figure Ialmenus has a languid neck (*languida ceruix*, 306). When he is killed, his mouth produces liquid instead of words: *proturbat mensas dirus liquor: undique manant | sanguine permixti latices, et Bacchus in altos | crateras paterasque redit* ('the grim liquid upset the tables before it: everywhere fluid mixed with blood seeps, and wine returns into the deep mixing bowls and goblets', 311–13). Calpetus is laid out already on the cold ground: *stratus humo gelida* (318) and speech dissolves for him too: *ecce iacentis | Inachius uates iugulum fodit, expulit ingens | uina cruor fractumque perit in sanguine murmur* ('look, the Inachian prophet stabs the throat of the man as he lies there, the torrent of blood forced out the wine and his broken muttering died in the blood', 321–3). The landscape itself is liquefied (10.298–302):

> stagnant nigrantia tabo
> gramina, sanguineis nutant tentoria riuis;
> fumat humus, somnique et mortis anhelitus una
> uoluitur; haud quisquam uisus aut ora iacentum
> erexit;

> The blackened pasture is inundated with gore
> and the tents are swayed by the bloody streams;
> the soil smokes and the gasps of sleep and death roll
> together; none of the fallen men lifted his gaze or his face.

Breath itself has become death, and the inability to lift up one's face is emphasised as an important part of the process of death.

Surprisingly early on in the fight, Thiodamas takes on attributes similar to those displayed by Tydeus in his aristeia in book 2, equally worn out by the simple excess of slaughter. He is a tiger to Tydeus' lion (10.286–95):

iam tarda manus, iam debile ferrum
et caligantes nimiis successibus irae.
Caspia non aliter magnorum in strage iuuencum
tigris, ubi inmenso rabies placata cruore
lassauitque genas et crasso sordida tabo
confudit maculas, spectat sua facta doletque
defecisse famem: uictus sic augur inerrat
caedibus Aoniis; optet nunc bracchia centum
centenasque in bella manus; iam taedet inanes
exhaurire animas, hostemque adsurgere mallet.

Now his hand is slow, his weapon is weak
and his anger is darkened by too much success.
Not otherwise does a Caspian tigress amongst the slaughter of great
cattle, when madness, placated by immeasurable blood,
has tired out her jaws and, filthy, jumbled her markings
with thick gore, watch her own deeds and grieve
that her hunger has failed: defeated in this way the augur wanders about
in Theban slaughter; now he would wish for a hundred arms
and a hundred hands for war; now he grows bored of draining out
empty souls, and would prefer the enemy to rise up.

There are clear similarities to the language describing Tydeus in
book 2, over and above the similarity of the situation.[65] Both passages focus on the jaws, and in both cases the characteristic physical
attributes of the animals have been erased by the blood from the
slaughter: the lion's mane is weighed down and the tiger's stripes
are hidden. Thiodamas becomes a version of Jupiter, bored with
destruction, and a version of Statius himself, whose own inadequacy to convey the mourning after is signified by the hundred-
mouths *topos* at 12.797–9:

> non ego, centena si quis mea pectora laxet
> tot busta simulque uulgique ducumque,
> tot pariter gemitus dignis conatibus aequem.

> Nor could I, even if some god opened my hundred-fold chest,
> match so many pyres of commoners and leaders at the same time,
> so many groans equally with worthy efforts.

[65] Mulder (1954) 341 points to the similarity between *ubi inmenso rabies placata cruore*
('when madness has been placated by immeasurable blood' 10.289) and *ubi sanguine
multo | luxuriata fames* ('when hunger has run riot with much blood', 2.676–7). Williams
(1972) 69 points out that the main intertext, *Aeneid* 9.339 f., is of a lion falling on sheep,
which strengthens the connection here.

Critics have deplored the episode as gratuitous violence.[66] In the passage itself, there is much to suggest that Statius was concerned with exploring and problematising the limits of heroism and masculinity. In the arming scene (10.253–61), each key member of the raiding party takes someone else's weapons: Thiodamas leaves his prophetic insignia and takes Polynices' helmet and breastplate; Capaneus donates his heavy sword to Actor, and Agylleus leaves behind his Herculean bow (10.259–61):

> permutat Agylleus
> arma trucis Nomii: quid enim fallentibus umbris
> arcus et Herculeae iuuissent bella sagittae?

> Agylleus exchanges
> his weapons for those of fierce Nomius: for how would the bow
> and arrows of Hercules help a war fought in deceiving shadows?

All these substitutions are open to more than one reading, on the practical and symbolic level. When Agylleus abandons the weapons of Hercules, the equivocation hinges on the phrase *fallentibus umbris* ('deceiving shadows'): is this a purely practical point, in which case the shadows are deceiving Agylleus himself and making it impossible to use the bow? Or is it a moral point, in which case there is no need for the bow and arrows when the shadows are providing cover for the raid and deceiving the Thebans?[67] Agylleus is giving up his heritage as son of Hercules to take up the weapons of a nobody. Throughout the raid, we are continually reminded of the problematic nature of Agylleus' descent from Hercules, which was already brought out in the wrestling. On his first mention in the episode, he is immediately identified as Herculean Agylleus (*Herculeum... Agyllea*, 249) and described in an ambivalent phrase: *hic robore iactat | non*

---

[66] Especially Williams (1972) 66: 'Statius seeks and achieves a gruesome and grotesque effect by ... the elaboration of grim details far beyond what a horror story requires ... the sense of pathos is practically always blunted by excess of descriptive horror.' See also: Vessey (1973) 303–7; Ripoll (1998) 323: 'cette boucherie facile et sans mérite sera tout sauf une démonstration de *uirtus*'.

[67] Williams (1972) 66 points out that Odysseus is actually given a bow and quiver to use in the Doloneia at *Iliad* 10.260–61. Is Statius here making a point of correcting Homer (how could you use a long-distance weapon like a bow effectively in the dark?), or making a point that the bow of Hercules in particular is not a deceptive weapon, as bows usually are?

cessisse patri ('this man boasts that he did not yield to his father in strength', 250–51). If we had not come across him before, we might accept his boast at face value: it is paired with a statement of fact about Actor (*hic aptus suadere*, 'this man is good at persuading', 250). Back in the wrestling, however, he is described as a *iactator* ('boaster', 6.837), and the truth of his boast is denied by the narrator precisely in the matter of *robur* ('strength'): *sed non ille rigor patriumque in corpore robur* ('but he did not have his father's rigour and strength of body', 6.840).[68] When he gives up his Herculean weapons, we are reminded of the way that Tydeus wrestles him into giving up the role of Hercules. During the fight, this is brought to our attention once more when he is called 'the son of mighty Hercules' (*magno satus Hercule*, 296), with the epithet 'mighty' attached to father, not son; the immediate implication might be that he is great through his descent from Hercules, but the wrestling has shown that he is great in size alone, and not in martial prowess.

Statius in the night raid is not simply providing a negative example of heroism, a case study in how it can go wrong; he is exploring the limits and the paradoxes of war. Victory is no guarantee of successful heroism or successful masculinity. Gender-related imagery is also used in the night raid to bring out its problematic nature. For instance, where Tydeus is compared to a lion, an emblem of masculinity,[69] Thiodamas is compared to a tiger. The gender of tigers is a slippery problem: the *OLD* classifies the word as 'f., (m.)'.[70] In this case, he is clearly a tigress, as the epithet *Caspia* demonstrates. And when Thiodamas and the raiding party return to the camp, there is another, rather more worrying, gender-bending simile (10.458–62):

> uolucrum sic turba recentum,
> cum reducem longo prospexit in aere matrem,
> ire cupit contra summique e margine nidi

---

[68] Williams (1972) 65 sees this as a discrepancy between Agylleus' view of himself and the narrator's view: 'Evidently his defeat at wrestling had not altered his opinion of himself, nor did he see himself as others saw him.'

[69] See for instance Gleason (1995) 62 on the Leonine man.

[70] The tiger is also an emblem of the oriental; the tigers whose death starts the war in *Thebaid* 7 had pulled the chariot of Dionysus in India, and are decked out luxuriously in purple and grapes (7.564–71, with Smolenaars (1994) 253–8).

extat hians, iam iamque cadat, ni pectore toto
obstet aperta parens et amantibus increpat alis.

So a crowd of recently born birds,
when they catch sight of their mother returning from afar through the air,
long to go to meet her and lean out gaping from the top edge
of the nest and would now be about to fall, if their parent with open wings
did not put her whole breast in the way and reproach them with loving
   wing-beats.

Not only does Thiodamas become a female, he becomes a female bird; the watching Argives become baby birds, gaping and about to fall. Their enthusiasm to watch becomes greed for food, so extreme as to be dangerous. Williams points to the 'gentleness' of this simile, but Thiodamas is bringing them results that are neither pleasant nor gentle. Thiodamas is an incongruous mother figure, bringing blood instead of milk and destruction instead of protection. In his moment of triumphant victorious return, he is strikingly feminised by Statius' imagery, just before the revelation of the deaths of Hopleus and Dymas will turn the joy of victory sour.

Death and heroism

If successful fighting in the *Thebaid* seems often to be tainted with the same bodily signs of defeat as unsuccessful fighting, can death redeem heroism? Statius' descriptions of the heroic body in death give us one answer to this question, and I want to look briefly at Parthenopaeus, Tydeus and Capaneus and their deaths. As Parthenopaeus lies wounded, on the point of death, Statius gives a lingering description of his body, which has all the qualities of the defeated hero (9.877–83):

at puer infusus sociis in deuia campi
tollitur (heu simplex aetas!) moriensque iacentem
flebat equum; cecidit laxata casside uultus,
aegraque per trepidos expirat gratia uisus,
et prensis concussa comis ter colla quaterque
stare negant, ipsisque nefas lacrimabile Thebis,
ibat purpureus niueo de pectore sanguis.

But the boy is carried by his allies to the pathless parts of the field
laid out (alas naïve in his youth!) and dying he weeps for his

235

fallen horse; his face released from its helmet has fallen,
and he breathes out sick grace through his terrified gaze,
and three times they grasp his hair and shake his neck, four times,
it [his head] refuses to stand, and, a crime lamentable for Thebes itself,
bright blood was flowing down his snowy chest.

The striking adjective *infusus* creates an image of Parthenopaeus
sprawling out, completely unable to hold his body together: he is
liquid already, yet the tears add to this fluidity.[71] Looseness is here
in the helmet (*laxata casside*) and sickness (*aegraque . . . gratia*);
more liquid in the blood that stains his perfect beauty, and cold
in the adjective *niueo* applied to his chest. Yet the most important
image here is the inability of his body to remain upright, the complete lack of rigidity. He must be carried; his head falls (*cecidit*),
and no matter how many times they pull his head upright by his
hair, his neck refuses to stand (*stare negant*). The efforts of his
friends to try and maintain some sort of uprightness in his neck are
emotionally charged: the *ter . . . quaterque* recalls the famous lines
in the *Aeneid* when Aeneas tries and fails to embrace Creusa and
Anchises.[72] Parthenopaeus loses his manhood in death, following
the model of Virgil's Euryalus, cut down like a flower in the field
(*Aeneid* 9.433–7), as we saw in chapter 2.[73] It is no coincidence
that Statius here describes him as *puer*: death sets him in stone,
forever just short of achieving manhood.

The death of Tydeus bears some similarity to the death of
Parthenopaeus.[74] He, too, is struck down in battle and carried to
the edge of the field, there to make his last demands of his friends
before he dies. The elements of the imagery are not encapsulated
in one passage, but throughout the whole description of his death,
from his fatal wound to his final cannibalism, the signs of defeat
and death recur. As he takes on the entire Theban army, he seems
to dissolve into liquid: *iam cruor in galea, iam saucia proluit ater |
pectora permixtus sudore et sanguine torrens*. ('Now there is blood
in his helmet, now a black torrent mixed with sweat and blood

---

[71] Cf. Vessey (1973) 301–2 on Parthenopaeus' death.
[72] *Aeneid* 2.792–3 and 6.700–701: *ter conatus ibi collo dare bracchia circum; | ter frustra
comprensa manus effugit imago.*
[73] See Fowler (1987); Skinner (1997).
[74] On the death of Tydeus, see Vessey (1973) 292–3; Ripoll (1998) 336–9.

drenches his wounded chest.' 8.711–12) When the spear of Melanippus hits Tydeus, the text signifies the seriousness of the wound
by piling up images of collapse: *nam flexus in ilia Tydeus | summis-
sum latus et clipei laxauerat orbem* ('for Tydeus, bending over his
groin, sank onto his side and let go the circle of his shield', 8.720–
21). He is clearly defeated and dying. When he summons up the last
of his strength to kill Melanippus despite his dissolution, the effort
makes the blood run: *perit expressus conamine sanguis* ('blood
dies, pushed out by the effort', 8.727). When his comrades carry
him from the battle, they have to prop him up: *summique in margine
campi | effultum gemina latera inclinantia parma | ponunt* ('they
place him on the furthest edge of the field propped up, twin shields
leaning on either side', 8.730–32). Just as with Parthenopaeus, his
friends display a need to keep him upright. As he slides towards
death, he feels the cold and further loses his uprightness: *sed et
ipse recedere caelum | ingentesque animos extremo frigore labi |
sensit* ('but he himself felt the sky go from him and his huge soul
slip away in the final cold', 8.733–5). There is an ironic connection
back to the wrestling match, both when Tydeus is propped up by
the shields as he and Agylleus were once propped up on each other
(*pendent per mutua fulti | bracchia*, 'they hang, propped up by each
other's arms', 6.862–3) and also when he is supporting himself on
the ground in the same way Agylleus did when exhaustion set in
(6.875).

When Capaneus dies, struck down by the thunderbolt of Jupiter,
he succeeds in holding his body together in death: he alone seems
to turn death into victory, to validate his masculinity in his attempt
to exceed it. His death is the remarkable death of a hero so stubborn
as almost to resist death itself: he remains standing until the end,
and retains the marks of the victorious hero so that he almost needs
a second thunderbolt (10.927–31, 935–9):

> talia dicentem toto Ioue fulmen adactum
> corripuit: primae fugere in nubila cristae,
> et clipei niger umbo cadit, iamque omnia lucent
> membra uiri. cedunt acies, et terror utrimque,
> quo ruat, ardenti feriat quas corpore turmas.
> [...]
> stat tamen, extremumque in sidera uersus anhelat,

237

pectoraque inuisis obicit fumantia muris;
nec caderet, sed membra uirum terrena relinquunt,
exuiturque animus; paulum si tardius artus
cessissent, potuit fulmen sperare secundum.

As he spoke such things, the thunderbolt, driven with the whole strength of
    Jupiter,
struck him: first his crest fled to the clouds,
and the black boss of his shield fell, and now all the limbs
of the hero are alight. The columns retreat, and there is terror on both sides
about where he will fall and which squadrons he will strike with his
    burning body.
[...]
He stands nevertheless, and breathes his last turned to the stars,
and throws his smoking chest against the hated walls;
he would not have fallen, but his earthly limbs abandoned the hero,
and his soul was stripped out; if his limbs had failed a little
later, he could have hoped for a second thunderbolt.

It is his armour which gives up first, his crest dissolving and his
shield falling as if they were parts of his body. The emphatic placing
of *stat tamen* and *nec caderet* at the beginnings of lines 935 and
937 points out just how remarkable it is that Capaneus manages to
remain upright despite being consumed by fire.[75] Like Tydeus, his
body is a deserter, its earthly limits in contrast with the more than
mortal proportions of his soul. It is no surprise that he is called a
uir twice in this passage.

Does the glory of what is achieved before death outweigh the
inevitable dissolution of masculinity in death? Tydeus is the clearest example of a strongly negative answer to this question. In the
moment of his death, his entire claim to heroism is undermined
by his cannibalism. The significance of his aristeia is erased by
his dying action. Other heroes, too, do not seem to achieve a satisfactory death. Apollo works hard to provide Amphiaraus with a
glorious death, trying to reread the manner of his death as advan-
tageous: *uade diu populis promissa uoluptas | Elysiis, certe non
perpessure Creontis | imperia aut uetito nudus iaciture sepulcro*
('Go, pleasure long promised among the Elysian peoples, you who
are certainly not about to suffer under the rule of Creon or lie naked

75 Williams (1972) 135.

with burial forbidden', 7.775–7).[76] However, this fate itself denies him the opportunity to die fighting, or indeed to die at all.[77] Diana, too, attempts to give Parthenopaeus a glorious death (9.662–7): yet he recognises as he dies that he has not crossed the boundary into manhood (9.891–2). Hippomedon is saved at the last from an ignominious death by drowning but is too weakened to fight on after his battle against the river (9.504–39). His death, too, is less than ideally glorious.[78] Polynices' and Eteocles' deaths are self-explanatory: but even the manner of the ultimate death-blow is degrading. Eteocles, like Lucan's Scaeva, fakes death in order to gain his chance at killing his opponent (11.552–73). This is the ultimate in bodily deception, and to die by deception is almost as unheroic as to kill by deception.

In Statius, it seems that epic heroism is always tainted either by defeat or excess. Is there an example of uncompromisingly positive heroism in the *Thebaid*, or is epic masculinity itself fatally flawed in Statius' version? Dymas is paradoxically successful in defeat when he achieves the narrator's approbation for his suicide. His death is clean and quick, with none of the bodily dissolution we have been examining above. He stabs himself: *horruit et toto praecordia protinus Arcas | impleuit capulo* ('the Arcadian shuddered and immediately filled his heart with his whole sword', 10.435–6), refuses to give away the Argive plans, and throws his dying body on top of Parthenopaeus as a form of burial: *sic ait, et magno proscissum uolnere pectus | iniecit puero* ('so he spoke and, having cut open his chest with a great wound, threw himself on the boy', 10.439–40). He is active and determined, and there is no great rush of blood and gore. The other great suicide of book 10, that

---

[76] Ripoll (1998) 226 suggests that the divine attempts to give their protégés a *magna mors* are ultimately empty. Ahl (1986) 2859 suggests that Apollo is actually responsible for Amphiaraus' descent to the Underworld; this is one of Statius' own alternative suggestions for the causation of the earthquake (809–16: *seu uati datus ille fragor*, 815) and would heighten the irony still further. Smolenaars (1994) 387–90.

[77] Throughout the beginning of book 8, Amphiaraus gradually fades into death: although Apollo attributed the causation of the earthquake to the Fates (7.774–5), they are taken by surprise by Amphiaraus' death, and only break off his thread at 8.11–13.

[78] The language of liquefaction characterises Hippomedon's death too: *manant* ('they are wet', 528); *soluitur* ('is loosed', 530); *laxat* ('relaxes', 530); *labant undarum e frigore gressus* ('his steps flag from the cold of the waves', 531). Cf. Vessey (1973) 297–8.

239

of Menoeceus, inspired by the goddess Virtus herself, is similarly clean (*Thebaid* 10.774–9):

sic ait, insignemque animam mucrone corusco
dedignantem artus pridem maestamque teneri
arripit atque uno quaesitam uulnere rumpit.
sanguine tunc spargit turres et moenia lustrat,
seque super medias acies, nondum ense remisso,
iecit et in saeuos cadere est conatus Achiuos.

Thus he speaks, and snatches his renowned soul with the glittering point
of his sword,
the soul which had long been scorning his limbs and sad to be held fast,
and he seeks it and breaks it with one wound.
Then he scatters the towers with blood and purifies the walls,
and threw himself on top of the centre of the battle-lines, with his sword
still not relaxed, and attempted to fall on the savage Argives.

Like Tydeus and Capaneus, he fights against the limits of his body; he takes it even further, in fact: Tydeus and Capaneus call their bodies deserters; Menoeceus scorns his body so much that he regrets his soul is kept in his body at all. His death again is active and determined (*arripit, rumpit*), clean and quick. The dissolution of his body and its collapse is presented and interpreted in a very different way: his blood is a libation which purifies rather than befouls; as he falls, he is brought to earth by Pietas and Virtus; even as he falls, his sword is still not relaxed (*nondum . . . remisso*). McGuire has argued that suicide provides an alternative form of heroism in the *Thebaid*, but that ultimately it too proves unsatisfactory and ineffective.[79] Despite the suicide's control over his own body, reflected in his death, that control does not extend to the wider text. Maeon's suicide in protest at Eteocles has no effect except to stop the tyrant killing him himself, and brings only silence. Dymas fails to protect Parthenopaeus' body, and his own body becomes a symbol of Argive defeat. Menoeceus saves Thebes, but only at the cost of causing Thebes to be defeated again, since his father Creon in his grief refuses burial to the Argives and brings down the wrath of Theseus.

The paradox of the *Thebaid* is that it is an epic which showcases defeat. The structure of the second half of the poem is a

79 McGuire (1997).

series of defeats and deaths: Amphiaraus, Tydeus, Hippomedon, Parthenopaeus, Capaneus, Adrastus (as he fails to stop the duel in book 11 and flees), Polynices and Eteocles (mutually defeating each other), and finally Creon.[80] Not only does Statius outdo Homer and Virgil in showing both sides of the battle, from the viewpoints of both victorious and defeated, but he also succeeds in creating a situation where both sides are defeated.[81] The primary function of book 12 is to restage the war so that Thebes too can be defeated, this time by Theseus.[82] The Statian hero exists only to undergo death and defeat.

[80] 'Statius' *Thebaid*...dwells preponderantly on the negative theme of generations cut off, as one hero after another is killed off in a kind of epic *Ten Green Bottles*.' Hardie (1993) 97.

[81] Ahl (1986) 2869 n. 57.

[82] Hardie (1993) 48 suggests that Theseus can be the one 'self-sufficient epic man' in Statius.

6

THE SWORD FIGHT

Introduction

We have now seen the lion's share of Statius' epic games: the two remaining events (fight in armour and archery) are both in different ways non-contests. The fight in armour is stopped before it begins, and the archery is an opportunity for Adrastus to display his skill without the threat of competition. Homer and Virgil provide precedents for ending with non-competitive displays. The Iliadic games finish with a javelin competition, which Achilles stops before it starts, in order to award the prize to Agamemnon. In the *Odyssey*, after Odysseus has humiliated the Phaeacian boys with his prowess in the discus, they diplomatically move to a display of dancing and ball skills, which, as we have seen above (pp. 173–6), is reflected in Virgil's display event, the *lusus Troiae*. In a sense, Virgil also reflects the Iliadic non-contest in his archery, which is won not by the best shot but by Acestes' omen, as we will see in chapter 7. In his non-contests, Statius is also engaging with this tradition. Each raises different issues, and we will begin by exploring the fight in armour in the context of gladiatorial games.

Gladiatorial spectacles have fascinated scholars as well as film-makers.[1] Social historians have tried to determine why they were so popular and all-pervasive in Roman culture of the imperial era.[2] Critics of Latin poetry, and epic in particular, have looked to them as a counterpart or even an inspiration for the spectacles of blood and violent death which progressively come to dominate Latin

---

[1] Most recently, *Gladiator* (2000) took several worlds by storm. Key recent works from amongst the vast array on gladiatorial games: Robert (1940); Auguet (1972); Ville (1981); Hopkins (1983) 1–30; Wiedemann (1992); Barton (1993); Plass (1995).

[2] Wiedemann (1992) suggests that imperial power and senatorial disempowerment are the main reasons; Barton (1993) takes a more psychological view, offering a stimulating insight into the angst, desire and horror aroused by gladiators in Roman writers.

epic.[3] How do Statius' games fit into the reality of the arena? What of actual representations of gladiatorial fights? Silius has a *bona fide* gladiatorial contest in his games in *Punica* 16. Statius' fight in armour never actually takes place. How do these texts relate to each other, to duels in epic battle and to real gladiatorial games? Silius takes the defining fratricidal battle of the *Thebaid* and restages it as a gladiatorial contest; his reading of Statius points out the way that Statius' fight is linked to the fights of Tydeus and Polynices in book 1 and the climactic duel of Polynices and Eteocles in book 11, presented by Jupiter as a gladiatorial combat.[4] Through these connections, we can begin to examine the multivalent relationship between games and war in the *Thebaid*, and question the central aim of the epic genre: heroic and poetic immortality.

The armed duel, according to one school of thought, is the event from which funeral games originated.[5] Yet the fight between Diomedes and Ajax in *Iliad* 23 (798–825) is a tendentious site: there are those who would like to exclude it entirely, and those who find its tone jarring.[6] Achilles marks it out as special, calling for the bravest to fight (802–4); the audience is overcome with θάμβος (wonder, admiration, 815).[7] The aim of the fight is to inflict a wound, and the prize is the armour despoiled from Sarpedon by Achilles.[8] Even here in the *Iliad*, the audience stop the fight just as

---

[3] See: Ahl (1976) 82–115; Williams (1978) 184–90; Segal (1983) 186–7; Heuzé (1985) 178–94; Most (1992) 401–3; Leigh (1997) 288–91; Zissos (2003).

[4] Legras (1905) 237 argues against any reference to gladiatorial games, on the grounds that imitation of Homer excludes it. Rather, the text simultaneously refers to Homeric and gladiatorial games, playing the two off against each other, even reading the Homeric fight as a predecessor for gladiatorial games.

[5] See Richardson (1993) 259.

[6] See, for instance, Willcock (1973) 2. See Richardson (1993) 259–60 on the chequered history of the text of the fight: 806 was athetised by Aristarchus; 824–5 were athetised by both Aristophanes and Aristarchus.

[7] θάμβος is a marked term which suggests an almost religious awe: see Aubriot (1989).

[8] It is not clear what this fight should be called. Willcock (1973) 2 refers to it as a fight in armour; Richardson (1993) 259 refers to it as an armed duel, but later talks of 'wounding with a spear thrust' (260). The description of the fight seems to combine elements of different types of fighting. Juhnke (1972) 113 refers to the fight in Statius as a 'Schwertkampf' (sword fight), but that in Homer as a 'Hoplomachie' (fight in armour). The actual weapons used in the Iliadic fight are not specified; closest to a description is ταμεσίχροα χαλκὸν ('flesh-cutting bronze', 803). The prize is a sword (μέγα φάσγανον, 'great sword', 824), and there are no descriptions of spear throws. The wording of the fighting seems to suggest a sword fight: they come near to each other (816) and Diomedes threatens Ajax's neck with the point of his weapon – even though it is described as a δόρυ (spear), he seems to be using it like a sword.

it looks likely that Diomedes will wound Ajax, because they are scared for Ajax (*Iliad* 23.822–3):[9]

καὶ τότε δή ῥ' Αἴαντι περιδείσαντες Ἀχαιοὶ
παυσαμένους ἐκέλευσαν ἀέθλια ἶσ' ἀνελέσθαι.

And then the Achaeans, fearing for Ajax,
ordered that they should stop and be given equal prizes.

Though a wound was the explicit aim of the fight, the audience are not in reality prepared to accept actual blood on view. Virgil excludes the event from the games in the *Aeneid* but displaces its ending onto the boxing, with Aeneas' intervention to save Dares from Entellus. Statius negotiates between the two, managing to have his duel and not fight it; Polynices and Agreus stand forward to fight, but Adrastus puts his foot down, and forbids it before a blow is struck (6.911–19):

sunt et qui nudo subeant concurrere ferro:
iamque aderant instructi armis Epidaurius Agreus
et nondum fatis Dircaeus agentibus exsul.
dux uetat Iasides: 'manet ingens copia leti,
o iuuenes! seruate animos auidumque furorem
sanguinis aduersi. tuque o, quem propter auita
iugera, dilectas cui desolauimus urbes,
ne, precor, ante aciem ius tantum casibus esse
fraternisque sinas (abigant hoc numina!) uotis.'

There are those who come forward to compete with naked iron:
and now Agreus from Epidaurus and the Dircaean exile,
not yet driven by the fates, are present, drawn up with their weapons.
But the leader Adrastus forbids it: 'A huge supply of death remains,
young men! Keep your courage and your eager madness
for the blood of the enemy. And you, on behalf of whom we have
depopulated our ancestral acres and our beloved cities,
do not, I beg, allow so great a right to chance before battle
and (may the gods drive this omen away!) to your brother's prayers.'

The sword fight is intimately linked to war and to Statius' war. Military vocabulary characterises the passage: *concurrere* (lit. run together) suggests joining battle; *instructi* (drawn up) would more naturally be used of armies, rather than single people; Adrastus is

---

[9] See above, p. 84.

called *dux* (leader, especially general); *copia* is often used more literally of military resources. Both the narrator and Adrastus are obsessively concerned with the coming war, and especially Polynices' destined battle with Eteocles. Polynices is not yet driven by the fates (*nondum fatis . . . agentibus*); he would like to compete but ultimately he can take it or leave it, whereas later he will be driven unavoidably by the Furies to fight Eteocles. His brother is imagined as already praying for his death, and to undertake the sword fight would be playing into his hands. *Desolauimus*, here used in a neutral way to convey the idea that the cities are empty since all the men have gone to war, ironically foreshadows the emotional reality of grief when they are all either dead or defeated. However, the 'eager madness for the blood of the enemy' (*auidum furorem | sanguinis aduersi*) is also a loaded way of describing the sword fight which assimilates it to what will happen in book 11 and to the love of war, especially civil war, which characterises the *Thebaid* in general. Further, the idea that he should not allow such a great influence to chance (*casibus*) before the war also suggests that the war itself is a sort of game. The sword fight, which does not happen, is a pre-emptive version of the duel in book 11, a fore-shadowing and reflection of the war itself, and a way of thinking about war as a gladiatorial battle writ large.

In terms of intertextuality, the key mode for this event is erasure. Virgil has essentially ignored and underplayed the Homeric sword fight by inserting its most important feature within a more sporting, less violent event. Statius does the opposite by drawing attention to its cancellation: like a crossed out word on a page, it tells you that it was once there but was deliberately removed. Statius is both intensifying the Homeric version (when the audience call for an end before Ajax is hurt) by bringing the intervention forward to before the battle begins, and constructing a narrative to explain why it is untold in the *Aeneid*: the duel is too close to war, and especially too close to death to allow it into the carefully constrained Virgilian arena.[10] This very closeness to war is what makes it so special and exciting for the Homeric audience, and so difficult for modern readers. Statius is conspicuously rewriting the event to show how

---

[10] Vessey (1970) 438 only notes the correspondence with the Homeric fight.

Virgil manipulates Homer, in the process placing himself closer to the original. When Silius restages the sword fight in his own games in *Punica* 16, he too is rereading Virgil in a tendentious way. We have seen above how Virgilian Silius' games are: only four events, chariots, running, fight and javelin, just as in the *Aeneid*. His placing of the fight puts it in the position of the Virgilian boxing, which, as we have seen, is the nearest Virgil comes to including the Homeric version. It seems very likely from the text of the fight itself that Silius was writing this passage at least with the *Thebaid* in mind.[11] What begins as a gladiatorial display narrows to focus on two brothers, fighting over kingship, who kill each other. In an even more clearly Statian touch, their two bodies are burnt on the same pyre but the flame divides (*Punica* 16.546–8):

nec manes pacem passi; nam corpora iunctus
una cum raperet flamma rogus, impius ignis
dissiluit, cineresque simul iacuisse negarunt.

Nor do their shades allow peace: for when a joint pyre
snatched their bodies with a single flame, the wicked fire
jumped apart, and the ashes refused to lie at the same time.

In Livy's version of these games (28.21), they are a *munus gladiatorium* ('gladiatorial games'; *gladiatorum spectaculum*, 'a show of gladiators') with *ludi funebres* tagged on. Silius echoes Livy in his comments on the appropriateness of the spectacle for the army and his moralising about the evils of ambition.[12] However, in Livy

[11] The *CHCL* has the *Punica* being written from AD 88 onwards and the *Thebaid* published in AD 91. Spaltenstein (1990) 416–38, in his commentary on the fight, frequently mentions correspondences with Statius but is careful to avoid suggesting who was imitating whom. As he points out, the myth of Polynices and Eteocles was well known, but it seems perverse to suggest that he could write at that time and in that place without some awareness at least of the *Thebaid*. Pomeroy (1989), however, has no compunction in seeing this episode in particular as a 'homage' to Statius (120), following Venini (1970b); Ahl (1986) 2814–16 also sees this as a clear echo of Statius.
[12] Livy 28.21: *insigne spectaculum exercitui praebuere* ('they offered a famous spectacle for the army'); Silius 16.531–2: *spectacula digna | Martigena uulgo suetique laboris imago* ('it was a spectacle worthy of the audience, born of Mars, and an image of their accustomed work'). Livy 28.21: *documentumque quantum cupiditas imperii malum inter mortales esset* ('evidence of how great an evil is the desire for rule among mortals'); Silius 16.533–4: *(quid iam non regibus ausum? | aut quod iam regni restat scelus?)* ('What has not now been dared by kings? or what crime now remains for a kingdom?'). Spaltenstein (1990) notes the correspondences and divergences from Livy.

the pair are cousins, not brothers, and rather than killing each other, the older, experienced cousin kills the younger; there is no mention of their burial. Silius' games are clearly in rivalry with Statius, and by essentially including the entire duel of Polynices and Eteocles as a gladiatorial spectacle within a set of funeral games, Silius turns the whole Thebaid into a game, an image of war for entertainment. He surpasses Statius by actually staging a sword fight, exceeds Homer and even Livy by killing off both his competitors, and yet retains a keen sense of otherness and disapproval about the spectacle. These were not criminals but people who should know better. Both Livy and Silius comment on the unusual high status of the gladiators, but Livy presents it as a display of nobility (28.21) while Silius represents the two as following some barbaric custom: *is genti mos dirus erat* ('that was the dire custom of their tribe', 16.537). Thus, Silius maintains a careful distance from the spectacle and rereads epic, with some distaste, as a gladiatorial display. This is hardly a homage to Statius but a clear display of rivalry.[13] If the games are a *Thebais in paruo*, a microcosm of the *Thebaid*, Silius miniaturises the whole poem still further by turning it into one fight within many as part of a gladiatorial display.

This reading of Statius' sword fight also shows an astute appreciation of the dynamics of the *Thebaid*. For the fight in armour is strongly linked to the dénouement of the epic and the duel between Polynices and Eteocles, foreshadowed by Polynices' fight with Tydeus in book 1.[14] I want to start by looking closely at the passage in book 1, and showing how it can be seen as a miniature set of games reaching a climax with the fight in armour, just as the games represent the second half of the *Thebaid*, and its own climax in the duel.

Tydeus and Polynices

When Tydeus and Polynices first meet in the entrance to Adrastus' palace and fight each other simply for the space, the text gestures

---

[13] Pomeroy (1989) reads it as homage.

[14] On the links between the two fights in 1 and 11 see: Bonds (1985). He does not make a connection with the fight in the games. Vessey (1973) 161 hints at a link through Adrastus' role as peacemaker.

towards moments in several events of the games, culminating in the sword fight.[15] Statius clearly signals here the importance of the contrast between games and reality in the *Thebaid*. In a simile, the two are compared to boys competing at the Olympic Games, yet it serves only to emphasise the differences between games and war.[16]

Even as the fight begins, Statius casts it like a game: it is *fortuna* who inspires them to compete, yet what she inspires is a bloody madness (*rabiem cruentam*, 1.408). From the beginning, this encounter is both game and war, both real and yet still protected from the true bite of reality by the intervention of an improvised umpire in the shape of Adrastus. The two make threats and strip off to fight (1.411–13):

> mox ut iactis sermonibus irae
> intumuere satis, tum uero erectus uterque
> exsertare umeros nudamque lacessere pugnam.

> Soon when their anger had swollen enough through boasting speeches, then indeed each stood up and revealed his shoulders and provoked naked battle.

The words *nudam...pugnam* ('naked...battle') look forward to *nudasque mouent in proelia uires* ('they stir up their naked strength for battles', 6.18), which first describes the games.[17] Both Parthenopaeus in the running and Tydeus in the wrestling strip off before they fight, as does Entellus in the Virgilian boxing.[18] The physical description that follows, however, makes a stronger link to Tydeus' wrestling match;[19] for here, too, Statius compares the size and spirit of the fighters (1.414–17):

---

[15] As well as Bonds (1985), see Vessey (1973) 92–100; Ahl (1986) 2852; Ripoll (1998) 321–2 on the fight in book 1.

[16] Ripoll (1998) 322 suggests that the lack of structure and rules in the fight and their lack of desire for praise (*cupido laudis*) shows how epic glory and *uirtus* is devalorised by the *Thebaid*.

[17] Heuvel (1932) 203 points to this connection but interprets the line as referring to a fight without armour and weapons ('*pugnam sine ueste et armis*').

[18] Parthenopaeus: 5.570; Tydeus: 5.835–6; Entellus: *Aeneid* 5.421–3. See Venini (1961b) 374.

[19] Heuvel (1932) 203 (also linking the description to Virgil's boxers and Valerius Flaccus' description of Amycus and Pollux); Vessey (1970) 435.

> celsior ille gradu procera in membra simulque
> integer annorum, sed non et uiribus infra
> Tydea fert animus, totosque infusa per artus
> maior in exiguo regnabat corpore uirtus.

> He was taller in size and in his long limbs and at the same time
> in his prime, but Tydeus was not beneath him in strength
> or spirit, and a greater manliness was poured through
> all his limbs and reigned in his scanty frame.

The longer version of this in the wrestling match (6.836–46) portrays Tydeus in much the same way; Polynices, however, is portrayed much more favourably than Agylleus (Tydeus' opponent in the wrestling). He is tall and *integer* (whole); Tydeus is only *non infra* (not beneath him), rather than actually superior.[20] However, the art of omission suggests that Polynices is not all that is ideal in a ruler: he is *integer* only in his age, for instance, not his mind or moral courage, and it is in Tydeus that *uirtus* rules.

Further, the fight looks forward to the boxing as well as the wrestling, when they shower blows on each other (1.418–20):[21]

> iam crebros ictus ora et caua tempora circum
> obnixi ingeminant, telorum aut grandinis instar
> Riphaeae, flexoque genu uacua ilia tundunt.

> Now they redouble frequent blows around the face
> and hollow temples and struggle against each other, the image of a shower
> of weapons or Riphaean hail, and they bruise hollow groins with bent knee.

There are verbal reminiscences of the passage in the boxing where Capaneus showers Alcidamas with punches (6.792–4):

> motu Spartanus acuto
> mille cauet lapsas circum caua tempora mortes
> auxilioque pedum

> The Spartan with sharp moves
> and the help of his feet watches out for a thousand deaths falling
> around his hollow temples.

---

[20] Note particularly that when Agylleus becomes exhausted in the course of the match, he is called *non integer* (6.872).

[21] Heuvel (1932) 204; he also sees a link here between the language of this image and the description of the chariot race at 6.422.

Both passages turn a Virgilian simile into a metaphor, refracting this passage from the boxing match in the *Aeneid* when Entellus attacks Dares with such ferocity that Aeneas stops the match (*Aeneid* 5.457–60):

> nunc dextra ingeminans ictus, nunc ille sinistra.
> nec mora nec requies: quam multa grandine nimbi
> culminibus crepitant, sic densis ictibus heros
> creber utraque manu pulsat uersatque Dareta.

> Redoubling blows, now with his right hand, now with his left.
> There is no delay, no rest: as clouds strike many blows on roofs
> with hail, so the hero is everywhere and beats and
> overwhelms Dares with densely packed blows from each hand.

Statius works with this image in the background, playing with the idea of it and hinting at it in his diction without directly alluding to it.[22] Instead, in the passage from book I he changes the hailstorm into a hail of weapons, of javelins and arrows, subtly moving the imagery from games to war. This image points us towards the wider matrix of storm imagery which is so important throughout the *Thebaid*, particularly emphasising that aspect of it which presents war as a storm, and not forgetting that Polynices has just struggled through a huge epic-stirring storm on his way to Thebes, one which has been read as an allegory for his state of mind,[23] but is also a foreshadowing of the war to come.

The contrast between games and war is also drawn out by the juxtaposition of the image of Olympic competition with a portrayal of the most brutal and dirty fighting, in words deeply significant for the rest of the *Thebaid*. For Statius follows his comparison of Polynices and Tydeus to boys competing at Olympia with a scrabble in which they attempt to scratch out each other's eyes (1.421–7):

> non aliter quam Pisaeo sua lustra Tonanti
> cum redeunt crudisque uirum sudoribus ardet
> puluis; at hinc teneros caueae dissensus ephebos

---

[22] In Apollonius, the storm of blows was compared to ship-builders banging in nails (*Argonautica* 2.79–85).

[23] Hill (1990) 107: 'if it has a significance it is just that of nature responding to the evil in men's hearts'. Hill also compares the storm to Virgil's epic storm at the beginning of the *Aeneid*.

concitat, exclusaeque exspectant praemia matres:
sic alacres odio nullaque cupidine laudis
accensi incurrunt, scrutatur et intima uultus
unca manus penitusque oculis cedentibus intrat.

Not otherwise, when the fifth year returns for the Pisaean
Thunderer and the dust burns with the raw sweat
of men; but there the discord of the stands stirs up the tender
young men, and the locked-out mothers wait for medals:
so they attack, keen in their hatred and lit up by no
desire for praise, and the claw of the hand probes
the innards of the face and enters deep into the yielding eyes.

This simile demands that the fight be read against and with the games in mind, yet the simile is oddly out of place. The point of contact is their eagerness to compete (and possibly their youth) but Statius is as keen to point out the differences as he is to claim similarities.[24] These boys fight for no love of glory, only hatred of each other.[25] There are no spectators here to urge them on, and they go for each other's eyes so that even they themselves will not be able to see the fight. What is more, in the simile, the watching mothers are *exclusae*, whereas here, both Polynices and Tydeus are locked out; it is as if we should think of them as the locked out lovers ignored by their prospective spouses (who only we know are within) and turning to self-destructive violence.[26] What is more, the mention of the *exclusae matres* reminds us that both have been excluded from their families, have precisely lost their mothers. In the face of Polynices' pedigree, there is an added twist: when he uses his new family to attempt to regain his old one, his mother becomes the (worrying) prize. This is a deeply ironic simile, and it is no surprise that the description of the fighting which follows should lay emphasis on Henderson's key word: *scrutatur* (literally, but rather boringly, 'investigate', 'search thoroughly').[27] The grim, horrific rummaging and digging around in flesh of fighting in the

---

[24] Heuvel (1932) 205–7.

[25] Ripoll (1998) 214 reads this as showing that glory has no place in Tydeus' motivations throughout the epic.

[26] Hershkowitz (1994) reads Polynices' rivalry with Eteocles as sexual rivalry, through the frequent bull similes.

[27] Henderson (1991) 57 and passim. Hill (1990) 109 also points to the significant echo of *scrutor*, used of Oedipus blinding himself at *Thebaid* 1.46–8, looking back to Seneca *Oedipus* 965.

Thebaid is ultimately symbolised by Tydeus' cannibalism, and this fight, with its undignified scrabbling, is a foretaste of the ends of both Tydeus and Polynices.

As the fight escalates, and they are about to go for their swords, we are presented with a rehearsal (as it were) of the fight in armour (1.428–31):

> forsan et accinctos lateri (sic ira ferebat)
> nudassent enses, meliusque hostilibus armis
> lugendus fratri, iuuenis Thebane, iaceres,
> ni rex[...]

> And perhaps they would have bared their swords, girded at
> their sides (so anger moved them), and you would lie,
> Theban youth, better dead by hostile arms, deserving the grief of your brother,
> if the king had not[...]

Here, too, the swords are naked, echoing the duel (*sunt et qui nudo subeant concurrere ferro*, 'there are those who come forward to compete with naked iron', 6.911), in a sort of inversion of the Greek athletic ethos, turning the purity of the naked athlete into the brutality of naked iron. This fight, however, is even more tentative than in book 6: the swords are not even unsheathed before Adrastus interrupts, not deliberately, but simply because he has been woken by the noise. Yet the same ideas are already there: Polynices' death would have been better than the war to come; the ever-present idea of the false grief of the brother.[28]

This moment of interruption by Adrastus is repeated in the duel between Polynices and Eteocles in book 11. Last but one in a long series of those who attempt to turn them aside from fratricide, followed only by the personification of Pietas herself, Adrastus rushes between the two as they are about to fight and makes a panicked speech of persuasion, full of echoes of the earlier speeches (11.429–35):

> tamen ille rogat: 'spectabimus ergo hoc,
> Inachidae Tyriique, nefas? ubi iura deique?
> bella ubi? ne perstate animis, te deprecor, hostis
> (quamquam, haec ira sinat, nec tu mihi sanguine longe),

---

[28] This also links the fight to Polynices' near-death in the chariot race (6.513–17). Heuvel (1932) 207; Vessey (1970) 436.

te, gener, et iubeo; sceptri si tanta cupido est,
exuo regales habitus, i, Lernan et Argos
solus habe!'

But he asks: 'Shall we watch this unspeakable act,
then, sons of Inachus and Tyrians? Where are rights and the gods?
Where is war? Don't persist in this state of mind, I beg you, enemy
(although, if anger allowed this, you would not be far in blood from me),
you, son-in-law, I even command; if your desire for rule is so great,
I take off my royal robes, go, have Lerna and Argos
on your own!'

When he asks *bella ubi?* ('where is war?') he specifically excludes
this from the true course of war. The duel has become a *nefas* not
even fit to be watched, the essence of the perversion of civil war,
fraternas acies ('brotherly battle lines') brought to a head. The
emphasis on spectatorship (*spectabimus*) suggests that the fratricide has become gladiatorial entertainment for the two armies. This
recalls the occasion where Polynices and Eteocles are described as
a *par* (pair), a gladiatorial term much used in Lucan's descriptions
of civil war.[29]

It comes in the mouth of Jupiter himself, as he forbids the gods
from watching (11.119–26):

> illas ut summo uidit pater altus Olympo
> incestare diem trepidumque Hyperionis orbem
> suffundi maculis, toruo sic incohat ore:
> 'uidimus armiferos, quo fas erat usque furores,
> caelicolae, licitasque acies, etsi impia bella
> unus init aususque mea procumbere dextra.
> nunc par infandum miserisque incognita terris
> pugna subest: auferte oculos!

> When the high father saw them from the top of Olympus
> raping the day and staining the panicked sphere of Hyperion
> with bloody spots, he begins thus with fierce words:
> 'We have seen armed men, in madness going as far as is acceptable,

---

[29] See Ahl (1976) 82–112; Masters (1993) 35, 44, 109–10, 155; Leigh (1997) 234–6.
Masters describes the gladiatorial imagery as 'central to Lucan's symbolism' (155);
Leigh argues against Ahl's interpretation of gladiatorial games as propitiation of
the dead by human sacrifice (235) and suggests instead a theory of metaliterary
amphitheatricality, where representations of passive spectatorship within the text provide a disruptive model for the reader which ultimately propels them towards action
(241–3).

heaven-dwellers, licensed columns, even if one man made blasphemous
war and dared to fall at my right hand.
Now an unspeakable pair come forward and a fight unheard of
on the wretched earth: turn your eyes away!'

While the word *par* on its own does not link the duel conclusively
to a gladiatorial fight, the emphasis on spectatorship throughout
the passage, the presentation of the fight as a spectacle too hor-
rible to watch, makes it clear that Jupiter is banning the gods
from the *munera* (gladiatorial games) of Polynices and Eteocles.
Jupiter's speech contrasts the speakable (and watchable) fighting
of the true war (122–3) with the unspeakable and unwatchable
match between the two brothers (125–6).[30] In the terms of Leigh's
reading of Lucan, Jupiter rebels against the passive spectatorship
of the amphitheatre of civil war, but rather than acting instead of
watching, he refuses even to watch.[31] His rhetoric is one of protect-
ing the cosmos from the sight which threatens to overturn values
as Phaethon physically overturned the world (it rapes the day and
stains the sun). Given Polynices' association with Phaethon noted
above (pp. 32–9), this cosmic imagery is very important.[32] This
decision to refuse to watch parallels Statius' own statement of
reluctance to be read (11.574–9):

> ite truces animae funestaque Tartara leto
> polluite et cunctas Erebi consumite poenas!
> uosque malis hominum, Stygiae, iam parcite, diuae:
> omnibus in terris scelus hoc omnique sub aeuo
> uiderit una dies, monstrumque infame futuris
> excidat, et soli memorent haec proelia reges.

> Go fierce souls and pollute dread Tartarus with death
> and consume all the punishments of Erebus!

---

[30] See Barton (1993) 85–106 on the paradoxes of watching gladiators. Seneca *Epistulae
Morales* 7 famously wrote to Lucilius about the dangers of watching the games: *nihil
uero tam damnosum bonis moribus quam in aliquo spectaculo desidere. tunc enim per
uoluptatem facilius uitia subrepunt.* ('Nothing, though, is so damaging for good morals
than to remain inactive watching some spectacle. For then vices creep in more easily
through pleasure.' 7.2–3) This has been read as evidence of philosophers' opposition
to gladiatorial games, but Seneca used gladiators as examples of philosophical virtue
and metaphors for the life of the wise man (*De Tranquillitate* 11.1–6; *Epistulae Morales*
37.1–2; *De Constantia Sapientis* 16.2; with Barton (1993) 11–46): watching and refusing
to watch were complex acts of cultural negotiation.
[31] See above, p. 98.   [32] See above, p. 32.

> But you, Stygian goddesses, now spare men from evil:
> may only one day in all lands, all ages
> have seen this crime, may this unspeakable omen fall out
> from the future, and may kings alone relate these battles.

His desire that only one day (*una dies*) should see the battle parallels Jupiter's desire to keep the skies unpolluted.[33] This anti-eulogy
makes impossible its own wishes, just as Lucan's reluctance to
fight the civil war is continually undercut by his own project in
writing it.[34] Here the Furies become his Muses, confirming the
poetic nature of their role in book 11, which will be examined
below.[35] It is an inversion of Virgil's famous address to the souls
of Nisus and Euryalus, damning Polynices and Eteocles to eternal punishment instead of blessing them with eternal paradise,[36]
wishing that his own poem may not perpetuate the evil by allowing
readers to see it over and over again, rather than proclaiming the
immortality of his protagonists along with the immortality of his
poetry.[37]

The sword fight is the penultimate event (or non-event) of the
games, and represents the duel of Polynices and Eteocles just as the
archery with its prophetic arrow represents the return of Adrastus
alone and defeated. It showcases the erasure of gladiatorial spectacle from Statius' games, and sets up a worrying link between
the glory of epic heroes and the glory of gladiators. Ultimately, do
we want the memorial that epic creates? Do we want to remem-
ber killing and slaughter and death? If that is the price of poetic
immortality, to present gladiatorial gore to readers down the ages,
is it worth it?

---

[33] For Ahl (1986) 2816, this passage shows that Statius was only too aware of parallels
between myth and reality; for Hardie (1993) 8, it represents Statius' 'condemnation of
epic's power to memorialize singular events.'

[34] Lucan's split voice is also manifested in delay; on delay in the *Thebaid*, see Vessey
(1973) 165–7; Brown (1994) 4–8.

[35] See below, pp. 301–5.

[36] Venini (1970a) 146 points out this reversal, comparing the passage in particular to Silius
Punica 2.696–8.

[37] Ahl (1986) 2889: 'There is, in effect, a civil war among the words in the account of
Maeon's suicide as elsewhere in Statius.'

GAMES AND WAR

Introduction

The reality which continually dominates epic games is war.[38] In Statius' games particularly, war threatens to break out during the games; both narrator and characters are continually looking forward to the war to come in the rest of the poem. The games are a microcosm of the war. In this section, we will analyse the complex relationship between games and war in the *Thebaid*. Vessey's model of foreshadowing is only one way of approaching it; games are also preparation, training and build-up for war. Games can be an analogy for war: war is a specialised situation, taking place in a separate area, often with recognised rules.[39] Games are also contrasted to war, however: the game situation is by definition a controllable one, where participation is voluntary.[40] War frequently threatens to intrude on Statius' games as they come close to going out of control.[41] Analogously, Statius' heroes continuously attempt to go beyond the bounds of war, breaking what rules of epic heroism there are. The following sections will examine these different

---

[38] The case of the Phaeacian games in the *Odyssey* might be read as a counter-example. These games are different in many ways from other epic games, as Cairns (1989) has shown. They are a peacetime activity taking place among citizens of the same city, and the Phaeacians are a notably unwarlike people. However, these too are surrounded by references to war. Before the games, Demodocus sings of the quarrel between Achilles and Odysseus (8.72–82), and the πήματος ἀρχή ... Τρωσί τε καὶ Δαναοῖσι ('beginning of grief for the Trojans and the Danaans'); after the boys have finished their games, they challenge Odysseus, and he draws our attention back to Troy and his role in the *Iliad*, using his prowess at sport to evoke his prowess as a warrior (8.202–33).

[39] Scarry (1985) enquires why war should be carried out in terms of pain, and international disputes are not settled by a dance contest. Huizinga (1949) reads war among other areas as developing from the play instinct. See also Caillois (1962). Plass (1995) links gladiatorial spectacle with civil war: 'violence under public auspices – "official violence," "war games" – is potentially as contradictory as "civil" war, at once "fratricidal" and "civilized."' (64) 'War was itself in many ways a show, made into a *spectaculum*.' (67)

[40] Huizinga (1949) 154 defines play as: 'an activity which proceeds within certain limits of time and space, in a visible order, according to rules freely accepted, and outside the sphere of necessity or material utility. The play mood is one of rapture and enthusiasm, and is sacred or festive in accordance with the occasion. A feeling of exaltation and tension accompanies the action, mirth and relaxation follow.' Huizinga also reads poetry as play. 'All poetry is born of play' (151).

[41] The text links the space for games with the space for war through the frequent reference to dust: the playing-field becomes a battlefield, as Von Stosch (1968) 13 points out.

facets of the relationship between games and war in the *Thebaid*: first, games as foreshadowing of war; second, games as training for war; third, war intruding on games; fourth, war as game. Finally, we will see how the war in the *Thebaid* goes beyond the rules and limits of war itself.

Foreshadowing

David Vessey's groundbreaking article on the games focused on the way they foreshadow the war.[42] Vessey was concerned to argue against the criticism of the *Thebaid* as episodic, a criticism which has frequently been levelled at the games in particular.[43] He suggests that various elements of the games are repeated in the war, so that the games become a complex series of omens for the deaths of all the heroes.[44] Apollo's intervention on behalf of Amphiaraus in the chariot race foreshadows his role in Amphiaraus' aristeia of book 7, when he actually becomes his charioteer. The hellish *effigies* which he uses to scare Arion is 'a foretaste of the nether regions', where Amphiaraus will arrive still alive in his chariot (427). There are problems with this tactic, however. These connections are somewhat nebulous; many of Vessey's elements of 'foreshadowing' are not omens of what is to come, but more intrusions of the mood of war into the games, such as the description of the battle of the Lapiths and the Centaurs on Amphiaraus' prize *crater* ('drinking bowl', 6.531–9, 428).[45] A clearer omen of Amphiaraus' fate, which Vessey does not note here, is the groaning of the earth in response to Amphiaraus' increasingly mad desire to beat even the driverless Arion: *dat gemitum tellus et iam tunc saeua minatur*

---

[42] Vessey (1970); see also Venini (1961a) 67; Vessey (1973) 209–29.

[43] E.g. Butler (1909) 213: 'He has therefore sacrificed the whole to its parts, and relies on brilliance of description to catch the ear of an audience, rather than on sustained epic dignity and ordered development of his story. [...] Statius' episodes do not cohere.' Vessey's two questions for his reading of the games are: 'Did Statius in fact show no originality in his treatment? Have the games no significance in the context of the whole epic?' (Vessey (1970) 426)

[44] Vessey (1970) 439 insists that this is their exclusive aim: 'Statius makes abundantly clear the premonitory intent of the whole narrative of the games.'

[45] For a sustained analysis of the poetics and wider significance of the prizes in the chariot race, see Lovatt (2002).

('the savage earth gives a groan and now already threatens', 527).[46]
The *iam tunc* clearly signals that this foreshadows the anger of the
earth to come.

The clearest examples of foreshadowing in the games come in
the speeches of the characters who read the events as omens as they
unroll. After Parthenopaeus loses the first foot race, his prayer to
Diana specifically asks her to take the power of meaning away
from the omen of his loss: *ne, quaeso, sinas hoc omine Thebas |
ire* ('do not, I beg, allow me to go to Thebes with this omen',
636–7).[47] The text, however, undermines this request: his loss was
caused by his hair (607–17), which had been vowed to Diana for
a safe return. At his eventual death, he returns to his hair (9.900–
902):

> 'hunc tamen, orba parens, crinem,' dextraque secandum
> praebuit, 'hunc toto capies pro corpore crinem,
> comere quem frustra me dedignante solebas.

> 'This hair, however, bereaved mother,' and with his right hand
> he held it out to be cut, 'take this hair, instead of my whole body,
> which you used to cut in vain despite my disdain.'

Although Parthenopaeus tries to undermine the power of the omen
to signify, the text vindicates the reading of his hair as an omen
of his death. Similarly, Adrastus, as we saw above, tries to control
the potential omen in the sword fight but succeeds only in creating a worse one (6.914–23). Adrastus is unable to distinguish
between the sword fight as a game and as part of war. He then
overinterprets his own paranoid actions, suggesting that they turn
the aborted fight into an omen of Polynices' death (*abigant hoc
numina!* 'May the gods drive this omen away!'). His reaction is to
create what the text presents as a clear omen: he garlands Polynices
victor, but has him announced not victor of the sword fight but victor of Thebes. The text labels *this* an omen: *dirae retinebant omina
Parcae* ('the dreadful fates held onto the omen').[48] The foreshadowing in Statius' games comes as much from the characters as

---

[46] Kytzler (1968) 6 does note this foreshadowing and links it with Apollo's prophecy to himself at 6.382.
[47] See Dominik (1994b) 117–18.
[48] See chapter 7 for a discussion of Adrastus as king.

from the narrator. Their minds are constantly on the war, so they read the events in the text as omens of what is to come. Often, as in these cases, and also in the final lines of the book, which will be examined below, the characters are at odds with the narrator in attempting to control the omens. The text privileges a narratorial interpretation which reads the omens in the worst light possible. In the archery, the leaders attempt to read the arrow as a physical phenomenon and avoid the issue of its significance as an omen (942–4). The narrator emphatically finishes the book with a reading of the arrow as a foreshadowing of Adrastus' flight: *penitus latet exitus ingens | monstratumque nefas: uni remeabile bellum, | et tristes domino spondebat harundo recursus* ('The huge disaster lies hidden and the ordained crime: only one man can return from this war, and the arrow promises this sad return to its master.' 943–5). These two final events, the sword fight and the archery, function almost entirely as omens and emphasise the importance of foreshadowing in the games.[49]

Vessey's reading of foreshadowing in other events is less convincing: he sees Phlegyas' practice throw and failure in reality as 'a parallel to Hippomedon's long triumph over the Thebans, followed, to his fellows' dismay, by his grim fate on the banks of the Ismenus';[50] Hippomedon's aristeia and death, however, are one continuous event, and his aristeia is not presented as practice for his battle with the river. He reads the boxing match as a demonstration of 'the same *furor* that leads Capaneus into his crazy battle with Jupiter in Book X' (433). He relates Tydeus' wrestling match to his aristeia in book 2. 'There also his heroic *uirtus*, his preternatural *uis* overcomes mighty odds.' (436) The only way to relate it to book 8 is via the simile of the lion in book 2 (437). The weakness of these arguments is primarily a result of strait-jacketing the relationship between games and war in the *Thebaid* in the model of 'foreshadowing'. Many of the intratextual references do not take the form of foreshadowing. 'Foreshadowing' as a word suggests that the games are merely a shadow of the war. However, the

---

[49] 'In the closing scenes of the funeral games, the premonitory nature of the account is not implicit but explicit.' (Vessey (1970) 438)

[50] Vessey (1970) 431.

relationship is a two-way one, a dialogue.[51] Most famously, in *Iliad* 22, war is compared to games (*Iliad* 22.159–66):

ἐπεὶ οὐχ ἱερήϊον οὐδὲ βοείην
ἀρνύσθην, ἅ τε ποσσὶν ἀέθλια γίγνεται ἀνδρῶν,
ἀλλὰ περὶ ψυχῆς θέον Ἕκτορος ἱπποδάμοιο.
ὡς δ᾽ ὅτ᾽ ἀεθλοφόροι περὶ τέρματα μώνυχες ἵπποι
ῥίμφα μάλα τρωχῶσι· τὸ δὲ μέγα κεῖται ἄεθλον,
ἢ τρίπος ἠὲ γυνή, ἀνδρὸς κατατεθνηῶτος·
ὣς τὼ τρὶς Πριάμοιο πόλιν πέρι δινηθήτην
καρπαλίμοισι πόδεσσι·

They were not competing then for a sacred ox
which is a prize for the feet of mortals,
but they were running for the soul of horse-taming Hector.
Just as when prize-winning whole-hoofed horses run around the goal
very swiftly. A great prize is set up,
either a tripod or a woman, when her husband has died.
So the two of them whirled three times around the city of Priam
on their quick feet.

Games are part of the world of normality, against which Homer is setting the war; in effect, games here are reality, war a surreal and horrific aberration.[52] War can be read as a sort of game, just as games can become a sort of war. In particular, the two are related by the ethos of heroism. The poetry of Homer gives undying glory to the successful warrior: the poetry of Pindar mobilises the same mechanisms on behalf of the successful athlete. This simile, however, underlines the differences between games and war as much as the similarities. Both are a striving for heroic glory but in games the prizes are monetary, while in war the lives of the competitors are at stake.

---

[51] Vessey (1970) 434 does hint at this dialectical relationship when he notes that the boxing is recalled in the lament for Alcidamas' death at 10.498–508. This only stimulates him (rather improbably) to read Capaneus as the cause of Alcidamas' death: 'As it happens, Capaneus was prevented from murdering Alcidamas in the games, but, nonetheless, he is indirectly responsible for his death in battle.'

[52] This simile marks out the battle between Achilles and Hector as something unusual, exceptional, possibly even unwarlike; in particular, the chase is unheroic. However, in other senses this is a super-battle, the ultimate epic duel and the model for many to come, including that between Turnus and Aeneas.

The training game

The opening lines of book 6 present the games as preparation for war (6.1–4):

nuntia multiuago Danaas perlabitur urbes
Fama gradu, sancire nouo sollemnia busto
Inachidas ludumque super, quo Martia bellis
praesudare paret seseque accendere uirtus.

Tradition the announcer slips through the Danaan cities
on much-wandering steps, proclaiming that the sons of Inachus
are consecrating a new tomb with customary rites and games on top of that,
through which warlike virtue prepares to foresweat war and to set itself alight.

The games are a 'foresweating' of the war, a way to prepare and to set their masculinity on fire.[53] It is *Fama*, the personification of the epic tradition herself, who introduces these new games. The games are essentially naked battles, as we have seen (6.18, see above, p. 44). The first simile of the book continues the links between games and war with imagery of practice and reality (6.19–24):

ceu primum ausurae trans alta ignota biremes,
seu Tyrrhenam hiemem, seu stagna Aegaea lacessunt,
tranquillo prius arma lacu clauumque leuesque
explorant remos atque ipsa pericula discunt;
at cum experta cohors, tunc pontum inrumpere fretae
longius ereptasque oculis non quaerere terras.

Just as when biremes daring to cross the unknown deeps for the first time
challenge either the Tyrrhenian storm or the Aegean pools,
first they try out their weapons on a tranquil lake and their rudder
and light oars and learn the dangers themselves;
and when they are an experienced cohort, then confidently they attack
the sea further and do not seek with their eyes the land that has been
snatched away.

Games stand in the same relationship to war here as a rowing lake does to the sea. Military vocabulary pervades the simile, making the presence of war clear: their accoutrements are *arma* (lit. weapons; Mozley translates as 'tackling'), the group of ships are a *cohors*,

---

[53] See Fortgens (1934) 35; Vessey (1973) 192, in a slight variation from 'foreshadowing', sees the games as a 'rehearsal for or anticipation of the war'. See also Brown (1994) 216–17.

and *inrumpere* is often used of military situations. This image is part of the seam of ship and storm imagery which runs through the *Thebaid*, in which storm often represents war and the ship represents the Argive expedition. For the dangers for which the ships are training (*ipsa pericula*) are the storms of the open sea. The ship was also an image for the poem throughout antiquity.[54] Statius himself uses this ship imagery of the *Thebaid* most strikingly at the end: *et mea iam longo meruit ratis aequore portum* ('and now my boat already deserves the harbour after the long sea' 12.809). In this simile, the poet and his poem are inexperienced, practising for reality, building up with the games towards the serious matter of war and self-consciously 'secondary'. The practice oars are light, like poetry refusing to be epic. At the same time, the image of a regatta reminds us of the Virgilian ship race, which Statius has noticeably chosen not to imitate. We have seen above how Statius' decision to go back to Homeric basics with the chariot race is a self-conscious challenge to the *Aeneid*. The games are practice for the real business of writing epic: war. Yet they also constitute an epic competition in themselves.

The value of athletics for military training was a strongly debated issue in the ancient world, and particularly in Rome.[55] The debate goes back into the classical Greek world: Xenophanes and a character in Euripides condemned athletes as worthless, while Plato represents the arguments in favour of athletics as military training, and the poetry of Pindar supports the military and heroic connection.[56] Romans generally took a stance of opposition to athletics as a form of military training.[57] However, Roman attitudes to

---

[54] Brown (1994) 217 reads the image as metapoetic. Ship as poem is similar to chariot as poem: see Kenney (1958) 206; Myerowitz (1985) 73–103. Nautical poetry metaphors in Ovid *Ars Amatoria* 1.772, 2.9–10, 3.26, 99–100, 500, 747–8; *Remedia Amoris* 70, 577–8, 811–12; *Fasti* 1.4, 466, 2.3, 863–4, 3.790, 4.18, 729–30. In other didactic poetry: Virgil *Georgics* 2.41–5; 4.116–17; Manilius *Astronomica* 2.59, 3.26. In other genres: Pindar *Olympian* 13.49; *Pythian* 2.62; Propertius 3.9.3–4; Horace *Carmina* 4.15.3–4.

[55] See König (2000) 49–76.

[56] König (2000) 49–52; Xenophanes in West (1972) 165–6 vol. 2; Euripides *Autolycus* frag. 282 (Nauck *TGF* 441). On Pindar, see Lee (1983); Perysinakis (1990). On Plato, see Kyle (1987) 137–40; physical training in educational schemes of *Republic* (3.403C–412B) and *Laws* (8.829E–834B). Morrow (1960) 297–398.

[57] Cicero *Pro Flacco* 71.90–92; *In Verrem* 2.2.7; *Tusculan Disputations* 4.70; *De Republica* 4.4 with Rawson (1992); Horace *Satires* 2.2.9–15 with Oliensis (1998) 41–63; Lucan *Bellum Civile* 2.270–72 with König (2000) 57 n. 41; Juvenal 3.58–80 with Braund (1988)

Greek sport and *gymnasia* were as complex as their general attitude to Greek culture.[58] While Cicero produced extensive criticism of Greek athletics in his work, he also had Greek statues imported to create an authentic atmosphere in his private *gymnasium*.[59] Archaeological remains support this evidence.[60] This stance of opposition is mainly held against Greek athletics in a festival context. Romans could still portray sport and physical exercise as useful training. According to Plutarch's life of Cato the elder, for instance, Cato insisted on educating his son himself, refusing to turn him over to a Greek slave, as was common practice (20.3).[61] He trained him using physical activities which were subtly distinct from the Greek athletic programme (Plutarch *Cato Maior* 20.4):

Not only did he teach his son to throw the javelin and fight in armour and ride a horse, but also to box with the fists, to bear the heat of the day and the cold weather and to swim forcefully across the eddies and rough waters of a river.[62]

The speech of Numanus Remulus in *Aeneid* 9 makes a similar training the recipe for the ideal Roman primitive (*Aeneid* 9.603–6):[63]

> durum a stirpe genus natos ad flumina primum
> deferimus saeuoque gelu duramus et undis;
> uenatu inuigilant pueri siluasque fatigant,
> flectere ludus equos et spicula tendere cornu.

> Our children, born from a hard root, we first bring down
> to the river and make them hard with the savage frost and the waves;
> the boys stay awake at the hunt and tire out the woods,
> their game is to drive horses and shoot arrows with the bow.

Camilla's upbringing, as described by Diana in *Aeneid* 11, shares in this rhetoric of ancient *uirtus* (11.570–84), although her appropriation of the ideals of manliness is fatally confused by her gender. She

---

11–15; Tacitus *Annals* 14.20 (see above, p. 42). See also Gruen (1984) 250–72; Alston (1998).

[58] König (2000) 52–8; see above, chapter 4, p. 166.

[59] Cicero *Letter to Atticus* 1.10.3.

[60] Neudecker (1988) 60–64: 'there are first-century AD paintings from Rome of young men undergoing gymnasium-style training.' König (2000) 54; Teja (1994).

[61] See Gruen (1993) 52–83 on Cato and Hellenism.

[62] οὐ μόνον ἀκοντίζειν οὐδ' ὁπλομαχεῖν οὐδ' ἱππεύειν διδάσκων τὸν υἱόν, ἀλλὰ καὶ τῇ χειρὶ πὺξ παίειν καὶ καῦμα καὶ ψῦχος ἀνέχεσθαι καὶ τὰ δινώδη καὶ τραχύνοντα τοῦ ποταμοῦ διανηχόμενον ἀποβιάζεσθαι.

[63] See above chapter 4, pp. 189–90.

carries a bow as well as a spear (*arcum*, 575), but this is no guarantee of virtue and manliness of archery. Even more confusingly, the young Latins are practising what seems like a full Greek athletic programme when the Trojans arrive in book 7 (*Aeneid* 7.162–5):[64]

> ante urbem pueri et primaeuo flore iuuentus
> exercentur equis domitantque in puluere currus,
> aut acris tendunt arcus aut lenta lacertis
> spicula contorquent, cursuque ictuque lacessunt.

> Before the city the boys and the young men in the flower of their youth
> are exercising horses and taming chariots in the dust,
> or they stretch their keen bows or hurl slow javelins
> with their arms and challenge each other to races and fights.

As I have noted above, there is no one simple and uncomplicated ideal of primitive Italy in the *Aeneid*.[65] A few lines after this, the palace of Latinus is described as *tectum augustum, ingens, centum sublime columnis* ('an august building, huge, high with a hundred columns' 170), which suggests a level of sophistication and civilisation far above the ideals of Numanus' speech. In Roman discourse of military training, therefore, some forms of sport are acceptable, others problematic. Horace in the *Satires*, however, makes a clear distinction between the Roman activities of military drill, exercising your horse and hunting, and the Greek activities of the palaestra (*Satires* 2.2.9–13):

> leporem sectatus equoue
> lassus ab indomito uel, si Romana fatigat
> militia assuetum graecari, seu pila uelox
> molliter austerum studio fallente laborem,
> seu te discus agit, pete cedentem aera disco –

> After chasing the hare or tired
> from the untamed horse, or, if Roman military exercises
> exhaust you and you are accustomed to go Greek, whether the swift ball
> or the discus gets you going, with enthusiasm softly deceiving you
> about the austere work, seek the retreating air with your discus –

Here, he picks out the discus as especially Greek and suggests that Greek sport is soft, although it too can provide exercise and lead

---

[64] Dickie (1985) 184 assimilates the two athletic Italian moments.
[65] See above, p. 147 n. 12.

to hard work (*austerum...laborem*).[66] Romans, though, should relish hard work for its own sake and not need it to be disguised in a cowardly fashion. We have seen, then, that the debate on the value of athletics for military training was wide-ranging and long-lived, Greek as much as Roman. The Roman stance was generally one of opposition, and athletics were implicated in Greek culture and the complex Roman attitudes towards it. On the other hand, sports that were separate from gymnasium culture and the festival context could be seen as essential for the creation of Roman military *uirtus* ('manhood') and *duritia* ('hardness').[67]

In this context, Statius' portrayal of his games as training could not be simple and straightforward. When he places his games on the positive side of this debate so emphatically at the beginning of book 6, this seems an unequivocally hellenising gesture. Later comments, however, create tensions and seem to gesture towards the debate. The essentially epic nature of his games adds another layer of complication: whereas the discus was never a Roman weapon, the Iliadic mass of metal corresponds, as shown above (p. 105), to the huge boulders thrown by epic heroes in battle. When Hippomedon substitutes a bigger discus, his speech claims preparation for war as the reason for the substitution (6.656–9). This reads the discus as a warlike event, and suggests that even this most Greek of events could be suitable for military training. The narratorial comment at the beginning of the running seems most clearly to acknowledge the existence of a debate. The running is described as least manly of events, but still useful in war for escaping when all else fails (551–3):

> agile studium et tenuissima uirtus,
> pacis opus, cum sacra uocant, nec inutile bellis
> subsidium, si dextra neget.

> a nimble enthusiasm and most slender courage,
> the work of peace, when the rites call, and not without use in war
> as protection, if your right hand turns you down.

---

[66] Muecke (1993): '*Graecor* conveys a sneer at the fashion of Greek athletics, but though the Greek ball-games may seem less arduous, they are still strenuous enough' 118.

[67] Alternatively, games could be seen as a displacement of war, rather than training for it. Poliakoff (1987) 114.

The phrase *pacis opus, cum sacra uocant* makes running not only a peacetime pursuit, but also puts it in the specific context of athletic festivals (*sacra*). This points towards Roman rhetoric separating military training from athletic festival activity. The next sentence brims with irony: reversing the usual rhetoric where running is only good for cowards, and running away is the ultimate act of unRoman cowardice, the narrator suggests that actually it is quite helpful to be able to run fast in battle if you need to escape. It is worth remembering that running and heroism have not always been incompatible. Achilles is the supreme runner, as Antilochus points out at *Iliad* 23.787–92, and part of Camilla's paradoxical *uirtus* is the ability to run extremely fast (*Aeneid* 7.808–11). Again, though, Camilla is a woman, and in both the *Aeneid* and the *Thebaid* running is the province only of boys.

The other event problematic in the context of war is archery. The bow is the weapon of Paris, and in Statius it becomes the weapon of Parthenopaeus; in Apollodorus' version of the games, he wins the archery contest.[68] In the *Iliad*, archery is associated with imagery of mothers and children.[69] Teucer is famously compared to a child hiding behind its mother's skirts when Ajax is protecting him with his shield: αὐτὰρ ὁ αὖτις ἰὼν πάϊς ὣς ὑπὸ μητέρα δύσκεν | εἰς Αἴανϑ ('but Teucer went back again to Ajax, like a boy to his mother', 8.271–2). When Pandarus wounds Menelaus at 4.104–47, he is described as 'foolish' (ἄφρονι, 104), and Athena protecting Menelaus from the wound becomes a mother brushing away a fly from a child: ὡς ὅτε μήτηρ | παιδὸς ἐέργη μυῖαν, ὅϑ᾽ ἡδέϊ λέξεται ὕπνῳ ('just as when a mother drives a fly away from her child, when he lies in sweet sleep', 130–31). The pains of childbirth are 'the arrows of Artemis'.[70] On the other hand, the bow is the weapon of Apollo, the weapon of Herakles and the weapon used as proof of manhood at the climax of the *Odyssey*.[71] In Roman thought, the bow is often the weapon of foreigners: at the end of *Aeneid* 12, when Jupiter sends his Dirae to incapacitate Turnus, they are compared to poisoned arrows shot by Parthians or Cydonians (*Aeneid* 12.856–8):

---

[68] Apollodorus 3.6.4.   [69] See Loraux (1981).   [70] Loraux (1981).
[71] It is also the weapon of Ion in Euripides' *Ion*: Goff (1988) 45 'Both Herakles and Ion hunt with the bow, the weapon of the solitary *ephebe*.'

non secus ac neruo per nubem impulsa sagitta,
armatum saeui Parthus quam felle ueneni,
Parthus siue Cydon, telum immedicabile, torsit,

No differently flies an arrow, driven through the cloud by a bow string,
an arrow which a Parthian has armed with the savage poison of wormwood,
a Parthian or a Cydonian shoots it, a weapon which will cause a wound that
cannot be cured.

Earlier in the book, Aeneas is wounded anonymously by someone
shooting an arrow (12.322–3). This refusal to claim heroic glory is
condemned as cowardice in the case of Arruns, who kills Camilla
from afar: his fear is emphasised at 11.805–7, 812–13, and he is
shot by the Nymph Opis with an arrow.[72] The bow, then, may be a
problematic weapon for the warrior hero, and it is no surprise that
the 'winners' of the archery contests in both the *Aeneid* and the
Thebaid are old men, no longer able to fight. Problematic events,
then, are won by those who are not fully men, whose age disquali-
fies them from heroism: the runners are too young, and the archers
too old. The idea of games as training for military action is tied
up with attitudes about what is Roman, what is Greek, what is
appropriately masculine and what is dangerously effeminate.

When Tydeus thinks about the relationship between games and
war at the beginning of the wrestling match, we are given a subtly
different version of the training model. Tydeus thinks of wrestling
as leisure, where war is work (6.828–33):

ille quidem et disco bonus et contendere cursu,
nec caestu bellare minor, sed corde labores
ante alios erat uncta pale. sic otia Martis
degere et armiferas laxare adsueuerat iras
ingentes contra ille uiros Acheloia circum
litora felicesque deo monstrante palaestras.

He was good at competing with the discus and in the running,
nor was he worse at fighting with the caestus, but anointed wrestling was set
above all other toils in his heart. So he was accustomed to spend
his leisure from war and to relax his armed rage,
wrestling against huge heroes on the shores of Achelous
in the fortunate wrestling grounds with the god showing how.

---

[72] Though Ripoll (1998) 223 sees Arruns along with Iapyx as examples of Virgilian heroes
who renounce glory.

He spent his *otia Martis*, his leisure from war, wrestling; to take part in sport is to relax.[73] This plays with Tydeus' status as hero par excellence: for him, heroism is just a job; it is what he does as a matter of course; the business of his life is war. However, the previous lines show some confusion in this categorisation. The opposition between games and war is undermined by the description of boxing as *caestu bellare*, 'to make war with the *caestus*'. The opposition between sport as leisure and the serious business of work is undermined by the way the wrestling is described as *labores ante alios*, 'work above all other types'. The text sets up the opposition between sport as leisure and war as work only to undermine it. The following section will examine how the games threaten to become war, before looking at how war can be seen as games.

War in the games

The ethos and atmosphere of war continually intrude into the games in the *Thebaid*.[74] Towards the end of the chariot race, competitive spirit becomes disturbingly warlike (6.454–9):

> rursus praecipites in recta ac deuia campi
> obliquant tenduntque uias, iterum axibus axes
> inflicti, radiisque rotae; pax nulla fidesque:
> bella geri ferro leuius, bella horrida credas;
> is furor in laudes, trepidant mortemque minantur,
> multaque transuersis praestringitur ungula campis.

> Again they slant headlong from the straight to the pathless
> parts of the field and stretch the track, again axles clash
> with axles, wheels with spokes; there is no peace, no trust:
> you would believe that war would be waged more lightly with iron, war,
>   horrid war;
> such is their madness for praise, they panic and threaten death,
> and many hooves press down on the crosswise fields.

In comparison, the passage in *Aeneid* 5, where the rowers are willing to give up their lives is not warlike in tone at all: *hi proprium*

---

[73] On Roman concepts of leisure see Toner (1995).
[74] See Hardie (1993) 52 on violence spilling over in the games of *Aeneid* 5.

decus et partum indignantur honorem | ni teneant, uitamque uolunt
pro laude pacisci, ('some are angry that they are not keeping hold of
their own glory and their share of honour, and want to bargain their
lives for praise', 229–30). Where those in the *Aeneid* would sacrifice their own lives, Statius' charioteers would take those of others. Statius evokes the Sibyl's prophecy of the Italian war through
bella, horrida bella (*Aeneid* 6.86), making it an encapsulation of
epic battle and pointing the reader both towards war and towards
the *Aeneid*, although *credas* ('you would believe') suggests, as
ever, both similarity and difference, an expression of disbelief in
his own hyperbole, even as it conjures up the idea of belief. Again,
the key word *leuius* ('more lightly') returns, this time casting the
war as less epic than the games. Here, the games are more warlike
than war itself.[75]

In the running, as we have seen (p. 58), the reaction of the
audience is so violent that it threatens to turn the games into a
civil war (6.618–20). As Adrastus attempts to make a judgement,
the language of war again describes the state of the crowd: *furit*
undique clamor | dissonus ('everywhere cacophonous shouting
rages', 625–6). At these moments when the order of the games
threatens to break down, the Argive army is divided along lines
of nationalities, as noted above (p. 177). Capaneus' speech at the
beginning of the boxing, as we have seen (p. 155), reads the potential violence in the games in terms of civil war (6.734–7). Since
his opponent must be one of his comrades, his death, if he died,
would be like death in civil war. The games are an ordered society,
even if they consist of people from many different nationalities,
and to bring war into the sphere of the games is to start a civil

---

[75] Vessey (1970) 428 points to the near-death of Polynices in the chariot race (6.513–17)
and the violence of the battle of the Lapiths and Centaurs depicted on Amphiaraus' prize
(6.531–9). The first is more clearly linked to the deaths of Phaethon and Hippolytus,
and the pretended death of Orestes, than to Polynices' actual death in the war. The
narrator's voice recalls the war by remarking how it could have been avoided: *quantum*
poteras dimittere bellum? (514), but war itself does not intrude into the games at this
moment. The ekphrasis is one step further removed, underlining the contrast as much
as the continuity, as Achilles' shield with its scenes of peace and the temple of Juno in
Carthage with its scenes of war do in the *Iliad* and the *Aeneid*. It is ominous in tone, but
it is not a foreshadowing, nor is it a portrayal of war intruding into games. On Polynices'
near-death and the myth of Phaethon, see above, pp. 32–9.

war. However, despite his awareness of this situation, Capaneus still attempts to kill his opponent and almost succeeds in starting this civil war. At the beginning of the boxing, Adrastus comments that the boxing is closest to war: *haec bellis et ferro proxima uirtus* ('this manhood is nearest to war and weapons', 730).[76] Yet this recognition fails to prepare him for the actual violence of Capaneus, making his analysis only too real. The order of Statius' games, the distinction between these games and war, is fragile and illusory. At all these points, the games are closer to war than an analogy for it: they threaten to break the boundaries of the comparison and become the real thing.[77]

War as game

We have seen above the famous simile from *Iliad* 22 comparing the combat of Hector and Achilles to an athletic event. The war in the *Thebaid* does not look back to the games so explicitly. Only when Amphion taunts Parthenopaeus at 9.779–87 are games mentioned, and this is in strongest possible contrast to true war. He insults Parthenopaeus by ordering him to 'play his battles at home': *proelia lude domi* (786). Yet the structure of the war is modelled on the games; each hero has a separate aristeia and fights in very different contexts and with different weapons. Amphiaraus drives his chariot and ploughs down enemies with the blades on its wheels; Tydeus fights singly and hand-to-hand in amongst the enemy; Hippomedon fights in the river; Parthenopaeus shoots a bow; Capaneus uses the

---

[76] Perhaps this is not simply a comment on the violence of Roman boxing, but also a self-conscious glance at the models for his boxing match: the match between Epeius and Euryalus in the *Iliad*, where Euryalus falls on the beach like a dead fish; the match between Odysseus and Irus, where Odysseus contemplates killing Irus; the match between Polydeukes and Amycus, where Polydeukes does in fact kill Amycus, and the match between Entellus and Dares, where Entellus only substitutes the death of an ox for Dares' death when Aeneas forces him to.

[77] It was not only in epic that games were close to war and violence. Pindar praises athletes in the same terms as warriors (*Pythians* 9.97–103; 10.55–9; *Isthmians* 1.50–51 with Perysinakis (1990)). See Brown (1994) 138 on Pindar and Statius. In inscriptions too, there are distinct similarities: both are praised for toughness and perseverance: Poliakoff (1987) 99. The response to athletes who broke the bounds of games was ambivalent; they were punished but also received a hero's honours. See Poliakoff (1987) 98, 123.

walls themselves as weapons, against the enemy; Polynices uses the whole range of weapons, ending in the sword fight that he was denied in the games, and Adrastus fights only with words. As demonstrated above, the audience also form a strong link between games and war, making war into a spectacle.[78] In particular, the audience in Valerius Flaccus' boxing match between Pollux and Amycus are strikingly similar to the audience of the fight between Eteocles and Polynices.[79] In the *Argonautica*, the shades of those whom Amycus had previously killed are sent up from Tartarus to watch the fight (*Argonautica* 4.258–60):

> et pater orantes caesorum Tartarus umbras
> nube caua tandem ad meritae spectacula poenae
> emittit; summi nigrescunt culmina montis

> And the Tartarean father sends out the shades of the slaughtered,
> who were begging him, at last to watch the spectacle of a deserved punishment
> from a hollow cloud; the peaks of the high mountain grow black.

In the *Thebaid*, the Theban dead come back to watch their own crimes surpassed by the fratricide (11.420–23):

> ipse quoque Ogygios monstra ad gentilia manes
> Tartareus rector porta iubet ire reclusa.
> montibus insidunt patriis tristique corona
> infecere diem et uinci sua crimina gaudent.

> The Tartarean ruler himself also orders the door to be opened
> so that the Theban dead can go to see the familial horrors.
> They sit on their ancestral mountains and pollute the day
> in a sad circle and rejoice that their own crimes are conquered.

This audience of the dead play on the closeness of games to war. War is a sort of game because it deserves an audience; it is a spectacle both for the dead and for the reader of the poem. This is a peculiarly deadly game, though, and it has the appropriate audience, the victims of murder in the *Argonautica*, and the perpetrators in the *Thebaid*. Both the boxing match in the *Argonautica* and the duel between Polynices and Eteocles come in a grey area between

---

[78] See above, chapter 2. Fortgens (1934) 127 points out the connection between the two descriptions of audiences in *Thebaid* 6 and 11.
[79] Venini (1970a) 114 also adds Lucan 7.768–70.

games and war. Single combats and duels are the most regulated type of war, but also the emblem of epic battle.

The other side of war

War, and particularly battle in epic poems, is a rule-bound activity. The reader is often presented with a combat between two people. These people usually begin by exchanging taunts and continue by exchanging spear throws. They might then attack each other with swords. Supplication is always a possibility, in which case there are recognised gestures: clasping the knees, for instance. After death, the armour may be taken, but the body should not be mistreated, and it should be allowed burial. The *Thebaid* is continually characterised by the way the rules of epic war are broken.[80] When Amphiaraus enters the Underworld alive, the king of Tartarus calls for an end to the rules of war: *pereant agedum discrimina rerum* ('may the rules of all things perish', 8.37).[81] He lists the atrocities as ways that the *Thebaid* will go beyond war and beyond epic (8.65–79):

> i, Tartareas ulciscere sedes,
> Tisiphone; si quando nouis asperrima monstris,
> triste, insuetum, ingens, quod nondum uiderit aether,
> ede nefas, quod mirer ego inuideantque sorores.
> atque adeo fratres (nostrique haec omina sunto
> prima odii), fratres alterna in uulnera laeto
> Marte ruant; sit qui rabidarum more ferarum
> mandat atrox hostile caput, quique igne supremo
> arceat exanimes et manibus aethera nudis
> commaculet: iuuet ista ferum spectare Tonantem.
> praeterea ne sola furor mea regna lacessat,
> quaere deis qui bella ferat, qui fulminis ignes
> infestumque Iouem clipeo fumante repellat.

---

[80] Ripoll (1998) 322–3 presents the Theban war as a war without rules, outside the norms: 'un guerre sans règles,' 'un conflit hors normes'. He argues that this is because it is a civil war, although, as we have seen in the boxing (chapter 4), the categories of foreign and civil war are confounded by Statius' Theban war. Not just civil war, but any war, and every epic war must join this 'naufrage collectif de la *uirtus belli*' (323).

[81] Vessey (1973) 263–4; Frings (1991) 85–105.

faxo haud sit cunctis leuior metus atra mouere
Tartara frondenti quam iungere Pelion Ossae.

Go, Tisiphone, avenge the Tartarean palace;
if ever you were most harsh with new horrors,
produce an unspeakable event, grim, unusual, huge, which the air
has not yet seen, for me to marvel at and your sisters envy.
Let it go so far that the brothers (may these be the first omens
of my hatred), the brothers rush on mutual wounds
in joyful war; may there be one who in the custom of mad wild beasts
horrifically gnaws his enemy's head, and one who will keep the dead
away from the final fire and will stain the heavens with the naked
ghosts: let that please the wild thunderer to watch.
Moreover so that madness does not provoke my realms alone,
look for someone to bear war against the gods, to repel the fires
of the thunderbolt and hostile Jupiter with his smoking shield.
I shall make it happen that all will have no lighter fear of stirring up
black Tartarus than of joining Pelion to leafy Ossa.

Here, Dis sets himself up as a patron ordering the action of the
rest of the epic (note particularly the programmatic *mouere* – by
literally stirring up Tartarus, Amphiaraus has stirred up the rest
of the poem). He asks Tisiphone to put on a spectacle (*edo* is the
standard verb used both for publishing poetry and for putting on
games) which is a novelty (*insuetum*, 'unwonted'; *quod nondum
uiderit aether*, 'which the heavens have not seen before'). Like
Statius, she exceeds her predecessors and makes her rivals (her
sisters) envious. Dis looks on and marvels. Gigantomachy is parallel to assaulting the Underworld, and both are portrayed as poetic
acts. Each act which goes beyond the rules of war is listed: first and
foremost, the fratricide; Tydeus' cannibalism; Creon's refusal of
burial; finally and most appositely, Capaneus' assault on heaven.
When Dis imagines Jupiter as audience watching the spectacle, he
sarcastically hopes that it will please him; but the adjective *ferum*
('wild') assimilates the ruler of the gods himself to Tydeus in his
bestial cannibalism (*rabidarum more ferarum*, 'in the custom of
wild beasts'). When Polynices and Eteocles finally do come out to
fight, the trappings of war are removed (11.409–15) as the *nigris
auidus regnator ab oris | intonuit* ('the greedy ruler thunders from
the black shores', 11.410–11). War in the *Thebaid* goes beyond

the bounds of acceptability: it breaks the rules of war; it is beyond epic. The games are too close to war for comfort; war too goes ever further away from the model of games. On a spectrum of order, the *Thebaid* moves from epic to chaos, from heroism to brute violence, from an ordered society to family killing each other – from games out to the other side of war.

7

THE ARCHERY

Introduction

The final event of Statius' games is the archery. The archery targets Adrastus, the sole participant in this non-game, and issues of kingship, control and interpretation. For the games are a controlled environment, and it is this element of control which differentiates them from reality. Historical games were also an arena for negotiations between the political controllers and their often rebellious subjects, as we have seen above. This chapter examines the archery match in relation to its Homeric and Virgilian predecessors and the Silian version; it shows that politics and control are essential to the interpretation of all these, and that the master of ceremonies (*editor*) strives, with more or less success, to control interpretation of events in the narrative, especially omens. The second section investigates the different roles of the *editores*, how they set the games up and establish their own control, and how they deal with controversy and dispute. The third section widens the discussion to include whole poems and look at how Achilles, Aeneas and Adrastus attempt, and often fail, to control the wider narrative, suggesting an analogous problem of poetic control.

The archery match

At *Iliad* 23.850–83, the archers shoot at a dove tied to a mast. Achilles specifically anticipates the improbable outcome, that one of the archers should hit the rope rather than the bird, and Teucer carries this out. Meriones then prays to Apollo and as the bird flies free, he brings it down, winning the match. When Virgil reworks this match, he takes on the entire apparatus of dove, mast and rope, as if specifically to transcend it. The first competitor hits the mast; the second hits the rope, and the third hits the bird. However, Acestes, who has nothing left to shoot, fires an arrow anyway. This arrow bursts into flames, forming an omen which Aeneas interprets as a sign of Jupiter's favour. Acestes thus wins the prize for archery, despite not playing the game by any foreseeable rule. He takes the unfairness of the Homeric game, where the first archer achieves a shot more difficult than what he was actually meant to achieve and yet loses (already made clear by Achilles' comment), and goes one step further: even the startling reassertion of fairness in the miraculous success of the second archer, who brings down the dove, is not as important as the divine symbol of the flaming arrow. This is a moment which ensures Virgil censure from sports historians down the ages. The game is less important than the manifestation of the divine: the symbolic nature of Acestes' victory transcends the logic of games.[1]

Statius' version seems to be ultra-Virgilian: all the Homeric apparatus of the dove, the rope, the missed shot, has gone. This is a display of intertextual subtraction: only the arrow and the omen remain.[2] For Adrastus is the only competitor, urged by the other princes to dignify the games with an exploit (6.924–8). He shoots an arrow across the circus at a tree but the arrow turns around in the air and returns back into the quiver. Statius marks this emphatically as an omen by speculating beforehand about the origin and futility of omens (934–7) and by putting the emphasis afterwards on different interpretations. This archery match is even further from a real match than the Virgilian version, with only one competitor, no prizes, and that one competitor not even accomplishing his aim: only the omen remains.

However, when one rereads it through the filter of the Iliadic javelin match, the final event in the games of *Iliad* 23, and Silius' reworking of it, this ultra-Virgilian archery match actually does go beyond Virgil and return to the realm of Homer. For Agamemnon

---

[1] Briggs sees this as symptomatic of Virgil's attitude to the games: 'Virgil sometimes includes his Homeric and Augustan parallels to the exclusion of specific details about the contests. That is, Virgil is more interested in identifying the captains in the boat-race as ancestors of great Roman families or in making clear parallels with the Homeric chariot-race than he is with giving the measurements of the boats, the length of the course, the number of crewmen, etc.' Briggs (1975) 283.

[2] Venini (1961b) 386.

stands up to compete in the javelin and Achilles immediately aborts the match, turning it into a compliment to the power of Agamemnon (*Iliad* 23.884–94):

Αὐτὰρ Πηλεΐδης κατὰ μὲν δολιχόσκιον ἔγχος,
κὰδ δὲ λέβητ᾽ ἄπυρον, βοὸς ἄξιον, ἀνθεμόεντα
θῆκ᾽ ἐς ἀγῶνα φέρων· καί ῥ᾽ ἥμονες ἄνδρες ἀνέσταν·
ἂν μὲν ἄρ᾽ Ἀτρεΐδης εὐρὺ κρείων Ἀγαμέμνων,
ἂν δ᾽ ἄρα Μηριόνης, θεράπων ἐὺς Ἰδομενῆος.
τοῖσι δὲ καὶ μετέειπε ποδάρκης δῖος Ἀχιλλεύς·
"Ἀτρεΐδη· ἴδμεν γὰρ ὅσον προβέβηκας ἁπάντων
ἠδ᾽ ὅσσον δυνάμει τε καὶ ἥμασιν ἔπλευ ἄριστος·
ἀλλὰ σὺ μὲν τόδ᾽ ἄεθλον ἔχων κοίλας ἐπὶ νῆας
ἔρχευ, ἀτὰρ δόρυ Μηριόνῃ ἥρωϊ πόρωμεν,
εἰ σύ γε σῷ θυμῷ ἐθέλοις· κέλομαι γὰρ ἔγωγε."

But the son of Peleus set out a long-shadowed spear
and a cauldron not burnt by fire, worth an ox, decorated with flowers,
bringing them for the contest; and spear throwing men stood up;
one was Agamemnon son of Atreus, powerful far and wide,
and the other Meriones, the excellent companion of Idomeneus.
And swift-footed god-like Achilles addressed them thus:
'Son of Atreus, since we know how much you stand out above all
and how much you are best in strength at throwing the spear;
but you take this prize as you go to the hollow
ships, and let us give this spear to the hero Meriones,
if you wish it in your heart. For I will order it.'

Achilles' decision is clearly political: the description of Agamemnon as powerful reminds us of the tension between power and heroism in the *Iliad* as a whole, and the word order of the first two lines of Achilles' speech adds to this tension, only differentiating between power and physical strength at ἥμασιν.[3] This scene is generally read as one of reconciliation, part of Achilles' reintegration into the ordered social world of the *Iliad*.[4] However, there is a tension here between the world of the games, where Achilles is in

---

[3] So much so that this use of δυνάμει is unique in Homer in carrying the sense of both political and physical power, according to Richardson (1993) 270. What is more, ἥμασιν is an absolute *hapax legomenon*, adding to the oddness of the equivocation.

[4] Richardson (1993) 202 compares the games to book 1: 'There Akhilleus was the protagonist in the dispute, whereas here by contrast he is the mediator and restorer of concord.' Cairns (1989) 236–7: 'the games of *Iliad* 23 have as one of their major functions to signal, confirm, and make as public as possible, the renewal of concord which had taken place between Achilles and Agamemnon in Book 19.'

total control, and the world of the war, where Agamemnon's power is a force to be reckoned with. This is the moment when Achilles seems to cede power back to Agamemnon, signalling the end of both his anger and his control of the poem. However, the way in which he summarily aborts the event, tactful though he is, must also assert his own power, at least within the frame of the games. Another possible subtext, in the delaying of the qualification of Agamemnon's power as power in throwing things, suggests that he is not the best in the wider context of the poem.

Silius makes the javelin the last event of his games in *Punica* 16, going back to Homer and making his own mediation between Homer and Virgil (16.575–91). First, Scipio's brother and Laelius name the dead and throw their spears; Scipio rewards them and then throws his own spear. His throw, too, becomes an omen: it stops in mid-flight, roots itself in the ground and metamorphoses into an instant oak tree; the prophets read this as an omen of great things to come (*ad maiora iubent praesagi tendere uates*, 'the prophets who know the future order him to stretch towards greater things', 16.590). His reworking of the Homeric event is telling: Agamemnon and Achilles are united in the person of Scipio, powerful both in games and war, erasing the tensions between different centres of power. The omen simultaneously corrects Virgil: this is an unequivocally positive omen, not only unambiguous, but arriving after Scipio has already completed the achievements that lead to his triumph at Rome (Silius puts that in the next paragraph, 16.594). Unlike Homer, Silius makes the event actually take place, but it is ritual, not competitive, like the *lusus Troiae*; even so, Scipio is the clear winner. His spear is victorious (*uictricem hastam*, 584) and he hurls it with 'great strength' (*magnis uiribus*, 584).[5] However, the inclusion of the preceding throws by Laelius and his brother mimics the structure of the archery matches, making three spear-throwers in all, mediating between the two spear-throwers (and two archers) in Homer and the four archers in Virgil.

Adrastus is offered the choice, by his princes, to do the archery or the javelin (927–8). He can choose between Homer and Virgil.

---

[5] Spaltenstein (1990) 437.

Adrastus chooses Virgil, but this introduction of the javelin reminds us of the wider parallels between the event in the *Iliad* and in the *Thebaid*. Both involve a negotiation between the king and his subjects, and in both there is no actual competition – in Adrastus' case because he is the sole competitor, and in Agamemnon's case because the competition is stopped. The way in which Adrastus moves from being master of ceremonies to being a participant in the last scenes of the book is accompanied by a change of role model: he moves from being Achilles, stopping the potentially embarrassing spectacle when he brings the sword fight to a premature end just before, to being an Agamemnon, pleased by the gesture of his subjects. The tone in this passage is completely different to the *Iliad*: we are in the territory of monarchy and flattery, where it becomes impossible to tell who is really in control, the king who inspires flattery, or the flatterer who persuades him to follow his advice.[6] The fact that Adrastus performs this non-event, which is supposed to make him equal in heroism to the other princes, only emphasises the contrast between them. Silius' Scipio, on the other hand, takes the initiative in both rewarding his representatives and coming forward himself to make a ritual act and display his own prowess.

Adrastus, however, chooses to do the archery, to be Acestes, suggesting that we reread Aeneas and Acestes in terms of power and politics. In the course of book 5 of the *Aeneid*, the portrayal of Acestes changes significantly. At the beginning of book 5, he is a primitive, wearing animal skins (5.37). This primitiveness is unstable, for he welcomes them with *gaza agresti* ('rustic treasures', 5.40): the rusticity suggested by *agresti* is offset by the grandeur of *gaza*, usually used of oriental treasure.[7] In Aeneas' speech, he becomes *hospes Acestes* ('our host Acestes', 36), and is a partner in Aeneas' sacrifice to his father (73). When he persuades Entellus to take part in the boxing, he becomes a rival centre of power within the frame of the games. By the end of book 5, with the founding of Acesta for those whose ships had been burned,

[6] On flattery, see: Bartsch (1994) 23–5, 148–87; Ahl (1984b) 81–5.
[7] *OLD gaza*: 'Treasure, esp. that of an eastern monarch.' Williams (1960) 47 describes the phrase as 'almost an oxymoron'.

Acestes has become a client king, an example to Aeneas of the successful act of founding. For while it is Aeneas who sets up the physical site of the city, Acestes gives out the laws (*Aeneid* 5.755–8):

> interea Aeneas urbem designat aratro
> sortiturque domos; hoc Ilium et haec loca Troiam
> esse iubet. gaudet regno Troianus Acestes
> indicitque forum et patribus dat iura uocatis.

> Meanwhile Aeneas marks out the city with the plough
> and allots the houses; this part he orders to be Ilium, this place
> Troy. Trojan Acestes rejoices in his kingdom
> and marks out the forum and gives laws to the elders who have
> been summoned.

It is no coincidence, then, that when Aeneas interprets the omen of the burning arrow, he calls Acestes 'father' (*pater*, 533) when he himself has been characterised by this epithet throughout the book.[8] Since Acestes is their host, a ruler in his own right and shortly to become Aeneas' first client king, there are not inconsiderable political motives behind Aeneas' interpretation of the omen and subsequent adjudication.

Interpreting the omens

Statius' rewriting of the omen and its interpretation in *Thebaid* 5 encourages us to open up a gap between the interpretation of the omen in *Aeneid* 5, which is in the voice of Aeneas, and the implications of Virgil's description. For Statius shows the leaders attempting to explain the phenomenon of the arrow, which has returned into the quiver, and specifically condemns their interpretations as *error*. He finishes the book with an emphatic authorially endorsed interpretation (6.942–6):

> multa duces errore serunt: hi nubila et altos
> occurrisse Notos, aduersi roboris ictu
> tela repulsa alii, penitus latet exitus ingens
> monstratumque nefas: uni remeabile bellum,
> et tristes domino spondebat harundo recursus.

8 *Aeneid* 5.129–30, 348, 424, 461, 545, 700.

The leaders weave many things in error: some say that it met clouds
and high north winds, others that the weapon was pushed back
by the blow of the tree opposite, but the huge outcome lies hidden deep within
and the omened crime: the arrow promised return from the war
only to one man, and to its lord a grim journey back.

In particular, the phrase *exitus ingens*, in the same emphatic position at the end of the line, links Statius' omen with the Virgilian
arrow (*Aeneid* 5.522–8):

> hic oculis subitum obicitur magnoque futurum
> augurio monstrum; docuit post exitus ingens
> seraque terrifici cecinerunt omina uates.
> namque uolans liquidis in nubibus arsit harundo
> signauitque uiam flammis tenuisque recessit
> consumpta in uentos, caelo ceu saepe refixa
> transcurrunt crinemque uolantia sidera ducunt.

> Now before the eyes occurrs a sudden omen of the future
> with great significance; the huge outcome taught us afterwards
> and the terrifying prophets sang the late omens.
> For the arrow, flying through the liquid clouds, burnt
> and marked its way with flames and, consumed, retreated
> into thin air, just as often stars fall out of the sky
> and run across it, flying and leading their tails.

Readers have responded in many different ways to the equivocal
nature of this passage: whether *terrifici* means arousing terror, as
it does for Heinze, or awe-inspiring, as Williams is keen to assert,
the ambiguity of the wording is undeniable.[9] The significance
of the image and the precise nature of the *exitus ingens* have been
the main bones of contention.[10] The way in which the flames of
Acestes' arrow are seen to relate to the rest of book 5 seems to
fit with a general pattern of optimistic or pessimistic interpretation. Those who see the flames as leading directly to the founding

---

[9] Heinze (1993) 133. Williams deals with 'the apparent contrast between *terrifici vates*
prophesying evil and Aeneas accepting the portent as a good omen' by insisting on
the natural awe inspired by prophets: 'it is nowhere suggested that the omen was evil.
The word *terrifici* refers to the natural awe which prophets inspire when they proclaim
omens.' Williams (1960) 141.

[10] Drew (1927) 45; Heinze (1993) 133–4; Williams (1960) 141; Putnam (1965) 84–5;
Galinsky (1968) 172–3, 177–8. A central issue is whether the omen is a reference to the
comet at Caesar's funeral games. On the comet, see: Ramsey and Licht (1997).

of Acesta will see them also as leading to the successful founding of Rome and the successful *imperium* of Augustus. On the
other hand, those who connect the flaming arrow to the burning
ships are more likely to see this omen as one which presages war
and destruction.[11] Reading through Statius slants me towards the
second complex of imagery, as well as highlighting the political motivations available to explain Aeneas' upbeat interpretation.
The *exitus ingens* for Statius is civil war and defeat; the omens are
too late because Virgil, Lucan and Statius are all condemned to
prophesy the destruction of the Roman republic after the event has
occurred; the road for Aeneas and for Rome is marked with the
flames of war and destruction, and meaning consumes itself, like
the flames that burn themselves out in the wind, blown on the wind
like empty promises.

Galinsky uses Aeneas' self-confident prophecy as an index of
his coming of age: '[b]oth in Books Five and Eight, Aeneas' companions are stunned while he is the only one who knows how to
interpret the portents.'[12] Adrastus, however, is not allowed a chance
at interpretation: he is the object of the omen, not the subject interpreting it. The *duces* are like commentators who attempt to explain
the events of a poem by reference to the physical circumstances
surrounding the events.[13] This is one sort of tendentious interpretation, one that misses the point of interpreting; rather than really
trying to understand what the omen means and acknowledging
that their expedition is fatally flawed, they find ways of explaining away the omen. Aeneas enacts another sort of interpretation,
reading the omen as the endorsement of his political allegiance.
Adrastus is not allowed to interpret at all: the meaning of the omen
'lies hidden deep inside' (*penitus latet exitus ingens*). Yet this does
not in the end encourage the privileging of the narratorial voice
over the voices of characters, but rather lays bare the tendentious
nature of all interpretation. There is no need to decide whether the
narrator's implications or Aeneas' interpretation are right, but that

---

[11] 'It is not only death which the symbolic arrow seems to predict but also destruction by
fire, an anticipation, it could be said, of the burning of the ships.' Putnam (1965) 85.
[12] Galinsky (1968) 172.
[13] Silius takes a different tactic: his *vates* (not Scipio, nor the other leaders) read the omen
unproblematically, and he backs it up by presenting its outcome immediately afterwards.

does not mean twisting both into a seamless homogeneity. When the narrator of the *Thebaid* bewails the inefficacy of omens, he is perhaps rather lamenting the way that omens are twisted to mean whatever the powerful want them to mean (6.934–7):

quis fluere occultis rerum neget omina causis?
fata patent homini, piget inseruare, peritque
uenturi praemissa fides: sic omina casum
fecimus, et uires hausit Fortuna nocendi.

Who would deny that omens flow from the hidden causes of things? The fates lie open to men, though it grieves them to observe them, and promises of the future sent ahead perish: thus we have made omens into chance and Fortune has drawn the strength to harm.

The *Thebaid* insists that interpretation is of supreme importance, but at the same time calls into question whether any interpretation can ever be satisfactory.[14]

CONTROLLING THE NARRATIVE

Introduction

The *editor* is the producer of the games, the master of ceremonies (*edo* is the standard verb used for putting on games and publishing poetry, giving a metapoetic edge to the role of the *editor*). This role is an important structural element of games, and unites them as a single spectacle, in counterpoint to the audience. He provides rules and gives judgements when those rules are challenged. The spectators correspond to the readers of the poem, the *editor* to the poet. He initiates and controls the spectacle, selects the elements and judges the outcomes. He negotiates with the audience and competitors, and both on occasion can challenge his authority. The *editor* also has a political significance: he is a figure of the king, a model monarch ruling over a model kingdom which extends just as far as the boundaries of that special area of space defined as the arena for games, where the rules of the games are the only laws of the land. In *Aeneid* 5 in particular, Aeneas is seen to represent

---

[14] Vessey (1970) 440 is worried by incongruity with 3.551–65, suggesting that the explanation lies in Statius' role as a 'rhetorical poet' who composed '*ad rem*'.

Augustus, or at least to provide a model of ideal authority for him.[15] The *editores* in our poems play very different roles, with implications for models of kingship as well as for the poet's control of the narrative.[16]

Producers of historical games were important political figures. Different types of games were organised, produced and paid for in different ways:[17] traditional Roman *ludi*, including the *ludi circenses* with their chariot races, were a responsibility of particular magistrates, paid for partly from the public purse and partly by the magistrate himself.[18] These *editores* gained political credit from putting on lavish spectacles, and attempts to restrict the ever-increasing spending are evidence of competitive conspicuous consumption in action.[19] Triumphal games and funeral games, whether gladiatorial, theatrical or athletic, were initiated, organised and funded by private individuals, also an important form of self-promotion and political capital.[20] Greek athletic games in the Roman world, as we have seen, began as part of these private spectacles, but when Augustus established recurrent festivals, such as the *Sebasta* and the *Actia*, these festivals were run along similar lines to festivals in the Greek world. The *agonothete* was a wealthy man chosen annually to hold the games, part of the civic responsibilities of the benefactor.[21] He was ultimately responsible (and financially responsible) but would have the aid of other officials: at Olympia, the *hellanodikai* acted as referees and umpires, as well as being in charge of training, organising the heats and

---

[15] For positive readings of Aeneas as Augustus in the games see: Drew (1927) 42–59; Galinsky (1968) 182; Cairns (1989) 248 ('the *sanctus pater*... becomes at once Anchises, Aeneas, and, in foreshadowing, Augustus'); e.g. Drew (1927) 57 'how affable and hail-fellow-well-met are the two, Aeneas and Augustus, yet abate not one jot of their regal dignity.'

[16] Brown (1994) 173 makes the equation between king and poet: 'The narratological function of the king is analogous to that of the epic poet, Apollo's disciple.' Hypsipyle is another poet figure in her guise as narrator, a narrator who controls the narrative at one level (in the Lemnian story) but loses control at another (in the wider poem) (Brown (1994) 94–128).

[17] See Balsdon (1969) 261–7.   [18] Beacham (1999) 3–4.

[19] See: Balsdon (1969) 262; Futrell (1997) 29–33; Potter and Mattingly (1999) 320–21.

[20] See: Wiedemann (1992) 6–8; Beacham (1999) 15–16.

[21] For clear evidence on how an *agonothete* was chosen, see Mitchell (1990) on the *Demostheneia* at Oenoanda. In this case, the *agonothete* was not financially responsible: the terms of the bequest included enough to cover the staging of the festival. His main responsibility was organisation.

putting competitors into classes; there was a *boule* which heard appeals.[22] At the *Sebasta*, the *agonothetai* heard the oath of the contestants before they competed, and distributed the prizes.[23] It was an honour to take this role and was recorded in inscriptions.[24] Domitian's *Capitolia* had the special distinction of being presided over by the emperor himself, while the *Quinquatria*, held each year at his Alban villa, were produced by an official chosen by lot from a college set up specifically for the purpose.[25]

The organisation of games was a model of wider civic and political organisation. In Rome, these arrangements changed during the first century AD. Under the empire, it was dangerous for private individuals to build up too much prestige and popular support by this method as by others. In particular, *munera* became part of the official and public realm, and were held under the auspices of the emperor.[26] Emperors also acted as *agonothetai* at Greek games: Claudius and Titus, for instance, both acted as *agonothetai* at the *Sebasta*.[27] It is no surprise, then, that representations of the *editor* in epic games changed substantially from Virgil to Statius. This section looks at representations of *editores* in games and war in Homer, Virgil and Statius.

Achilles in *Iliad* 23

In the *Iliad*, there is continual tension between Achilles' control of the games and his acknowledgement that Agamemnon has control

---

[22] There is an inscription (*IG* IV² 1.98) which says that Philon the Corinthian has been fined by the *agonothete* and the *hellanodikai* and that the *boule* confirmed on appeal that he must pay it. Pausanias 6.23–4 mentions the *hellanodikai* matching the runners, pentathletes and fighters. Pausanias 6.3.7 mentions a disputed result, in which two out of the three *hellanodikai* were fined by the *boule* for giving victory to the wrong man. Pausanias 5.9.4–6 discusses the way that the organisation of the Olympic Games has changed over the years. See Miller (1991) 63–78. See also Harris (1964) 151–69 and, for a more up-to-date account, Decker (1995) 116–29.

[23] Caldelli (1993) 33, 34.   [24] Caldelli (1993) 36.

[25] Caldelli (1993) 108–12, at least until the third century. Suetonius *Domitian* 4. See also Alex Hardie (2003) 128–9.

[26] Wiedemann (1992) 8: 'As early as the 20s BC, Augustus restricted the praetors to two gladiatorial shows during their year of office, with a maximum of 120 participants. [...] From Domitian's time on, no gladiatorial games could any longer be presented at Rome except by the emperor or by a relative or magistrate on his behalf.' See also Futrell (1997) 44–6.

[27] Geer (1935) 214–15; Leiwo (1995) 46.

in the wider sphere of the war. The characters and audience are rebellious under his control, but any democratisation is appearance only: Achilles is a strong, hands-on ruler of his spectacle. The way he initiates the games sets the tone for his role in the rest (*Iliad* 23.257–70):

αὐτὰρ Ἀχιλλεὺς
αὐτοῦ λαὸν ἔρυκε καὶ ἵζανεν εὐρὺν ἀγῶνα,
νηῶν δ᾽ ἔκφερ᾽ ἄεθλα, λέβητάς τε τρίποδάς τε
ἵππους θ᾽ ἡμιόνους τε βοῶν τ᾽ ἴφθιμα κάρηνα
ἠδὲ γυναῖκας ἐυζώνους πολιόν τε σίδηρον.

ἱππεῦσιν μὲν πρῶτα ποδώκεσιν ἀγλά᾽ ἄεθλα
θῆκε γυναῖκα ἄγεσθαι ἀμύμονα ἔργα ἰδυῖαν
καὶ τρίποδ᾽ ὠτώεντα δυωκαιεικοσίμετρον,
τῷ πρώτῳ· ἀτὰρ αὖ τῷ δευτέρῳ ἵππον ἔθηκεν
ἑξέτε᾽ ἀδμήτην, βρέφος ἡμίονον κυέουσαν·
αὐτὰρ τῷ τριτάτῳ ἄπυρον κατέθηκε λέβητα
καλόν, τέσσαρα μέτρα κεχανδότα, λευκὸν ἔτ᾽ αὕτως·
τῷ δὲ τετάρτῳ θῆκε δύω χρυσοῖο τάλαντα,
πέμπτῳ δ᾽ ἀμφίθετον φιάλην ἀπύρωτον ἔθηκε.

But Achilles detained the people and sat them down in a broad circle,
and brought prizes from the ships, cauldrons and tripods,
horses, mules, oxen with strong heads,
well-belted women and grey iron.
   And first of all he set up glorious prizes for the fastest
charioteers, an excellent woman to take away, skilled in crafts,
and a tripod with handles that held twenty-two measures,
for the winner; but again for the man in second place he brought a horse,
six years old, unbroken, pregnant with a mule foal;
and for the third he set out a fine cauldron,
which had never been used, containing four measures, still white;
and for the fourth, he brought two talents of gold,
for the fifth he set out a reversible bowl untouched by fire.

In this passage, Achilles exercises a very personal control over the crowd and the mechanics of establishing the prizes. At 257–8, the verbs that one would expect to describe the crowd instead describe Achilles: the crowd do not wait and sit themselves. Achilles makes them stop and sit down. The continual and repeated emphasis on τίθημι suggests that Achilles is personally and physically placing the prizes on display.[28] In the archery, he sets up the mast and dove himself, as well as organising the prizes (23.850–55). He announces each event in direct speech.[29] This special power of control is his through his connection to Patroclus and his grief: it starts with the organisation of the funeral pyre and continues through the games. However, he is careful to gesture towards the authority of both Agamemnon and the collective council of the princes. When he first takes control at 23.152–60, he asks Agamemnon to order the Achaeans to cease from mourning and have a meal, emphasising Agamemnon's power (Ἀτρεΐδη, σοὶ γάρ τε μάλιστά γε λαὸς Ἀχαιῶν | πείσονται μύθοισι, 'son of Atreus, for the people of the Achaeans will be most greatly persuaded by your words', *Iliad* 23.156–7). He addresses his speeches and announcements to Atreides and the Achaeans (236, 272, 658, except in the javelin, where the speech is solely addressed to Atreides), and even suggests that the audience's approval will be needed to ratify the winner of the boxing match (661). When Antilochus challenges his decision, motivated by personal pity, to give the second prize in the chariot race to Eumelus despite his accident, Achilles seems to bow to the rule of fairness by delineating public and private: the prizes are irreparably in the public domain, and can only be allocated by the conventions of the games, but he is at liberty to give whatever private gifts he wants to those who fail to win through bad luck. Yet when Achilles gives the fifth prize to Nestor in the chariot race (616–52) and awards an extra prize to Antilochus for praising his own running (785–97), it suggests that favour towards Antilochus could also have been at work when he agreed to abide by the rules. In the sword fight, too, it is the audience who put an end to the fight, but Achilles goes against their expressed wishes that Diomedes and Ajax should receive equal prizes, and awards the prize to Diomedes (822–5). In Achilles, we have an *editor* who is closely and personally involved with the organisation of the spectacle, who masks his control with careful gestures to both

---

[28] Even though this is often read as a special athletic meaning (to propose prizes in the games): *LSJ* τίθημι def. A.3.a.

[29] *Iliad* 23.272–86, 657–63, 707, 753, 802–10, 831–5 (except the javelin, which is discussed above, p. 278).

Agamemnon and the audience, but whose power is personal and arbitrary, founded on the authorising power of his grief.

Aeneas in *Aeneid* 5

When Aeneas first initiates the twin ceremonies of sacrifice to Anchises and memorial games, his style is emphatically personal (*habebo*, 'I will hold', 50; *ego agerem*, 'I myself will do', 51; *exsequerer strueremque*, 'I will accomplish and I will build', 54).[30] His commands both include his audience in jussive subjunctives and order them with imperatives. Yet when the games are actually set up, Aeneas plays no active role: the description is impersonal and passive (*locantur*, 'they are placed', 109; *tuba canit*, 'the trumpet blows', 113). He makes far fewer direct announcements than Achilles (only at 304–14 and 363–4) and even announces the victory of Cloanthus in the ship race 'through public criers' (*praeconis*, 245). He does still set up the mechanics of the archery competition himself, but it is clear that for a Roman audience this was counterintuitive, and it is presented as a heroic feat rather than a simple act of organisation: *ingentique manu malum de naue Seresti | erigit* ('He erected the mast from the ship of Serestus with his huge hand', *Aeneid* 5.487–8). His physical positioning during the events following the ship race also emphasises his power and his separation from the rest of the audience. After he has led the audience to the new circus, he sits on a raised structure in the middle (*exstructoque resedit*, 'he sat down on a stand', 290). When Dares is about to take the prize in the boxing uncontested, he stands literally at Aeneas' feet: *Aeneae stetit ante pedes* ('he stood before the feet of Aeneas', 381). The *editor* in this idealised Roman world (if that is what it is) holds firm power and prestige without dirtying his hands with the business of organisation. Aeneas' official role is also emphasised by the epithets which describe him in terms of father and son relations, either as son of Anchises, underlining the continuity of ancestral authority, or *pater*, suggesting Augustus' title *pater patriae* ('father of the fatherland'), and implying that

---

[30] Cairns (1989) 239 describes Aeneas as 'the discreet and genial president of his games'.

the control of the king over his kingdom is similar to that of the Roman father over his family.[31]

Aeneas' interactions with the characters are equally different from Achilles', with the emphasis on responsible leadership rather than personal favour. When he gives Sergestus a prize despite the disaster in the ship race, it is not through pity like Achilles, but to reward him for managing to salvage his ship and bring it in: *Serges-tum Aeneas promisso munere donat | seruatam ob nauem laetus sociosque reductos* ('Aeneas gives the promised prize to Serges-tus, happy because he preserved his ship and led back his team', 282–3). When he arbitrates between the runners, he carefully follows the distinction already established by the exchange between Antilochus and Achilles, awarding the official prizes as declared but acting generously towards those brought down by bad luck. We have seen above the moral ambivalence of Aeneas' judgement about Nisus' foul in the running; Aeneas here is more arbitrary than Achilles. Ultimately, Aeneas' effective control is displayed at the end of the boxing, when, as we have seen, a word from him is enough to end the fight: *dixitque et proelia uoce diremit* ('He spoke and parted the battle with his voice.' *Aeneid* 5.463). There is ambiguity here about whether Aeneas physically intervenes in the boxing, or whether his words are so effective that they seem like actions. In itself, *diremit* could mean interrupt or physically divide, which gives Aeneas' words even more the force of action. However, whether acting, or by speaking alone, the image of the father imposing an end (*pater...finem imposuit*, 5.461–3) is a compelling demonstration of effective power and control.

Adrastus in *Thebaid* 6

Aeneas is a Roman *editor*, maintaining his dignity and his distance, controlling effectively and officially, without dirtying his hands. In Adrastus, this lack of involvement goes even further.[32] Achilles

---

[31] Epithets: *pater*: 129–30, 348, 424, 461, 545, 700, 827; *satus Anchisa*: 244, 424; *Anchisi-ades*: 407. See Nugent (1992): 257–8, 260–1 on paternalism and patriarchy in *Aeneid* 5.

[32] His role as *editor* brings Adrastus into comparison with Aeneas: he is more usually compared to Latinus, or Evander. Brown (1994) 166–8.

personally annouces six of the eight events in direct speech; Aeneas directly announces two out of four events: Adrastus only announces one out of seven events.[33] This is symptomatic of the way he generally recedes into the background. At the beginning of book 6, it is the 'sons of Inachus' who organise the funeral and the games (*Inachidas*, 6.3).[34] Amphiaraus, not Adrastus, commands the building of the funeral pyre for Opheltes (84–5). At 249–50, Fama seems to take control of the proceedings, calling the spectators to watch in the language later used for Adrastus calling the competitors to compete: *iamque auidum pugnas uisendi uulgus inermes | (fama uocat cunctos) aruis ac moenibus adsunt | exciti* ('and now the crowd greedy to see the unarmed battles (*fama* calls them all) are present and stirred up in the fields and on the walls', 6.249–50). Rumour (or tradition) has more power than the *editor* himself.

The chariot race symbolises Adrastus' lack of power and control: the focus is on his horse, not on him (301), and his chariot is driven by someone else, Polynices. When he advises Polynices on how to drive, he is described as *rector* ('driver', 315), a deeply ironic epithet which underlines the connection between his inability to drive and his inability to rule. It was Polynices who really initiated the war and is really driving the chariot to its destruction, as he drives the army to its own destruction. Even his speech and judgement is not effective: in the boxing, his intervention is panicked and must be backed up by the physical force of Tydeus and Hippomedon (807–12); in the foot race, when war threatens to break into the race, all Adrastus does is doubt: *ambiguumque senis cunctatur Adrasti | consilium* ('the old man Adrastus delays as advice pulls him two ways', 6.626–7).[35] Here, Adrastus is

---

[33] In Silius' games, Scipio announces the games themselves (288–302) in a speech which is clearly modelled on Aeneas, and the running in direct speech, but none of the other events.

[34] In contrast, Silius' Scipio is a very hands-on leader during the funeral: *rector ducebat* ('the ruler led', 305); *ipse, tenens nunc lacte... aspergit* ('he himself, now holding the milk, scatters...', 308–9); *vocat... canit... refert... inchoat* ('he calls...he sings...he brings back...he begins', 310–13).

[35] Neither the gladiatorial fight nor the running in Silius have disputed outcomes, so there is little opportunity for Scipio to display his style of leadership. This may be deliberate: in Livy's version of the gladiatorial fight, Scipio tries to persuade the brothers not to fight. In Silius' version, he is not mentioned.

portrayed in the most negative light: he is an old man afflicted by delay and doubt. Although Achilles and Aeneas make decisions that are challenged and possibly wrong, at least they make decisions. Adrastus cannot make a decision at all, and instead forces the race to be rerun. To return to the announcing of events, at 834–5 it is *animosa Gloria* ('spirited Glory') who initiates the wrestling, and in the fight in armour, Statius takes this lack of control even further. Far from announcing and controlling the beginning of events, Adrastus has to stop an event which starts against his will. At the very beginning of the games, after the *pompa* ('procession'), it is Courage (*Virtus*) who starts the games: *tandem satiata uoluptas | praestantesque uiros uocat ad sua praemia uirtus* ('At last, when pleasure had been satisfied, Manliness calls the outstanding men to her own rewards.' 294–5). What sort of a ruler is Adrastus? Perhaps Adrastus is an attempt to create a model of monarchy which is not tyrannous, in contrast to Eteocles. If so, he succeeds only in showing that weakness can be as tyrannous and arbitrary as strength, only less effective.

Weakness does not lead to fairness. At the end of the chariot race, in which Polynices has completely failed to control his chariot and has ended up almost dead on the race course, Adrastus gives him a prize simply because he is his son-in-law: *at generum famula solatur Achaea* ('but he consoles his son-in-law with an Achaean handmaiden', 549).[36] This nepotism is symptomatic of imperial family dynamics.[37] In the discus, when Adrastus does give a prize in consolation to Phlegyas, who would have won if not for the bad fortune of slipping, even in this reworking of Achilles and Eumelus, Aeneas and Sergestus, Adrastus manages to slant the focus so that the unfairness and potential discord is emphasised, while allowing no space for actual negotiations.[38] For he says (6.726–30)[39]:

[36] Scipio is also nepotistic in his rewards for his brother and Laelius for throwing their javelins: *ipse etiam, mentis testatus gaudia uultu, | ductor, ut aequauit meritis pia pectora donis…* ('the leader himself, even, bearing witness with his face to the joy of his mind, when he had matched their pious breasts with deserved gifts…' 580–81).

[37] On the problem of dynastic succession and first century epic, see Hardie (1993) 91–4.

[38] Scipio in *Punica* 16 gives a consolation prize to Atlas, the charioteer who suffers a *naufragium* ('shipwreck') through the dangerous driving of his competitor, Durius, explicitly out of pity for his age. There is no hint that anyone else should have any say in the matter.

[39] Frings (1991) 169.

'at tibi' ait 'Phlegya, casu frustrate sinistro,
hunc, quondam nostri decus auxiliumque Pelasgi,
ferre damus, neque enim Hippomedon inuiderit, ensem.
nunc opus est animis: infestos tollite caestus
comminus; haec bellis et ferro proxima uirtus.'

'To you, Phlegyas, frustrated by your unfortunate fall,
we give this sword, once the glory and aid of our Pelasgus
to bear, and Hippomedon will not envy you.
Now there is need for courage: raise the hostile boxing gloves
at close quarters; this courage is nearest to war and iron.'

Rather than taking personal responsibility for his decision, he makes it seem falsely inclusive by saying *damus* in the first person plural; the only we here is a royal we. His confidence that Hippomedon would not envy this consolation prize is misplaced: we have seen Hippomedon envious at the great practice throw, and secretly pleased at the slip.[40] Adrastus gives no option or space for negotiation: he moves straight into the next event. This is symptomatic of the weak ruler: his worry that Hippomedon might challenge his decision leads him to make absolutely sure that there is no opportunity to do so. Thus, the *Thebaid* suggests that weak rule leads to its own tyranny.

Finally, his actions at the end of the sword fight leave us in no doubt that Adrastus is not only weak and often mistaken, but dangerous in both weakness and mistakes. For when he has forbidden Polynices to risk his life and the expedition in a sword fight, his attempt to console him creates an omen as bad as the returning arrow. His attempt to control the narrative on one level leads to effects he cannot understand on another (6.918–23):

'ne, precor, ante aciem ius tantum casibus esse
fraternisque sinas (abigant hoc numina!) uotis.'
sic ait, atque ambos aurata casside ditat.
tum generum, ne laudis egens, iubet ardua necti
tempora Thebarumque ingenti uoce citari
uictorem: dirae retinebant omina Parcae.

'Do not, I beg, allow so great a right to chance before battle
and (may the gods drive this omen away!) to your brother's prayers.'
So he speaks and enriches both men with golden helmets.

Then, so that his son-in-law would not lack praise, he orders his high temples
to be garlanded and him to be proclaimed victor of Thebes
with a huge shout: the terrifying Fates held on to the omen.

It is his paranoia, his desire to avoid adverse omens, which causes
him to create one, just as it is his weakness which leads to the
arbitrariness of his decisions. If he were confident enough in his
rule to allow challenges, he would open a space for negotiation
which would keep his rule from tyranny. This is the fair face of
monarchy in Statius' *Thebaid*, neither effective nor just, merely
weaker in his arbitrariness. As the next section will show, Achilles
and Aeneas may be effective in controlling their limited domains in
the games, but this only contrasts more strongly with their inability
to control the wider poems. Statius' figure of king and poet cannot
even control the games effectively: the *Thebaid* is a study of power
out of control.

Control and narration in *Aeneid* 12 and *Thebaid* 11

In the games, the *editor* is a powerful controlling force, a figure
of the ideal king and the poet organising his material in an effective and ordered way. Outside the arena of the games, however,
the *editor* has less stable and certain power. Of the three *editores*
discussed above (Achilles, Aeneas and Adrastus), Achilles has the
most problematic relationship with control of the narrative. His
secure position in the role at the games contrasts with the tensions
between him and Agamemnon over control of events outside the
games. The action of the whole poem is propelled by this tension:
Achilles' desire for control leads him first to blame Agamemnon
for the plague and then to persuade Zeus to change the dynamics of
battle in his favour. Yet this control is double-edged: in this way, he
inadvertently causes the deaths of both Patroclus and himself. This
issue is thus central to the *Iliad* (it does not fall within the scope of
this project to examine it in detail here). For the sake of concise-
ness, I will examine only the *Aeneid* and *Thebaid* in depth, and I
will focus in both cases on the climactic duels, which I have already
shown to be an important point of comparison to the games. In both
Aeneid 12 and *Thebaid* 11, the limitations of the *editor*'s control

295

over events play a significant role in their unfolding. Language of composition and narration suggests a metapoetic reading of these tensions. I will begin by examining the events of *Aeneid* 12, take a brief look at images of power associated with Adrastus throughout the *Thebaid*, and finish with a discussion of Adrastus' final failure in *Thebaid* 11.

Aeneid 12: duelling with the narrative

The duel begins in a way that is instantly evocative of the games: the sun rises (5.104–5; 12.113–15) and men make arrangements for the day (5.109–13; 12.116–20). In both cases, Aeneas is not directly involved with creating the ordered setting for events to come; his leadership is shown in the calm and ordered way in which his men work without him. The armies are positioned, drawn up by ranks; the sacrifice follows due ritual. When Aeneas swears his oath, his speech orders the cosmos and the gods, while he pledges political order for the union of the two peoples (12.175–94). The preparations for the duel are a vision of order, good leadership and an ordered cosmos.[41] When things fall apart, however, Aeneas reacts to his loss of control with disbelief and fury (*Aeneid* 12.311–22):

> At pius Aeneas dextram tendebat inermem
> nudato capite atque suos clamore uocabat:
> 'quo ruitis? quaeue ista repens discordia surgit?
> o cohibete iras! ictum iam foedus et omnes
> compositae leges. mihi ius concurrere soli;
> me sinite atque auferte metus. ego foedera faxo
> firma manu; Turnum debent haec iam mihi sacra.'
> has inter uoces, media inter talia uerba
> ecce uiro stridens alis adlapsa sagitta est,
> incertum qua pulsa manu, quo turbine adacta,
> quis tantam Rutulis laudem, casusne deusne,
> attulerit;

> But dutiful Aeneas was stretching out his unarmed right hand,
> no helmet on his head, and calling to his men with a shout:
> 'Where are you rushing? What sudden discord rises?

---

[41] Cf. *Iliad* 3.276–80, 19.258–65; Williams (1973 (repr. 1987)) 449.

O restrain your angers! The treaty has been made and all the rules
agreed. It is my right to meet him alone.
Allow me to do it and don't be afraid. I will make this treaty
with a firm hand; now these rites owe Turnus to me.'
In the middle of this speech, among these very words,
behold, an arrow, shrieking on its wings, flew at the hero,
shot by which hand, driven by what wind,
who brought such great glory to the Rutulians, whether chance or a god,
nobody knows.

This speech is a desperate attempt to regain control, a picture of
Aeneas standing up to the irresistible impetus of war, which he
presents strongly as civil war (*quo ruitis* echoes Horace *Epode* 7
and *discordia* reinforces the reference).[42] The short sentences, the
imperatives, the emphatic alliteration and the positioning of *mihi*,
me, and *ego* make this speech impassioned: however, this is still
far from the panic displayed by Adrastus at 6.809–12. The syntax
remains unbroken; Aeneas speaks in whole sentences. His speech
is a picture of emphatic certainty, certainty that he will eventually
make good the treaty, which contrasts strongly with the narratorial
uncertainty over where the arrow came from. Yet the arrow stops
him speaking: it is as if the noise it makes as it flies towards him
represents the noise of battle drowning out his words.[43] Ultimately,
this desperate attempt to control the surge of battle is futile; the
speech is heard by no one, and Aeneas only leaves himself open
to attack, putting words against weapons.

When he finally returns to battle, we see Juturna consolidating
the control of the narrative which she snatched with the rebellion
of the Rutulians. She literally seizes the reins of the narrative when
she takes control of Turnus' chariot (12.468–72), and is presented
choosing the shots like a director (*Aeneid* 12.477–85):

> similis medios Iuturna per hostis
> fertur equis rapidoque uolans obit omnia curru,
> iamque hic germanum iamque hic ostentat ouantem
> nec conferre manum patitur, uolat auia longe.
> haud minus Aeneas tortos legit obuius orbis,
> uestigatque uirum et disiecta per agmina magna

---

[42] Williams (1973 (repr. 1987)) 458.
[43] This arrow is described in very similar terms to the simile describing the arrival of the
Dira to paralyse Turnus at 12.856–60: the two are assimilated as victims.

uoce uocat. quotiens oculos coniecit in hostem
alipedumque fugam cursu temptauit equorum,
auersos totiens currus Iuturna retorsit.

Just so Juturna is carried by her horses through the middle
of the enemy and flying in her swift chariot, wanders everywhere,
and now she displays her brother here, now there, triumphant,
and does not allow him to join battle, and flies way off the course.
No less Aeneas, equally in the way, reads their twisted tracks,
traces the man and calls him through the disorganised columns
with a loud voice. Whenever he caught sight of his enemy and
tried to catch the flight of his wing-footed horses by running,
every time Juturna swerves the chariot back on itself.

Like the poet, Juturna chooses what her audience will see, in order
to keep them hooked on the narrative, following whether they like
it or not, and to convey a particular message: in this case, the
tantalising image of Turnus triumphant but slightly out of Aeneas'
reach. Statius links this episode to the aristeia of Amphiaraus,
where Apollo takes over the reins of his chariot, suggesting that
Juturna is a poet figure. Both Turnus and Amphiaraus seem not to
recognise their divine charioteers at first, but claim in the end that
they have known them all along (*Aeneid* 12.632–4; *Thebaid* 7.779–
81). Apollo is inevitably a poet figure, contriving the remarkable
death of Amphiaraus as well as his spectacular aristeia, as we have
seen.[44] Juturna, too, takes control of the narrative here, thwarting
Aeneas and his desire for a Trojan reworking of the *Iliad*, for
a successful closure. Unavoidably, though, like Achilles before
her, Juturna's efforts to control the narrative cause only greater
destruction and confusion. Eventually, Aeneas refuses to follow
her chariot of song, to carry out the role of obedient reader and
viewer, but decides to attack the city itself. Juturna has succeeded
only in bringing out his brutality, in turning this effort to control
and civilise epic into an even closer reworking of the *Iliad*.

At this point, the poet, too, seems to be struggling with the
narrative, reluctant to enact the story in its telling (12.500–504):

Quis mihi nunc tot acerba deus, quis carmine caedes
diuersas obitumque ducum, quos aequore toto
inque uicem nunc Turnus agit, nunc Troius heros,

---

[44] See above, p. 258.

expediat? tanton placuit concurrere motu,
Iuppiter, aeterna gentis in pace futuras?

What god now will lay out in song so many bitter things for me, so many different
slaughters and the deaths of leaders, whom Turnus in his turn now drives
across the whole plain, and now the Trojan hero in his turn?
Did it please you, Jupiter, that tribes who will be at peace for eternity
should struggle in such great confusion?

The narrator is incapable of telling this bitter story: with the verb
expedire, the text brings together explaining and achieving, linking
the telling of the story with the creating of the actions.[45] This
invocation displaces responsibility for the poem onto the gods,
who bring it about as well as enable the telling of it. Implicitly,
this war (marked once more as civil and prefiguring civil wars) is
the choice of Jupiter, a source of pleasure for him. The narrator's
disbelief creates a distance between his choices for the story and his
characters' actions: this passage shows a split voice in the *Aeneid*
similar to the split voice of Lucan in the *Bellum Ciuile*.

Adrastus, storms and horses

While Aeneas seems to need to fight to regain control of the narrative, Adrastus' control never was that secure. Throughout the
Thebaid, the text presents us with a series of conflicting images
which show Adrastus veering from effective king in the model of
Aeneas and Augustus, to a weak and ineffective old man, suddenly more like Latinus. In this section, I will discuss two passages to give a flavour of the complexity and ambivalence of this
imagery.

The first passage comes from book 5, when the Argives return
to Nemea with Hypsipyle and announce the death of the king's
baby son, Opheltes. Amphiaraus calms the king's mad rage, but
the Argive armies hear a rumour that Hypsipyle has been killed
and start to riot against the king. Adrastus is described calming
the riot (5.699–709):

---

[45] See Lieberg (1982) on the *topos* of poets actually creating what they write about. This
argument is crucial to Masters' reading of the split voice in Lucan (Masters (1993)).

alipedum curru sed enim sublimis Adrastus
secum ante ora uirum fremibunda Thoantida portans
it medius turmis et, 'parcite, parcite!' clamat,
'nil actum saeue, meritus nec tale Lycurgus
excidium, gratique inuentrix fluminis ecce.'
sic ubi diuersis maria euertere procellis
hinc Boreas Eurusque, illinc niger imbribus Auster,
pulsa dies regnantque hiemes, uenit aequoris alti
rex sublimis equis, geminusque ad spumea Triton
frena natans late pelago dat signa cadenti,
et iam plana Thetis, montesque et litora crescunt.

But Adrastus, high on his chariot of winged horses, carrying
the daughter of Thoas with him, before the rage-filled faces of the men,
goes through the middle of the squadrons and shouts: 'Spare them! Spare them!
Nothing was done savagely, Lycurgus does not deserve such
slaughter, behold, the finder of the welcome river!'
Thus when Boreas and Eurus on one side overturn the sea
with divergent storms and Auster black with rainclouds on the other,
the day is repelled and the hurricanes rule, the king of the deep sea
high on his horses comes, and double Triton, swimming at the foamy
reins, gives a broad sign to the falling sea
and now Thetis is flat and the mountains and shore grow.

This comparison reverses the statesman simile at *Aeneid* 1.148–53, showing Adrastus as a strong ruler and linking him to the Roman context of the Virgilian simile.[46] Though *turmis* suggests that the riot is among his own troops, the previous description of the disturbance places it firmly in an urban context: Lycurgus looks back to the citadels (*arces*, 689); war rages in the buildings (*tecta*, 691); the buildings are attacked just as in *Aeneid* 1 (*Aeneid* 1.148–50; *Thebaid* 5.695). This slippage between a mutiny among the troops and an uprising of the citizens links Adrastus more strongly to the statesman in Virgil's simile. The imagery of the storm simile is also reminiscent of Virgil's storm.[47] There is a significant difference, here, however. Adrastus is not merely the strong statesman calming riot with his personal charisma: he brings certainty and truth in the face of panic and rumour. For the two

[46] On the statesman simile: Harrison (1988).
[47] Both foreground the winds as the cause of storm; verbal echoes include: *procellis* both at the end of the line (*Aen.* 1.85; *Theb.* 5.704); Statius' *pulsa dies* ('the day repelled', 706) recalls Virgil's *ponto nox incubat atra* ('black night covered the sea', 89).

opposing winds are equivalent to the two opposing rumours about and attitudes to Hypsipyle, but when Adrastus brings her physical presence, he takes charge of the truth, in charge of the narrative as well as calming the storm and the riot.

The second passage, however, uses similar imagery to convey exactly the opposite impression of Adrastus. At the funeral of Opheltes, the mourning seems to accuse the Argives, and Adrastus attempts to console Lycurgus (6.45–53):

> ipse, datum quotiens intercisoque tumultu
> conticuit stupefacta domus, solatur Adrastus
> adloquiis genitorem ultro, nunc fata recensens
> resque hominum duras et inexorabile pensum,
> nunc aliam prolem mansuraque numine dextro
> pignora. nondum orsis modus, et lamenta redibant.
> ille quoque adfatus non mollius audit amicos
> quam trucis Ionii rabies clamantia ponto
> uota uirum aut tenues curant uaga fulmina nimbos.

Adrastus himself, whenever he was allowed and the stupefied house
fell silent, when the storm was intermitted, consoles the father
with his speeches of his own accord, now listing the fates,
the hard circumstances of human life and its unavoidable thread,
now another child and a little treasure still remaining, if the powers
above are favourable. He had not yet put a limit on his beginnings when
   lament returned.
But he also heard these friendly addresses no more gently
than the madness of the fierce Ionian cares about the shouted prayers
of men at sea or the wandering thunder cares about the insubstantial clouds.

Here, Adrastus seems to start a storm rather than calm it, for his blundering consolations stir up a new blast of mourning. Suddenly, he moves from being Neptune calming the waves to playing the role of the sailor about to drown at sea, begging futilely for the mercy of the sea. His speech is worse than ineffective: it has the opposite effect to the one desired, stimulating renewed mourning rather than calming.

Adrastus and the Furies in *Thebaid* 11

Can Adrastus control the narrative in book 11 any better than Aeneas in *Aeneid* 12? Where Aeneas was primarily battling with

Juturna for control, with a dark Jupiter in the background, Adrastus ineffectually flails against the combined forces of the two furies, Tisiphone and Megaera. Jupiter removes the gods even from the audience, and only the forces of hell remain on the field. At the beginning of book 11, Tisiphone decides that she needs renewed inspiration to achieve closure (*fraterna claudere quaerit | bella acie*, 'she seeks to close the fraternal wars in battle', 11.58–9) and calls on her sister Megaera to help her, underlining the way she has taken over the role of poet by her echo of the opening words of the poem (*fraternas acies*, 'fraternal battle lines', 1.1).[48] In her speech to Megaera, she presents herself as both poet and triumphant general. The bodies and blood are her triumphant insignia (*meae uires, mea laeta insignia*, 'my strength, my joyful standards', 83). She is driven by 'madness' like a poet (*furores*, 77); she claims responsibility for the episodes of Tydeus (85–8) and Capaneus (88–91), talking about them as if she was both impersonating them and creating them; at 95–6, she says that Megaera will be more effective because her hair has recently drunk at the fountain of Cocytus, as if gaining hellish poetic inspiration (*exultantque recentes | Cocyti de fonte comae*, 'your hair exults freshly in the fountain of Cocytus'); at 97, she makes a claim of novelty (*non solitas acies... paramus*, 'I am organising unusual columns'); climactically, she labels the fratricide their 'greatest work' (*grande opus!* 100).[49] The Furies take control of the narrative in *Thebaid* 11, an alternative centre of poetic power, as Dis is an alternative to Jupiter throughout the *Thebaid*.[50]

It is no surprise, then, that when Adrastus tries to take control of the situation again, it is the Furies who thwart him. They have inspired Polynices to fight his brother and, in an impassioned speech, he bewails the lateness of his decision to fight him, now that almost all their forces are already defeated, with Adrastus as audience (11.155–92). Yet at the end he turns to thoughts of his

---

[48] Cf. Vessey (1973) 161, though he does not note the presentation of the Furies as poet figures.

[49] Venini (1970a) 32 points out the Senecan heritage of the claim of novelty, though not their self-consciously poetic nature; she interprets *grande opus!* as referring solely to the difficulty of their task: the fact that it needs explanation is some justification here for 'reading it hard'.

[50] Ahl (1986) 2858–63; Hardie (1993) 79–80.

death and funeral, and Argia his wife (11.187–92). Throughout the *Thebaid*, Polynices has been peculiarly sensitive to the needs of his audience, manipulating them effectively with his mastery of rhetoric, but here his audience nearly master him. He joins Adrastus in empathetic weeping at 11.193. Unlike Aeneas, Adrastus does not attempt to take back control of the narrative by increasing his violence and brutality: he remains gentle, and uses only words to attempt to persuade Polynices. The key word *mulcere* brings us back to the simile in *Aeneid* 1 where the statesman soothes the breasts of the riotous people (*pectora mulcet*, 1.153), but this measure of success for Adrastus is futile as the Fury intervenes physically, slamming the helmet over Polynices' head so he cannot even hear the persuading words, and throwing him on his horse so that he is surprised still as he finds himself outside the camp.[51] The Furies' control over events is emphasised still further as the two brothers approach each other (11.403–6):

> iamque in puluereum Furiis hortantibus aequor
> prosiliunt, sua quemque comes stimulantque monetque.
> frena tenent ipsae phalerasque et lucida comunt
> arma manu mixtisque iubas serpentibus augent.

> Now with the Furies encouraging, they jump forward on the dusty
> plain, and their companions spur them on and warn them.
> The Furies themselves hold the reins and arrange the trappings and
> the bright weapons with their hands and increase the crests by
>   mixing in their serpents.

Once more, the image of holding the reins represents control of the narrative: the Furies here are bizarre mixtures of the second in a duel and a costume artist, clearly as interested in creating an image of warlikeness as in driving the minds of the men.

Adrastus makes one more final attempt to stop the fratricide, to take the reins from the Furies, to assert his kingship, after Antigone and Jocasta have done their best (11.424–46). He is characterised here by his age and kingship, both presented as worthy of respect

---

[51] Venini (1970a) 62 points out the violence and materiality of Megaera's actions. She interprets Polynices' pallid state as the traditional pallor preceding death (204), and links the description to Turnus at *Aeneid* 12.221. His paleness suggests to me his surprise and reluctance to be there.

(*regnis multum et uenerabilis aeuo*, 'very respectable in both kingship and age' 427), holding on to the reins as he attempts to take
back control again (*medias inmittit Adrastus habenas*, 'Adrastus
set his reins for the middle').[52] He even commands Polynices to
stop, layering his speech with imperatives (*ne perstate*, 'don't persist', 431; *te, gener, et iubeo*, 'you, son-in-law, I even order', 433;
i, Lernan et Argos | solus habe, 'go, have Lerna and Argos on your
own', 434–5). Yet this is one fight that he cannot stop, when the
editores are now the Furies, and ultimately even his kingship is
fruitless. He offers to give up his kingdoms to stop the fight, precisely undercutting the orders even as he gives them: why should
Polynices obey the orders of someone demanding that he take
power over them? Again, the storm imagery returns, this time in
an image which recalls the boxing (11.435–8):

> non uerba magis suadentia frangunt
> accensos sumptisque semel conatibus obstant,
> quam Scytha curuatis erectus fluctibus umquam
> Pontus Cyaneos uetuit concurrere montes

> The persuasive words do not break them in their burning
> any more or stand in the way of their decisions once taken
> than the Scythian sea, standing up with curved waves,
> ever stopped the Cyanean mountains from clashing.

Alcidamas fighting Capaneus is compared to a mass of water hurling itself at a rock. This is subtly different, the clashing rocks suddenly becoming mountains in an echo of *Aeneid* 8.691–3, not the
tide wearing away even the rocks, but the liquid unable to block the
movement of solids: the rocks move, and the tide can do nothing
about it. Now violence fatally overcomes words; brutality overcomes skill. Adrastus' exit is accompanied by a disturbing image:
as he leaves, he is like Hades arriving in the Underworld.[53] So he
figuratively joins Amphiaraus and Oedipus in the Underworld and
seems to become part of the Furies' plot, even driving into their
space.[54] Yet, as Hardie has shown, even the Furies ultimately lose

---

[52] Vessey (1973) 164.
[53] Vessey (1973) 164 links Adrastus and Oedipus; Ahl (1986) 2858.
[54] Cf. Vessey (1973) 264: 'Dis is the infernal Jupiter, an aspect of the supreme being who presides over the whole universe.'

control of this fight, surpassed by their subject-matter and assimilated in their lack of control both to the powerless Adrastus and the absent gods.[55] In the end, the momentum of the action is out of control, and the chariot of song careers onwards, empty still.

The producers of games were important politically and symbolically: they form the centre of power in the cosmos of the arena, and become a model of kingship and narrative control. In the *Aeneid*, Aeneas' control over the games, his creation of an inclusive and univocal consensus among competitors and audience, stands in sharp contrast to his failure of control in *Aeneid* 12. Statius takes this several stages further: control in the games is fragile; dissent and disharmony characterise the audience. Adrastus abdicates control completely in the wider narrative, as do the gods, and even the Furies. It is not clear that Statius himself is even in control of this poem as it veers chaotically into digression and excess. The teleological drive of epic narrative carries us into ever more horrific atrocity; there is no moral centre to this poem.

---

[55] Hardie (1993) 44: 'The brothers meet each other in single combat only because they have become more Fury-like than the Furies themselves, who take on the role of passive spectators like Virgil's Latinus.'

CONCLUSION

We come into the home straight, finishing line in sight, last burst of desperate energy; or step up to the podium for the medal ceremony, tearfully anticipating the national anthem; or face the post-match post-mortem, with commentators mournfully musing about the decline of athletics; or should this rather be the closing ceremony, mayoral speeches, children dancing, processions of athletes? The riots back home, several wounded, one dead? The aftermath, clearing up the litter and wondering what to do with the stadium? Or the surprise drug test results and the redistribution of the medals? Like the *Thebaid*, a festival of games has many possible endings.

Perhaps, then, a final procession. Virgil in the *Georgics* creates a poetics of play: one end is in the *sphragis*, when he represents himself as playing while Octavian fights (*Georgics* 4.559–66):

> Haec super aruorum cultu pecorumque canebam
> et super arboribus, Caesar dum magnus ad altum
> fulminat Euphraten bello uictorque uolentis
> per populos dat iura uiamque adfectat Olympo.
> illo Vergilium me tempore dulcis alebat
> Parthenope studiis florentem ignobilis oti,
> carmina qui lusi pastorum audaxque iuuenta,
> Tityre, te patulae cecini sub tegmine fagi.

> I was singing this song about the care of fields and herds
> and trees, while great Caesar was thundering at deep
> Euphrates in war and giving laws as victor to the willing
> peoples and setting out on the way to Olympus.
> At that time sweet Parthenope was nourishing me, Virgil,
> flourishing in the inglorious enthusiasms of leisure,
> who played with the songs of shepherds and daring in youth
> sang of you, Tityrus, under the shade of a broad beech.

This has been called 'an exercise in self-diminution'. To be a poet at play is to embrace 'a triviality which is representative

307

of Alexandrian programmatics'.[1] Yet this poet at play, pursuing leisurely activities at Naples, the site of Augustus' games, must deliberately look back to the games and his own representation as victor at the beginning of book 3 (*Georgics* 3.17–20):

> illi uictor ego et Tyrio conspectus in ostro
> centum quadriiugos agitabo ad flumina currus.
> cuncta mihi Alpheum linquens lucosque Molorchi
> cursibus et crudo decernet Graecia caestu.

> There, I myself, victor, displayed in Tyrian purple,
> will drive a hundred four-horse chariots to the river.
> All Greece, leaving the Alpheus for me and the groves of Molorchus,
> will compete in races and with the violent boxing glove.

Morgan represents the *sphragis* as a retreat on Virgil's behalf from too hubristic a claim of assimilation to Octavian as *triumphator*. But it also reminds us of his poetic triumph. In the *Aeneid*, the downbeat end plays off against the upbeat end-in-the-middle. When Virgil translates Greek games to Rome, it is the act of a cultural imperialist, putting Greek culture to his own uses. Going back to *Cosmos and Imperium*, Hardie says: 'The *Aeneid* is at one level a colossal exercise in definition, seeking to define the Roman epic as the new *Weltgedicht* through an act of appropriation or of literary imperialism, whereby the world of Greek culture and literature (understood as the realization of what was always potentially present in Homer) is pressed into the service of the new age in Rome'.[2] The triumph of emperor is the triumph of poet, the triumph of Roman empire over Greece and Greek culture. However, there is another aspect to Virgil's self-presentation as victor in *Georgics* 3: he is an *editor* of games. As Versnel points out, the *editor* of *ludi* wore the same costume of Jupiter Optimus Maximus as the *triumphator*.[3] The verb *agitabo* contains both the idea of personally driving a chariot and the idea of setting chariot races in motion. And the conquest of Greece, bringing the Muses to Italy, also looks back to M. Fulvius Nobilior's celebration of the first set of Greek games at Rome.

---

[1] Morgan (1999) 214.   [2] Hardie (1986) 1–2, cited by Morgan (1999) 59.
[3] Versnel (1970) 129–31.

Statius has an actual triumph in book 12: when the Argive women are waiting to ask for Theseus' help in forcing Creon to allow them to bury their husbands, Theseus returns victorious from war with the Amazons (*Thebaid* 12.519–39). This is a Roman triumph which reads the Greeks as Romans and shows clearly how Statius is using his mythical Greece as a site for articulating Roman concerns.[4] The joyful audience, the procession of spoils and the *triumphator* in his chariot add up to a very Roman occasion. Braund says: 'Theseus... is Romanised from Greek myth into the position of the supreme Roman *paterfamilias*, the emperor: he is thus cast in the role of the tamer of barbarism and the representative of civilisation.'[5] The figure of Theseus is an alternative model of kingship to Adrastus and Eteocles, and an alternative centre of drive and power for the end of the poem. There has been considerable recent debate about closure in the *Thebaid*, whether Theseus truly achieves it, about *clementia*, whether he properly embodies it, and whether if so it is a tyrannous virtue.[6] In Vessey's reading, Theseus redeems the poem.[7] Braund also reads Theseus positively: he is a new Jupiter, *justly* angry.[8] Ripoll, too, sees him as the 'truly "positive hero" of the work'.[9] Others, however, emphasise the jarring elements in his portrayal:[10] the references to Ariadne (12.676) and Aegeus (12.624–6), his avidity for war (595, 599), his assimilation to Creon and to the dead brothers through the bull simile (601–5).[11] He certainly dominates the war, whether the war is a repetition or a reversal of the original war.[12] He is solidly in control until the final moment when the grieving women take over the

---

[4] Thanks to Mary Beard for this thought.　　[5] Braund (1996) 13.

[6] On *clementia* in the *Thebaid* cf. Burgess (1972).

[7] Vessey (1973) 307–16 on Theseus and the end of the *Thebaid*: 'Theseus is the great peace-maker, who because he is both just and merciful is alone able to draw a close to the dark tale of human sin, passion and madness.' (308); 'The *Thebaid* is an epic not of sin but of redemption, a chronicle not of evil but of triumphant good.' (316).

[8] Braund (1996) 3: 'Statius is evidently concerned to present Theseus' anger as just.'

[9] Ripoll (1998) 19.

[10] See Ahl (1986) 2894–8; Dominik (1994a) 92–8: 'Like Adrastus, Theseus seems concerned with natural justice. But his treatment of women and violent undertaking of war against Thebes introduce a disturbing aspect into the notion of a just ruler.' (93); Hershkowitz (1994) 144–7; Dietrich (1999).

[11] Hershkowitz (1994) 145 'The simile implies that Theseus cannot be isolated from the sexually-charged conflict that has produced and been produced by the *furor* of Thebes.'

[12] Braund (1996) 3: 'the initiative, the control, the power to make things happen, are firmly vested in Theseus.'

narrative in more than one sense.[13] Theseus can be viewed as in some sense a referee, an arbiter for the war, coming in from outside to resolve the poem.[14] He is not presented as a poet figure, but he is a version of Amphiaraus as well as a *triumphator*, driving a chariot with four white horses, like Amphiaraus in the chariot race, and a version of Adrastus as *editor* of the games.[15] However, the triumph itself focuses on and empathises with the defeated barbarian women, sympathetically steadfast, holding on to their identity when Statius' male heroes have melted and fallen away.[16] This is the only representation of victory in the *Thebaid*, and it brings together themes of gender, ethnicity and spectacle that have been continually recurring throughout this book. The Roman project of taming the world is not endorsed by Statius; *imperium* brings only the breakdown of boundaries, the dissolution of order. Epic heroism becomes an impossibility; women become men; men become women. As far as poetics are concerned, the attempt by the poet to grapple with the realities of political power and the violence of war leaves poetry completely overwhelmed. Theseus' triumph over barbarian women leads to a war which enacts defeat for the victors and allows endless unassuaged mourning. If Virgil's downbeat endings belie the ultimate optimism of his poems, Statius' end in reconciliation, and mock-modest poetic survival is completely overwhelmed by the darkness and horror of the nihilistic representation of power out of control which is the *Thebaid*.

[13] Dietrich (1999) reads the end of the *Thebaid* as a feminine affair, with the grief of the women and the narratives of Argia and Antigone valorising a female anti-epic perspective. However, I have argued elsewhere (Lovatt (1999)) that this female voice is equally undercut by the destructive potential of grief and the imagery which associates grieving women with witches and maenads.

[14] Hardie (1993) 47: 'the man Theseus has taken over the role of supreme arbiter that the real Jupiter had abrogated when he withdrew from the action'; Braund (1996) compares 'Theseus as a kind of tragic *deus ex machina* – a superhuman outsider who alone can cut the knot' (18) – to Aeneas when he 'preserves the "rules of war" (*iura belli*) and makes war to achieve peace' (17).

[15] See Hardie (1997) 153 n. 50 on the triumph as funeral (*Aeneid* 11.53–4; Lucan 3.288–92; *Thebaid* 12.88, 578–9). On triumphs, see Versnel (1970), esp. 115–29 on links with funerals. Braund sees this Romanisation of Theseus in his role as *triumphator* as the key to his power over the narrative. Braund (1996) 14: 'Statius' Romanisation of Theseus puts him in control of events – and of the narrative too. As a figure of supreme power, it is he and he alone who can bring the narrative to a close.'

[16] Though Ahl (1986) 2893–4 points to the chilling force of the *nondum*.

APPENDIX: SUMMARY OF EPIC GAMES

Homer: *Iliad* 23

1. Chariot race 262–650	Eumelus; Diomedes; Menelaus; Antilochus; Meriones. Nestor advises Antilochus. Eumelus in the lead; Apollo knocks Diomedes' whip away; Athena replaces it and wrecks Eumelus; Antilochus passes Menelaus dangerously; spectators argue over who is winning; Diomedes wins, followed by Antilochus. Achilles wants to offer second prize to Eumelus but Antilochus protests; Menelaus complains about Antilochus' dangerous driving. Achilles gives extra prize to Nestor.
2. Boxing 651–99	Epeius and Euryalus. Epeius boasts; Euryalus takes up challenge. Epeius knocks out Euryalus.
3. Wrestling 700–739	Ajax and Odysseus. Stalemate, broken by Ajax, which gives Odysseus the opportunity to throw him. Both fall. Achilles stops fight in third round and gives equal prizes.
4. Running 740–97	Oilean Ajax, Odysseus, Antilochus. Ajax ahead, Odysseus prays to Athena, who trips Ajax. Odysseus wins, Ajax second. Antilochus compliments Achilles, who gives him an extra prize.

5. Fight in armour 798–825	Telamonian Ajax and Diomedes. Audience stops the fight before anyone is wounded because they are afraid for Ajax. Diomedes wins most important prize.
6. Discus 826–49	Polypoetes, Leonteus, Telamonian Ajax, Epeius. Epeius makes laughable throw; Leonteus goes further; Ajax further still; Polypoetes wins.
7. Archery 850–83	Dove tied to ship mast: hit dove to win. Teucer and Meriones. Teucer hits cord; Meriones hits flying dove.
8. Javelin 884–97 (end)	Agamemnon and Meriones. Achilles stops contest and awards first prize to Agamemnon.

Virgil: *Aeneid* 5

1. Ship race 114–285	Mnestheus captaining Pristis; Gyas captaining Chimaera; Sergestus captaining Centaurus; Cloanthus captaining Scylla. Gyas takes lead, followed by Cloanthus. Cloanthus overtakes Gyas by going very close to the *meta*; Gyas throws his helmsman overboard. Sergestus goes too close and wrecks his ship. Mnestheus encourages rowers, overtakes Gyas, and presses hard on Cloanthus. Cloanthus prays to the gods of the sea, and Portunus pushes him home. Prizes: Cloanthus *chlamys*; Mnestheus the breastplate of Demoleos; Gyas two silver cauldrons. Sympathy prize for Sergestus for bringing his crew home safely.
2. Running 286–361	Nisus, Euryalus, Diores, Salius, Patron, Helymus, Panopes, many unnamed.

Nisus winning followed by Salius, Euryalus, Helymus, and Diores. Nisus slips on blood of sacrifice, trips Salius to give victory to his beloved Euryalus.

Salius complains so Aeneas gives him an extra prize. Nisus complains too and is similarly rewarded.

3. Boxing
362–484

Dares, Entellus.

Dares displays himself and almost walks off with the prize unopposed, but Acestes persuades the veteran Entellus to compete. They negotiate over boxing gloves. Entellus tries for big blow, misses and falls; Acestes helps him up; he is so angry that he rains down blows on Dares and Aeneas has to stop the fight.

He sacrifices his prize ox instead of killing Dares.

4. Archery
485–544

Hippocoon, Mnestheus, Eurytion and Acestes.

Hippocoon strikes mast, Mnestheus breaks rope, Eurytion kills dove. Acestes shoots arrow into air; it bursts into flames.

Aeneas reads this as positive omen and awards prize to Acestes.

5. *Lusus Troiae*
545–603

Ascanius and other Trojan boys perform display of cavalry manoeuvres, between dance and imitation of war.

Statius: *Thebaid* 6

1. Chariot race
296–549

Polynices, Amphiaraus, Admetus, Thoas, Euneos, Chromis and Hippodamus.

Polynices veers wide round the turning-post, but overtakes Amphiaraus and Admetus again; Thoas falls; Chromis wrecks Hippodamus; Apollo raises monster to wreck Polynices; Amphiaraus tries to overtake the driverless Arion, but fails.

Amphiaraus wins the bowl of Hercules; Admetus gets second prize (*chlamys*). Adrastus gives Polynices a consolation prize.

2. Running 550–645	Idas, Alcon, Phaedimus, Dymas, many others, Parthenopaeus. Parthenopaeus in the lead from Idas; at the last moment, Idas grabs his hair and pulls him back. Parthenopaeus protests and Adrastus orders the race to be rerun. Parthenopaeus wins.
3. Discus 646–730	Many unnamed competitors; Hippomedon replaces discus with a bigger one; only Phlegyas and Menestheus want to compete. Phlegyas does huge practice throw; but slips on the real throw and drops it at his feet. Menestheus cautious but successful throw. Hippomedon throws further. Hippomedon wins but Phlegyas gets extra sympathy prize.
4. Boxing 730–825	Capaneus issues challenge; Alcidamas the Spartan accepts. Capaneus continually attacking, Alcidamas avoiding; Alcidamas makes successful blow to forehead; Capaneus goes mad. Brief rest. Capaneus goes for big blow, misses, falls, and Alcidamas takes pot shot. Capaneus gets up raging, and Adrastus asks Tydeus and Hippomedon to stop the fight before Alcidamas is killed.

5. Wrestling 826–910	Tydeus and Agylleus. They fight for a long time; Agylleus gets tired while Tydeus stays fit; Tydeus goes for legs, fails, and Agylleus crashes down on him, but he escapes, picks him up, holds him above his head, and throws him down.
6. Sword fight 911–23	Polynices and Agreus. Adrastus stops the fight before it can happen. Awards both a golden helmet and crowns Polynices victor of Thebes.
7. Archery 924–46	Other leaders ask Adrastus either to do javelin or archery as display. He elects to shoot an arrow at a tree, but the arrow bounces off and returns to his quiver. The leaders debate what it means, but the narrator reads it as an omen that only A. will return from the war.

Silius: *Punica* 16

1. Chariot race 312–456	Cyrnus with lead horse Lampon; Hiberus driving Panchates; Durius driving Pelorus; Atlas driving Caucasus. Cyrnus takes the lead, followed by Hiberus, with Durius and Atlas neck and neck. Hiberus overtakes Cyrnus; Durius wrecks Atlas, passes Cyrnus and challenges Hiberus, but at the last moment drops his whip. Hiberus wins.
2. Running 457–526	Tartessus, Hesperus, Baeticus, Eurytus, Lamus, Sicoris and Theron. Eurytus followed by Hesperus. Theron comes from the back and passes Hesperus, who in his fury pulls him back by the hair allowing Eurytus to win.

3. Gladiatorial fights 527–56	Various volunteer gladiators; two brothers fight to the death for their father's crown, kill each other, and flames divide on common pyre.
4. Javelin 557–74	Burnus, Glagus, Aconteus, Indibilis, Ilerdes. Throwing at a target. Burnus wins, Ilerdes second, Aconteus third.
5. Honorific javelin 575–91	Scipio's brother and Laelius honour the dead with spear throws. Scipio himself throws a spear, which stops in mid-flight and turns into a tree. Prophets interpret this as omen of great things to come.

BIBLIOGRAPHY

Adams, J. N. (1982) *The Latin Sexual Vocabulary*, London
Ahl, F. (1976) *Lucan: An Introduction*, Ithaca
   (1984a) 'The Art of Safe Criticism in Greece and Rome', *AJP* 105: 174–208
   (1984b) 'The Rider and the Horse: Politics and Power in Roman Poetry from Horace to Statius', *ANRW* 2.32.1: 85–102
   (1986) 'Statius' *Thebaid*: A reconsideration', *ANRW* 2.32.5: 2803–912
Alston, R. (1998) 'Arms and the Man. Soldiers, Masculinity and Power in Republican and Imperial Rome' in L. Foxhall and J. Salmon, eds. *When Men were Men: Masculinity, Power and Identity in Classical Antiquity*, 205–23, London
Anderson, W. S. (2002) 'Trojan, Dardanian, Roman: The Power of Epithets in the *Aeneid*' in W. S. Anderson and L. N. Quartarone, eds. *Approaches to Teaching Vergil's Aeneid*, 53–9, New York
Arieti, J. A. (1975) 'Nudity in Greek Athletics', *CW* 68: 431–6
Arnold, I. R. (1960) 'Agonistic Festivals in Italy and Sicily', *AJA* 64: 245–51
Asquith, H. C. A. (2001) *Silver Epic Catalogues*, diss., Durham University
Aubriot, D. (1989) 'Remarques sur l'usage de *thambos* et des mots apparentés dans l' "Iliade"', *Orpheus* 10: 249–60
Auguet, R. (1972) *Cruelty and Civilization: The Roman Games*, London
Baker, R. J., ed. (1990) *Propertius 1*, Armidale, Australia
Balsdon, J. P. V. D. (1969) *Life and Leisure in Ancient Rome*, Oxford
Barthes, R. (1993) *Mythologies*, London
Barton, C. (1993) *The Sorrows of the Ancient Romans: The Gladiator and the Monster*, Princeton
Bartsch, S. (1994) *Actors in the Audience: Theatricality and Doublespeak from Nero to Hadrian*, Cambridge, Mass.
   (1997) *Ideology in Cold Blood: A Reading of Lucan's Civil War*, Cambridge, Mass.
Beacham, R. C. (1999) *Spectacle Entertainments of Early Imperial Rome*, New Haven
Beard, M., North, J. and Price, S. (1998) *Religions of Rome*, Cambridge
Berger, M., Wallis, B. and Watson, S., ed. (1995) *Constructing Masculinity*, New York
Beye, C. R. (1969) 'Jason as Love-hero in Apollonius' *Argonautica*', *GRBS* 10: 31–55

BIBLIOGRAPHY

Bollinger, T. (1969) *Theatralis Licentia: Die Publikumsdemonstrationen an den öffentlichen Spielen im Rom der früheren Kaiserzeit und ihre Bedeutung im politischen Leben*, Winterthur

Bolton, J. D. P. (1948) 'Was the Neronia a Freak Festival?', *CQ* 42: 82–90

Bonds, W. S. (1985) 'Two Combats in the *Thebaid*', *TAPA* 115: 225–35

Bowditch, L. (1994) 'Horace's Poetics of Political Integrity: Epistle 1.18', *AJP* 115: 409–26

Bowker, L. H., ed. (1998) *Masculinities and Violence*, London

Braund, S. (1988) *Beyond Anger: A Study of Juvenal's Third Book of Satires*, Cambridge

(1996) 'Ending Epic: Statius, Theseus and a Merciful Release', *PCPS* 42: 1–23

Brenkman, J. (1976) 'Narcissus in the Text', *Georgia Review* 30: 293–327

Briggs, W. W. (1975) 'Augustan Athletics and the Games of *Aeneid* 5', *Stadion* 1: 277–83

Brod, H., ed. (1987) *The Making of Masculinities: The New Men's Studies*, Boston

Brown, J. (1994) *Into the Woods: Narrative Studies in the Thebaid of Statius with Special Reference to Books IV–VI*, diss., Cambridge

Brown, P. (1988) *The Body and Society: Men, Women, and Sexual Renunciation in Early Christianity*, New York

Brown, R. (1987) 'The Palace of the Sun in Ovid's *Metamorphoses*' in M. Whitby, P. Hardie and M. Whitby, eds. *Homo Viator: Classical Essays for John Bramble*, 211–20, Bristol

Burgess, J. F. (1972) 'Statius' Altar of Mercy', *CQ* 22: 339–49

Butler, H. E. (1909) *Post-Augustan Poetry: From Seneca to Juvenal*, Oxford

Caiani, L. (1990) 'La pietas nella "Tebaide" di Stazio. Mezenzio modello di Ippomedonte e Capaneo', *Orpheus* 11: 260–76

Caillois, R. (1962) *Man, Play and Games*, London

Cairns, F. (1989) *Virgil's Augustan Epic*, Cambridge

Caldelli, M. L. (1993) *L'Agon Capitolinus: Storia e Protagonisti dall'Istituzione Domizianea al IV Secolo*, Rome

Cameron, A. (1973) *Porphyrius the Charioteer*, Oxford

(1976) *Circus Factions: Blues and Greens at Rome and Byzantium*, Oxford

Cantarella, E. (1992) *Bisexuality in the Ancient World*, New Haven

Cerutti, S. (1993) 'The Seven Eggs of the Circus Maximus', *Nikephoros* 6: 167–76

Clauss, J. J. (1993) *The Best of the Argonauts: The Redefinition of the Epic Hero in Book 1 of Apollonius' Argonautica*, Berkeley

Clavel-Lévêque, M. (1984) *L'Empire en Jeux: Espace Symbolique et Pratique Sociale dans le Monde Romain*, Paris

Coarelli, F. (1980) *Roma: Guide Archeologiche Laterza*, Bari

Coarelli, F., Gregori, G. L., Lombardi, L., Orlandi, S., Rea, R. and Vismara, C. (1999) *Il Colosseo*, Milan

Coleman, K. M., ed. (1998) *Statius Silvae IV*, London

Connell, R. (1995) *Masculinities*, Cambridge

Conte, G. B. (1986) *The Rhetoric of Imitation: Genre and Poetic Memory in Virgil and other Latin Poets*, Ithaca

Corbeill, A. (1997) 'Dining Deviants in Roman Political Invective', in J. Hallett and M. Skinner, eds. *Roman Sexualities*, 100–128, Princeton

Costabile, F. (1978) *Municipium Locrensium*, Naples

Crowther, N. B. (1980–81) 'Nudity and Morality: Athletics in Italy', *CJ* 76: 119–23

 (1982) 'Athletic Dress and Nudity in Greek Athletics', *Eranos* 80: 163–8

 (1983) 'Greek Games in Republican Rome', *AC* 52: 268–73

Culler, J. (1980) 'Prolegomena to a Theory of Reading' in S. Suleiman and I. Crosman, eds. *The Reader in the Text*, 46–66, Princeton

Cuypers, M. P. (1997) *Apollonius Rhodius Argonautica 2.1–310*, diss., Leiden

Dällenbach, L. (1989) *The Mirror in the Text*, Oxford

Davis, G. (1983) *The Death of Procris: 'Amor' and the Hunt in Ovid's Metamorphoses*, Rome

Decker, W. (1995) *Sport in der griechischen Antike*, Munich

DeForest, M. M. (1994) *Apollonius' Argonautica: A Callimachean Epic*, Leiden

Dewar, M., ed. (1991) *Statius Thebaid IX*, Oxford

 (1994) 'Laying it on with a Trowel: The Proem to Lucan and Related Texts', *CQ* 44: 199–211

Dickie, M. (1985) 'The Speech of Numanus Remulus (*Aeneid* 9.598–620)', *PLLS* 5: 165–222

Dietrich, J. (1999) 'Thebaid's Feminine Ending', *Ramus* 28: 40–53

Dominik, W. J. (1994a) *The Mythic Voice of Statius*, Leiden

 (1994b) *Speech and Rhetoric in Statius' Thebaid*, Hildesheim

Dover, K. (1980) *Plato Symposium*, Cambridge

Drew, D. L. (1927) *The Allegory of the Aeneid*, Oxford

Duckworth, G. (1967) 'The Significance of Nisus and Euryalus for *Aeneid* IX–XII', *AJP* 88: 129–50

Duff, J. W. (1964) *A Literary History of Rome in the Silver Age*, London; New York

Edmondson, J. (1996) 'Dynamic Arenas: Gladiatorial Presentations in the City of Rome and the Constructions of Roman Society during the Early Empire' in W. Slater, ed. *Roman Theater and Society*, 69–112, Michigan

Fantham, E. (1992) *Lucan. De Bello Ciuili Book 2*, Cambridge

 (1996) *Roman Literary Culture*, Baltimore; London

 (1999) 'The role of Lament in the Growth and Death of Roman Epic' in M. Beissinger, J. Tylus and S. Wofford, eds. *Epic Traditions in the Contemporary World: The Poetics of Community*, 221–36, Berkeley; London

Farrell, J. (1999) 'The Ovidian *Corpus*: Poetic Body and Poetic Text' in P. R. Hardie, A. Barchiesi and S. Hinds, eds. *Ovidian Transformations*, 127–41, Cambridge

Farron, S. (1993) *Vergil's Aeneid: A Poem of Grief and Love*, Leiden

Fedeli, P., ed. (1980) *Sesto Properzio: Il Primo Libro delle Elegie*, Florence

319

Feeney, D. C. (1991) *The Gods in Epic*, Oxford

Feldherr, A. (1995) 'Ships of State – *Aeneid* 5 and Augustan Circus Spectacle',
ClAnt 14: 245–65

(1998) *Spectacle and Society in Livy's History*, Berkeley; London

(2002) 'Stepping Out of the Ring: Repetition and Sacrifice in the Boxing
Match in *Aeneid* V' in D. S. Levene and D. P. Nelis, eds. *Clio and the
Poets: Augustan Poetry and the Traditions of Ancient Historiography*, 61–79,
Leiden

Fontenrose, J. (1959) *Python: A Study of Delphic Myth and its Origins*, Berkeley

Fortgens, H. W., ed. (1934) *P. Papinii Statii de Opheltis funere carmen epicum,
Theb. Lib. VI 1–295, versione Batava commentarioque exegetico instructus*,
diss., Groningen

Fowler, D. (1987) 'Vergil on Killing Virgins' in M. Whitby, P. Hardie and M.
Whitby, eds. *Homo Viator: Classical Essays for John Bramble*, 185–98,
Bristol

(2000) 'Epic in the Middle of the Wood: *mise en abyme* in the Nisus and
Euryalus Episode' in A. Sharrock and H. Morales, eds. *Intratextuality*, 89–
113, Oxford

Foxhall, L. and Salmon, J., eds. (1998a) *Thinking Men: Masculinity and its Self-
representation in the Classical Tradition*, New York

(eds.) (1998b) *When Men were Men: Masculinity, Power and Identity in Classical Antiquity*, London

Fränkel, H. (1945) *Ovid: A Poet between Two Worlds*, Berkeley

Frécaut, J.-M. (1972) *L'Esprit et l'Humour chez Ovide*, Grenoble

Frings, I. (1991) *Gespräch und Handlung in der Thebais des Statius*, Stuttgart

Futrell, A. (1997) *Blood in the Arena: The Spectacle of Roman Power*, Austin

Galinsky, G. K. (1968) 'Aeneid V and the *Aeneid*', *AJP* 89: 157–85

(1972) 'Hercules Ovidianus (*Met.* 9.1–272)', *WS* 85: 93–116

(1975) *Ovid's Metamorphoses: An Introduction to the Basic Aspects*, Berkeley

(1990) 'Hercules in the *Aeneid*' in S. J. Harrison, ed. *Oxford Readings in
Vergil's Aeneid*, 277–94, Oxford

Gardiner, E. N. (1955) *Athletics of the Ancient World*, Oxford

Geer, R. M. (1935) 'The Greek Games at Naples', *TAPA* 66: 208–21

Gernet, L. (1955) 'Jeux et droit: remarques sur le XXIII chant de l'*Iliade*' in *Droit
et Société dans la Grèce Ancienne*, 9–18, Paris

Gillis, D. (1983) *Eros and Death in the Aeneid*, Rome

Gilmore, D. (1990) *Manhood in the Making: Cultural Concepts of Masculinity*,
New Haven

Gleason, M. W. (1995) *Making Men: Sophists and Self-representation in Ancient
Rome*, Princeton

Goff, B. (1988) 'Euripides' *Ion* 1132–1165: the Tent', *PCPS* 34: 42-54

Golden, M. (1998) *Sport and Society in Ancient Greece*, Cambridge

Gossage, A. (1969) 'Virgil and the Flavian Epic' in D. R. Dudley, ed. *Virgil*,
67–93, London

Gotoff, H. C. (1984) 'The Transformation of Mezentius', *TAPA* 114: 191–218

Graver, M. (1998) 'The Manhandling of Maecenas: Senecan Abstractions of Masculinity', *AJP* 119: 607–32

Griffin, J. (1980) *Homer on Life and Death*, Oxford
(1985) *Latin Poets and Roman Life*, London

Gruen, E. S. (1984) *The Hellenistic World and the Coming of Rome*, Berkeley
(1993) *Culture and National Identity in Republican Rome*, London

Hardie, A. (1983) *Statius and the Silvae: Poets, Patrons and Epideixis in the Greco-Roman World*, Liverpool
(2003) 'Poetry and Politics at the Games of Domitian' in A. J. Boyle and W. J. Dominik, eds. *Flavian Rome: Culture, Image, Text*, 125–48, Leiden

Hardie, P. R. (1986) *Virgil's Aeneid: Cosmos and Imperium*, Oxford
(1988) 'Lucretius and the Delusions of Narcissus', *MD* 20: 71–89
(1993) *The Epic Successors of Virgil*, Cambridge
(1994) ed. *Virgil: Aeneid IX*, Cambridge
(1997) 'Closure in Latin Epic' in D. H. Roberts, F. M. Dunn and D. Fowler, eds. *Classical Closure: Reading the End in Greek and Latin Literature*, 139–62, Princeton
(2002) *Ovid's Poetics of Illusion*, Cambridge

Harriott, R. (1969) *Poetry and Criticism before Plato*, London

Harris, H. A. (1964) *Greek Athletes and Athletics*, London
(1972) *Sport in Greece and Rome*, London

Harrison, S. J. (1988) 'Vergil on Kingship: The First Simile of the *Aeneid*', *PCPS* 34: 55–9
(ed.) (1991) *Vergil: Aeneid 10*, Oxford
(1992) 'The Arms of Capaneus: Statius' *Thebaid* 4.167–77', *CQ* 42: 247–52

Heinze, R. (1993) *Virgil's Epic Technique*, Bristol

Henderson, A. A. R. (1970) '*Insignem conscendere currum* (Lucretius 6.47)', *Latomus* 29: 739–43

Henderson, J. (1991) 'Statius' Thebaid/Form Premade', *PCPS* 37: 30–80
(2002) 'A doo-dah-doo-dah-dey at the races: Ovid *Amores* 3.2 and the Personal Politics of the Circus Maximus', *Classical Antiquity* 21: 41–65

Hershkowitz, D. (1994) 'Sexuality and Madness in Statius' *Thebaid*', *MD* 33: 123–47
(1998a) *The Madness of Epic: Reading Insanity from Homer to Statius*, Oxford
(1998b) *Valerius Flaccus' Argonautica: Abbreviated Voyages in Silver Latin Epic*, Oxford

Heuvel, H. (1932) *Publii Papinii Statii Thebaidos Liber Primus*, Zutphen

Heuzé, P. (1985) *L'Image du Corps dans l'Oeuvre de Virgile*, Paris

Hill, D. E., ed. (1983) *P. Papinii Stati Thebaidos Libri XII*, Leiden
(1990) 'Statius' *Thebaid*: A Glimmer of Light in a Sea of Darkness' in A. J. Boyle, ed. *The Imperial Muse. Ramus Essays on Roman Literature of the Empire. Flavian Epicist to Claudian*, Bendigo

Hinds, S. (1987) 'Generalising about Ovid', *Ramus* 16: 4–31

(1998) *Allusion and Intertext*, Cambridge

Holmes, N. (1999) 'Nero and Caesar: Lucan 1.33–66', *Classical Philology* 94: 75–81

Holzberg, N. (1998) '*Ter quinque volumina* as *carmen perpetuum*: The Division into Books in Ovid's *Metamorphoses*', *MD* 40: 77–98

Hopkins, K. (1983) *Death and Renewal*, Cambridge

Horsfall, N. M. (1990) 'Numanus Remulus: Ethnography and Propaganda in *Aeneid* 9.598 ff.' in S. J. Harrison, ed. *Oxford Readings in Vergil's Aeneid*, 305–15, Oxford

ed. (1995) *A Companion to the Study of Virgil*, Leiden

Howland, R. L. (1954) 'Epeius, Carpenter and Athlete', *PCPS* 183: 15–6

Huizinga, J. (1949) *Homo Ludens*, London

Humm, M. (1997) *Feminism and Film*, Edinburgh

Humphrey, J. H. (1986) *Roman Circuses. Arenas for Chariot-racing*, Berkeley

Hunter, R. L. (1988) '"Short on Heroics": Jason in the *Argonautica*', *CQ* 38: 436–53

(1989) 'Bulls and Boxers in Apollonius and Vergil', *CQ* 39: 557–61

(1993) *The Argonautica of Apollonius*, Cambridge

Innes, D. C. (1979) 'Gigantomachy and Natural Philosophy', *CQ* 29: 165–71

Jal, P. (1963) *La guerre civile à Rome*, Paris

James, P. (1986) 'Crises of Identity in Ovid's *Metamorphoses*', *BICS* 33: 17–25

Janan, M. (1988) 'The Book of Good Love: Design and Desire in *Metamorphoses* 10', *Ramus* 17: 110–37

Juhnke, H. (1972) *Homerisches in römischer Epik flavischer Zeit. Untersuchungen zu Szenennachbildungen und Strukturentsprechungen in Statius' Thebais und Achilleis und in Silius' Punica*, München

Jüthner, J. (1969) *Philostratos über Gymnastik*, Amsterdam

Kaimio, J. (1979) *The Romans and the Greek Language*, Helsinki

Keith, A. M. (2000) *Engendering Rome: Women in Latin Epic*, Cambridge

Kenney, E. J. (1958) 'Nequitiae poeta' in N. I. Herescu, ed. *Ovidiana*, 201–9, Paris

Kimmel, M. S., ed. (1987) *Changing Men: New Directions in Research on Men and Masculinity*, London

Klinnert, T. C. (1970) *Capaneus–Hippomedon: Interpretationen zur Heldendarstellung in der Thebais des P. Papinius Statius*, Berlin

Knight, V. H. (1995) *The Renewal of Epic: Responses to Homer in the Argonautica of Apollonius*, Leiden

Knoespel, K. J. (1985) *Narcissus and the Invention of Personal History*, London

König, J. (2000) *Athletic Training and Athletic Festivals in the Greek Literature of the Roman Empire*, diss., Cambridge

Kuhn, G. G., ed. (1964) *Claudii Galeni Opera Omnia*, vol. IV, Hildesheim

Kyle, D. G. (1987) *Athletics in Ancient Athens*, Leiden

Kyriakidis, S. (1994) 'Invocatio ad Musam (*Aen.* 7.37)', *MD* 33: 197–206

Kytzler, B. (1968) 'Beobachtungen zu den Wettspielen in der Thebais des Statius',
   Traditio 24: 1–15
   (1969) 'Imitation und Aemulatio in der Thebais des Statius', *Hermes* 97: 209–
   32
Langdon, M. K. (1990) 'Throwing the Discus in Antiquity: The Literary
   Evidence', *Nikephoros* 3: 177–82
La Penna, A. (1996) 'Modelli efebici nella poesia di Stazio' in F. Delarue et al.,
   eds. *Epicedion*, 161–84, Poitiers
Lawall, G. (1966) 'Apollonius' *Argonautica*: Jason as Anti-hero', *YCS* 19: 121–69
Lee, H. M. (1983) 'Athletic Arete in Pindar', *Ancient World* 7: 31–7
Lee, M. O. (1979) *Fathers and Sons in Virgil's Aeneid*, Albany
Legras, L. (1905) *Étude sur la Thébaïde de Stace*, Paris
Leigh, M. (1997) *Lucan: Spectacle and Engagement*, Oxford
Leiwo, M. (1995) *Neapolitana: A Study of Population and Language in Graeco-
   Roman Naples*, Helsinki
Lennox, P. G. (1977) 'Virgil's Night-episode Re-examined: *Aeneid* IX, 176–449',
   Hermes 105: 331–42
Lieberg, G. (1982) *Poeta Creator*, Amsterdam
Lloyd, G. E. R. (1966) *Polarity and Analogy: Two Types of Argumentation in
   Early Greek Thought*, Cambridge
Lomas, K. (1993) *Rome and the Western Greeks 350 BC–AD 200: Conquest and
   Acculturation in Southern Italy*, London
Loraux, N. (1981) 'Le lit, la guerre', *L'Homme* 21: 37–67
Lovatt, H. V. (1999) 'Competing Endings: Re-reading the End of Statius' *Thebaid*
   through Lucan', *Ramus* 28: 126–51
   (2001) 'Mad about Winning: Epic, War and Madness in the Games of Statius'
   Thebaid', *MD* 46: 103–20
   (2002) 'Statius' Ekphrastic Games', *Ramus* 31: 73–90
   (2004) 'Epic Games and Real Games in Virgil's *Aeneid* 5 and Statius' *Thebaid*
   6' in S. Bell and G. Davies, eds. *Games and Festivals in Classical Antiquity*,
   107–14, Oxford
Ludwig, W. (1963) 'Plato's Love Epigrams', *GRBS* 4: 59–82
Lyle, E. B. (1984) 'The Circus as Cosmos', *Latomus* 43: 827–41
Lyne, R. O. A. M. (1978) *Ciris: A Poem Attributed to Vergil*, Cambridge
   (1990) 'Vergil and the Politics of War', in S. J. Harrison, ed. *Oxford Readings
   in Vergil's Aeneid*, 316–38, Oxford
MacClancy, J., ed. (1996) *Sport, Identity and Ethnicity*, Oxford
Mader, G. (1997) '*Duplex nefas, ferus spectator*: Spectacle and Spectator in
   Act 5 of Seneca's *Troades*' in C. Deroux, ed. *Studies in Latin Literature and
   Roman History VIII*, 319–51, Bruxelles
Makowski, J. (1989) 'Nisus and Euryalus: A Platonic Relationship', *CJ* 85: 1–15
Malkin, I. (1994) *Myth and Territory in the Spartan Mediterranean*, Cambridge
Mariscal, G. L. and Morales, M. S. (2003) 'The Relationship Between Achilles
   and Patroclus According to Chariton of Aphrodisias', *CQ* 53: 292–5

Markus, D. (1997) 'Transfiguring Heroism: Nisus and Euryalus in Statius' *Thebaid*', *Vergilius* 43: 56–62

Markus, D. D. (2003) 'The Politics of Epic Performance in Statius' in A. J. Boyle and W. J. Dominik, eds. *Flavian Rome: Culture, Image, Text*, 431–67, Leiden

Masters, J. M. (1993) *Poetry and Civil War in Lucan's Bellum Civile*, Cambridge

Mayer, M. (1887) *Die Giganten und Titanen in der antiken Sage und Kunst*, Berlin

McDonnell, M. (1991a) 'Athletic Nudity among the Greeks and the Etruscans' in *Spectacles sportifs et scéniques dans le monde Étrusco-italique*, Rome

(1991b) 'The Introduction of Athletic Nudity: Thucydides, Plato, and the Vases', *JHS* 111: 183–93

(2003) 'Roman Men and Greek Virtue' in R. Rosen and I. Sluiter, eds. *Andreia: Studies in Manliness and Courage in Classical Antiquity*, 235–62, Leiden

McGuire, D. T. (1997) *Acts of Silence: Civil War, Tyranny, and Suicide in the Flavian Epics*, Hildesheim; Zurich; New York

McNelis, C. (2002) 'Greek Grammarians and Roman Society During the Early Empire: Statius' Father and his Contemporaries', *ClAnt* 21: 67–94

Messner, M. A. (1987a) 'The Life of a Man's Seasons: Male Identity in the Life Course of the Jock', in M. S. Kimmel, ed. *Changing Men*, 53–67, London

(1987b) 'The Meaning of Success: The Athletic Experience and the Development of Male Identity', in Brod. H., ed. *The Making of Masculinities*, 193–209, Boston

(1992) *Power at Play: Sports and the Problem of Masculinity*, Boston

Miles, G. B. (1999) 'The *Aeneid* as Foundation Story' in C. Perkell, ed. *Reading Vergil's Aeneid: An Interpretive Guide*, 231–50, Norman, Oklahoma

Millar, F. (1977) *The Emperor in the Roman World*, London

Miller, S. G. (1991) *Arete: Greek Sports from Ancient Sources*, Berkeley

Mitchell, S. (1990) 'Festivals, Games and Civic Life in Roman Asia Minor', *JRS* 80: 183–93

Montserrat, D., ed. (1998) *Changing Bodies, Changing Meanings: Studies on the Human Body in Antiquity*, London

Moorton, R. F. (1989) 'The Innocence of Italy in Virgil's *Aeneid*', *AJP* 110: 105–30

Morgan, L. (1998) 'Assimilation and Civil War: Hercules and Cacus' in H. P. Stahl, ed. *Vergil's Aeneid: Augustan Epic and Political Context*, 175–98, London

(1999) *Patterns of Redemption in Vergil's* Georgics, Cambridge

Morrow, G. R. (1960) *Plato's Cretan City: A Historical Interpretation of the Laws*, Princeton

Most, G. (1992) '*Disiecti membra poetae*: The Rhetoric of Dismemberment in Neronian Poetry' in R. Hexter and D. Selden, eds. *Innovations of Antiquity*, 391–419, New York; London

Moulton, C. (1974) 'Similes in the *Iliad*', *Hermes* 102: 380–97

Mouratidis, J. (1984) 'Anachronism in the Homeric Games and Sports', *Nikephoros* 3: 11–22

Mozley, J. H. (1928) *Statius with an English Translation*, Cambridge, Mass.

Muecke, F. (1993) *Horace. Satires II with an Introduction, Translation and Commentary*, Warminster

Mulder, H. M. (1954) *Publii Papinii Statii Thebaidos Liber Secundus*, Groningen

Mulvey, L. (1975) 'Visual Pleasure and Narrative Cinema', *Screen* 16.3: 6–18

Myerowitz, M. (1985) *Ovid's Games of Love*, Detroit

Nelis, D. (2001) *Vergil's Aeneid and the Argonautica of Apollonius Rhodius*, Chippenham, Wiltshire

Neudecker, R. (1988) *Die Skulpturenausstattung römischer Villen in Italien*, Mainz am Rhein

Newman, J. K. (1967) *The Concept of Vates in Augustan Poetry*, Brussels

Nisbet, R. G. M. and Hubbard, M. (1970) *A Commentary on Horace Odes Book 1*, Oxford

Nugent, S. G. (1992) 'Vergil's "Voice of the Women" in *Aeneid* 5', *Arethusa* 25: 255–92

Ogilvie, R. M. (1980) *Roman Literature and Society*, London

O'Hara, J. J. (1996) *True Names: Vergil and the Alexandrian Tradition of Etymological Wordplay*, Ann Arbor

O'Higgins, D. (1988) 'Lucan as *Vates*', *ClAnt* 7: 208–26

Oliensis, E. (1998) *Horace and the Rhetoric of Authority*, Cambridge

Otis, B. (1963) *Virgil: A Study in Civilized Poetry*, Oxford
      (1970) *Ovid as an Epic Poet*, Cambridge

Papanghelis, T. (1986) *Propertius: A Hellenistic Poet on Love and Death*, Cambridge

Parker, H. N. (1999) 'The Observed of All Observers: Spectacle, Applause, and Cultural Poetics in the Roman Theatre Audience' in B. Bergman and C. Kondoleon, eds. *The Art of Ancient Spectacle*, 163–80, New Haven; London

Parkes, R. E. (2002) *A Commentary on Statius, Thebaid 4.1–308*, diss., Oxford

Parry, A. (1966) 'The Two Voices of Virgil's *Aeneid*' in S. Commager, ed. *Virgil: A Collection of Critical Essays*, 107–23, Englewood Cliffs

Pavlock, B. (1985) 'Epic and Tragedy in Vergil's Nisus and Euryalus Episode', *TAPA* 115: 207–24.

Penley, C. (ed.) (1988) *Feminism and Film Theory*, New York

Perkell, C. (1997) 'The Lament of Juturna: Pathos and Interpretation in the Aeneid', *TAPA* 127: 257–86

Perysinakis, I. N. (1990) 'The Athlete as Warrior: Pindar's *P*.9.97–103 and *P*.10.55–59', *BICS* 37: 43–9

Pietsch, C. (1999) *Die Argonautika des Apollonios von Rhodos*, Stuttgart

Plass, P. (1995) *The Game of Death in Ancient Rome: Arena Sport and Political Suicide*, Wisconsin

Poliakoff, M. B. (1987) *Combat Sports in the Ancient World: Competition, Violence and Culture*, New Haven

Pomeroy, A. (1989) 'Silius Italicus as "*doctus poeta*"', *Ramus* 18: 119–39

Porter, J. I., ed. (1999) *Constructions of the Classical Body*, Ann Arbor

Potter, D. S. and Mattingly, D. J. (1999) *Life, Death, and Entertainment in the Roman Empire*, Ann Arbor

Potz, E. (1993) 'FORTUNATI AMBO: Funktion und Bedeutung der Nisus/ Euryalus-Episode in Vergils *Aeneis*', *Hermes* 121: 325–34

Prince, G. (1980) 'Introduction to the Study of the Narratee' in J. Tompkins, ed. *Reader Response Criticism*, 7–25, London; Baltimore

Putnam, M. C. J. (1965) *The Poetry of the Aeneid: Four Studies in Imaginative Unity and Design*, Cambridge, Mass.

(1995) 'Possessiveness, Sexuality and Heroism' in *Virgil's Aeneid: Interpretation and Influence*, 27–49, Chapel Hill; London

Quint, D. (1993) *Epic and Empire*, Princeton

Ramsey, J. T. and Licht, A. L. (1997) *The Comet of 44 B.C. and Caesar's Funeral Games*, Atlanta, Georgia

Rawson, E. (1969) *The Spartan Tradition in European Thought*, Oxford

(1991) '*Discrimina ordinum*: The *lex Julia theatralis*' in F. Millar, ed. *Roman Culture and Society*, 508–45, Oxford

(1992) 'The Romans' in K. J. Dover, ed. *Perceptions of the Ancient Greeks*, 1–28, Oxford

Richardson, N. (1993) *The Iliad: A Commentary. Volume VI: Books 21–24*, Cambridge

Richlin, A. (1983) *The Garden of Priapus: Sexuality and Aggression in Roman Humor*, New Haven

Ripoll, F. (1998) *La Morale Héroïque dans les Épopées Latines d'Époque Flavienne: Tradition et Innovation*, Louvain; Paris

Robert, L. (1940) *Les Gladiateurs dans l'Orient Grec*, Paris

(1970) 'Deux concours Grecs a Rome', *CRAI*: 6–27

Rosati, G. (1983) *Narciso e Pigmalione: Illusione e Spettacolo nelle Metamorfosi di Ovidio*, Firenze

(2002) 'Muse and Power in the Poetry of Statius' in E. Spentzou and D. Fowler, eds. *Cultivating the Muse: Struggles for Power and Inspiration in Classical Literature*, 229–52, Oxford

Saunders, C. (1927) 'The Volscians in Virgil's *Aeneid*', *TAPA* 58: 92–9

Saylor, C. (1990) 'Group Versus Individual in Vergil *Aeneid* 9', *Latomus* 49: 88–94

Scarry, E. (1985) *The Body in Pain: The Making and Unmaking of the World*, Oxford

Schetter, W. (1960) *Untersuchungen zur epischen Kunst des Statius*, Wiesbaden

Segal, C. (1983) 'Boundary Violation and the Landscape of the Self in Senecan Tragedy', *Antike und Abendland* 29: 172–87

Segal, L. (1997) *Slow Motion: Changing Masculinities, Changing Men*, London

Sherwin-White, A. N., ed. (1966) *The Letters of Pliny*, Oxford

Simpson, M. (1969) 'The Chariot and the Bow as Metaphors for Poetry in Pindar's Odes', *TAPA* 100: 438–73

Skinner, M. B. (1997) *'Ego mulier*: The Construction of Male Sexuality in Catullus' in J. Hallett and M. Skinner, eds. *Roman Sexualities*, 129–50, Princeton

Smolenaars, J. J. L., ed. (1994) *Statius Thebaid VII: A Commentary*, Leiden

Snijder, H., ed. (1968) *P. Papinius Statius, Thebaid: A Commentary on Book III with Text and Introduction*, Amsterdam

Spaltenstein, F. (1990) *Commentaire des Punica de Silius Italicus*, Geneva

Stirrup, B. (1976) 'Ovid's Narrative Technique', *Latomus* 35: 97–107

Suleiman, S. and Crosman, I., ed. (1980) *The Reader in the Text*, Princeton

Svenbro, J. (1984) 'La découpe du poème. Notes sur les origines sacrificielles de la poétique grecque', *Poétique* 58: 215–32

Taisne, A.-M. (1994) *L'esthétique de Stace: la peinture des correspondances*, Paris

Tanner, R. G. (1986) 'Epic Tradition and Epigram in Statius', *ANRW* 2.32.5: 3020–46

Teja, A. (1994) 'Gymnasium Scenes in the Stuccoes of the Underground Basilica di Porta Maggiore', *International Journal of the History of Sport* 11: 86–96

Thomas, R. F. (1982) *Lands and Peoples in Roman Poetry*, Cambridge

Thompson, L. and Bruère, R. T. (1970) 'The Virgilian Background of Lucan's Fourth Book', *CPh* 65: 152–72

Thornham, S., ed. (1999) *Feminist Film Theory*, Edinburgh

Thuillier, J.-P. (1975) 'Denys D'Halicarnasse et les jeux Romains (Antiquités Romaines, VII, 72–73)', *MEFRA* 87: 563–81

(1980) 'La nudité athlétique: Grèce, Etrurie, Rome', *Nikephoros* 1: 29–48

(1982) 'Le programme "athlétique" des *Ludi Circenses* dans la Rome republicaine', *REL* 60: 105–22

(1985) *Les Jeux Athlétiques dans la Civilisation Etrusque*, Rome

(1996a) *Le Sport dans la Rome Antique*, Paris

(1996b) 'Stace, *Thebaide* 6: les jeux funèbres et les réalités sportives', *Nikephoros* 16: 151–67

Tissol, G. (1997) *The Face of Nature: Wit, Narrative and Cosmic Origins in Ovid's Metamorphoses*, Princeton

Toll, K. (1997) 'Making Roman-ness and the Aeneid', *ClAnt* 16: 34–56

Tompkins, J. (1980) 'The Reader in History: The Changing Shape of Literary Response' in J. Tompkins, ed. *Reader Response Criticism*, 201–32, Baltimore

Toner, J. P. (1995) *Leisure and Ancient Rome*, Cambridge

Toynbee, J. M. C. (1971) *Death and Burial in the Roman World*, London

Turner, B. S. (1984) *The Body and Society*, Oxford

Van Nijf, O. (1999) 'Athletic Festivals and Greek Identity in the Roman East', *PCPS* 45: 176–200

Venini, P. (1961a) 'Studi sulla Tebaide di Stazio. La composizione', *RIL* 95: 55–88

(1961b) 'Studi sulla Tebaide di Stazio. L'imitazione', *RIL* 95: 371–400

(1970a) *P. Papini Stati Thebaidos Liber Undecimus*, Firenze

(1970b) 'Silio Italico e il mito tebano', *RIL* 41: 778–83

Vernant, J.-P. (1981) 'A "Beautiful Death" and the Disfigured Corpse in Homeric Epic' in F. I. Zeitlin, ed. *Mortals and Immortals: Collected Essays*, 50–74, Princeton

Versnel, H. S. (1970) *Triumphus: An Inquiry into the Origin, Development and Meaning of the Roman Triumph*, Leiden

Vessey, D. W. T. C. (1969) *The Sources of the Thebaid*, diss., Cambridge

(1970) 'The Games in Thebaid VI', *Latomus* 29: 426–41

(1973) *Statius and the Thebaid*, Cambridge

(1982) 'Flavian Epic' in E. Kenney, ed. *Cambridge History of Classical Literature*, 558–96, Cambridge

(1986) '*Pierius menti calor incidit*: Statius' Epic Style', *ANRW* 2.32.5: 2965–3019

Veyne, P. (1990) *Bread and Circuses*, London

Vian, F. (1952) *La Guerre des Géants: le Mythe avant l'Époque Hellénistique*, Paris

Ville, G. (1981) *La Gladiature en Occident des Origines à la Mort de Domitien*, Rome

Von Moisy, S. (1971) *Untersuchungen zur Erzählweise in Statius' Thebais*, Bonn

Von Stosch, G. (1968) *Untersuchungen zu den Leichenspielen in der Thebais des P. Papinius Statius*, Dusseldorf

Walters, J. (1993) *Ancient Roman Concepts of Manhood and their Relation with other Markers of Social Status*, diss., Cambridge

(1997) 'Invading the Roman Body: Manliness and Impenetrability in Roman Thought' in J. P. Hallett and M. B. Skinner, eds. *Roman Sexualities*, 29–43, Princeton

Warde-Fowler, W. (1918) *Virgil's Gathering of the Clans*, Oxford

Weinstock, S. (1971) *Divus Julius*, Oxford

West, M., ed. (1972) *Iambi et Elegi Graeci*, Oxford

Wheeler, S. M. (1999) *A Discourse of Wonders*, Philadelphia

(2002) 'Lucan's Reception of Ovid's *Metamorphoses*', *Arethusa* 35: 361–80

Wiedemann, T. (1992) *Emperors and Gladiators*, London

Willcock, M. M. (1973) 'The Funeral Games of Patroclus', *BICS* 20: 1–11

Williams, C. (1999) *Roman Homosexuality: Ideologies of Masculinity in Classical Antiquity*, New York; Oxford

Williams, G. (1978) *Change and Decline: Roman Literature in the Early Empire*, Berkeley

Williams, R. D., ed. (1960) *P. Vergili Maronis Aeneidos Liber Quintus*, Oxford

(ed.) (1972) *P. Papini Stati Thebaidos Liber X*, Leiden

(ed.) (1973 (repr. 1987)) *The Aeneid of Virgil: Books 7–12*, London

Willis, W. H. (1941) 'Athletic Contests in the Epic', *TAPA* 72: 392–417

Wise, V. M. (1977) 'Flight Myths in Ovid's *Metamorphoses*: An Interpretation of Phaethon and Daedalus', *Ramus* 6: 44–59

Wiseman, T. P. (1987) *Roman Studies*, Liverpool

Wistrand, E. (1956) *Die Chronologie der Punica des Silius Italicus*, Göteborg

BIBLIOGRAPHY

Wörrle, M. (1988) *Stadt und Fest in kaiserzeitlichen Kleinasien. Studien zu einer agonistischen Stiftung aus Oenoanda*, Munich

Wyke, M., ed. (1998) *Parchments of Gender: Deciphering the Bodies of Antiquity*, Oxford

Yavetz, Z. (1969 (new edition 1988)) *Plebs and Princeps*, New Brunswick

Zanker, P. (1988) *The Power of Images in the Age of Augustus*, Ann Arbor

Zeitlin, F. I. (1990) 'Thebes: Theater of Self and Society in Athenian Drama' in J. J. Winkler and F. I. Zeitlin, eds. *Nothing to do with Dionysus?*, 130–67, Princeton

Zetzel, J. E. G. (1997) 'Rome and its Traditions' in C. Martindale, ed. *The Cambridge Companion to Virgil*, 188–203, Cambridge

Zissos, A. (2003) 'Spectacle and Elite in the *Argonautica* of Valerius Flaccus' in A. J. Boyle and W. J. Dominik, eds. *Flavian Rome: Culture, Image, Text*, 659–84, Leiden

INDEX OF PASSAGES DISCUSSED

331

GENERAL INDEX